Current Trends in Textlinguistics

Research in Text Theory
Untersuchungen zur Texttheorie

Editor
János S. Petöfi, *Bielefeld*

Advisory Board
Irena Bellert, *Montreal*
Maria-Elisabeth Conte, *Pavia*
Teun A. van Dijk, *Amsterdam*
Wolfgang U. Dressler, *Wien*
Peter Hartmann, *Konstanz*
Robert E. Longacre, *Dallas*
Roland Posner, *Berlin*
Hannes Rieser, *Bielefeld*

Volume 2

Walter de Gruyter · Berlin · New York
1978

Current Trends in Textlinguistics

Edited by
Wolfgang U. Dressler

Walter de Gruyter · Berlin · New York
1978

Library of Congress Cataloging in Publication Data

Main entry under title:

Current trends in textlinguistics.

    (Research in text theory ; v. 2)
    Bibliography: p.
    Includes index.
    1. Discourse analysis – Addresses, essays, lectures.

I. Dressler, Wolfgang. II. Series.
P302.C8   410   77-14357
ISBN 3-11-006518-5

CIP-Kurztitelaufnahme der Deutschen Bibliothek

Current trends in textlinguistics / ed. by Wolfgang U. Dressler. –
Berlin, New York : de Gruyter, 1977.

    (Research in text theory ; Vol. 2)
    ISBN 3-11-006518-5

NE: Dressler, Wolfgang U. [Hrsg.]

© Copyright 1977 by Walter de Gruyter & Co., vormals G. J. Göschen'sche Verlagshandlung –
J. Guttentag, Verlagsbuchhandlung – Georg Reimer – Karl J. Trübner – Veit & Comp., Berlin 30.
Printed in Germany
Alle Rechte des Nachdrucks, der photomechanischen Wiedergabe,
der Herstellung von Photokopien – auch auszugsweise – vorbehalten.
Satz und Druck: Passavia Passau
Bindearbeiten: Lüderitz & Bauer, Berlin

Contents

Introduction

Wolfgang U. Dressler
Universität Wien

The development of textlinguistics and discourse analysis on the international scene has been characterized by a relative seclusion (or independence, to put it more positively) of certain trends. Many authors in the field continue to consider and even to cite only their own contributions and those of their teachers, pupils, or collaborators most of the time. E.g. Soviet textlinguistics is virtually unknown[1] in the West[2], although considering its scope (more than 700 titles) and early start (nearly 30 years ago), Soviet textlinguistics surpasses all other textlinguistic traditions; on the other hand not too much of the huge Western literature on the subject is known by linguists in the Soviet Union. Nor do the very few introductions cover the whole field (cp. note 2): E.g. Kallmeyer (1974) and Mortara (1974) concentrate on certain Continental European trends only. Nor is there any up-to-date bibliography[3]. These facts have hampered the development of the subject and have led to much duplication.

Therefore this volume has the function and the ambition of bringing contributions from various authors and widely divergent schools together in one place and to inform the reader about the recent developments within various trends. Thus he should be able to compare their basic tenets and methods, judge their respective achievements and plunge into detail problems with the help of the bibliographies. As there has not been a strict complementary distribution of topics, there is a certain overlap among several chapters of this volume. In this way it should be easier for the reader to confront various schools of thought.

Even if certain authors are well-known for their work on text or discourse, their achievements are often identified with a certain stage of their development. This is particularly the case with Z.S. Harris, whose pioneering early work is widely known, whereas his later innovations have for the most part not been noticed by fellow textlinguists.

This is not the place to sketch the history of textlinguistics. This has been done at various places[4], and notably many contributions to this volume (particularly H. Rieser) give surveys not only of recent developments, but also of the

---

[1] Maybe with the exception of Estonian semiotics.
[2] Here also the present writer must confess his shortcomings, since Dressler (1973) contains only references to five Russian publications in textlinguistics.
[3] Dressler – Schmidt (1973) was a first attempt without a successor or replacement.
[4] Cp. also the forthcoming reader (Dressler 1977).

earlier background. And as the various chapters of this volume speak for themselves, it is not necessary to introduce or summarize them.

Most of the authors of this volume adhere to the concept of textlinguistics proper, insofar as they view written and spoken texts as the minimal free unit of language. Others prefer using the looser and less obliging term discourse.

Circumstances have forced certain modifications of the original plan for this volume. Harvey Sacks was to write a contribution on the sociolinguistic domain of textlinguistics; after his tragic accident and death, which means a great loss to our field, his friend E. Schegloff has been so kind to provide an article on conversational analysis which includes many pragmatic and sociolinguistic problems H. Sacks would have had to deal with. Thus Schegloff's contribution differs from the others in that it concentrates on practical analysis instead of giving a survey. He and S. Kuno must be thanked most warmly for their last-minute readiness to collaborate in this volume.

Limitations of space have been much resented by many contributors. In the case of T. A. van Dijk and W. Kintsch this has led to a considerable narrowing of their original topic 'The psycholinguistic dimension of text grammar'. However only in this way can the reader understand the problems of this new and fascinating research area. H. Rieser was to write on the Constance project of text grammar; but in the mean-time this project has been dissolved, so that he preferred to place his approach into the context of the development of text grammar in general.

Readers might be astonished to find two titles on semiotic problems. Since J. S. Petöfi preferred to go beyond his original assignment to write on semantics, the reader now has the opportunity to compare widely diverging approaches without there being much overlap. Also in other cases overlap has not been specifically avoided: e.g. van Dijk's (1972) book is referred to in various chapters of this volume, but always viewed from different angles.

A deplorable lacuna is the lack of any contributions from the German Democratic Republic, which I was unable to obtain. This is particularly unfortunate, since both theoretical work done in textlinguistics[5] and practical applications for pedagogical purposes[6] have reached a high level of quality there.

This volume is the successor of a more ambitious earlier project which was planned to contain much longer contributions by more than thirty authors. Economic constraints have forced the exclusion of two types of chapters:

1) Supplementary contributions in special areas which are already represented in the volume: E.g. chapters on tagmemic and stratificational discourse analysis, about which the reader can find information in the chapters written by Longacre – Levinsohn and Grimes; information about stratal theories other than the systemic-functional model, e.g. work done by P. Sgall's group (men-

---

[5] As in the series *Studia Grammatica* and in Lang's (1973) still unpublished dissertation.

[6] Cp. the series *Textlinguistik* of the Pädagogische Hochschule Dresden, which is hardly available abroad.

tioned in Palková – Palek's chapter); non-verbal aspects of discourse – in addition to Nöth's chapter see e.g. Yngve 1970 and Vance 1974.

2) More regrettable is the exclusion of areas where not much (or still too little) textlinguistic work has been done so far, but where more and deeper textlinguistic studies would be highly profitable. The extension of the generally recognized domains of textlinguistics and discourse analysis (also for the purpose of practical application) would be very desirable e.g. in:

a) The acquisition of textual competence by the child: Already Weir's (1962) book has been very illuminating as to the nature of the acquisition process. Several specialists are now working on this subject, e.g. S. Ervin-Tripp (University of California, Berkeley). Since the acquisition process continues until adulthood (similar to lexical competence), analysis of texts produced by pupils in various school-types is a natural consequence (cp. Sinclair – Coulthard 1975, Conrady 1976).

b) Studies of the acquisition of text competence are the basis for the pedagogical use of textlinguistics. E.g. in West Germany, several attempts have been made to introduce textlinguistics into the school system, especially for education in the mother tongue[7].

c) Contrastive textlinguistics had a good start with Gleason (1968). Later particularly Hinds (e.g. 1972) worked on contrastive textgrammar (of Japanese and English, cp. A. Kawashima for Japanese and German). Such studies can be used for the practice, criticism, and teaching of translation (cp. Dressler 1974).

d) The role of the lexicon in and of lexicography for a text grammar has been widely neglected, with the notable exception of J.S. Petöfi (see his chapter in this volume), who proceeded from the thesaurus conception of documentary analysis.

e) Such work is one of the necessary prerequisites for the wider usage of textlinguistic approaches in computational linguistics, e.g. for the purposes of automatic text reduction (automatic abstracting etc., cp. Sevbo 1969).

f) Not only the acquisition (a), but also the loss or the disturbances of textual competence can throw light on important problems of textlinguistics. For schizophrenia see the articles by Nöth (1974, 1976) and Leodolter (1975).

In aphasiological studies the disturbance of text competence, especially in syndromes of 'dynamic aphasia' has been investigated by Luria (1976) and his collaborators; Cvetkova (1968, 1972) has included the rehabilitation of text competence into her pioneering programs of aphasia therapy. Textlinguistic studies are now under way at various centres, e.g. by D. Engel (Universität Konstanz), W. Huber (Technische Hochschule Aachen), W. U. Dressler and J. Stark (Universität Wien, cp. 1977). Since aphasia is a differential disturbance of linguistic and cognitive capacities, aphasiological evidence can show us conditions of text generation and analysis and their relations to non-linguistic functions of the brain (cp. Luria 1976).

---

[7] Cp. Beisbart 1976, Herrmann 1976. Also foreign language teaching is considered in East German publications, such as in *Textlinguistik* (see note 6), cp. Liebsch 1976.

A final word about the language problem: It has been decided to publish the whole volume in English, although nearly two thirds of the authors are non-native users of English and live in countries where English is not a language of every-day life. If one subtracts the three anglicists among them, still half of the contributors do not have a native command of English. Responsibility for English style is with the single authors, although I have introduced some corrections. But, in distinction to other editors, I have not aimed at the task of complete englishing. In the age of increasing computer-generated English texts and of English becoming the major international language of linguistics, a volume presumably written for a majority of non-English readers by a majority of non-English authors does not need to contain only contributions in fully idiomatic English, particularly because in certain countries it is rather difficult to produce texts in such a perfect English.

In a variation of Terentianus Maurus one might say "Habeat sua fata libellus!". May this small book[8] help in spreading knowledge of the aims, results, uses, and problems of textlinguistics!

References

Beisbart, O. et al. 1976. Textlingustik und ihre Didaktik. Donauwörth, Auer.

Conrady, P. 1976. Schüler im Umgang mit Texten. Kronberg, Scriptor.

Cvetkova, L. S. 1968. K teorii vosstanovitel'nogo obučenija. Prace Psychologiczne-Pedagogiczne 204, 13. 81–90.

Cvetkova, L. S. 1972. Vosstanovitel'noe obučenie pri lokal'nyx poraženiax mozga. Moscow, Medicina.

van Dijk, T. A. 1972. Some Aspects of Text Grammars. The Hague, Mouton.

Dressler, W. 1973. Einführung in die Textlinguistik[2]. Tübingen, Niemeyer.

Dressler, W. 1977 (forthcoming). ed.: Wege der Textlinguistik. Darmstadt, Wissenschaftliche Buchgesellschaft.

Dressler, W. 1974. Der Beitrag der Textlinguistik zur Übersetzungswissenschaft: Übersetzer und Dolmetscher (ed. V. Kapp, Heidelberg, Quelle und Meyer) 61–71.

Dressler, W. – S. J. Schmidt. 1973. edd.: Textlinguistik: Kommentierte Bibliographie. Munich, Fink.

Dressler, W. – J. Stark. 1977. Störungen der Textkompetenz bei Aphasie: Kurzfassung. in: Textlinguistik und Semantik (edd. W. Meid – K. Heller, Innsbruck, Institut für Sprachwissenschaft). 265–268.

Gleason, H. A. 1968. Contrastive Analysis in Discourse Structures: Monograph Series on Languages and Lingustics 21. 39–63.

Herrmann, W. 1976. Situation und Norm: Zur Problematik pädagogischer Textbewertung mit Beispielen für ein neues Prüfungsverfahren. Kronberg, Scriptor.

Hinds, J. 1972. Discourse Constraints on Syntax. in: From Soundstream to Discourse (= Papers from the 1971 Mid-American Linguistic Conference, edd. H. Hays – D. Lance, Columbia, Missouri) 115–124.

Kallmeyer, W. et al. 1974. Lektürekolleg zur Textlinguistik. 2 vol., Frankfurt, Athenäum-Fischer.

Lang, E. 1973. Sudien zur Semantik der koordinativen Verknüpfung. Diss. (Dr. scient.), Berlin, Humboldt Universität.

---

[8] And it is really a small *libellus,* in view of the tasks of and the enormous literature on textlinguistics.

Leodolter, R. 1975. Gestörte Sprache oder Privatsprache: Kommunikation bei Schizophrenen: wiener linguistische gazette 10/11. 75–96.

Liebsch, H. 1976. Textlinguistische Probleme unter schulpraktischem Aspekt: Probleme der Textgrammatik (= Studia Grammatica XI) 183–194.

Luria, A. R. 1976. Basic Problems of Neurolinguistics. The Hague, Mouton (Russian original of the first part: A. R. Lurija, Osnovnye problemy nejrolingvistiki. Izdatel'stvo Moskovskogo Universiteta 1975).

Mortara, B. G. 1974. Aspetti e problemi della linguistica testuale. Torino, Giappichelli.

Nöth, W. 1974. Textsituation, Pragmatik und Kommunikationsstörungen in der Schizophrenie: Orbis 23. 1–38.

Nöth, W. 1976. Textkohärenz und Schizophrenie: Zeitschrift für Literaturwissenschaft und Linguistik 29.

Sevbo, I. P. 1969. Struktura svjaznogo teksta i avtomatizacija referirovanija. Moscow, Nauka.

Sinclair, J. – Coulthard, P. 1975. Towards an Analysis of Discourse: The English Used by Teachers and Pupils. London, Oxford University Press.

Vance, S.-M. 1974. Conversational Alternation and the Topic of Conversation. PhD Thesis, University of Chicago.

Yngve, V. H. 1970. On getting a word in edgewise: Papers from the 6th Regional Meeting, Chicago Linguistic Society 567–578.

On the Development of Text Grammar*

Hannes Rieser
University of Bielefeld

1 Pregenerative approaches towards discourse analysis

Harris' preface to the Phoenix edition of *Structural Linguistics* (1960) contains two important additions to the distributional method, which mark the end of classical structuralism. First he proposed to describe a language by means of a set of kernel sentences and transformations operating on these kernel sentences, thereby yielding the sentences of the language (cf. Harris [⁸1969], pp. vi–vii). With the aid of these tools subtle syntactic and semantic relations between sentences could be described and ambiguities explained (cf. Harris [1968], pp. 49–157). Another point of his was to stress that linguistic analysis earlier had not gone beyond the limits of the sentence and that the methods known had not allowed to describe the structural relations between sentences or parts of different sentences. The tools necessary for describing connected pieces of writing or talking were provided by discourse analysis which Harris had suggested in two works in 1952 (reprinted in Harris [1970], cf. also Harris [1968], pp. 146–152).

Even though Harris' notion of transformation had a persistent impact on the developments within linguistic theory, especially because of the explanatory power Chomsky attached to it, discourse analysis did not gain much attention, despite the fact that the problems treated within the frame of discourse analysis had also been pointed out by Bloomfield (cf. Bloomfield [¹⁰1969], p. 170) before Harris, and e.g. by Lyons [²1969], p. 174) after Harris.

The only generally known discussion of Harris' discourse analysis is in Bierwisch (1965), reprinted in Bierwisch (1971). Bierwisch admitted that the linguistic analysis of structures extending beyond the sentence had to be regarded as an unsolved problem, but he was not prepared to accept Harris' proposals, because in his opinion the notion of discourse was not explicated within his theory. The structural methods used were not appropriate for the objects chosen and yielded ad hoc results. With the help of discourse analysis it was not possible to distinguish between acceptable sequences of sentences and

---

* This paper is a slightly revised version of the second chapter of a German manuscript, entitled "Zur empirisch motivierten semantischen Beschreibung von Texten". It was translated by Fritz Neubauer and the author. The whole German paper will be published in the series *Papers in Text Linguistics* (Buske, Hamburg 1976/77).

random accumulations of disconnected sentences, nor did it provide *one* correct analysis of a discourse but several possible ones. Bierwisch's alternative consisted in demanding from a text theory to explicate the notion 'text in L' in analogy to Chomsky's 'sentence in L' and to determine what constituted the connection between the sentences of a discourse. Thus Bierwisch was among the first to formulate what was later known as the *coherence problem* or coherence principle in the literature, even though he did not put forward any suggestion of his own on this subject. But he did discuss the methodological shortcomings of Harris' approaches without finding much attention. A careful consideration of his criticism would have avoided some of the misguided developments in what was later called text linguistics.

In Europe the linguistic analysis of texts was first undertaken in the early sixties (cf. Hartmann [1964]). In European linguistics, American distributionalism had not found many followers and Harris was hardly known, due to the strong influence Indo-European studies, philology and the different European variants of structuralism (Saussure, Martinet, the Prague School, the Copenhagen School) had.

Nor did the kind of homogeneous research community later formed by the adoption of Chomskyan theories in the midsixties exist at that time. The initial justifications given for text linguistic approaches were quite similar to those put forward by Harris in America. It was pointed out that suprasentential regularities could not be reconstructed by traditional morphological and syntactical tools. This coincided with an intensive discussion of the methodological and fundamental questions in the philologies, where the central topic was, whether an intersubjectively valid interpretation of texts was possible. Stimulated by Russian and French structuralism, R. Ingarden (cf. Ingarden [³1965]) and R. Wellek (cf. Wellek-Warren [⁶1968]) it was concluded that a reliable interpretation should be based on the description of text structure. Since none of the philologies provided any descriptional tools, support was expected to come from linguistics, which, however, at that time was not able to reconstruct the syntax and semantics of texts either. Semantics, especially, was in a poor state then. These two vital aspects, the problems of supra-sentential relations and of text-interpretation in literature had great influence on the further development of text linguistics and on the direction of research.

From this it can easily be seen why text linguistics in its early days was descriptively oriented and did not have an integrating formal basis. The only attempt to use structuralist methods in a narrow sense occurred in Harweg (1968). He concentrated on text coherence, more specifically on 'substitution by pro-forms'. 'Pro-form' here stood for expressions of identical or different morphological form designating the same object and replacing each other in texts under certain conditions. Similar facts had already been discussed by Harris. It is interesting to note that despite the purely syntactic approach used by Harris as well as by Harweg the justification for these substitution procedures was essentially of a semantic nature.

As to Harweg's proposals, it remained unclear how his pro-forms related to other means of creating text coherence, such as tense and time reference. Harweg's approach resulted in an 'open' taxonomy of pro-forms, and these pro-forms could be used to connect sentences. In effect, it consisted in a pure classification procedure, which was duly criticized even by linguists working in the field of descriptive linguistics. Nevertheless, it has to be mentioned that Harweg has made a valuable contribution to research into the mechanisms of text structure, especially since there is still no theory accounting for the facts discovered by him.

On the other hand, one may object to Harweg's ideas on the same grounds as to Harris' discourse analysis: They do not allow an intuitively adequate decision on whether a particular utterance can be regarded as a text or not, nor do they explain what properties a piece of natural language must have to constitute a text.

2   Generative text grammar

2.1   Interpretative approaches

At the end of the sixties it was generally agreed that a text grammar should specify the notion 'text in L' as originally demanded by Bierwisch and attempts were made to use the theoretical framework provided by generative grammar to achieve this aim. This is only natural, as it is one of the most important goals of generative grammar (following the model of recursively defined artificial languages) to provide a classification procedure which distinguishes between sentences and non-sentences. Generative grammar was also used to describe the different degrees of acceptability and to explain why these different degrees of acceptability should occur. This could be done by extending these notions and by finding corresponding text terms for syntactic well-formedness and semantic acceptability. It is therefore not surprising that the very first attempts at setting up text grammars were strongly influenced by Chomsky's theory and Katz and Fodor's semantics (cf. Isenberg [1971], Petöfi [1971a], Rieser [1973]). Certainly, generative grammar has always been a few steps ahead of text linguistics so far as technicalities are concerned, but this is not so with respect to the discovery of empirical facts. On the contrary: the scope of generative grammar is a priori reduced, and problems are only recognized as significant if they can be solved with the means provided by the theory. Much of the success of generative grammar is due to the strategy to exclude unfavourable examples, if at all possible. Naturally, this does not leave room for comprehensive heuristic investigation.

Those text grammarians who nevertheless tried to extend the scope of generative grammar did so by postulating that not sentences but texts should be considered the natural domain of generative grammar (cf. e.g. Isenberg [1971] and van Dijk [1972]). This presupposes that basic concepts in linguistic theory such as 'competence' and 'performance' would have to be formulated in relation to texts, sentence competence and sentence performance should be based on text competence and text performance (cf. van Dijk [1972], p. 3). The effort to find sound empirical evidence for this hypothesis, resulted in a collection of syntactic and semantic data (cf. e.g. Dressler [1972]). They were supposed to constitute a part of all the explicanda for a linguistic text theory.

Since certain of these facts occurring regularly in sentences, such as the use of pronouns and pro-adverbs could only be explained by regarding the sentences in question as 'constituents' of texts, text grammarians could not see any objective necessity for an *autonomous* sentence grammar. Sentence grammarians usually commented – if they commented at all – that these phenomena could well be treated within the framework of sentence grammars, *once sentence grammars would be fully* developed (cf. Dascal–Margalit [1974]).

One of the formal differences between the Chomsky theory and interpretative text grammar consisted in the introduction of rules which allowed a text symbol to expand into symbols for sentence sequences. These symbols for sentence sequences could then be expanded into sentence symbols (cf. Rieser [1973]). These rules were supposed to reflect the 'hierarchical' organization of supra-sentential structures. Another type of rule was used to account for the complicated cases of coreference between sentences. These rules were either regarded as locally restricted transformations (cf. Rieser [1972]), or as conditions formulated in some suitable meta-language. *It is a definite inadequacy of interpretative text grammar, however, that only coherence information explicitly appearing in surface structure can be handled succesfully.* Implicitly provided coherence information necessary e.g. for time reference, local reference, maintenance of quantitative or qualitative standards, the observation of cause and event relations, and for the insertion of the missing parts into elliptical constructions could not be reconstructed by interpretative text grammatical models then. These shortcomings led to attempts to use alternative models based on generative semantics, but recent developments in syntax and semantics, especially the contributions of Montague and Suppes have reopened the possibility of solving these problems within text grammar (cf. Suppes [1973] and Gabbay [1973]).

2.2   Text grammar versus sentence grammar

There are some parallels between the discussions about an optimal text grammar and the most powerful sentence grammar. This is certainly not surprising, because text grammarians agree that, naturally, a text grammar cannot exist without integrating parts of sentence grammar. Thus genuine research into text linguistics starts where sentence grammar fails to provide adequate explanations for linguistic phenomena.

We can thus formulate two conclusions: The empirically deficient state of the known sentence-grammatical theories justifies the demand for text grammars. The question, whether text grammar constitutes a separate discipline could only be decided on the basis of a future highly powerful sentence grammar.

Thus, at present a rational ('Popperian') decision is not possible nor will it be in the near future. In the meantime it may be settled by the research of linguists, other academics interested in this field, or by interference of the research management.

As has been pointed out already, there has been considerable convergence between the aims and methods of philosophical logic and of current text grammar, this becomes especially evident in the kind of context logic developed lately.

The integrative capacity of text grammar led to considerable difficulties from the very beginning, because the basic assumptions of sentence grammars, which were accepted explicitly or implicitly also in text grammar, carry with them the foundational problems connected with these assumptions such as the choice of a semantic component, the application of the transformational apparatus, how to make use of syntactic and semantic features, the formulation of strategies for text analysis, and whether one should use meaning postulates or definitions in the lexicon. It has remained true that the more comprehensive and empirically motivated tasks are formulated for a text grammar, the greater is the tendency to integrate different formal techniques and methods into this text grammar. The increase in integrative power then enormously multiplies the foundational problems, thus too much integration may lead to pointless syntheticism and permanent ad hoc modifications. It is therefore one of the important future tasks of textgrammatical research not to lose control of the accumulated foundational problems and to reduce them step by step. This can only be achieved by observing rigid formal standards without abandoning the empirical basis.

2.3   Generative semantics expanded

In 1971 Isenberg considered the possibility of basing text grammars on the proposals made by generative semanticists (Isenberg [1971]). Petöfi (1971a) assumes an intermediate position between an interpretative grammar and generative semantics in his proposals for a text grammar. This can be inferred from his proposal to assign a linguistic-semantic *and* logico-semantic interpretation to deep structure. "Interpretation" in this case stands for "mapping one artificial language onto another artificial language". The lexicon proposed in Petöfi (1971a) aims at integrating a Katz-Fodor type of lexicon with a Fillmore type of lexicon.

Petöfi continued this line of research (Petöfi [1971b]), and surveyed critically all the sentence-grammatical models presented until 1971 discussing elaborately the linguistic phenomena these grammars are able to handle. He gave the following reasons for pursuing research in text linguistics: First, the existing sentence grammars could not provide a homogeneous treatment of such well-known linguistic phenomena as pronominalization or topic-comment relation. Secondly, nor could all other linguistic phenomena referred to by descriptively oriented text linguists be explained within the framework of existing sentence grammars. In the first case sentence grammarians could not achieve what they set out to do, i.e. the theory was internally refuted, in the second case, the theory could not handle facts presented from outside. This led Petöfi to the conclusion that a new theory would have to be put forward. In this paper Petöfi also questioned some of the basic assumptions of grammatical theory by proposing that a comprehensive grammatical text theory should contain and make a distinction between a speaker-related component and an addressee-related component. Thus generative semantics sentence grammar and the Chomsky-Katz-Fodor type of an interpretative sentence grammar could be integrated, *provided a homogeneous notation could be found for this integrated version.*

Petöfi (1971b) contained a chapter on lexicology which clearly went beyond the proposals for linguistic lexicons made until then. Even though he subsequently concentrated more and more on questions related to the lexicon component within the textgrammatical program he also presented proposals for the setting-up of workable algorithms for formation rule systems and transformational systems in Petöfi (1971b), concrete systems open to detailed criticism were only presented later in Petöfi (1973).

By 1972 the standard work on text grammatical *problems* was van Dijk (1972). Whereas in Petöfi (1971b) the elaboration of text grammars was mainly motivated by grammatical considerations (cf. above), van Dijk tried to present methodological as well as grammatical and empirical arguments for text grammars. In the main the empirical arguments consisted of a revision of Chomsky's notion of 'competence' supported by hypotheses from psycholinguistic research. The grammatical arguments showed that co-referentiality, pronominalization, tense and time reference, local reference, semantic relations between sentences, connectives, topic-comment etc. could only be handled successfully within the framework of a text grammar. The methodological argument was based on the intuitively justifiable assumption that discourses should be regarded as the 'natural domain' of a grammar rather than sentences.

These empirical and grammatical arguments led to a detailed reformulation of the tasks for an adequate text grammar. van Dijk's most important point consisted in his so-called 'macro-structure hypothesis', which can be paraphrased as follows: local restrictions occur in discourses, they determine the coherence between the sentences within a sentence sequence. Micro-restrictions or micro-structures such as e.g. the restrictions on pronouns, pro-adverbs, and connectives are examples of such local restrictions. Apart from these microrestrictions there are also more global restrictions which are determined by the primary and secondary topics of the discourse, they are called 'macro-restrictions' or sometimes 'macro-structures' (emphasising changes from the restrictions to their 'cause', i.e. to the different topics in a text).

van Dijk's assumption that the macro-restrictions determine at least a part of the micro-restrictions, e.g. those existing on the lexical level, is quite plausible. Unfortunately, so far no attempt has been made to relate macro-structures and micro-structures, even though this should be one of the main concerns of any text grammar. Such a text-grammatical approach can also be used to handle the linguistic problems within the theory of literature, as is pointed out by van Dijk (1972).

All the works mentioned in this chapter so far can be safely placed within generative semantics. They did not present theories meant for falsification but merely research without explanations in the strict sense of the word or predictions of any kind, which could only be discussed on the basis of their plausibility. Thus is many cases objections against them are based on tactical considerations rather than on scientific facts.

It is still the great advantage of the text grammars based on generative semantics that they can account for the difference between deep structure coherence and surface structure coherence (cf. the distinction made by van Dijk between microstructure and macro-structure). Thus texts incoherent on a surface structure level frequently show a high degree of deep structure coherence: time references and local references may be provided only implicitly without any realization on the surface. This, of course, is very important for the semantic interpretation.

It is clear, however, that the works discussed also show the characteristic shortcomings of generative semantics, e.g. no explicit distinction between syntax and semantics is made. The formation rules of logic function only as a guiding principle, and the logical rules of deduction are not applied at all. The syntactic notion of entailment is not defined in these systems. Thus, by ignoring semantics all intuitions about text structure have to be put into the syntax. Another point is that the central rôle of the lexicon would require adequate insertion rules. Furthermore it remains unclear how the various transformational components necessitated by the relative remoteness from surface structure are supposed to interact. General transformational theory has not been developed as far yet.

2.4   Recent developments in text grammar: Between generative semantics and logic

In van Dijk (1973) the deep structure constituting the base of a text grammar, originally presented by him in 1972, was worked out in greater detail in the form of a "natural logic", called "text logic". This text logic is supposed to generate the logical representation of sentence sequences and to specify the derivation rules acting on logical forms. van Dijk tried to define the notions of 'derivability', 'premise', and 'entailment' for the natural logic proposed. He also discussed in detail the characteristic differences between the currently used formal languages and the natural logic. For instance, the sentences of texts were regarded as theorems derivable from axioms, meaning postulates, definitions and previously derived theorems by means of derivation rules. It was argued that such derivation rules could only be applied in a non-ad-hoc way, if the logical structure of natural language connectives, of names, and of quantifying expressions could be reconstructed. The semantics – structurally corresponding with syntax – should assume the form of a model-theoretic interpretation. Even though this was quite a revolutionary approach for 1973 (especially as far as using derivation rules and the semantics were concerned), it gained little attention.

van Dijk suggested that the traditional logical systems would have to be changed to correspond with the properties of natural languages. The behaviour of the natural language connective *and* served as a prime example for the different behaviour of natural language connectives (*and* is not commutative) and their classical logic counterparts. As a consequence van Dijk came to the conclusion that a richer logical language would have to be developed to meet the requirements of linguistic theory. The notion 'coherence' was partially explained by the notion 'derivability'. Further developments of this research program are presented in van Dijk (1974).

Petöfi (1973) constitutes a revised and enlarged version of his 1971c version with his intermediate version (Petöfi [1972]). As did van Dijk, Petöfi also tried to develop a machinery for the description of text coherence. Even though they started from similar intuitions, Petöfi did not use the deductive parts of logical systems as a guiding principle. His approach was further revised and minimally changed in the meantime, the latest published version is contained in Petöfi (1975). There a text semantic representation consists of the following components:

The set of descriptions of objects referred to in the text,
the set of propositions represented in the text,
the set of text sentences,
the set of the so-called 'thematic nets'; there is a corresponding thematic net to every object, a thematic net contains all the propositions describing some property of a discourse object,
the net of time reference,
the set of communicative nets; a communicative net contains all the propositions realized in a communication situation,
the reference-relation-diagram, which fixes the relationship between the discourse objects.

It can easily be seen that coherence is the central aspect in this paper. These components contain entities determining surface coherence as well as entities establishing deep structure coherence, the program practically fixes the ontology of a text.

For later discussions other aspects of Petöfi (1975) are of a greater importance. In Petöfi (1973) it was suggested already that semantic representations should be treated modeltheoretically. (Petöfi-Rieser [1974] was devoted to this very problem.). This clearly implied that the original idea of using the methods of generative semantics had been abandoned. After Petöfi (1973) a series of investigations concerned with various related topics was started, this included the discussion of the foundation of case grammar as used in Petöfi (1973), of presupposition and entailment (cf. Petöfi-Rieser [1973b]), of lexicon structure and semantic questions (cf. Petöfi-Rieser [1974]). Rieser (1976) constitutes the most comprehensive application and extension of Petöfi (1973).

The proposals contained in Petöfi (1975) are theoretically more far-reaching than those contained in Petöfi (1973). Petöfi now claims that the grammatical component of a text theory should generate intensional structures. This clearly indicates that the parameters normally only included in a pragmatic interpretation (cf. Cresswell [1973], pp. 173–189) are put into the object language. Consequently, the model-theoretic interpretation manages with partial functions not depending on various points of reference. This approach faces the following problems: The notion 'derivation' has to be defined. Either a direct interpretation of the intensionalized syntax proposed has to be given or this language has to be translated into a language suitable for a model-theoretic treatment. Also the semantic notion of 'entailment' has to be defined. – Thus almost all explanation takes place in the syntax, the semantic metalanguage plays only a subsidiary rôle, because in case of standard contexts it merely contains expressions corresponding as closely as possible to object language expressions.

A suitable transformational component has not yet been devised for van Dijk's or for Petöfi's model, nor for the investigations based on these works such as e.g. Rieser (1976). A general evaluation of these lines of research cannot take place before a suitable model theory can be constructed and a transformational component capable of mapping logical structures onto the morphological structures of a particular natural language is devised. These problems are still unsolved and only future research can show whether there is an adequate solution. I is clear, however, that van Dijk as well as Petöfi have already greatly contributed to explicate the notions "text coherence" and "text in L". Further attempts of setting up text grammars should therefore consider their proposals.

2.5   Methodological issues

2.5.1   Criticism from the neighbouring disciplines

The weight empirical data should have was amply discussed in text linguistics, but in spite of this not enough attention was paid to the wealth of intuitively well-known empirical parameters and their explicit analysis. Thus one of the potentially most powerful directions in text linguistic research was not put into practice. The analysis of the factors involved in the production and reception of texts and the development of neatly set up research programs based on comprehensive analysis was neglected. One could speak of a repetition of the same kind of methodological misdirection which had led to the hardly justifiable scope restrictions in sentence grammar earlier on: The task of text lingustics was supposed to be the reconstruction of the syntactic and semantic structure inherent to discourses, but these discourses were regarded as something given, as a completed product and object of research. This idealization practically led to the disregard of the temporal dimension of discourse production. Generalizations based on such a working principle, especially in semantics, are naturally open to serious criticism. Text linguistics had thus missed the chance to offer an attractive, fruitful, and real alternative to sentence grammars and their superficial successes. Only recently more interesting semantic phenomena such as 'correction', 'backwards-interpretation' etc. have been discussed, but so far no general explanatory model has been proposed.

These and similar shortcomings were naturally also seen by critics of text linguistics in its initial stages who were working on literary theory (cf. Wienold [1972], pp. 65–139, semiotics, and language philosophy [cf. Schmidt [1973]). Text linguists realized that there were lots of unsolved methodological problems and that the tasks of text linguistics had been defined too narrowly from the outset. Due to the lack of instruments necessary for the treatment of more promising explicanda, this insight had little immediate effects. The instruments have not improved very much since then. What *has* become clear, however, is that there is not one unique explicandum 'text', but various different explicanda requiring different explanatory devices. In hindsight it can be said that text linguists tried to apply formal apparatuses too early, perhaps because in general the rôle of formalization in theory construction was grossly overrated. Also, everybody tried to use formalisms without reconsidering whether this was really appropriate. Only the recent works by Schiffer, Grice, Stenius etc. as well as other foundational studies have schown that the relation between formalization and theory construction is not easily solved. The precise explication of one's linguistic intuitions should come first, and only then does formalization make sense. Formalization alone cannot be equated with having a theory (cf. Scott [1973]), nor can it be used – as is frequently the case – to cover up the neglecting of empirical data.

It is a serious question, indeed, whether the still unsolved problems in text grammars already allow formal explications. This applies especially for text coherence and the semantic component.

2.5.2   Criticism from within the discipline

From the outset text grammar was also criticized by sentence grammarians. A rather subtle contribution along these lines was Lang (1972), who commented that the facts mentioned by text grammarians did not justify the conclusion that texts rather than sentences should be considered the domain of a grammar. He did admit, though, that the facts discovered by text linguistics necessitated a modification of the descriptional tools available. It can be gathered that he thought of a significant expansion of generative transformational grammar. As a result of text grammar certain structural relations would have to be explained within the framework of linguistic descriptions. Even though a considerable number of text linguists were quoted in Lang (1972), many of their arguments were not really dealt with. He concentrated mainly on criticizing Isenberg (1971). Arising from his criticism he advanced some arguments for a text theoretic approach. Among these was the hypothesis that the property of 'texthood' was determined by clusters of linguistic *and* communicative features and would therefore have to be reconstructed by *separate* theories and subsequently *integrated* into a text theory. In his opinion the traditional descriptional tools could be expanded to form the grammatical component of such an integrated theory. This also applied for the component describing the coherence phenomena which were dealt with in great detail in Lang (1974). Compared to the proposals contained in van Dijk (1974) Lang's treatment appears to be somehow inadequate, especially in his handling of the semantics.

van Dijk's (1972) methodological, grammatical, and psycholinguistic proposals were severely attacked by Dascal-Margalit (1974). They did not aim at writing a learned review of van Dijk (1972), but tried to criticize him as *the* representative for text linguistic research. By identifying him with text linguistics in general they thought of being able to refute all existing text-grammatical research programs by refuting some of van Dijk's arguments. Dascal and Margalit put forward several well-founded arguments against text linguistics in general. Much weight was given to Bar-Hillel's strict distinction between an observation level and the theoretical level. According to Dascal and Margalit, it follows from that that the notion 'sentence' is the theoretical correspondence to the observational term 'discourse', and that there is not really any reason to introduce a theoretical construct 'text'. Even though they strongly recommended sticking to a sentence-grammatical framework, they did not even try to show how the linguistic phenomema treated by van Dijk could be explained, nor were recent works in logic and linguistic theory supporting text grammar taken into account (cf. Petöfi-Rieser [1976] on this subject). It was nevertheless a positive result of Dascal and Margalit's article that the discussion about methodological arguments was reopened and showed that one's intuitions about properties of discourses were not as uniform as the text grammarians had assumed. Obviously, their pre-theoretical assumptions had been guided by traditional descriptive linguistics, academic background knowledge and some not explicitly stated theoretical principles. In addition it became clear that the hypothesis about the range of data that could possibly be covered by an optimal sentence grammar vary considerably. So far, however, surprise developments in sentence grammar have not yet taken place and nobody can tell what the semantic or pragmatic components of sentence grammars would look like.

3 Montague grammar and text grammar

From the remarks on the various approaches it should have become clear that philosophical logic has exerted considerable influence on grammatical theory and on text grammar as well. This is especially true of the terminology and the approach towards semantics. This process was initiated by works like e.g. Keenan (1970). Kummer (1972a) was one of the first text grammarians to propose an integration of recent work on transformational grammar and intensional logic. According to Kummer a text grammar should allow to define "coherent text in a language L". He concentrated on the analysis of texts, and especially on the reconstruction of syntactic relations between anaphoric expressions and proposed to use a kind of surface syntax together with a calculus to generate logical forms. Surface structures are mapped into canonical forms by means of transformations. The surface structures prior to the translation are similar to the structures generated by standard transformational grammar. Coherence rules operate on the canonical forms to specify anaphoric and other relations between sentences. Kummer also proposed a model-theoretic treatment for the canonical forms, in order to provide an explicit semantics. He assumed (as van Dijk) that the coherence problem could only be solved if the grammar contained appropriate deduction rules. The important question of mapping syntactic structures into logical (or canonical) forms which had not been discussed by van Dijk is also treated in Kummer (1972a). Kummer's subsequent works deal with logical forms and valid inferences (cf. e.g. Kummer [1972b]), but so far he has not tried to reconstruct a larger fragment of a natural language with the apparatus he proposed in Kummer (1972a).

Ballmer (1975) is the latest work in text linguistics. He already refers to the discussion Bierwisch vs. Harris, Lang vs. Isenberg, and Dascal-Margalit vs. Dijk and comes to the conclusion that there is no real demarcation between sentence grammars and text grammars. He does not try to solve this question and assumes a rather pragmatic attitude by regarding sentence grammar as the theoretical foundation of a text grammar. But since sentence grammars fail to describe many of the properties of natural language these well-known phenomena have to be treated within a text-grammatical program. These phenomena include co-reference, sentence connectives, macrostructures and corrections of interpretations resulting from information given in the ensuing part of the discourse. These are exactly the problems discussed by text grammarians since Harweg (1968), and Ballmer comments that no satisfactory solutions have been found for them. He suggests that a careful selection of language fragments (i.e. of texts with specific properties) could lead to progress. Such a fragment may e.g. consist of texts containing expressions used for time reference (like "now", "then", and "yesterday", "tomorrow" and the corresponding tense markers). A grammar capable of describing the syntax and semantics of such a fragment (and therefore also fragments of a similar structure) he calls "language reconstruction systems". It can easily be seen that this strategy corresponds to the strategies proposed by Montague and Thomason. As guiding principles for adequate solutions Ballmer insists on maintaining the standards set up by Montague, because neither generative grammarians nor text grammarians can exhibit adequate solutions in a strict sense, and even some linguistic and logical research in the Montague tradition shows various shortcomings as a result of using an inexact notion of transformation or too artificial or too small fragments.

Ballmer concentrates on the development of suitable sentence grammars, which he calls "punctuation grammars", because the different punctuation marks are regarded as special morphemes and are of central importance for the syntax and semantics. Punctuation grammar is set up like a categorial grammar and the special morphemes trigger off the particular types of transformations such as e.g. permutation or insertion in the syntax, and they function as speech act operators or hypersentences in the semantics. A sharp distinction between sentences and texts is no longer necessary. Ballmer leaves open the question how larger semantic and thematic units in texts can be reconstructed (cf. the arguments in Kutschera [1974] on his subject) and how the intuitions mentioned in Petöfi (1975) can be treated. As a result of Ballmer's concentration on methodology and the development of more powerful sentence grammars, coherence theory, which ought to be the central task of text linguistics, is not given due attention, instead he tries to solve some of the problems usually regarded as belonging to philosophical logic or traditional sentence grammar. As in any other science, ist is sometimes the case that some problems are not really accepted as problems and just left aside.

4   Current trends (1976)

The current trends in text grammar do not follow a clear direction. The first stage, i.e. the development of new descriptional tools, is completed, because Montague grammar has shown that it is necessary and feasible to develop still more rigid descriptional tools. Ballmer has made some steps in this direction by applying it to a few text-linguistic problems. van Dijk is now working on empirical tests in support for the macro-structure hypothesis and on questions of empirical pragmatics. Ballmer announced some research on methodology and on the evaluation of different types of sentence grammars. Petöfi and Rieser concentrate on the lexicological and semantic problems arising from the description of larger corpora and continue their work on methodological questions in connection with the set-up of a text theory. Kummer has turned towards the foundation of linguistic theory by means of action theory (cf. Kummer [1975]).

Bibliography

Ballmer, T.Th.: 1975, *Sprachrekonstruktionssysteme*. Kronberg/Ts.: Scriptor.
Bierwisch, M.: 1971, Review of Z.S.Harris' *Discourse Analysis Reprints*. In: Ihwe (ed.) 1971, pp. 141–154. 1st impression 1965.
Bloomfield, L.: [10]1969, *Language*. London: Allen & Unwin. 1st impression 1933.
Cresswell, J.M.: 1973, *Logics and Languages*. London: Methuen.
Dascal, M.-A.Margalit: 1974, A New 'Revolution' in Linguistics-'Text Grammars' vs. 'Sentence-Grammars'. In: *Theoretical Linguistics*. Vol. 1 (1974), No. 1/2, pp. 195–213.
van Dijk, T.A.: 1972, *Some Aspects of Text Grammars*. The Hague: Mouton.
–: 1973, Text Grammar and Text Logic. In: Petöfi-Rieser (eds.), 1973a, pp. 17–79.
–: 1974, *'Relevance' in Logic and Grammar*, Ms. University of Amsterdam.
van Dijk et al.: 1972, *zur bestimmung narrativer strukturen auf der grundlage von textgrammatiken*. Hamburg: Buske.
Dressler, W.: 1972, *Einführung in die Textlinguistik*. Tübingen: Niemeyer.
Gabbay, Dov M.: 1973, Representation of the Montague Semantics as a Form of the Suppes Semantics. In: Hintikka et al. (eds.), 1973, pp. 395–413.
Gülich, E.–W.Raible (eds.): 1972, *Textsorten*. Frankfurt: Athenäum.
Harris, Z.S.: [8]1969, *Structural Linguistics*. Chicago, London: University of Chicago Press. 1st impression 1947.
–: 1968, *Mathematical Structures of Language*. London: John Wiley.
–: 1970, *Papers in Structural and Transformational Linguistics*. Dordrecht–Holland: Reidel. in this volume: Discourse Analysis, pp. 313–349; Discourse Analysis. A Sample Text, pp. 349–373; Culture and Style in Extended Discourse, pp. 373–383.
Hartmann, P.: 1964, Text, Texte, Klassen von Texten. In: *Bogawus 2,* pp. 15–25.
Harweg, R.: 1968, *Pronomina und Textkonstitution*. München: Fink.
Hintikka, K.J.J. et al. (eds.): 1973, *Approaches to Natural Languages*. Dordrecht–Holland: Reidel.
Ihwe, J. (ed.): 1971, *Literaturwissenschaft und Linguistik,* Vol. 1, Frankfurt: Athenäum.
–: 1973, *Literaturwissenschaft und Lingustik,* Vol. 2, Frankfurt: Athenäum.
Ingarden, R.: [3]1965, *Das literarische Kunstwerk*. Tübingen: Niemeyer. 1st impression 1931.
Isenberg, H.: 1971, Überlegungen zur Texttheorie. In: Ihwe (ed.), 1971, Vol. 1, pp. 150–173.
Keenan, E.L.: 1970, *A Logical Base for a Transformational Grammar of English,* MS. University of Pennsylvania.
Kummer, W.: 1972a, Outlines of a Model for a Grammar of Discourse. In: *Poetics 3* (1972), pp. 29–56.
–: 1972b, Aspects of a theory of argumentation. In: Gülich-Raible (eds.), 1972, pp. 25–50.
–: 1975, *Grundlagen der Texttheorie*. Reinbek: Rowohlt.
von Kutschera, F.: 1974, *Grundzüge einer logischen Grammatik*. MS. University of Regensburg.
Lang, E.: 1972, Über einige Schwierigkeiten beim Postulieren einer "Textgrammatik". In: Ihwe (ed.), 1973, pp. 17–51.
–: 1974, *Studien zur Semantik der koordinativen Verknüpfung*. Phil. Diss. Ostberlin.
Lyons, J.: [2]1969, *Introduction to Theoretical Linguistics*. Cambridge: CUP.
Petöfi, J.S.: 1971a, Probleme der ko-textuellen Analyse von Texten. In: Ihwe (ed.), 1971, Vol. 1, pp. 173–213.
–: 1971b, *Transformationsgrammatiken und eine kotextuelle Texttheorie*. Frankfurt: Athenäum.
–: 1971c, 'Generativity' and 'Textgrammar'. In: *Folia Linguistica V* (1972), pp. 277–309.
–: 1973, Towards an Empirically Motivated Grammatical Theory of Verbal Texts. In: Petöfi-Rieser (eds.), (1973a), pp. 205–276.
–: 1975, Beyond the sentence, between linguistics and logic. In: *Style and Text*. Stockholm: Skriptor.

20   H. Rieser

Petöfi, J. S.–D. Franck (eds.): 1973, *Präsuppositionen in Philosophie und Linguistik*. Frankfurt: Athenäum.
Petöfi, J. S.–H. Rieser (eds.): 1973a, *Studies in Text Grammar*. Dordrecht–Holland: Reidel.
Petöfi, J. S.–H. Rieser: 1973b, 'Präsuppositionen' und 'Folgerungen' in der Textgrammatik. In: Petöfi-Franck (eds.), 1973, pp. 385–495.
–: 1974, *probleme der modelltheoretischen interpretation von texten*. Hamburg: Buske.
–: 1976, Some Arguments Against Counter Revolution. On Marcelo Dascal's and Avishai Margalit's "A New 'Revolution' in Linguistics? – 'Text-Grammars' vs. 'Sentence-Grammars'"; to appear in *Linguistics*.
Reichenbach, H.: ²1966, *Elements of Symbolic Logic*. New York: Free Press. 1st impression 1947.
Rieser, H.: 1972, Model (1). In: van Dijk et al. (1972), pp. 27–77.
–: 1973, Probleme der Textgrammatik II. In: *Folia Linguistica*, Vol. VI (1973), pp. 28–46.
–: 1974, Textgrammatik und Interpretation. In: Petöfi-Rieser (1974), pp. 61–155.
–: 1976, *Aspekte einer partiellen Texttheorie*. Untersuchungen zur Textgrammatik mit "nicht-linear" festgelegter Basis unter besonderer Berücksichtigung des Lexikon- und des Fachsprachenproblems. MS University of Bielefeld.
Schmidt, S. J.: 1973, *Texttheorie*. München, W. Fink, UTB.
Scott, D.: 1973, Background to Formalization. In: Leblanc (ed.), pp. 224–274.
Suppes, P.: 1973a, Semantics of Context-free Fragments of Natural Languages. In: Hintikka et al. (eds.), 1973, pp. 370–395.
–: 1973b, Comments on Montague's Paper. In: Hintikka et al. (eds.) 1973, pp. 259–262.
Wellek, R.-A. Warren: ⁶1968, *Theorie der Literatur*. West-Berlin: Ullstein. 1st English impression 1942.
Wienold, G.: 1972, *Semiotik der Literatur*. Frankfurt: Athenäum.

The Semiotic Framework of Textlinguistics

Winfried Nöth
Ruhr-Universität Bochum

1   *Semiotics and Textlinguistics*

Before the semiotic framework of textlinguistics can be analysed, it is necessary to distinguish clearly the province of semiotics from that of textlinguistics. Textlinguistics is the branch of linguistics in which the methods of linguistic analysis are extended to the level of the text. This might seem a trivial statement, but semiotics is also concerned with texts, and it is important to realize that textlinguistics and semiotics use the term "text" in different ways. While textlinguistics is only concerned with the texts of a natural language, semiotics considers instances of verbal as well as non-verbal communication as texts.

1.1   The Field of Semiotics

Semiotics is concerned with sign systems or *codes*. Thus, by definition the study of semiotics includes language, the most elaborated system of signs, as well as other non-linguistic codes. This makes the field of semiotics appear rather unlimited. A recent bibliography of semiotics (Eschbach 1974) contains more than 10,000 titles covering the most diverse areas from non-verbal communication to the philosophy of language. A survey of some monographs which explicitly lay claim to a semiotic approach seems to confirm this picture of a rather heterogeneous field: there are semiotic approaches to animal communication (Sebeok 1972), theology (Grabner-Haidner 1973), epistemology (Klaus 1963; Resnikow 1968), basic research in mathematics (Hermes 1938), film analysis (Knilli 1971; Metz 1972), psychiatry (Shands 1970), communication theory (Ruesch 1972), architecture (Eco 1972), aesthetics (Bense 1967), mass communication (Koch 1971), advertisements (Nöth 1975) and literature (Trabant 1970; Wienold 1972; Coquet 1973; Segre 1973). The question which might be raised in view of this diversity is: where does semiotics end and where do other disciplines of research begin (cp. Eco 1972: 28–44; Koch 1974)? Only one aspect of this problem can be dealt with in this paper: what is an appropriate dividing line between semiotics and textlinguistics and where is there a possible overlap between the two provinces?

1.2   Two Roads to Semiotics

The field of semiotics has been approached from two main directions. The first direction is that of *general semiotics*. This is the direction taken by Peirce, Morris (1971), Bense (1967) and others. It begins with the elaboration of a general theory of signs (SEM) and continues to analyse on the basis of this theory various linguistic (L) and non-linguistic sign systems or codes (cp. the definition of "codes" in: Nöth 1975: 70–80). Diagram 1 (cp. Koch 1972) shows the difference between this approach to semiotics (1a) and the second approach (1b) which might be called the approach of *linguistic semiotics* or semiology:

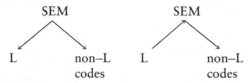

Diagram 1: Heuristics of semiotics: the approach of general semiotics (1a; left) compared to the approach of linguistic semiotics (1b; right).

The road of linguistic semiotics is the one outlined by Saussure and followed by Hjelmslev and the French structuralists. Since language is the most important sign system and "nothing besides language is more appropriate to make the nature of the semiological problem understood" (Saussure 1969: 34), linguistic semiotics begins with linguistics in order to set up by means of *analogy* a general model of semiotics (cp. Koch 1971: 24). This general model can then be applied to other sign systems. The heuristic priority of linguistic analysis in semiological research even leads R. Barthes (1967a: 11) to the conclusion that non-linguistic semiotics should be considered "a second-order language" which does not exist independently of language. A further conclusion which is derived from this thesis is the reversal of the common semiotic hierarchy (cp. diagram 1) according to which linguistics is part of semiotics. Thus, for Barthes *(ib.)* "linguistics is not part of the general science of signs, even a privileged part, it is semiology which is a part of linguistics". We do not support this thesis (cp. Nöth 1972: 111–8) which seems to imply a confusion of heuristics and systematics. We shall try instead to come to a more distinct delimitation between the fields of linguistics and semiotics.

1.3   Delimitation of Linguistics and Semiotics

There is, among French structuralists, a tendency to identify narrative, poetic or literary analysis based on certain linguistic principles with semiotics. One of the reasons that text analysis is no longer considered to be part of linguistics is that the linguistic model used by the French structuralists does not go beyond the level of the sentence (cp. Martinet's [1960] levels: phoneme, moneme and phrase). Thus, everything transgressing the level of the sentence is no longer considered to be the object of linguistic but of semiotic analysis. Units of semiotic description, explains Barthes (1967a: 11), are "no longer monemes or phonemes, but larger fragments of discourse... Semiology is therefore perhaps destined to be absorbed into a *trans-linguistics,* the materials of which may be myth, narrative, journalism, or on the other hand objects of our civilization, in so far as they are *spoken* (through press, prospectus, interview, conversation...)". We shall call this conception of semiology which includes text analysis *semiotics in the broader sense.*

Linguistics which is based on a model which includes the level of the text (and which is the approach of the contributors to this volume) has to draw a different dividing line between linguistics and semiotics. If text analysis – as textlinguistics – is considered part of linguistics, semiotics has to be understood in a *narrower sense.* This is the approach to semiotics used in this paper. It assumes that textlinguistics provides an appropriate model to give an adequate analysis of the linguistic structures of a text. On the other hand, this approach realizes that non-linguistic codes constitute a semiotic framework of texts which cannot be dealt with appropriately by textlinguistic analysis.

2   Three Semiotic Frameworks of Textlinguistics

We cannot give here a complete account of all the semiotic codes which constitute the semiotic framework of texts. We shall have to restrict ourselves to the outline of the three possible types of frameworks of textlinguistics (§ 2; a more detailed model of the place of linguistics within the framework of semiotics and other disciplines is outlined by Koch 1971; 1973) and to some examples of analyses (§ 3) which require taking into account the semiotic framework of textlinguistics.

2.1   Framework 1: The Outer Semiotic Framework of Textlinguistics

Let us take the term "framework" literally in order to show in the form of diagrams the possible semiotic frameworks of textlinguistics, which will be marked by means of a thick line. Diagram 2 shows the outer semiotic framework of textlinguistics:

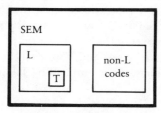

Diagram 2: Framework 1: the outer framework of textlinguistics

Textlinguistics is first considered a part of linguistics (L). Thus, texts are at first to be described within the framework of L. Within the framework of L, the following structures will be analysed among others: phonemes, morphemes, words, syntactic structures like noun phrases and verb phrases, semantic structures (sememes), and textual structures like topics and comments. Besides these structures which are specific for language, the structures of texts are determined by a number of structures which are common to all semiotic codes. These structures are located within the framework of semiotics (SEM) and thus constitute the outer framework of texts. Structures which are specific for non-linguistic codes are excluded from consideration within framework 1 of textlinguistics.

Two dimensions of semiotics are of prime importance within the framework 1 of textlinguistics: semantics and pragmatics. While almost all pragmatic structures of texts are not specific to language and therefore part of the semiotic framework, the semantic structures of texts are mostly specific to language and belong only in part to the semiotic framework. Among the pragmatic structures of framework 1 are those situational factors which are described in models of the communication theory: the addresser who sends a message to the addressee via a channel, the attention (focus) of the participants who select the structures of the message, the feedback between the participants etc. (cp. Koch 1971; Nöth 1975: 39–60). The questions which concern the communicational situation of text production and text reception have to be resolved within this semiotic framework of textlinguistics.

Among the semantic structures of framework 1 are those which have to be analysed within a general theory of signs. The analysis of the triadic structure of the sign is an example of a general semiotic analysis which must also be applicable to the study of the linguistic sign. Peirce's elaborate typology of signs based on the triadic sign model was set up within this general framework. According to this typology (cp. Nöth 1977), the linguistic sign, since it is in arbitrary relation to its referent, is to be classified as a *symbolic* sign. In texts, however, types of signs can occur which are non-specific of language: indexical expressions (cp. Bar-Hillel 1954), e.g. demonstrative or possessive pronouns, or iconic expressions, e.g. onomatopoetic words. Peirce considered the indexical or iconic use of words as an example of sign degeneration, since in this case signs with a high degree of arbitrariness (symbols) are used as signs with a lower degree of arbitrariness (icon or index).

Within the framework 1 of textlinguistics, the problems involved in the analysis of texts from the point of view of a general typology of signs are one of the main concerns of "textsemiotics", a direction of semiotics represented by Bense (1967: 58–79; 1969: 91–6) and Walther (1962; 1965). The linguistic foundations of these problems were outlined by Jakobson (1965).

2.2   Framework 2: Semiotic Codes Represented Within Texts

Language is a code which enables its users to communicate about communication. Thus, the linguistic code (L) can be used in the form of texts to represent structures of non-linguistic codes (code x). If we consider kinesics, the communication system of body motion (cp. Birdwhistell 1973), as an example of a non-linguistic code, the text genre of the novel gives many examples of a linguistic representation of this non-linguistic code. While in the case of the novel (framework 2a; cp. diagram 3), the representation of non-semiotic structures constitutes only part of the text, there are texts which represent nothing except the structures of a non-linguistic code (framework 2b). The Old-English manuscript *Indicia Monasterialia* (cp. Kluge 1885; Barley 1974) which describes a code of hand signs which was used in Anglo-Saxon monasteries, is an example of this type of framework where one code is only "translated" into the code of language.

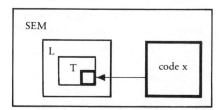 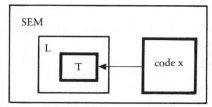

Diagram 3: Framework 2: a non-linguistic code x is represented partly within a text (framework 2a, left) or the text translates code x (framework 2b, right).

2.3   Framework 3: L-Texts in Contiguity With Non-L-Texts

While the novel is a typical example of the importance of framework 2 in text analysis, framework 3 must be taken into consideration in the case of drama analysis (cp. Kowzan 1968). Let us take kinesics again as an example of a non-linguistic code. This is the semiotic code on which the gestures of the actors in a drama are based. These gestures are represented directly, not indirectly by means of language as in case of framework 2. Drama uses the kinematic code at the same time or in contiguity with the linguistic code which is used in the dialogues of the actors. This relation is shown in diagram 4:

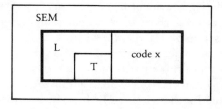

Diagram 4: Framework 3: a linguistic text in contiguity with the structures of a non-linguistic code x

The case of framework 3 is not restricted to drama analysis. It is, in fact, a very frequent type of framework, which has to be taken into consideration in the analysis of texts in most of the modern media: the comics (cp. Hünig 1974), cinema, advertisement, television etc. A typical example of text analysis within framework 3 is R. Barthes's *Système de la mode* (1967b).

3   Analyses of the Semiotic Framework of Textlinguistics

The relevance of the three frameworks of textlinguistics for textual analysis will be demonstrated in the following examples of semiotic analyses of texts.

3.1   Semiotic Study of Myth and Magic

The structural study of myth is often considered a paradigm of semiotic text analysis. Myth, defined as a "sacred tale" (Leach 1970: 54), is a text and thus an object of textlinguistic analysis. Which semiotic framework is used in the structural study of myth?

3.1.1   The Semiotic Framework of Myth in the Analyses of the French Structuralists

In his analysis of myth, Lévi-Strauss (1968) has taken the road outlined in diagram 1b. His text-analytic procedures use the heuristics derived from the linguistic model of phonology (Trubetzkoy; Jakobson): in analogy to the phonological analysis of distinctive features, Lévi-Strauss (*ib.*) analyses the recurrence of binary oppositions of semantic units in texts. In the Oedipus myth e.g., the following oppositions are established: *overrating* vs. *underrating (of blood relations)* and *denial* vs. *persistence (of autochthonous origin of man)*. Also in analogy to phoneme-analysis a minimal unit of textual analysis is introduced which is called the *mytheme*.

Although Lévi-Strauss's studies of myth fail to fulfil many requirements of a strictly textlinguistic approach, there are nevertheless similarities to two approaches to textlinguistics. One is the approach of Greimas's (1966) structural semantics, which is equally based on the analysis of binary oppositons of semantic units. The second approach is that of Harris's (1963) *discourse analysis*. This similarity is evident in Lévi-Strauss's analysis of the Oedipus myth, where he sets up a chart of recurrent semantic units similar to the "reduction tables" set up by Harris (*ib.: 43 ff.*).

The procedures of analysis mentioned so far do not yet fall within the framework of semiotics (in the narrower sense) since they only deal with the code of language. An interpretation of myth within the semiotic framwork 1 has been given by Roland Barthes (1957: 215 ff.). He describes myth as a general phenomenon of everyday life which occurs (*ib.: 221*), when a *sign* within a "primary semiological system" which consists of *signifier (signifiant) + sig-*

nified (signifié) loses its primary *signified* and acquires a new *signified* within a "secondary semiological system". An example is a newspaper photograph (*ib.*: 223) which primarily signifies a "young negro with a French uniform and a French Tricolour in the background". Its secondary, mythical meaning is "colonialism" or "*grandeur française*". This is an example of visual myth (thus, within the framework of a non-linguistic code), but the same mythological structure can be found in oral or written texts.

In R. Barthes's interpretation, myth is not analysed as a narrative. The concept of myth is used instead rather metaphorically. In fact, in other contexts (1967a), he equates the same process of signification within a "secondary semiological system" with "connotation", "metalanguage" and "ideology". This shows that his analysis of myth provides a semiotic framework which is too general to allow specific structures of the myth as a text to be discovered.

Let us now consider the analysis of myth within the semiotic framework 2a of texts. In *The Raw and the Cooked,* Lévi-Strauss (1970: 160–5, 240–1) deals more explicitly with the non-linguistic codes of communication which are of importance in the analysis of myth: among these, the sensory, acoustic, visual, gustatory and olfactory codes are the most important ones. Others are, e.g., the sociological, the aesthetic, the astronomical and the cosmographic codes. Lévi-Strauss maintains that the principles governing in the use of these codes are similar to those underlying the use of language. This seems to be a consequence of an approach to semiotics following road 1 b without arriving at an independent general model of semiotics and without even taking into consideration the possible necessity of other non-semiotic frameworks of description. We cannot go into further details of these problems which regard the outer framework of semiotics and not of textlinguistics. Also, it is not possible to go into further details of the semiotic study of myth in this paper. We shall, instead, turn to the structural study of charms (cp. Nöth 1977) and try to outline the semiotic framework of this genre related to myth.

3.1.2   Semiotic Analysis of Anglo-Saxon Magic

Let us consider the following example of an Anglo-Saxon charm in the New-English translation (cp. Grattan, Singer 1952: 159):

Write this along the arms against *dwarf:* + T[rinity] + Omega + Alpha + and grate celandine into ale. S. Marcutus, S. Victorius.

The magic power of this charm against *dwarf* – which is probably either a nightmare or fever (Storms 1948: 168) – can be analysed within the three frameworks of semiotics. It is a charm which uses linguistic (*write...*) as well as non-linguistic codes. *Grating celandine into ale* and drinking this potion seems to be a purely medical and thus non-semiotic device. The medical usefulness of this remedy is, however, most doubtful. Its physiological effect is probably completely ineffective against the causes of the disease. It is, therefore, more adequate to assume that this remedy is not used because of its physiological effects but rather because of its semiotic value. The act of *grating celandine into ale* may be considered as a sign for dispelling the disease. It is a sign within a non-linguistic medico-magical code according to which the cutting, pounding or grating of plants (cp. Storms, 1948: 29) is used as an iconic sign (based on similarity between signifier and signified) for the physical "destruction" of the disease.

The study of this non-verbal medico-magical code underlying the Anglo-Saxon charms is an example of textual analysis within framework 2. The code is reported in the Anglo-Saxon manuscripts by means of language. In the actual situation, however, in which the Anglo-Saxon magician used this charm as a medical device, both codes, the linguistic and the non-linguistic, were used in contiguity. The non-linguistic device of *grating celandine into ale* was accompanied by the linguistic device of using sacred formulas. Thus, we have an example of framework 3 of textual analysis.

The use of language in our Anglo-Saxon charm is not a "normal" one. It deviates significantly from the conditions under which normal language use occurs. The description of this deviation requires taking into account the semiotic framework 1 of textual analysis. Three instances of semiotic analysis within this framework shall be discussed:

(1.) The words used by the magician, especially *Omega + Alpha,* are not used in their denotational sense with the signified "Greek letters" but with the connotational sense of "something sacred". This is an observation within the framework of semiotics in the broader sense. (For Roland Barthes, this would be an example of myth.) For semiotics in the narrower sense, however, this feature of language use falls within the framework of linguistic semantics, which should be able to supply a model of language including such factors as denotation and connotation. The following features of language in the above charm fall within the framework of semiotics in the narrower as well as in the broader sense.

(2.) The situational conditions of sign use deviate significantly from those of the normal conditions. Among the minimum conditions of sign use is the requirement of the existence of an addresser and an addressee of the sign. Is this condition fulfilled in our charm? The addresser is probably the magician (perhaps also the patient himself). He writes the holy words along the patient's arm and orally invokes the saints. Who is the addressee of this message? It is evidently not the patient but either his diseased body or more probably the dwarf who is believed to have caused the disease. In both cases, the addressee is not on the same level as the addresser. Neither the patient's body nor the dwarf can give a linguistic response to the message, and while the former is physiologically existent, the latter is only existent within the magico-medical code.

(3.) Another semiotic aspect of the magico-medical situation concerns the communicational function of the sign used. The words T[*rinity*] + *Omega + Alpha* which roughly mean "something holy" are not only used in order to communicate this meaning to the addressee. The receiver, who embodies an "evil force", is supposed to be affected directly by the "holiness" of the written and spoken words. The channel of communication, in this case, is the skin of the patient. The words written on the skin of the patient are used in the same way as a physician today uses an ointment. Thus, language is used in order to obtain a physiological effect *directly* without the intervention of a person who first understands the message. Language is used in a non-semiotic way. This is the most extreme instance of that process which Peirce has called "degeneration of signs". –

In conclusion, although it is not possible to go into all details of the semiotic framework of charms in this paper, some further aspects concerning the pragmatic dimension of the charms should be mentioned. Although we have said that the words used in our charm are not actually addressed to a human addressee, this is only true on a level which might be called the surface level of analysis. On a deep level, it is evident that the charm does have a communicative function and is indeed addressed to the patient. The meaning of this message is a psychotherapeutic one. It signalizes help and gives confidence and hope to the patient. This is the only level on which the magician can be sucessful in his therapy: the improvement of the psychic state of the patient can result in an improvement of his physiological state.

3.2   The Semiotic Framework of Poetry Analysis

"Many poetic features belong not only to the science of language but to the whole theory of signs, that is, to general semiotics." With this statement, R. Jakobson (1960: 351) refers to the semiotic framework of poetry analysis. The semiotic structures of poeticalness are primarily situated within the semiotic framework 1 of textlinguistics. Since we cannot give a complete outline of the semiotic framework of poetry in this paper, we have to confine ourselves to the analysis of two semiotic aspects of poeticalness which concern the pragmatics of poetic communication (3.2.1) and the semantic problem of the poetic sign (3.2.2).

3.2.1   Pragmatics of Poetic Communication

What is the difference between poetry and everyday casual language? Most theories of poetry answer this question with reference to the linguistic structure of the text. In poetry, according to these theories, language is either used in deviation from a linguistic norm, or the textual units are distributed according to certain patterns of recurrence. Other theories characterize the essence of poetry as consisting of a certain type of non-trivial ("sublime") informational content. These theories would probably characterize the following text (Porter 1972: 90) as non-poetic:

> *North Indian Lamb Curry*
> 3 tbsps. vegetable oil
> 1 large onion, thinly sliced

3 cloves garlic, crushed
1 tbsp. grated ginger
2 tbsps. ground coriander
[...]

A linguistic description that takes into account only the textual features would have to classify this text as a cookery recipe and not as a poem. And yet the text is published in an anthology of *Found Poems* so that we have to assume that at least the author of this anthology and some of its readers are willing to accept this text as a poem. What, then, is the difference between the text considered as a cookery recipe and the text considered as a poem?

Since the textual structures do not change when the recipe is considered as a poem, the framework of textlinguistics has to be abandoned in favour of a situational or semiotic framework in order to describe the poeticalness of the above text. Within this semiotic framework we can observe that the poeticalness of this text depends on the *focus* (cp. Koch 1971), the mode of attention of the author or the reader of the poem. It is not the text but the situational framework that changes when the author/reader takes a different attitude towards the text.

The factors determining the pragmatic framework of poetic communication have received special attention by two schools of textual theory: the Russian Formalists and the Prague Structuralists. According to the Russian Formalists (cp. Erlich 1965: 181), poetic language is opposed to 'practical' or informative language. In everyday speech, language has a practical, communicative function. Since no attention is paid to language itself, everyday speech becomes *automatized*. Poetry, on the other hand, uses language as a device of 'making strange' (Šklovskij *ib.:* 176–7). The communicative function of language is relegated to the background in order to attain a "new way of seeing" (cp. Lachmann 1970). The distinction between automatization and deautomatization or foregrounding made by the Prague Structuralists (cp. Garvin 1964) gives a similar basis for the theory of poeticalness.

The poetic focus of the reader dissociates the above text from its practical use as a cooking recipe and gives rise to a "new way of seeing" which makes the text a poem. This new poetic perception of a text normally used for practical purposes is a general semiotic phenomenon. The same transformation from practical to aesthetic communication occurs in other semiotic codes: within the code of sculpture, Marcel Duchamp's *objets trouvés* are a well known example of this transformation, and the genre of the *event* (cp. Nöth 1972) is an example of the transformation of most trivial, everyday segments of practical behaviour into pieces of art. This shift from a practical to an aesthetic way of perceiving things has been outlined within the framework of aesthetics. According to E. Bullough's (1912: 89) famous theory of "psychical distance", aesthetic perception occurs through "the cutting out of the practical sides of things and our practical attitude to them". Šklovskij, too, referred to the effect of poetry as creating "a distance between us and the appearances" (cp. Lachmann 1970:

243). This congruence between the statements about poeticalness and the basis of aesthetic perception within non-linguistic codes means that the pragmatic dimension of poetic communication is not specific to language but is situated within the general framework of semiotics.

3.2.2   Semiotics of the Poetic Sign

If it is possible, within the pragmatic dimension, to transform a cooking recipe into a poem merely by reading the text with a different focus, what is then the result within the semantic dimension of the text? Is there a change of meaning, too? A reinterpretation of the theories set up by the Russian Formalists and the Prague Structuralists from the semiotic point of view seems to lead to this conclusion.

"In poetic language", Mukařovský (1964: 19) points out, "foregrounding achieves maximum intensity to the extent of pushing communication into the background as the objective of expression and of being used for its own sake; it is not used in the services of communication but in order to place in the foreground the act of expression, the act of speech itself." And R. Jakobson (1960: 356) writes: "The set (*Einstellung*) toward the *message* as such, focus on the message for its own sake, is the *poetic* function of language." These theories of the poetic language are basically in accordance with the theories of general aesthetics which state that art is perceived for itself alone. E. Panofsky, e.g., writes: "We experience an object aesthetically, when we look at it ... without relating it, intellectually or emotionally to anything outside itself" (in: Kirby 1969: 37).

Applied to our *found poem,* this means that the cooking recipe, considered as a poem, no longer communicates those meanings that are related to "cooking". The text, instead, communicates itself and thus acquires a special sign function. The normal function of a sign is to denote something beyond itself. The sign is not identical with its referent. In contradistinction, the "focus on the message for its own sake", which characterizes the poetic sign, means that the poetic sign is identical with its referent.

In "Esthetics and the Theory of Signs", Morris (1939) defined the aesthetic sign as a special type of an iconic sign. Iconic signs are signs that have certain similarities or common features with their referents. The definition of the aesthetic sign as one which has similarities with its referent seems to be incompatible with the definition of art as directing one's focus to the sign itself, not to the referent. While the former theory seems to be indebted to the principle of mimesis as the basis of art, the latter seems to stand in the tradition of "art for art's sake" (cp. Todorov 1975). Morris himself was aware of these two divergent conceptions in the theory of the aesthetic sign, and tried to resolve this divergence within his theory of value.

Yet, within the typology of signs, the two theories of the aesthetic sign – that which puts the emphasis on iconic representation, and that which emphasizes identity of sign and referent – are not altogether incompatible. Since an icon is related to its referent because of common features, semiotics also distinguishes various degree of iconicity (cp. Morris 1971: 98-9, 273) depending on the degree of correspondence between the features of the sign with those of the referent. Accordingly, signs with the highest possible degree of iconicity are those signs of which the features are in complete congruence with the features of the referent. This is the case with signs that are identical with their referent. Thus, the concept of the iconic sign does provide an adequate semiotic framework for the two divergent theories of the aesthetic sign, and resolves the difference between them as a matter of degree.

Why does poetry use signs referring to no other referent than these signs themselves? Is this autological use of language not a pathological way of communication? There are two answers to this problem. One is that the focus on the language instead of on its referent is only the beginning of poetic analysis and leads to the discovery of more poetic features within the text that can be described in textlinguistic analysis. The other answer is of a metalinguistic kind and was already partly given by Jakobson (1972: 415). Why is it, he asked, that in poetry, a word is experienced as a word and not as a mere representation of its referent? "Because, along with the immediate awareness of the identity of the sign and the referent (A is A_1), we also need the immediate consciousness of the incomplete identity (A is not A_1); this antinomy is essential since without contradiction, there is no movement of concepts, no movement of signs, the relation between concept and sign becomes automatized, the events come to a standstill, and the perception of reality withers away." – This means that the autological use of language in poetry can be a means of bringing into awareness the basic semiotic problems of meaning and reference. Poetry thus converges with semiotics.

In conclusion, it must be emphasized that neither the semiotic definition of the poetic sign nor the pragmatic analysis of poetic communication is sufficient to determine all structures of poeticalness. There are more poetic structures that have to be determined within the framework of textlinguistics. But nevertheless, as our example of the *found poem* has demonstrated, there are texts which cannot be dealt with as poems, unless the semiotic framework of poetry analysis is taken into consideration.

Bibliography

Bar-Hillel, Yehoshua. 1954. Indexical Expressions. *Mind* 63, 359–74
Barley, Nigel F. 1974. Two Anglo-Saxon Sign Systems Compared. *Semiotica* 12, 227–37
Barthes, Roland. 1957. *Mythologies*. Paris: du Seuil
Barthes, Roland. 1967a. *Elements of Semiology*. London: Cape
Barthes, Roland. 1967b. *Système de la mode*. Paris: du Seuil
Bense, Max. 1967. *Semiotik*. Baden Baden: Agis
Bense, Max. 1969. *Einführung in die informationstheoretische Ästhetik*. Reinbeck: Rowohlt
Birdwhistell, Ray L. 1973. *Kinesics and Context*. Harmondsworth: Penguin
Bullough, Edward. 1912. 'Psychical Distance' as a Factor in Art and as an Aesthetic Principle. *British Journal of Psychology* 5.2, 87–118

Coquet, Jean Claude. 1973. *Sémiotique littéraire*. Paris: Mame
Eco, Umberto. 1972. *Einführung in die Semiotik*. München: Fink
Erlich, Viktor. 1969. *Russian Formalism*. The Hague: Mouton
Eschbach, Achim. 1974. *Zeichen-Text-Bedeutung, Bibliographie zu Theorie und Praxis der Semiotik*. München: Fink
Garvin, Paul L. 1964. *A Prague School Reader on Esthetics, Literary Structure, and Style*. Washington: Georgetown UP
Grabner-Haidner, Anton. 1973. *Semiotik und Theologie*. München: Kösel
Grattan, J.H.G., Charles Singer. 1952. *Anglo-Saxon Magic and Medicine*. London: Oxford UP
Greimas, Algirdas-Julien. 1966. *Sémantique structurale*. Paris: Larousse
Harris, Zellig S. 1963. *Discourse Analysis Reprints*. The Hague: Mouton
Hermes, Hans. 1938. *Semiotik. Eine Theorie der Zeichengestalten als Grundlage für Untersuchungen von formalisierten Sprachen*. Leipzig: Hirzel
Hünig, Wolfgang. 1974. *Strukturen des Comic Strip*. Hildesheim, New York: Olms
Jakobson, Roman. 1960. Linguistics and Poetics. *Style in Language,* ed. Thomas A. Sebeok. Cambridge, Mass.: MIT Press, 350–77
Jakobson, Roman. 1965. A la recherche de l'essence du langage. *Diogène* 51, 22–38
Jakobson, Roman. 1972. Was ist Poesie? *Texte der russischen Formalisten, Bd II,* ed. W.-D. Stempel. München: Fink, 393–417
Kirby, Michael. 1969. *The Art of Time*. New York: Dutton
Klaus, Georg. 1963. *Semiotik und Erkenntnistheorie*. München: Fink[4]: 1973
Kluge, F. 1885. Zur Geschichte der Zeichensprache. *Internationale Zeitschrift für allgemeine Sprachwissenschaft* 2, 116–40
Knilli, Friedrich, ed. 1971. *Semiotik des Films*. München: Hanser
Koch, Walter A. 1971. *Varia Semiotica*. Hildesheim, New York: Olms
Koch, Walter A. 1972. Vorwort zur deutschen Ausgabe. Christian Metz. *Semiologie des Films*. München: Fink, 11–6
Koch, Walter A. 1973. Einleitung. *Perspektiven der Linguistik I,* ed. W.A. Koch. Stuttgart: Kröner, XI–LV
Koch, Walter A. 1974. Semiotik und Sprachgenese. *Perspektiven der Linguistik II,* ed. W.A. Koch. Stuttgart: Kröner, 312–46.
Kowzan, Tadeusz. 1968. Le signe au théatre. *Diogène* 61, 59–90
Lachmann, Renate. 1970. Die 'Verfremdung' und das 'Neue Sehen' bei Viktor Šklovskij. *Poetica* 3, 226–49
Leach, Edmund. 1970. *Claude Lévi-Strauss*. New York: Viking
Lévi-Strauss, Claude. 1968. The Structural Study of Myth. C. Lévi-Strauss. *Structural Anthropology*. London: A. Lane-Penguin, 206–31
Lévi-Strauss, Claude. 1970. *The Raw and the Cooked*. London: Cape
Martinet, André. 1960. *Eléments de linguistique générale*. Paris: Colin
Metz, Christian. 1972. *Semiologie des Films*. München: Fink
Morris, Charles. 1939. Esthetics and the Theory of Signs. *Journal of Unified Science* 8. 131–50
Morris, Charles W. 1971. *Writings on the General Theory of Signs*. The Hague: Mouton
Mukařovský, Jan. 1936. L'art comme fait sémiologique. *Actes du 8me congrès international de philosophie, Prague*. 1065–72
Mukařovský, Jan. 1964. Standard Language and Poetic Language. *A Prague School Reader on Esthetics, Literary Structure, and Style,* ed. P.L. Garvin. Washington: Georgetown UP, 17–30
Nöth, Winfried. 1972. *Strukturen des Happenings*. Hildesheim, New York: Olms
Nöth, Winfried. 1975. *Semiotik. Eine Einführung mit Beispielen für Reklameanalysen*. Tübingen: Niemeyer
Nöth, Winfried. 1977. *Dynamik semiotischer Systeme*. Stuttgart: Metzler
Peirce, Charles Sanders. 1931–35; 1958–60. *Collected Papers of Charles Sanders Peirce,* Vol. 1–6, ed. Charles Hartshorne, Paul Weiss, Vol 7–8, ed. Arthur W. Burks. Cambridge, Mass.: Harvard UP.
Porter, Bern. 1972. *Found Poems*. New York: Something Else Press

Resnikow, Lasar Ossipowitsch. 1968. *Erkenntnistheoretische Fragen der Semiotik*. Berlin: Deutscher Verlag der Wissenschaften

Ruesch, Jurgen. 1972. *Semiotic Approaches to Human Relations*. The Hague: Mouton

Saussure, Ferdinand de. 1969. *Cours de linguistique générale*. Paris: Payot

Sebeok, Thomas A. 1972. *Perspectives in Zoosemiotics*. The Hague: Mouton

Segre, Cesare. 1973. *Semiotics and Literary Criticism*. The Hague: Mouton

Shands, Harley C. 1970. *Semiotic Approaches to Psychiatry*. The Hague: Mouton

Storms, G. 1948. *Anglo-Saxon Magic*. The Hague: Nijhoff

Todorov, Tzvetan. 1975. Literature and Semiotics. *The Tell-Tale Sign,* ed. T.A.Sebeok. Lisse: de Ridder, 97–102

Trabant, Jürgen. 1970. *Zur Semiologie des literarischen Kunstwerks*. München: Fink

Walther, Elisabeth. 1962. Textsemiotik. Max Bense. 1962. *Theorie der Texte*. Köln: Kiepenheuer & Witsch, 65–9

Walther, Elisabeth. 1965. Semiotische Analyse. *Mathematik und Dichtung,* ed. Helmut Kreuzer, Rul Gunzenhäuser. München: Nymphenburger V., 143–57

Walther, Elisabeth. 1974. *Allgemeine Zeichenlehre*. Stuttgart: dva

Wienold, Götz. 1972. *Semiotik der Literatur*. Frankfurt: Athenäum

A Formal Semiotic Text Theory as an Integrated Theory of Natural Language (Methodological Remarks)

János S. Petöfi
University of Bielefeld

1   Basic problems for an integrated theory

1.1   It is a common feature of contemporary linguistics that efforts are undertaken to devise a so-called 'integrated theory' to provide a homogeneous framework for research into different aspects of language.

Since natural languages form an intricately structured organic system and integrate various combinations of phenomena, they by their very nature prove that it is possible to integrate descriptions of their different aspects. What can be discussed and actually is discussed are the reasons for considering certain aspects while others are left out, and the motivations for this decision.

1.2   A short characterization of some of the main trends in contemporary linguistics can serve as an introduction into the discussion about a particular scope of integration:

(1) By applying the method of American descriptive linguistics or of other structuralist schools the scope of aspects investigated is from the outset limited to the analysis of certain oppositions occurring on various levels; research is based on a *corpus* and results in a taxonomy.

(2) The method used in generative linguistics enables one to integrate descriptions of the phonological, syntactic, and linguistico-semantic aspects. (Katz and Postal use the term 'linguistic' to refer to this integration in Katz–Postal 1964.) Research in generative linguistics deals with the notion *'competence'* which also requires psychological explanation.

(3) Speech act theory can be seen as a necessary addition to (and modification of) generative linguistic theory. Research concentrates on the different *conventions* on which speech acts are based.

(4) Montague grammar can be seen as a correction of generative linguistic theory. Montague extended the scope of generative grammar to include logico-semantics and formal-pragmatics into his theory. The research strategy consists in the gradual extension of descriptions of language *fragments* (artificial mini-corpora selected for a given purpose) until a linguistic, logico-semantic and formal-pragmatic description accounts for the entire individual language.

(5) Text linguistics deals with the question whether it is necessary to analyse *structures beyond the frame of the sentence.* With respect to the methods used, the different text linguistic programs vary as do the various schools of sentence-centered grammars.

(6) The main concern of the theory of verbal communication and of non-formal pragmatic studies is the analysis of natural languages in communication-al settings, including the treatment of intentional meaning. In this context it is usual to speak of so-called *'communicative competence'* (it is not clear whether it has psychological implications or not).

(7) The theory of verbal communication was further expanded by its application to the analysis of literature to include research in and description of *text production* and *text reception.*

Explicit formal methods have been developed only in generative linguistics and Montague grammar.

1.3   When looking at this spectrum of linguistic schools it becomes clear that if we aim at constructing an integrated formal theory at this stage, the scope of this theory can and must be wider than the scope of generative linguistics, but it cannot possibly cover all the aspects mentioned above. If one accepts that the treatment and the scope of semantics are the decisive criteria, speech act theory, Montague grammar and text linguistics should be considered in the first place as being of importance in the establishment of an integrated formal theory. The central methodological properties of such a theory can be described as follows.

(a) Utterances with text character (i.e. discourses) are the basic language units to be investigated by the theory.
Motivation:
(1) Only discourse can reflect all phenomena in an act of communication,
(2) native speakers of a natural language also know the conventions that have to be used in a discourse,
(3) many properties of an utterance cannot be described within a sentential frame.

(b) The theory covers the phonological, syntactic (including linguistico-semantic aspects), (logico-)semantic and (formal-)pragmatic aspects of discourses.
Motivation:
(1) These aspects together form the complete set of semiotic aspects,
(2) research into these aspects implies investigating a whole range of different conventions, including also speech acts conventions,
(3) Montague's descriptions of language fragments seems to confirm that it is possible to elaborate a logico-semantic theory for natural languages, not only for formal languages; this implies that it must also be possible to devise a theory which aims at describing all semiotic aspects within a homogenous framework.

(c) The object of description is the knowledge native speakers have about the aspects mentioned in (b).

Motivation:

(1) This knowledge comprises the knowledge about the system of phonological, syntactic, semantic, and pragmatic conventions necessary for the production and reception of discourses within a language community,

(2) it includes knowledge about the drawing of inferences from utterances/discourses,

(3) this kind of knowledge does not imply the existence of a disputable psychic substratum as required for the application of the term 'competence' in generative linguistics.

(d) The term 'discourse' in this context is to be understood as referring to a given utterance of text character and not to an utterance being produced just now (for the time being, we avoid dealing with objects mentioned in 1.2. [6] and [7]). This restriction on the range of objects can be motivated by the following considerations:

(1) Text production and text reception can be investigated indirectly, even under this restriction,

(2) if we want to analyse communication processes, we need an integrated theory as outlined here.

(e) The goal of description is the representation of the knowledge defined in (c) by an explicit system of rules (or in other words, the *rational reconstruction* of the conventions existing within a language community).

Motivation:

(1) Only the explicit description enables an intersubjectively valid exchange of ideas about language systems,

(2) only an explicit description of natural language can allow further progress in the analysis of the system and function of natural languages.

(f) The integrated semiotic theory characterized in (a) to (e) can be called *a formal semiotic text theory,* and its task can be defined as the explication of the notion 'coherent text in L'.

Remark:

In this context it is better to operate with two different notions 'coherent text in L': a theoretical notion ('coherent text in L_T', where L_T stands for the theoretical language of the text theory) and an empirical notion ('coherent text in L_O', where L_O stands for the object language itself). Linguistic research must aim at reducing the discrepancy between these two notions to near-identity.

The corpora used as a basis for the construction of a formal semiotic text theory are partly natural corpora-discourses, partly artificially produced fragments for the purpose of representing a specific aspect.

2   The structure of a formal semiotic text theory

The methodological principles discussed in the preceding chapter do not affect the actual structure of a formal semiotic text theory. The could be realized in differently constructed text theories.

In the following paragraphs I want to discuss some of the major methodological aspects of the structure of a particular formal semiotic text theory: the so-called 'text-structure world-structure theory' (with the German abbreavation TeSWeST).

2.1   The TeSWeST aims at describing the syntactic, semantic and pragmatic structure of natural language texts. In detail this means
(a) the assigning of (all possible) syntactic (intensional-semantic) representations to natural language texts,
(b) the world-semantic (extensional-semantic) interpretation of the individual intensional-semantic representations,
(c) the generating of syntactic (intensional-semantic) representations, and
(d) the comparing of a text, of the intensional-semantic representation of a text, and of the extensional-semantic representations of a text with other texts, the intensional-semantic representations of other texts, and the extensional-semantic representations of other texts, respectively.

Since these points represent a generalization of what a logical theory has aimed at, the structure of the TeSWeST must necessarily be analogous to logic. This applies not only to the structure of the theory's components, but also to the relation between the different components. There are two reasons why I speak of analogy rather than identity with logic:
(1) The aims of the TeSWeST are much more general than the aims of a logical theory, and
(2) the range of objects to be described by the TeSWeST (i.e. natural language texts) is much wider than the range of natural language objects described by logical theories so far.

Given this difference between logical theories and the TeSWeST, then it follows that the traditional structure of a logical theory, i.e. logical syntax plus logical semantics, must be replaced by a much more complex structure in the TeSWeST, at least at the present stage of research. This complex structure is shown in Figure 1 (where the direction of the analysis is indicated by arrows).

The main components of the TeSWeST are
the Text Grammatical Component (TGrC),
the World-Semantic Component (WSeC), and
the Lexicon Component.

The WSeC dominates the structure of the TeSWeST. The WSeC directly or indirectly determines the structure and functions of the other components.

The task of the Logico-Syntactic Formation Component (LoSynFC) is to construct syntactically well-formed formulae (logico-syntactic representations [LoSynR]) and to define logico-syntactic inferences (LoSynInf).

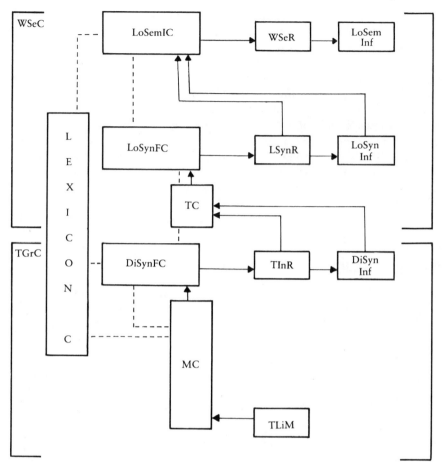

Figure 1

Explanation of abbreviations used:

DiSynFC   Disambiguating Syntactic Formation Component
DiSynInf   Disambiguated syntactic inferences
LoSemIC   Logico-Semantic Interpretation Component
LoSemInf   Logico-semantic inferences
LoSynFC   Logico-Syntactic Formation Component
LoSynInf   Logico-syntactic inferences
LoSynR   Logico-syntactic representations
MC   Mapping Component
TC   Translation Component
TGrC   Text Grammatical Component
TInR   Intensional-semantic text representations
TLiM   Linear text manifestations
WSeC   World-Semantic Component
WSeR   World-semantic representations

The task of the Logico-Semantic Interpretation Component (LoSemIC) is to carry out the world-semantic (extensional-semantic) interpretation of the LoSynR-s (the result of which is a world-semantic representation [WSeR]) and to draw world-specific logico-semantic inferences (LoSemInf).

The TGrC must contain a Disambiguating Syntactic Formation Component (DiSynFC) to enable the construction of unambiguous (intensional-semantic) text representations [TInR] based on the analysis or generation of natural language texts. The TInR-s should be translatable into a logico-syntactic language. Apart from the formation rules of the TInR-s the DiSynFC also contains rules for drawing disambiguated syntactic inferences (DiSynInf). The TGrC must also contain a Mapping Component (MC) which maps the TInR-s to natural language texts (linear text manifestations [TLiM]) or the TLiM-s to all admissible TInR-s.

(A Translation Component (TC) must guarantee the transition from DiSynFC to the LoSynFC.)

The Lexicon Component contains syntactic and semantic information and is closely connected with both the TGrC and the WSeC.

2.2   After this short characterization of the components of the TeSWeST, let us now turn to the methodological principles governing the structure of the TeSWeST and the strategy which has to be followed when constructing it.

(a) The WSeC and the TGrC must be separated from each other; the TGrC must also be able to function as an autonomous component.

   (a1) The separation of the TGrC from the WSeC (i.e. the linguistic from the logical component, or, in other words, the construction of a DiSynFC parallel to the LoSynFC) is justifiable from two points of view ($1\alpha - 1\delta$ and 2):

      (1α) The rule systems of logical syntaxes in use so far are not suitable for the description of natural languages, because the logical formulae assigned by them to natural language utterances are only capable of representing a part of the syntactic information found in natural language utterances. The reconstruction of the remaining part of the syntactic information is – without any apparent reason! – regarded as a task of the semantic component (cf. e.g. how the arguments of predicates are interpreted syntactically as ordered tuples, and how they are interpreted semantically);

      (1β) even without these shortcomings the rule systems referred to in (1α) ought to be enlarged to become suitable for describing natural languages; however, at present one cannot predict to what extent the set of logical signs (and consequently also the set of philosophical logics) can be enlarged;

      (1γ) but even if we had at our disposal all the philosophical logics necessary for the syntactic description and semantic interpretation of natural languages, and all problems within the particular logics had

been solved, this would still not mean that all these logics could
function without major difficulties as subsystems within a highly
complex system;

(1δ) many of the fundamental questions arising from the application of
model-theoretical interpretations to natural language discourses
have not yet been solved, not even within the already existing
philosophical logics.

As a consequence of (1α) to (1δ) one can only expect a necessarily slow
further progress in the construction of the WSeC, which would also retard
the elaboration of the TGrC if it is not separated from the WSeC. But such
a delay would have grave consequences in many different respects, also for
the elaboration of the WSeC.

(2) The separation of the two components is not only reasonable from
a technical point of view as pointed out above. It is a justifiable
demand that all the linguistico-semantic aspects of natural languages
(e.g. paraphrasability, translation from one language into another
etc.) should be describable without a logico-semantic apparatus.
(Thus on the one hand we need a specially constructed DiSynFC (cf.
[b1]) and on the other hand also the structure and the function of the
Lexicon Component has to be defined in a special way (cf. [d].)

(a2) If we separate the TGrC from the WSeC the following condition has to
be fulfilled: The rule system of the TGrC must enable the construction of
such TInR-s that are unambiguously translatable into LoSynR-s constructed by means of a (future) LoSynFC. (In the present stage of
logico-linguistic research the structure of this LoSynFC would be close
to modal predicate logic syntaxes.)

By fulfilling this condition the demand formulated in (a1) (2) can be
fulfilled without impeding the corresponding development of syntactic,
linguistico-semantic and logico-semantic research. (The results of purely
linguistic studies can be directly used for the analysis of problems with
the world-semantic interpretation.)

(b) The central methodological principles governing the TGrC are as follows:

(b1) The rule system of the DiSynFC, and the accordingly produced TInR-s
must meet the following conditions:

(1) The TInR-s must be canonical representations indifferent to the
surface structure of actual utterances/discourses of the particular
natural language; this is a precondition

(α) for a theoretically acceptable and optimal handling of paraphras-
ing (i.e. the replacement of utterances/discourses by semantically
identical but structurally different utterances/discourses) which
occur in all natural languages;

(β) for carrying out optimally diachronic and synchronic (stylistic,
dialectological, socio-linguistic) comparisons within a given
natural language, and

(γ) for fulfilling the theory's claim to (an at least limited) universality.

(2) The TInR-s must be able to represent completely the syntactic information contained explicitly or implicitly in natural language utterances.

(3) The structure of the TInR-s must allow

(α) their easy construction,

(β) an easy derivation of DiSynInf-s from them and

(γ) their systematic decomposition and the arrangement of the constituents into various kinds of classes while retaining the information where they originated from (this last requirement is, above all, indispensable for the semantic interpretation of discourses).

(4) The TInR-s must contain all the information necessary to optimally carry out the semantic interpretation; this means that if possible nothing should happen in the WSeC but the assignment of the appropriate denotata to the individual elementary signs of the TInR and the construction of the interpretation of the utterance in question out of these denotata.

(5) The TInR-s must allow the explication of 'coherent text in L'; this means that

(α) in case of analysis they must contain all the information necessary for deciding whether the TInR obtained as the result of the analysis is a representation of a coherent discourse of the natural language L or not,

(β) in case of synthesis the DiSynFC must only generate representations of coherent discourses.

(b2) The MC must meet the following requirements:

(1) In case of synthesis it must enable

(α) the derivation of such TLiM-s that manifest the intension represented by the given TInR and only this;

(β) the derivation of such TLiM-s that manifest the intension represented by the given TInR, but are ambiguous;

(γ) the derivation of such TLiM-s that do not entirely manifest the intension represented by the given TInR, however, when analysing these derived TLiM-s, among the admissible TInR-s that can be assigned to these TLiM-s, the originally given TInR can also be reconstructed.

(2) In case of analysis it must enable

(α) the discovery of the appropriate TInR (or TInR-s) with respect to all TLiM-s enumerated in (b2) (1);

(β) the synthesis of all DiSynInf-s adequately derived from the obtained TInR-s.

(c) As to the WSeC, only two general methodological principles can be formulated at present:

(c1) The LoSemIC must be capable of operating with a flexible notion of 'world'. 'Flexible' here means that
- (1) the set of world-complexes that can be assigned as interpretational models to the given TInR-s in the course of the world-semantic interpretation should represent a good approximation to the intuitively possible world-complexes
- (2) different kinds of consistency conditions (among them also the condition of inconsistency) should be admissible for the sub-worlds of the world-complexes.

(c2) The LoSynFC must be capable of representing fully and unambiguously all information that are contained in the TInR-s. (Only in this case is it possible to speak of a TC at all.)

(d) The Lexicon Component
- (d1) must enable the functioning of the MC, DiSynFC, TC, and of the LoSemIC,
- (d2) as to the functioning of the DiSynFC
    - (1) the Lexicon Component must correspond to a traditional unilingual dictionary plus an encyclopedia of a limited size; in other words this means that
        - (α) it should provide an *optimally large* part of common-sense knowledge, which would guarantee an optimal derivability of implicatures from individual utterances/discourses in standard contexts;
        - (β) it should provide an *optimally structured* part of common-sense knowledge: it must assign appropriately structured and the adequate type of explicantia (functioning as definientia in the Lexicon Component) to the individual explicanda (functioning as definienda in the Lexicon Component);
    - (2) the Lexicon component must meet the formal requirements demanded by the TGrC; in other words this means that
        - (α) the structure of the explications (definitions in the Lexicon Component) must enable the smooth derivation of implicatures of the kind mentioned above,
        - (β) the Lexicon Component must be a syntactic-semantic valency lexicon and operate with canonical syntactic-semantic categories as its elementary units (not with surface structure categories).

Even though I did not explicitly describe how the various methodological principles are connected, I hope that it is evident.

2.3   In this context I also want to discuss briefly the explication of the notion 'coherent text in L_T'. The TeSWeST can explain it on two levels: on the TInR level and on the WSeR level. (On the level of TLiM certain intuitively coherent texts do not form a coherent chain, grammars only operating with structures close to TLiM are therefore incapable of describing the coherence of these texts.)

On the level of the TInR the canonical representation of an object language text forms a hierarchical connexion. Since it is the case that the so-called 'connective elements' play the central role in creating the coherence necessary to form this connexion, the main task of text theoretical research consists in the analysis and description of the structure of these connective elements. 'Connective element' here refers to so-called 'canonical connective elements'. The following three questions arise in this context:

(a) What are the canonical connectives (and other elements of the canonical structure such as e.g. temporal information) into which the object language connectives (including punctuation marks) are to be translated?

(b) How can the possible argument places of canonical connectives be specified (semantically, pragmatically)?

(c) Into which logical signs must the TC translate the canonical connectives?

The explicit definition of what constitutes 'macro-structures', a term which is often used for object language texts, depends, after all, on the answers to the question (b).

With respect to the WSeC 'coherence' refers to the internal coherence of the individual subworlds of the world system and to the coherence of the world system itself that can be assigned as an interpretation to the text under analysis. At present there is not much that could be said about the relation between coherence on the TInR level and coherence on the WSeR level. It seems to be clear, however, that the coherence of a TInR ist neither a necessary nor a sufficient condition for the coherence of the WSeR which is assigned to this TInR.

3   Concluding remarks

3.1   There are two reasons why at the present stage of logico-linguistic research it is important to discuss the possibility of constructing an integrated theory and the problems associated with the structure of an integrated theory:

(i) The object under investigation, i.e. natural language texts (discourses) is so complex that its description can only be adequate if different aspects of the relation between its individual structural elements are described, and this can only be achieved by an integrated theory.

(ii) Linguistic and logico-linguistic research economy is another decisive question, because logico-semantic interpretation requires a rather complex apparatus, even if the description is restricted to certain utterance types of sentence character.

The framework of an integrated theory assures that the same attention is devoted to making the particular sub-apparatuses, necessary for the description of different aspects, compatible with each other, as is taken up by discussions about the internal structure of these sub-apparatuses.

3.2   There are two possible methods of constructing an integrated theory: one can either set out from an existing apparatus (with its limitations but well-known scope) and try to modify it to the extent required by the object under investigation, or one can start with what is required for the description of the object and try to devise an apparatus accordingly.

In this paper on the methodological questions of a formal semiotic text theory I have kept in mind both aspects. In my outline of the text grammatical component I started with the requirements for the description of the object, I left open, however, how the so-called 'world-semantic component' should be set up. Perhaps this solution is acceptable to linguists (in a narrow sense) and logicians/logico-linguists. It is obvious that what is important for the linguists is the description of natural language, while logicians and logico-linguists can only be interested in the enlargement of the scope of the existing apparatuses, even if this enlargement has its limits. In the long run, however, all attempts of expanding existing methods can contribute to the construction of an apparatus required for our purpose.

Logico-linguistic research has, without doubt, already decisively contributed to recent improvements in the analysis of natural languages. It is, however, also clear that there is still a long way to go to the establishment of an integrated theory as outlined in this paper. In order to stimulate this kind of formal semiotic research it is necessary to intensify the dialogue between linguists (in a narrow sense) and logico-linguists on the one hand, and between representatives of different schools in both camps on the other hand. The methodological principles discussed in this paper are also meant to promote such an intensified exchange of ideas.

3.3   Finally I would like to make a remark on a terminological question. In discussions about methodology it has been stated that there is no need for a text theory, since an appropriately constructed sentence-grammar would also be capable of describing discourse structures (cf. Dascal–Margalit 1974; Petöfi–Rieser 1976). It is not important, in my opinion, whether the *theoretical construct* that can be assigned to an object language text (to a discourse) as a representation is called 'sentence' or 'text'. The essential thing is that the apparatus in question should be capable of providing an adequate description of object language *texts*. It can naturally not be denied that one can attempt to reach this aim by enlarging the apparatus which was originally devised for the description of object language sentences. It must naturally also be clear that the resulting expanded apparatus will no longer be very similar to the original sentence grammar.

If we accept that one of the main tasks of the linguistics is to provide a syntactic, semantic and pragmatic description of object language *texts,* and this should not be difficult to accept (even for sentence-grammarians), the insistence on using the term 'sentence-grammar' as the name of the appropriate discourse-centered apparatus can only be motivated by tactical considerations.

(More about the overall structure and particular aspects of the TeSWeST can be found in Petöfi 1973, Petöfi–Rieser 1974, Petöfi 1975, Rieser 1976; an elaborated and in some points modified version of the 1973 rule system of the DiSynFC ist contained in Petöfi 1976; questions about the Lexicon Component are treated in Petöfi–Bredemeier 1976.)

References

Dascal, M. – A. Margalit: 1974, "A New 'Revolution' in Linguistics? – 'Text-Grammars' vs. 'Sentence-Grammars'". *Theoretical Linguistics,* vol. 1, n. 1/2, pp. 195–213.

Katz, J. J. – P. Postal: 1964, *An Integrated Theory of Linguistic Description.* Cambridge, Mass.: M.I.T.

Montague, R.: 1974, *Formal Philosophy: Selected Papers of Richard Montague,* edited and with an introduction by R. Thomason. New Haven: Yale University Press.

Petöfi, J. S.: 1973, "Towards an Empirically Motivated Grammatical Theory of Verbal Texts." In: Petöfi–Rieser (eds.) 1973, pp. 205–275.

–: 1975, *Vers une théorie partielle du texte.* Papers in Textlinguistics, no. 9. Hamburg: Buske.

–: 1976, Structure and Function of the Grammatical Component of the Text-Structure – World-Structure Theory. In: Guenthner, F. – S. J. Schmidt (eds.) *Proceedings of the First Bad Homburg Workshop on Formal Semantics.* Dordrecht: Reidel (Forthcoming).

Petöfi, J. S. – H. Rieser, 1974, *Probleme der modelltheoretischen Interpretation von Texten.* Papers in Textlinguistics, no. 7. Hamburg: Buske.

–: 1976, Some Arguments Against Counter-Revolution. On M. Dascal's and A. Margalit's "A New 'Revolution' in Linguistics? – 'Text-Grammars' vs. 'Sentence-Grammars'". *Linguistics* 188, pp. 11–22.

Petöfi, J. S. – J. Bredemeier (eds.): 1976, *Das Lexikon in der Grammatik, die Grammatik im Lexikon: Beiträge zur Struktur des Lexikons und Zur Texttheorie.* (Forthcoming)

Petöfi, J. S. – H. Rieser (eds.): 1973, *Studies in Text Grammar.* Dordrecht: Reidel.

Rieser, H.: 1976, *Aspekte einer partiellen Texttheorie.* Untersuchungen zur Textgrammatik mit "nicht-linear" festgelegter Basis unter besonderer Berücksichtigung des Lexikon- und des Fachsprachenproblems. Manuskript. Bielefeld.

Searle, J. R.: 1969, *Speech Acts.* An Essay in the Philosophy of Language. Cambridge: Cambridge University Press.

Some Problems of Communicative Text Theories*

Siegfried J. Schmidt
University of Bielefeld

0.1 Opening remarks

In this paper I do not intend to give a survey of the different approaches to research in the domain of so-called communicative text theories. Such a survey would demand more space than is available here; furthermore, several books containing such surveys have recently been published (e.g. Henne 1975; Braunroth et al. 1975; Schlieben–Lange 1975).

I therefore mean to discuss unsolved problems that should be tackled by theories of this kind over the next few years.

To begin with I shall characterize the framework in which the problems of communicative text theories should be located.

1 *"Communicative text theories": a cover term for a complex field of research*

1.1 Linguistic research over the last decade – divergent as the different standpoints may be – has been characterized by one recurrent feature: an orientation towards what is commonly called "communication". Despite the many differences in approach, what all recent attempts to construct a theory of natural languages seem to have in common is that they are communication-oriented, that is to say they aim to construct theories which allow the linguist to describe and explain, within the framework of a homogeneous theory, the internal structure of sentences and texts as well as the conditions and rules underlying successful communication. This aim implies a development of linguistic research in several respects:

(a) the field of research has had to be *modified* and *amplified:* from isolated words or sentences the interest has shifted to texts in social contexts;

(b) the construction of theories that are more powerful than any of the tradi-

---

* The term "communicative text theory" has been proposed by Dressler who invited me to deliver a contribution with the title "communicative text theory". – I am indebted to the members of my DFG Research Group "Theorie der Literarischen Kommunikation" (Finke, Kindt, Wirrer, Zobel) for their critical remarks, to B. and J. Wirrer and especially to Käthe Henke for stylistic advice.
[1] For details see the survey in Schmidt (^{2}1976)

tional linguistic models and that therefore allow us to explain *more* (and more complicated) linguistic facts;

(c) the construction of theories that give *better* explanations of the problems than any of the theories so far available;

(d) a new appreciation of the *interrelation* of linguistic theories.

1.2   The reasons that led linguists to try to construct communicative text theories are well-known. I shall therefore restrict myself to a number of general points:

(a) in the fifties and sixties it became apparent that structuralist and generative linguistics had failed to explain transphrastic problems (e.g. anaphoric connections between sentences) as well as other problems essential to linguistic communication (e.g. presuppositions). This failure motivated many linguists to ask whether linguistics up to Chomsky's "Aspects" had perhaps been operating with too restricted a model of language, relying as it did on a model which defined language as a system of signs and the speaker as an abstract automaton.

(b) The fact that many linguists concentrated their investigations on phonological, syntactical and syntactic-semantic analyses favoured the view that generative linguistics was based on a reductionist fallacy, a view supported by the works of philosophers of language like Wittgenstein, Austin and Searle and works by Marxist psychologists like Sève, Wygotski and Leont'ev; these works opened up a new approach to language as "verbal communication", which was interpreted as a form of social interaction.

(c) The increasing interest in the political implications of scientific research confronted linguists with the question of how to define the relation of linguistics to social reality and how to justify its aims of research and the social and scientific assumptions on which it was based.

(d) The new approach to language as a form of social interaction encouraged empirical research in spoken everyday language, its rules, conventions and special features. Labov for instance formulated his motivation for empirical research as follows: "The penalties for ignoring data from the speech community are a growing sense of frustration, a proliferation of moot questions, and a conviction that linguistics is a game in which each theorist chooses the solution that fits his taste or intuition. I do not believe that we need at this point a new 'theory of language'; rather, we need a new way of doing linguistics [...]". (1970: 85)

(e) First (descriptive) analyses of verbal communication supported the hypothesis that a natural language is not at all a homogeneous system but a framework that integrates very different kinds of "languages", i.e. ways to communicating by means of verbal signs. Consequently the analysis of speech variation became an important object of linguistic research.

1.2.1   Of course this sketch of the various reasons for an orientation of linguistic research towards phenomena of communication is far from complete;

but that is not the purpose of my paper. The questions I want to discuss are these:

What are the results of linguists' orientation towards verbal communication? What sorts of problems have appeared in this field of research? What are the problems that should be solved in further research work?

1.3   The present situation in linguistic research on verbal communication is complicated and a detailed report of all the different approaches would be a task in its own right, as the following list of topics may indicate:
(a) analysis of argumentation structures (Kummer, 1972)
(b) elaboration of conversational postulates (Grice, 1975)
(c) definition of the notion of convention (Lewis, 1969)
(d) text typology on the basis of models of communication (Gülich and Raible, 1975)
(e) models of text-processing (Wienold 1972)
(f) development of context grammars (van Dijk, 1974, 1976)
(g) analysis of rules of everyday communication and their social impact (Labov, 1970)
(h) action-theoretical models of language and communication (Kummer, 1975).

For the purpose of the present paper a typological survey will suffice especially as this volume contains a number of articles dealing with different aspects of text theories.

1.3.1   One type of research in this domain (e.g. that of Wunderlich and Maas) may be characterized as an elaboration of speech act theories. These theories are methodologically linked with the sociology of interaction (Mead and his followers), the ethnomethodology (from Schütz to Cicourel, Dell Hymes, Gumperz, Garfinkel, Goffman, Sacks and others) and/or Marxist theories of action and communication (see the report by Braunroth et al., 1975). Some favourite topics in this domain, which borders on socio-linguistics and is normally called "linguistic pragmatics", are analysis of sequences of speech acts; analysis of the situational elements of communication; analysis and definition of concepts like 'intention' and 'convention', analysis of meta-communicative signals, etc.[2].

---

[2] See e.g. some bibliographies and readers:

R. Meyer-Hermann, 1974, Vorarbeitung zu einer Bibliographie zur Sprechakt-Theorie (und Annexes) Mimeo: Universität Bielefeld

J.E. Grimes and D.J. Cranmer, 1972, Bibliography on discourse and related topics. Mimeo: Cornell University, College of Arts and Sciences, Ithaka, New York.

A. Eschbach, 1974, Zeichen-Text-Bedeutung.
Bibliographie zur Theorie und Praxis der Semiotik. München: Fink (Kritische Information Bd. 32)

W. Dressler und S. J. Schmidt, eds., 1973, Textlinguistik. München: (Kritische Information Bd. 4)

P.P. Giglioli, ed., 1972, Language and social context. Harmondsworth: Penguin

D. Wunderlich, Hrsg., 1972, Linguistische Pragmatik. Frankfurt/M.: Athenäum

1.3.2   A second type of research in this field tries to develop formal text grammars which take into consideration intensional and modal logic, modal theories, and logic of action. These text grammars are communicative text grammars in so far as they try to answer syntactic as well as semantic and pragmatic questions[3] in the framework of a homogeneous theory (cf. Petöfi, 1975).

Petöfi and Rieser for example claim that "[...] the most important phenomena usually referred to as 'pragmatic', like choice of pronouns, temporal and local deixis, relations of time and tense, presupposition and inference, successful and unsuccessful speech acts can only be treated in connection with those structures of natural languages that have been intensively discussed in linguistics ever since the coming into existence of generative semantics; this refers to phenomena like disambiguation, the stating of paraphrastic relations between utterances, definition and quantification in natural languages, encyclopedic and linguistic information in the lexicon, analysis of performative verbs and so on." (1974: VIII)[4] [my translation]

1.3.3.   A third type of research elaborates ideas and models of the logic of action in the light of text-theoretical considerations. Thus the investigations by von Wright (1967, 1975) and Nowakowska (1973) have influenced recent work on action theory by Brennenstuhl (1975) and work on text theory by Kummer (1975), who, in addition, tries to integrate materialistic psychology (Leont'ev, Sève, Rubinstein, Wygotski).

1.3.4   "[...] a formal reconstruction of an assumed system of rules enabling native speakers to relate one or more discourses of a natural language with one or more appropriate contexts, and conversely [...]" is – according to van Dijk (1976:26) – the proper task of formal pragmatics. Using his text grammar (1972), sketches of a context grammar (1974, 1976) and work on the philosophy of action (1974a, 1975a) as a theoretical basis, van Dijk has started to cooperate with psychologists (Kintsch) in order to develop tools for use in experimental research on text grammars. Results so far concern the form and functions of textual macro-structures and convincingly show the necessity and effectiveness of interdisciplinary empirical research in this field (see van Dijk and Kintsch 1975; van Dijk et al. 1975).

2   Some general problems of communicative text theories

2.1   As the rough typology in section 1 has shown a number of different approaches have been used in the various attempts to a arrive at phenomena of

---

[3] For a detailed analysis of the relation between these semiotic concepts see Petöfi (1974), whose position I share in this respect.

[4] See e.g. M. Rüttenauer, ed., 1972, Textlinguistik und Pragmatik. Hamburg: Buske (Papiere zur Textlinguistik, Bd. 3)
J. S. Petöfi and R. Rieser, eds., 1973, Studies in text grammar. Dordrecht: Reidel
J. S. Petöfi and S. J. Schmidt, eds., 1977, Texttheorie. Berlin: W. de Gruyter (in press)

verbal communication. To the present writer the main problems in the construction of communicative text theories become evident from the following:

- the field under investigation is extremely complex; it is noticeable that almost no writer on communicative text theories has started his work with a detailed and explicit description of the domain of research concerned. The result is – in my opinion – that there is hardly a communicative text theory that explicitly evaluates the kinds and dimensions of abstractions it works with – abstractions that, of course, are indispensable to theory construction;
- while formal text theories fulfil the requirement of explicit formal representation, they are still far from explaining the functioning of natural languages in social contexts and the mechanisms of social communication processes; speech act theories on the other hand usually lack formal stringency;
- all communicative text theories work with unsatisfactory models of action and communication: the degree of idealization of these models is too high, and/or the scope of application is too unspecific. Most models of communication are no more than item-collecting models (e.g. Wunderlich, 1971, and Schmidt, 1973) without proper specification of the relations between the items;
- up to now no agreement on the structure of communicative text theories has been achieved in terms of the general norms of analytical philosophy of science;
- communicative text theories must be firmly based on the empirical investigation of communication processes. The works of Labov and his colleagues are only a first step in the right direction; more work must follow (and is being undertaken in several places, e.g. research projects at the University of Bielefeld by Kallmeyer and Schütze, Meyer-Hermann and others).

2.1.2   On the whole is has to be admitted that as far as constructing communicative text theories in the proper sense of the term is concerned we are still at the very beginning. But fortunately the first steps have been taken: the need for such theories is widely acknowledged; the complexity of the research involved has become obvious; the formal problems constructing appropriate theories have become apparent.

3.   Specific problems of communicative text theories

3.0   In this section I shall discuss three specific problems which – in my opinion – show that the different approaches (as characterized in section 2) should be integrated towards a solution of the problems involved in explaining verbal communication.

I have chosen the subjects I shall discuss in this chapter for the following reasons:

(1) Nearly all theories of verbal communication use concepts like *'situation'*

or *'context of communication'* without providing a clear explanation of these concepts.

Intuitive concepts like these seem to point to elements that are essential to any kind of communication and should therefore be precisely characterized in a theory of verbal communication.

(2) Verbal communication in social contexts is not simply about verbal texts but is about socially formed and acknowledged *types* of texts. Disciplines investigating texts (like literary criticism, theology, etc.) are waiting for textlinguistic proposals on how to define and characterize types of texts in an adequate way. Thus text typology is one of the fields where linguists have to fulfil interdisciplinary tasks (apart from the genuine linguistic interest in questions of text typology).

(3) A linguistic theory that claims to offer an adequate explanation of the process of verbal communication has to answer the question of how people *understand* verbal texts. Consequently the problem of the understanding of verbal texts (including the processus of reception and interpretation) is one of the central subjects of linguistics. Perhaps one might even say that linguistic theories can be ranked according to their ability to explain the complex process of understanding.

3.1   On the analysis of complex situations of communication

3.1.1.   In the presentations of my own concept of a communicative text theory[5] I have put forward the general idea that every speaker and hearer engaged in a communication process is strongly influenced by what I have called the "komplexe Voraussetzungssituation" (complex of relevant factors making up the situational context). This expression served as a cover term for the whole set of elements constituting the *situation* of a speaker or hearer at a certain time t_i and at a certain place l_i: elements like, for example (1) available semiotic codes and rules of successful verbal behaviour in communication situations, conversational postulates etc.; (2) economic situation; (3) social situation (including the personal history of socialization, social role, etc.); (4) political situation; (5) cultural situation (including the education and knowledge of speakers and hearers); (6) sets of hypotheses concerning the communication situation, the communication partners and their possible reactions; (7) speakers' and hearers' intentions and so on.[6] It is in the framework of this complex set of factors that a speaker constitutes his special intentions as to the propositional content and the communicational effect of his text production and text utterance ("Mitteilungs- und Wirkungsabsicht") that is to say his "communication strategy".

My reason for introducing the concept of "komplexe Voraussetzungssituation" into a communicative text theory was my disatisfaction with communica-

---

[5] See my (1973)
[6] For a detailed description see my (1976).

tion models like that of Jakobson. What I wanted to emphasize was the fact that every speech act (or communication act) is embedded in complex social activity (which I used to call communication-action-game: "kommunikatives Handlungsspiel") (1973).

A rather similar approach can be found in Marxist communicative text theories, e.g. in the work of Schmidt and Harnisch who define the concept of "communication strategy" as follows: "By communication strategy we understand a plan for an optimal realization of communicational intentions, a plan which respects the objective and subjective elements and conditions involved in processes of communication and which determines the internal and external structure of a text; the verbal text is derived from this strategy." (Schmidt, 1972; my translation).

According to Schmidt and Harnisch, communication strategies are realized in spoken as well as written texts. Such texts cannot be fully understood and adequately analysed without an analysis of the elements influencing the communication strategy. Such influencing elements are, among others, the consciousness of the speaker, his intentions, his intellectual grasp of the situation, his background knowledge, his linguistic competence, his knowledge of the communication partner(s), the social relations between speaker and hearer, social and moral norms accepted by the speaker and hearer, his degree of consciousness concerning the application of communication strategies, and so on (see the report on Schmidt and Harnisch in Braunroth et al., 1975: 284 ff).

3.1.2   It can be assumed that there is a high degree of agreement among text theoreticians that a proper treatment of communication acts and especially an adequate semantic analysis of literary or political texts is impossible if proper attention is not paid to the social and individual conditions that actually influence the production and reception of texts in communication processes. The question, however, is how text theories can account for such problems: Is it for example possible to reconstruct the complex (network of) factors as "worlds" (in the sense that logic uses the term), consisting of systems of presuppositions? How much information about specific situations can be incorporated into the lexicon of a text grammar? How is it possible to gain empirical data constituting complex situations? What kinds of methods are required (and how can they be developed) if we are to be enabled to infer from texts the various elements making up a complex situation or to predict how known influencing factors will regulate text production/reception?

Possibly a first step towards the solution of these and other related problems might be to construct a standard model of text production (or text reception, respectively, see section 3.3) which would contain as many influencing elements as can be found or imagined at the moment. Such a model ought to contain not only lists of items but also a representation of relations between the items and some sort of hierarchical order according to the degree of recurrence of the items in communication processes and/or the degree of influence on text production/reception. This model might function as a heuristic device which would take into account all social, psychological, logical and encyclopedic aspects relevant to the theoretical reconstruction or the formal representation of individual communication acts or the meaning of an individual text. Without such a component no communicative text theory will – in my opinion – be able to provide methods for a critical analysis of texts that are relevant for social interaction (political, literary, scientific or religious texts, advertisements etc.).

3.2   Some problems of setting up a typology of texts

3.2.1   It is one of the basic assumptions of communicative text theories (apart from the above mentioned assumption of the necessary social embeddings of texts) that texts in social communication always appear as manifestations of a socially recognizable *text-type*. If – as was stated in section 1.1 – a communicative text theory acknowledges as its basic aim the construction of a theory that is empirically adequate and formally consistent it must make provision for the representation of *all* types of text.

What are the implications of this basic assumption?

(a) If a text theory chooses to accept the above mentioned assumption, it has to answer the question whether the rules for text production and text analysis it has formulated are applicable to *all* types of texts or only to a few types. This, of course, is a problem that touches on the methodology the theory is based on: did it gain its rules as a result of inductive generalization over a representative corpus of different text types? Or were the rules formulated as a result of a systematization of the linguist's intuitive linguistic competence?

(b) All disciplines which describe, analyse, and/or interpret verbal texts (like literary criticism, theology, law, history, philosophy, etc.) constantly make use of pre-theoretical concepts of text types ('discussion', 'letter', 'lecture', 'prayer', etc.). All these disciplines are (or should be) interested in a stricter definition of text types which may be empirically tested. – If communicative text theories were to take not only their own problems but also their interdisciplinary task seriously they would have to try to answer such questions.

(c) Furthermore, problems of text typology have obvious social implications. Among others Gülich and Raible (1975: 147) have mentioned that "[...] linguistic barriers are probably less due to a lack of grammatical competence than to the fact that certain speakers are unable to make use of certain text types, either actively or passively." [my translation] The competence which is necessary to produce, understand, and process meaningful sequences of sentences must – according to Sanding (1972: 13) – include a competence to produce, understand and process *types* of texts.

If these and similar hypotheses are correct, the construction of adequate text typologies is of great relevance to didactics and social psychology in so far as it clarifies how such a competence can be developed and what types of texts are in use under what conditions in what social groups.

(d) Finally, text theoretical research up to now has shown that several important problems of communicative text theories – like the coherence of texts, the analysis of macro-structures in narratives or the acceptability of texts – cannot be solved without a solution of the problem of text typology. (e.g. the expectations of recipients concerning different ways of understanding scientific versus literary texts or social norms regarding the acceptability of news bulletins versus poems.)

3.2.2   How can the problems of text typology best be solved? There are two basic possibilities: Either one starts with pre-theoretically characterized types of texts (as objects under observation) and tries to produce a formal reconstruction of the heuristically assumed types by means of a consistent text theory; or one constructs an efficient text theory which allows the production of text types as theoretical constructs, which may then be empirically tested.

If we leave aside these general problems for the moment then some general principles of research strategy in this field seem to be acceptable: bearing in mind that the orientation of communicative text theories is towards verbal texts in contexts of communication, any specification of text types has to respect text internal as well as text external aspects and markers (this hypothesis is emphasized by nearly all scholars working in this field. For a survey cf. Gülich and Raible, eds., 1972). External markers (e.g. characteristics of the communication situation, medium, expectations of recipients, the social norms and conventions for the combination of external and internal markers) should – for general philosophical reasons – be derived from an explicit model of communication; internal markers (as for example stylistic devices, choice of tenses, choice of meta-communicative signals, of illocutionary indicators, of stereotypes for opening and finishing a text, etc.) can only be specified in the framework of an explicit text theory.

Another methodological device is the classification of text types according to *function* (cf. Hartmann 1964:23) for – as Gülich and Raible (1972:5) have pointed out – there is a correlation between the configuration of internal and external markers and the function of a text.

But here we meet another problem: attributing communicative functions (or illocutionary forces) to texts will not be possible until we have a text-context-grammar (in the broader sense) which provides rules for the correlation between communicative text functions and the choice and clustering of internal markers. In addition, following this line of research, the problem of possible and/or expectable hierarchies of communicative text functions must be solved; because one text can fulfil different communicative functions in one and the same situation (e.g. persuade *and* warn) or parts of a text may fulfil different partial functions (which may conflict with the function of the text as a whole).

Some further problems can only be touched on: e.g. the problem of the modification or innovation of communicational text functions (e.g. in experimental literature), or the problem of the depth of typespecification for different purposes of applied linguistics.

I think it has become clear that text typology is a necessary and complicated aspect of communicative text theory. A number of special problems have been raised in order to underline that text typology must try to do justice to its object, texts in communicational settings. This is possible only if the typology analyses the communication function of texts in situations and if it pays special attention to the intentions of the speaker and the expectations of the hearer (both involved in their respective complex situations; cf. section 3.1) *and* to those correlates in text-structures (text internal markers) which enable a recipient to recognize what type of text the speaker is intending to produce.

3.3   Models of text reception

3.3.1   A short glance at the discussion during the last few years shows that the problems of text reception and text processing are favourite topics of current research and need further clarification. Here again a few hints must be sufficient:

(a) In the last section (3.2.1) I have mentioned the hypothesis that a recipient has to be able to recognize the type of text he is hearing or reading in order to understand it correctly (cf. Schmidt 1973).

(b) Wienold (1972) has directed the linguist's attention to the fact that readers attribute meanings to texts, and he has tried to characterize different sorts of text processing operations ("Textverarbeitungsoperationen"; cf. Wienold and Rieser, 1974).

(c) The question of *how* readers understand texts has also been discussed by literary scholars (e.g. Iser, 1975) as well as by scholars working in the field of artificial intelligence (see authors like Schank & Colby, eds. 1973, Schank, Rieger, Winograd, etc.).

The present state of research in this field can be characterized as follows:

(1) One group tries to construct orientation models which list and characterize the elements of the reception process which are intuitively regarded as relevant (e.g. Kindt and Schmidt, 1974).

(2) Another group tries to construct simulation models by means of artificial intelligence research in order to simulate processes of reception with the help of data processing machines (see the survey in Samlowski, 1974).

(3) A third group works with socio-psychological experiments to discover regularities in reception processes; e.g. the analysis of macro-structures (see Kintsch, 1974, and van Dijk and Kitsch, 1975).

Here again I cannot go into the details of the different approaches (see my survey in Schmidt, 1975). I can only try to draw the reader's attention to some problems and perhaps indicate possible ways of dealing with them.

3.3.2   A theory of text reception which tries to reconstruct the concept of 'understanding' texts has – in my opinion – to account for the following components, which must be theoretically defined and integrated into a *model of understanding* testable by empirical research[7]:

(1) The reception of verbal texts – and in the following remarks I shall restrict myself to the reception of *written* texts – obviously starts with the psycho-physiological process of text perception (Wahrnehmung). This process is influenced by individual and social factors (like the state of the recipient at the time of reading or his socialization history) which determine the selectional and modificatory operations involved in perceiving a written text-formula (= written text-material). That is to say the graphic stimuli of the text-formula are perceived by the recipient, compared with stored information and recognized as representations of meaningful signs of a particular language.

(2) For all processes connected with perception or following perception we have to take into consideration Hörmann's criterion of "sense constancy": "We expect what we hear [or read] to make sense, and we analyse the incoming message so as to conform to this criterion. The course and kind of analysis we apply is geared to the goal of making (or keeping) sense. This is what we mean by sense-constancy." (1975:5) Furthermore we have to account for the fact that – in accordance with the axiom of the necessary social embedding of all texts – the "[...] simultaneous perception of a verbal utterance and of its meaningful general background is the nucleus of understanding." (l.c.:9)

(3) The perceived signs are then processed in the reader's consciousness with the purpose of assigning conceptual structures to configurations of signs. Hypothetically one might postulate a specific operation that would mediate between psychological apperception and semantic (or conceptual) interpretation: a *syntactic* analysis.

The syntactic analysis would contain two sorts of operations:
– a segmentation of the structure assigned to the text into elementary units
– a syntactic disambiguation that integrates these units into syntactically coherent complexes.

(4) The syntactic analysis is partially integrated into the *semantic* analysis which assigns conceptual structures to the syntactically analyzed structure (for further details see Kindt, 1975).

This complex operation may perhaps be characterized in the following way (see Schmidt, 1975a):

(a) analytically one might postulate a process of linear *intensional* interpretation where a recipient decides (during the linear reading of the textformula) which cognitive structure stored in his memory he assigns to syntactically analyzed structures according to information he picks up from the co-text and con-text;

(b) in addition one might postulate a process of *extensional* interpretation where the recipient has to decide whether the intensionally interpreted

---

[7] It must be emphasized that the following sketch does *not* try to reconstruct the *psychological* process of understanding in actu; it only presents components of such a model which need further qualification. – This sketch relies on papers by Kindt and Schmidt (1974) and Petöfi (1974).

structures/elements of structures can be referentially related to a real or fictive world.

(5) The intensional and extensional interpretation processes (which may be enlarged by the operations of commenting on intensional and commenting on extensional interpretation, as proposed by Petöfi, 1974a, whenever problems arise in the interpretation processes or certain interpretations have to be justified by the recipient) provide the information which is organized by the recipient into a meaningstructure or "world" coherent for the reader at t_i.

(6) By way of drawing inferences from the world he has assigned to the analyzed textstructure, the recipient may enlarge the world to reach a higher degree of "plasticity".

The postulated operations (5) and (6) are dominated by the reduction and systematization of information provided by macro-structures (cf. van Dijk and Kintsch). If van Dijk's hypotheses are correct then macro-structures are built up *during* the process of understanding and are stored in the memory, where they serve as a clue for the retrieval of semantic information a recipient has obtained from the text. The stored macro-structures do not remain stable in the memory but are integrated into so-called "fact-and-knowledge-systems"; consequently we must imagine such memory stores to be in a state of permanent modification. Thus the "understanding" of any informational process potentially modifies the whole system (or certain parts of the system) of conceptual structures stored in the recipient's memory.

3.3.3   This, of course, is no more than a very tentative proposal to investigate the process of understanding verbal texts; it does not, for example, take into consideration all the projection and rereading processes which occur in actual processes of text understanding, influenced by information the recipient may take or actually does take from the situational context and his own complex situation.

All that this sketch was intended to do was to raise a few questions relating to the sort of problems which must be solved by a communicative text theory which seriously intends to construct a theory of *text*-semantics. Without an explicit model of understanding processes any such theory lacks an empirical basis. On the other hand a text-semantics like Petöfi's provides a great number of suggestions on how to combine empirical research work on understanding with the construction of formal text grammars (cf. Petöfi's papers in Petöfi and Rieser, 1974).

3.4.1   I hope these short remarks have shown that the construction of a comprehensive communicative text theory is still a mere "promesse de fortune" and that the different approaches currently under discussion need to be integrated into a unified and homogeneous theory. This, in my opinion, demands better interdisciplinary cooperation, the elaboration of a common theoretical base and comparable systems of representation leading to a common framework for research into which results can be integrated; it finally demands an increase in the number of empirical investigations carried out so that the theory can rely on an adequate data base.

References:

Braunroth, Manfred; Seyfert, Gernot; Siegel, Carsten; Vahle, Fritz. 1975. *Ansätze und Aufgaben der linguistischen Pragmatik.* Frankfurt/Main: Athenäum (FAT 2091)
Brennenstuhl, Waltraud. 1975. *Handlungstheorie und Handlungslogik.* Kronberg/Ts.: Scriptor.
van Dijk, Teun A. 1972. *Some aspects of text grammars.* The Hague: Mouton.
van Dijk, Teun A. 1974. *"A note on the partial equivalence of text grammars and context grammars".* in: Marvin, D. Loflin and James Silverberg (eds), Discourse and influence in cognitive anthropology. The Hague: Mouton
van Dijk, Teun A. 1974a. *Philosophy of action and theory of narrative.* Mimeo: University of Amsterdam.
van Dijk, Teun A. 1976. *"Pragmatics, presuppositions and context grammars."* in: Siegfried J. Schmidt (ed.). Pragmatik/Pragmatics II. München: Fink (53–82)
van Dijk, Teun A. 1975a *"Action, action description and narrative".* in: New Literary History, T. 6. 374–394.
van Dijk, Teun A. and Kintsch, Walter. 1975. *Recalling and summarizing stories.* Mimeo.
van Dijk et al. 1975. *Recalling and summarizing complex stories.* Mimeo: University of Amsterdam.
Grice, H. Paul. 1975. *"Logic and conversation".* in: Peter Cole and Jerry L. Morgan (eds.) Syntax and semantics. Vol. 3: Speech acts. New York–San Francisco–London: Academic Press (41–58).
Gülich, Elisabeth and Raible, Wolfgang. 1975. *"Textsorten-Probleme".* in: Linguistische Probleme der Textanalyse. Jahrbuch des Instituts für Deutsche Sprache in Mannheim. Düsseldorf: Pädagogischer Verlag Schwann (144–197).
Gülich, Elisabeth and Raible, Wolfgang (eds.) 1972. *Textsorten.* Differenzierungskriterien aus linguistischer Sicht. Frankfurt/Main: Athenäum.
Hartmann, Peter. 1964. *"Text, Texte, Klassen von Texten".* in: Bogawus, T. 2 (15–25).
Henne, Helmut. 1975. *Sprachpragmatik.* Tübingen: Niemeyer.
Hörmann, Hans. 1975. *The concept of sense constancy.* Mimeo. University of Bochum.
Iser, Wolfgang. 1975. *"Der Lesevorgang. Eine phänomenologische Perspektive."* in: Rainer Warning (ed.) Rezeptionsästhetik. München: Fink (253–276).
Kindt, Walther and Schmidt, Siegfried J. 1974. *Textrezeption und Textinterpretation.* Vorlage zum ZIF-Colloquium "Die Rolle der Grammatik in der nicht-automatisierten und automatisierten Textverarbeitung". University of Bielefeld (in press).
Kindt, Walther. 1975. *Ein Rezeptionsmodell.* Mimeo: DFG-research-project "Theorie der Literarischen Kommunikation". University of Bielefeld.
Kintsch, Walter. 1974. *The representation of meaning in memory.* New York: Erlbaum
Kummer, Werner. 1972. *"Aspects of a theory of argumentation".* in: Elisabeth Gülich and Wolfgang Raible (eds.). Textsorten. Frankfurt/Main: Athenäum (25–49).
Kummer, Werner. 1975. *Grundlagen der Texttheorie.* Reinbek b. Hamburg: Rowohlt.
Labov, William. 1970. *"The study of language in its social context".* in: Studium generale 23 (30–87).
Lewis, David. 1969. *Convention: A philosophical study.* Cambridge/Mass.: Havard U.P.
Nowakowska, Maria. 1973. *Language of motivation and language of action.* The Hague: Mouton (Janua Linguarum. Series Maior 67).
Petöfi, Janos S. 1974. *"Semantics – pragmatics – text theory".* Mimeo: University of Bielefeld.
Petöfi, Janos S. 1975. *Von der Satzgrammatik zu einer logisch-semantischen Texttheorie.* Mimeo: University of Bielefeld.

60   S. J. Schmidt

Petöfi, Janos S. 1974a. *"Grammatische Beschreibung, Interpretation, Intersubjektivität"*. in: Janos S. Petöfi and Hannes Rieser, Probleme der modelltheoretischen Interpretation von Texten. (29–59).

Petöfi, Janos S. and Rieser, Hannes. 1974. Probleme der modelltheoretischen Interpretation von Texten. Hamburg: Buske (papers in text linguistics, vol. 7)

Samlowski, Wolfgang. 1974. *Konzepttheorie. Ein praktischer Beitrag zur Textverarbeitung und Textrezeption.* Working paper 12. Istituto per gli studi semantici e cognitivi. Castagnola.

Sandig, Barbara. 1972. *"Zur Differenzierung gebrauchssprachlicher Textsorten im Deutschen"*. in: Elisabeth Gülich and Wolfgang Raible, eds., Textsorten. Frankfurt/M.: Athenäum (113–124).

Schlieben-Lange, Brigitte. 1975. *Linguistische Pragmatik.* Stuttgart–Berlin–Köln–Mainz: Kohlhammer.

Schmidt, Siegfried J. 1973. *Texttheorie.* Probleme einer Linguistik der sprachlichen Kommunikation. München: Fink. (^{2}1976) (UTB 202)

Schmidt, Siegfried J. 1975. *Zur Klärung des Begriffs 'Literarische Kommunikation'.* Mimeo: DFG-research-project "Theorie der Literarischen Kommunikation". University of Bielefeld.

Schmidt, Siegfried J. 1975a. *Textanalyse und Textinterpretation.* Studienbrief. Deutsches Institut für Fernstudien. Tübingen (in preparation).

Schmidt, Siegfried J. 1976. *Zum Aufbau einer Theorie der Literarischen Kommunikation.* Mimeo: University of Bielefeld.

Schmidt, Wilhelm and Harnisch, Hanna. 1972. *"Kategorien und Methoden einer marxistisch-leninistischen Sprachwirkungsforschung"*. in: Wilhelm Schmidt (ed.) Sprache und Ideologie. Halle (65–110).

Wienold, Götz. 1972. *Semiotik der Literatur.* Frankfurt/M.: Athenäum.

Wienold, Götz and Rieser, Hannes. 1974. *Vorüberlegungen zur Rolle des Konzepts der Textverarbeitung beim Aufbau einer empirischen Sprachtheorie.* Diskussionsvorlage zum ZIF-Colloquium "Die Rolle der Grammatik in der nicht-automatisierten und automatisierten Textverarbeitung". University of Bielefeld (in press).

Wunderlich, Dieter. 1971. *"Pragmatik, Sprechsituation, Deixis"*. in: LiLi, I, 1/2, 153–190.

von Wright, Georg H. 1967. *"The logic of action"*. in: Nikolas Rescher (ed.) The logic of decision and action. Pittsburgh.

von Wright, Georg H. 1974. *Erklären und Verstehen.* Frankfurt: Athenäum.

Cognitive Psychology and Discourse: Recalling and Summarizing Stories

Teun A. van Dijk – Walter Kintsch
University of Amsterdam, University of Colorado

1 Discourse in Psychology: A Short Survey

1.1 Parallel to the elaboration of text grammars in linguistics, there has been increasing attention in psychology for the cognitive processing of discourse. This development is a natural consequence of theoretical and experimental work on meaningful material, i.e. on semantic information processing, begun in the sixties, which completed psychological research on morphonological and syntactic structures of sentences in the generative-transformational paradigm. It was soon understood that the processing of syntactic structures depends on underlying semantic structures of sentences, and that memory for verbal utterances is predominantly semantic (Kintsch 1972, 1977, and other contributions in Tulving and Donaldson, eds. 1972.). Similarly, it now seems obvious that the interpretation of sentences is a function of the verbal and non-verbal context in which a sentence is uttered, and that the conceptual knowledge structure of our memory not only depends on the interpretation of isolated sentences, but also on the understanding and processing of whole discourses. In this paper we will briefly sketch the main tenets of this psychological approach to discourse, and report some of our own theoretical and experimental findings in this field, in particular with respect to the ability to recall and summarize stories.

1.2 One of the first psychologists who systematically studied discourse processing was F.C. Bartlett. In his influential book *Remembering* (1932) he describes a series of experiments in which an American Indian story had to be recalled after various delays by the same test person, or serially reproduced by several test persons, i.e. each test person had to tell the story as he recalled it to a next test person. He found that recall for details of description, style or mode of presentation of the story was very weak through the various reproductions of the same test person, but that the general outline of the story, once established, is remarkably constant even after long delays (of months or even years). Elements of the story which were poorly understood for cultural reasons, were transformed to more familiar structures. Recall is not mere reproduction, but involves reasoning and explaining. In other words, memory and hence recall is essentially *constructive* and is based on rationalisations of different sorts and on the current knowledge, interests and emotional attitude of the subject with respect to the story and its content. From these and the many other experiments he carried out on remembering, Bartlett formulated a theory of recall which still influences most current work in this domain. One of the key notions is that of *schema,* which is characterized as an active principle in our memory, (re-)organizing elements of recall into structured wholes. In perception and language understanding we interpret and recall all new information with respect to our established schemata, which are both cognitively and socially determined.

Paul (1959) replicated some of Bartlett's experiments many years later, focusing attention especially on a better experimental design, more adequate, discourse analysis, and on the variables of degree of explication and familiarity of the stories. Discourse with a higher degree of internal explication is better recalled, whereas more unfamiliar themes tend to lead to more incoherent reproductions than familiar themes of a story. Paul discovered two systematically different styles of recall: some subjects tend to rather good and faithful reproduction of the original story, whereas others leave away detail, import their own elements (e.g. explications) and tend to skeletonize more than the better retainers. Characteristically, the latter group better recalls non-explicated stories. Although our insight into memory for discourse at present is constantly increasing, little is known about these individual differences in recall due to different styles, interests, preferences and knowledge (schemata).

1.3   Partly within, partly outside the Gestalt tradition of Bartlett and within the so-called verbal learning paradigm in cognitive psychology of the fifties and sixties, some scattered experiments were carried out, which brought little systematic theoretical insight and explication, but at least provided a number of facts to be explained.

Thus Cofer (1941) in his early experiments with prose passages also taken from folk tales established the well-known fact that verbatim learning of prose is much more difficult than what the called logical learning, i.e. the learning of the essential idea of a passage, especially when the passages are long.

Gomulicki (1956) paid more detailed attention to the elements which are deleted in reproductions of prose passages, and found that the probability of recall of an element is directly related to the degree of contribution of that element to the total meaning of the passage. The process of understanding a passage involves a ranking of importance of the various elements, and more in general abstraction from the detailed input. Thus, in narratives the units of agent and action are better recalled than descriptions due to their different importance or relevance for the story. Retention of elements from discourse may of course be enhanced or impaired by various means. Slamecka (1959), for example, found that interpolated passages with a similar topic reduced retention of the original passage. Whereas many of the experiments carried out pertained to learning of individual words, ideas or sentences from discourse (see e.g. Newman & Saltz, 1960), Lee (1965) attempted to demonstrate that what we learn from discourse essentially depends upon its global (he uses the term molar) hierarchical structure. Expressions of high level structure are for example the initial paragraph with the outline of the story, the title, and the summary or conclusion. Below we will give a theoretical explanation of these and similar findings and assumptions.

Similarly, Lachman & Dooling (1968) distinguished between processes of word understanding and recall and those involving categories, themes or summaries of whole discourses, which are core units around which the lexical units are organized. Pompi & Lachman (1967) are more specific and postulate special surrogate structures, involving themes, images, schemata, abstracts or summaries, and which do not directly depend on the meanings of the individual words. This idea will also be elaborated theoretically below.

That thematic or schematic representation of the content of discourse as it is represented for example in titles directly influences understanding, especially of vague or ambiguous passages, was demonstrated by Dooling & Lachman (1971): subjects had no difficulty interpreting such passages if a title was given, but could hardly understand about what the passage was without such a title. It follows, as was shown also in several papers in educational psychology, that the use of titles, outlines, summaries and thematic words within the passage positively influences understanding, organization in memory and recall of the discourse.

1.4   More systematic research on the cognitive properties of discourse followed in the early seventies. Many of the contributions to the Carroll & Freedle (1972) volume treated aspects of discourse and their influence on the organization of memory and recall. Whereas it is firmly established, at least since the experiments of Sachs (1967), that comprehension and long term memory are basically semantic, it now becomes imperative to investigate the structures of semantic information in discourse and memory, what levels of semantic interpretation should be distinguished, and why some semantic information is better recalled than other. Thus, Freedle (1972), in the volume mentioned, attacks the difficult problem of topic understanding or construction in discourse and the relations between topics and so-called key-words. Continuing the basic ideas of Bartlett, Crothers (1972) also assumes that memory structures and recall of discourse are determined by the over-all structure or gist of the discourse, and he identifies this structure with that of the superior nodes in a hierarchical tree. His data, however, did not confirm his hypothesis probably because of the type of hierarchical structures postulated (see Crothers 1975). Frederiksen (1972), finally, shows that superordinate processing also must take place in the processes of inference and recall of logical arguments, but that the context, i.e. the specific tasks required from the subject, may heavily influence the nature of the structures assigned or the inferences drawn, a point which is emphasized especially by Rothkopf (1972) in the same volume.

1.5   Some of the problems and hypotheses mentioned above have been treated in our own earlier work on discourse. Referring to Bartlett, van Dijk in various papers and his dissertation (1972) assumed that the notion of *macro-structure,* to be explicated in more detail below, representing the global organization of the semantic structure of a discourse, makes explicit notions such as theme, plot, idea, or schema, used in earlier psychological work, and that such macro-structures organize both the production and the comprehension, storage and recall of complex verbal structures such as discourses. Kintsch, in a series of papers collected in Kintsch (1974), shows that discourse comprehension is semantic, propositionally based, and that surface structure complexity only influences understanding under specific reading time restrictions. Important is the experimental confirmation of the assumption that all processes involved in discourse understanding, question answering, problem solving, recall and recognition, etc. are not only based on those propositions which are explicitly expressed in the discourse, but also on those which are deductively or inductively implied by expressed propositions. That is, discourse comprehension has an important inference-making component.

2   Current Research on Discourse, Cognition and Knowledge

2.1   The interest for discourse processing is spreading rapidly at the moment. Various dissertations, monographs and volumes of articles have appeared or are in print, which show a more acute feeling for the necessity of a theoretical framework for the earlier data and assumptions; many of the intuitive notions used before were felt inadequate. These actual developments take place in cognitive and educational psychology on the one hand and in artificial intelligence on the other hand, in both cases closely linked with advances in linguistics, rhetorics, philosophy and philosophical logic, within the broader framework of what now is being called cognitive science.

2.2   Barnard in his dissertation (1974) tried to explain certain recall properties of prose on the basis of its cohesion, a notion he established operationally, not theoretically: a discourse is more cohesive if more subjects re-construct it from the set of its scrambled sentences. In free recall the more cohesive texts, under this definition, were not better recalled however, as measured by the number of idea units (undefined) and inaccuracies. Similarly he assessed the global thematic structure of discourse by having subjects delete what they intuitively think are the less important sentences of the next. When more than half of the subjects agree on the most thematic sentences these are also recalled better. Barnard also talks about two levels of discourse comprehension, first the interpretation of individual proposition and second the formation of sub-units of sets of propositions, organized hierarchically. Meyer (1975) in her dissertation takes a more theoretical approach to the representation of discourse structure. Sequences of sentences from a discourse are assigned a hierarchical structure based on rhetorical categories denoting the specific relations between the sentences, such as specification, explication or cause. Her experiments show that the sentences located high in this hierarchical structure are better recalled and more resistent against forgetting. One of the problems in this kind of research is the explanation of memory elements which are not explicitly expressed in the discourse, but which, by inference or construction, nevertheless may occur in the recall protocols. Comprehension and recall of discourse, and of semantic information in general, is in part based on imported implied elements coming from particular or general schemata representing our knowledge of the kind of discourse, the topic treated and the context of use (task, problem). (For comments on Meyer and for further experiments, see Thorndyke, 1975.)

2.3   This role of our knowledge of the world, as it is represented in memory, in the understanding of discourse has received attention in recent work in artificial intelligence. Charniak (1972) in his computer simulation of the interpretation of children stories clearly demonstrates that the interpretation of each sentence of a story involves a large amount of conventional knowledge about objects, actions and transactions and their usual pre-conditions and consequences. This knowledge, just as the meaning postulates of the lexicon of a language, need not be explicitly expressed in the text. Each sentence (information) is interpreted with respect to a certain topic initiated earlier in the discourse and invoking a 'demon' which inspects following sentences for information which belongs to the knowledge structure it covers. For instance, the concept of 'birthday' activates a demon involving such elements as 'birthday-cake', 'games' and 'presents', which then may coherently be expected in the following part of the discourse. Similarly, at a lower level, for the structure of birthday games or present giving.

Minsky (1975) in a highly influential paper has generalized these results for information processing in general, and introduces the notion of a *frame*. Although the precise nature of frames is not yet very clear, they function as abstract units of data and procedures (rules) in the organization and interpretation of data. The existence of a frame for 'chair', 'room', 'story', etc. guarantees that we always know, recognize or interpret an object to be a chair (or the same chair) even if we see it under many different transformations (e.g. various angles). Similarly, we are able to interpret and recognize the abstract schema (plot) of stories under many linguistic or narrative transformations of detail. Frames may be devised for different kinds of knowledge of the world. Thus, Schank (1975), using the term *script,* shows that action and the comprehension of action discourse with respect to the concept RESTAURANT depends on the conventional data structure we have available about restaurants and eating in restaurants: the usual place-time properties of restaurants and restaurant visits, the usual persons and their typical roles and actions, and the possible courses of action in calling a waitress, ordering food, eating, paying and leaving. (See also the other contributions in Bobrow & Collins, eds. 1975.) Below we will not so much be concerned with the actual structure of frames or scripts, but rather with their uses or functions in the comprehension, organization and retrieval of information from discourse.

2.4   From this brief description of some work in psychology and artificial intelligence about discourse processing a great number of hypotheses, notions, suggestions, problems and experimental variables emerge.

Clearly, first of all, we need a sound theory and grammar of discourse structure, because the different properties of this structure determine all aspects of cognitive processing. Assuming that we know how sentences (surface morphonological and syntactic structures) are assigned conceptual and propositional meaning structures, it should be investigated how propositions are interpreted relative to each other, how they are combined into larger semantic units, and how these are organized in memory, and finally how our conventional knowledge, personal style and interests, and the specific pragmatic context of action and interaction (the tasks to be carried out) determine these processes of understanding, memory organization, integration with extant knowledge, and retrieval in (re-)production.

It will be our task in the following sections to attack some of these problems by devising a theoretical framework which can explain the results of a number of experiments carried out with a particular type of discourse, viz. stories.

3   Discourse, Macro-structures and Narrative

3.1   Due to space limitations we are unable to specify here the full theoretical framework reconstructing the ability of language users to partially reproduce and summarize previously acquired information from discourse. The assumption, however, is that discourse processing (understanding, organization, retrieval) is a function of the structures assigned to the discourse during input. We are aware of the fact that recall and summarizing are also a function of the relations between the acquired information and existing knowledge, interests, intentions, etc., but these factors will not be investigated in this paper. The theoretical framework necessary to describe and explain the important linguistic and cognitive phenomena mentioned above is a complex one. It consists of several sub-theories: (for more details, cf. van Dijk, 1977a).
(i) a theory of discourse, consisting of
    a) a grammar of discourse, with at least
      – a theory of semantic representations (propositions) for sentences and sequences of sentences (micro-structure);
      – a theory of semantic representations for global discourse structures (macro-structures);
      – a theory relating micro-structures with macro-structures;

b) a more general theory of (non-linguistic) discourse structures, with specific theories for different kind of discourse; in our case e.g. a theory of narrative structures; this theory of narrative structures is itself based on a theory and logic of action and action description;

(ii) a theory or model of discourse structure processing, in particular of semantic information, i.e. for comprehension/interpretation, storage in memory, memory transformations, retrieval, and (re-)production and use/application.

(iii) a more general theory for complex cognitive information processing, in which the ability to process discourse is related to our ability to perceive/interpret and memorize complex events and actions after visual input, and to plan or organize and execute complex actions, both bodily and mental (reasoning, problem solving).

It goes without saying that this is too ambitious a program. For details of some fragments we refer to other contributions in this book.

3.2   Since we assumed that discourse processing is a function of the structures assigned to the discourse during input, our first task is to find a sound representation of discourse structures. Earlier it has been emphasized that although morphonological and syntactic structures of sentences play a role in comprehension, they are not regularly stored in long term memory (except for some stylistic exceptions) so they will be neglected here, as well as the grammatical rules and cognitive operations under which they interact with semantic representations. Similarly, we will not be concerned with the pragmatic structures of the communicative contexts, e.g. the properties of speech acts (underlying intentions, purposes, knowledge, etc. of language users), in which discourses are or may be produced and interpreted. It is undoubtedly the case that the actual meaning assigned to a sentence or discourse in conversation depends on context variables, especially when we understand 'meaning' to comprise also the 'function' of the discourse (as a promise, threat, etc.). Hence we will focus on the proper semantic structure of discourse, as it is invariant for all possible contexts, assuming that these semantic structures are the basis for all particular meanings and interpretations in context.

3.3   The semantic structure of discourse is the formal reconstruction of what is non-technically called the 'information' or 'content' of a discourse. Above it has been briefly announced that we distinguish between two different levels of meaning in discourse, viz. between that of its actual sentences and sequences of sentences, and that of parts of the discourse or of the discourse as a whole. The latter kind of meaning structures will be called macro-structures, and will be discussed below.

At the micro-level the semantics assigns sequences of *propositions* to the sequence of sentences of the discourse. Several propositions may be expressed by one sentence, depending on certain semantic, pragmatic, stylistic (and cognitive and social) factors not to be discussed here, or must be expressed by a sequence of sentences.

Propositions are taken to have the usual form: n-place predicate, *n* arguments, preceded by quantifiers binding variables, and by operators of various kinds (modalities). Propositions combine in *compound* propositions and *sequences* of propositions, which are pairwise *connected,* e.g. as expressed by connectives in natural language. Connection conditions are based on relations between *facts,* viz. the denotata of (asserted) propositions in possible worlds, and relative to a *topic of discourse* (for detail, see van Dijk, 1977a, Ch. 3). Connection is a specific kind of *coherence,* defined over sequences of propositions, not only in terms of relations between facts, in some possible world and relative to a topic of discourse, but also in terms of intensional and extensional relations between 'parts' of propositions (quantifiers, predicates, arguments, etc.), studied elsewhere in this collection.

A distinction is made between an *implicit text base* and an *explicit text base* underlying a discourse, where the first is actually expressed, and the second is a theoretical construction in which also those propositions are postulated which are necessary to establish coherence, e.g. meaning postulates and propositions from our knowledge of the world coming from frames as discussed above. These interpolated propositions are those which are 'presupposed' by the propositions expressed in the discourse, and constitute the basis of the *relative interpretation* of the expressed propositions of the discourse.

3.4   The global meaning of a discourse is represented by *semantic macro-structures.* These will also be represented as propositions. Hence we need semantic mappings, which we call *macro-rules,* in order to relate micro-structures with macro-structures (for detailed discussion and linguistic and cognitive motivation for these kind of structures, see van Dijk, 1977a, b). Characteristic of macro-structures is that they are *entailed* by the sequence of propositions (micro-structure) of the discourse. Their function is to *reduce* and *organize* information. That is, they delete and combine sequences of propositions, under certain specified conditions. Due to their *recursive* nature, macro-rules generate not one macro-structure, but *several macro-structures* at increasingly more global levels of semantic representation, where *the* macro-structure is the top-most macro-structure. A general constraint on macro-rules is that no proposition may be deleted which is a presupposition for a subsequent (macro-)proposition in the discourse. We distinguish provisionally four macro-rules, which are not formalized here:

MR-1: DELETION

> Of a sequence of propositions we may delete all those denoting an accidental property of a discourse referent (under the general constraint: if not necessary for the interpretation of following propositions).

MR-2: GENERALIZATION

> Of a sequence of propositions we may substitute any subsequence by

a proposition defining the immediate super-concept of the micro-propositions.

MR-3: SELECTION

Of a sequence of propositions we may delete all propositions which represent a normal condition, component or consequence of a fact denoted by another proposition (according to general postulate or frame).

MR-4: CONSTRUCTION

Of a sequence of propositions we may substitute each subsequence by a proposition if they denote normal conditions, components or consequences of the macro-proposition substituting them.

We see that in rules MR-1 and MR-2 the information is *irrecoverably* lost, whereas in MR-3 and MR-4 information is partly (inductively) recoverable by general knowledge of postulates and frame knowledge concerning normal conditions, components and consequences.

Examples: MR-1: ⟨Mary played with a ball. The ball was blue⟩ ⇒ ⟨Mary played with a ball⟩; MR-2: ⟨Mary played with a doll. Mary played with blocks, ...⟩ ⇒ ⟨Mary played with toys⟩; MR-3: ⟨I went to Paris. So, I went to the station, bought a ticket, took the train, ...⟩ ⇒ ⟨I went to Paris (by train)⟩; MR-4: ⟨I went to the station, bought a ticket, ...⟩ ⇒ ⟨I traveled (to Paris) by train⟩.

Many details and specific constraints are omitted here. One of them, for instance, is that the rules must remain as specific as possible, i.e. define immediate super-sets, super-concepts, etc. In the next section, it will be shown how these general semantic rules organizing the meaning of discourse also at higher levels of representation, are also crucial in cognitive information processing, e.g. in understanding discourse.

3.5   Next, we need more specific structures defining the characteristics of stories, because they also determine the cognitive processing of the discourse, viz. *narrative structures*. Note that these are not specifically linguistic (semantic) but are mapped on semantic structures. More in particular the categories involved are to be connected with *macro-structures* of discourse. That is, one category may dominate a whole sequence of propositions, as represented by one macro-proposition. These categories are well-known and need not be spelled out here (e.g. SETTING, COMPLICATION, RESOLUTION, EVALUATION, MORAL, and further categories defining the hierarchical syntax of narrative, see e.g. van Dijk, 1975 for an example). The specific narrative structures may be called *super-structures* in order to account for the fact that they also operate globally, but are distinct from semantic macro-structures. Narrative categories are based on more general notions from the *theory of action* and *action description,* which defines the notion of an act, the conditions of success of an act, conditions, components and consequences of acts, different types of acts, and the ways in which acts are described in natural language discourse (for detail, see van Dijk, 1976a, and reference given there). In these terms we not only are able to define notions such as auxiliary action/helper, obstructing action/antagonist, etc. but also the basis for the operation of semantic macro-rules on action discourse in general (because we know what conditions/causes, components and consequences of actions are). For instance, since intentions and purposes are necessary conditions or components of actions, descriptions of them may be deleted.

Similarly, we are able to define *levels* of *completeness* of action description, relative to the number of actions or the globality of the actions represented. Most natural action discourses, thus, are *incomplete,* simply because it is mostly semantically impossible and pragmatically irrelevant to describe all actions of a given course of action. Thus, natural discourse may also be *over-complete* when too many details are given relative to the level of description, or *sub-complete* when certain actions are not described which must be known in order to be able to understand other actions.

3.6   Finally, some remarks are necessary about the relations between *macro-structures* and *frames* (see also van Dijk 1977b). A frame, essentially, is a structure of conventional knowledge about typical situations, events or activities. Macro-rules are organizing principles of complex information processing; macro-structures only exist with respect to more detailed levels of information. Since a frame is a complex unit of information, handling it properly requires that it has a macro-structure. In that case the macro-structure has a general, conventional nature, whereas the macro-structure of individual discourses has a particular nature (except again the categories and rules organizing macro-structures conventionally, as in narrative discourse).

One of the frames used in the (re-)production and interpretation of the story by Boccaccio used in our experiments reported below, is for example that of TRADE. Such a frame must have a macro-structure something of the following form:

$$\text{MERCHANT}(X) \ \& \ \text{MERCHANT}(Y) \ \& \ \text{EXCHANGE}(X, Y, Z) \ \&$$
$$\text{GOODS}(Z) \ \& \ \text{PURPOSE}_X(\text{MAKE PROFIT}(X) \ (\ldots)$$

That is, such a global structure may partially coincide with the conceptual information of the meaning postulates of the lexicon. The frame, then, specifies the different (inter-)actions involved in the exchange, the conditions of success or failure (e.g. competition), the kind of goods which are tradable, the means of transport used depending on the particular time and culture, etc. The global organization of a frame allows us to distinguish what are its central or relevant properties, i.e. the essential components, and especially allows the *application* of the frame at different levels of generality or detail. In order to understand a sentence like 'International trade has gone back last year due to the economic crisis in the world' in a newspaper economic article, we need not activate our whole TRADE-frame, but only its 'top-level', i.e. macro-information ('international exchange of goods as a component of economic structures', say).

A flexible use of the nearly too powerful tool of conceptual conventional

frames therefore requires rules of application specifying for each kind of situation or (con-)text, which information from the frame is required.

In a story about a merchant who wants to become rich by international
trade, we may expect a certain number of propositions denoting facts which are
consistent with the conventional TRADE-frame, e.g. buying goods, shipping
them, trying to sell them. Hence, conversely, a macro-structure of that part of
the discourse may simply be 'X WANTED TO TRADE', according to MR-4.
Similarly, much information may also be left implicit in the discourse, due to
our general frame knowledge. In other words, a discourse must at least express
that information which does not belong to the frame, the information which is
inconsistent with the preferred or normal course of events (going bankrupt after
unsuccessful trading), and information which entails the essential information
of the frame (otherwise we would be unable to identify the particular frame). In
(inter-)action frames like that of TRADE, we also know what the preferred
optimal final state should be. If this final state is not realized the discourse must
mention it, and this at the same time defines a condition for the narrative
category of Complication, which only allows unexpected events. What is
a normal course of events for a certain situation, then, is to be formulated in our
reconstruction of the cognitive and conventional frames used in the interpretation and transformation of the world.

3.7   We are now in a position to specify the macro-rules operating for action
discourse in general and narrative discourse in particular, because we now
know which sort of propositions are relevant in an appropriate action description and which are not, with respect to a certain level of information abstraction
(see van Dijk 1975). Given an action discourse, then, the following types of
propositions may in general be abstracted from:
(1) descriptions of reasons, purposes and intentions for actions and the mental
     consequences of actions (by our general knowledge of action and rule MR-2
     or 4);
(2) descriptions of alternative possible courses of events;
(3) descriptions of auxiliary actions which are normal (by theory of action, and
     MR-2);
(4) descriptions of properties of states (time, place, objects, individual persons)
     which do not condition further action (by MR-1);
(5) meta-descriptions: propositions announcing, repeating, resuming or com-
     menting other propositions (general principle of non-redundancy);
(6) description of dialogue (by MR-2 if taken as auxiliary for further action; by
     MR-4 if subsumable by general speech act concept).
The application of these rules (which are not complete and somewhat too
strong) yields a macro-structure for an action discourse. The narrative
categories further require that each category must be represented in macro-
structure. In other words: macro-structures of narrative discourses themselves
have a narrative structure.

3.8   The theoretical framework outlined above will be the basis for a description of the cognitive processes involved in the production, comprehension and interpretation, storage and retrieval of discourse in general and of narrative discourse (stories) in particular. It describes the abstract nature of the operations of establishing connections between propositions as expressed by the discourse, the establishment of coherence relations, and the assignment of several macro-structures, possibly with different hierarchically ordered narrative functions. The macro-structures as postulated have important cognitive functions. Not only do they enable the interpretation of complex semantic information, but at the same time they organize this information in memory, and define which information is relatively important and which is relatively unimportant.

On the one hand this provides an explanation of forgetting, and retrievability in recall and recognition. On the other hand the macro-rules may be viewed as reconstructing active procedures of information reduction as they occur in abstracting and *summarizing* (see also Rumelhart, 1975). A summary, then, will be taken as a discourse expressing a macro-structure of another discourse. Note that such a summary has the usual properties of natural discourses: connection, coherence, but also implicitness and relative incompleteness. That is, it only indirectly reflects an abstract macro-structure. The same holds for the strategies and procedures of actual processing: the rules postulated above are only abstract reconstructions of them.

4   Psychological process assumptions

There is today no satisfactory psychological processing theory of text comprehension and memory, and we are not about to offer one here. Instead, our strategy is to use the model for the representation of texts that was outlined in the previous sections as a tool with which informative experiments can be designed. It is hoped that these experiments will provide us with the basic empirical foundation of knowledge about text processing that is a necessary precondition for theorizing. In essence, we shall use the representational model to tell us where to look for interesting psychological effects. Previous work has concentrated upon the micro-structure of text bases, neglecting the other factors that have been discussed. This was done by working with relatively short paragraphs of text for which the macro-structure out of context is relatively unimportant. In these studies we were concerned with how people infer propositions from the text, how these propositions are connected and ordered. The theory makes certain claims about the representations that result from these processes. Hence we could explore whether the cognitive operations involved in reading comprehension and memory reflect important aspects of these hypothesized representations. Most of these results have already been published in Kintsch (1974) and Kintsch et al., (1975).

In Section 7 some as yet unpublished work will be reported that has been performed during the last years both at the University of Amsterdam and at the University of Colorado. These experiments are concerned primarily with the role of the macro-structure in text comprehension and memory. Three related hypotheses have been investigated. These hypotheses follow directly from the theoretical discussions above.

(i) What is stored in memory (besides some specific information about words and sentences, or other physical aspects of the text which will be neglected here) corresponds to the macro-structure of the text, with some of the micro-structure propositions subordinated under the macrostructure categories. In recall, the subjects use the macro-structure as a retrieval cue for the detailed propositional information about the text. Abstracts or summaries are (possibly variable) expressions of the macro-structure.

Table 1 shows a hypothetical (incomplete) example of a memory representation for a story from Boccaccio's *Decameron*. Macro-structure propositions are written out in natural language, micro-structure propositions are indicated only as P's.

(ii) In order to understand narratives subjects must have available as part of their general knowledge a conventional narrative schema. This schema is used to organize the text base.

In our example, the schema consists of those parts of Table 1 that remain after all story-specific information is deleted (e.g. the labels inside the boxes are erased, as well as the micro-structure propositions at the bottom). Comprehending a story can thus be compared to filling in the empty slots in a pre-existing story schema.

(iii) The construction of a macro-structure is a necessary component of comprehension; hence macro-structures are established during reading, rather than at the time of recalling or summarizing a story.

If these three hypotheses can be confirmed, they would have important implications for a processing model of narratives. The outline of such a model would be as follows. We start with a document, the written narrative, and we end up with a document, either a recall protocol, or a summary of the story. Reading the story involves a certain set of perceptual processes that need not concern us here, and three distinct linguistic-conceptual processes: (1) the decoding of the text into words, phrases, and sentences, i.e. the linguistic analyses proper; (2) propositions are inferred from this linguistic material, that is the conceptual meaning is constructed from the verbal text; this is the micro-structure of the text; (3) the micro-structure propositions are organized into higher order units by semantic macro-rules and with the help of a conventional story schema; the units are labelled, and these labels are the macro-structure propositions. The same rules and other rules (e.g. narrative transformations) may again operate upon these macro-structure propositions, creating a hierarchy of macro-structures (corresponding to more and more general summaries of the story). These three processes must occur at least in part sequentially, but they are certainly highly interactive.

Right after reading a narrative, traces from all these processing activities remain in the reader's memory: visual memory traces (what the text looked like, where on a page a certain sentence was, etc.), linguistic memory traces (some actual words and phrases used in the text), micro-structure propositions (the detailed content of the story), as well as macro-structure propositions (the over-all organization of the story in terms of its main events). All of these memory traces may persist in time, but usually the task demands of reading are such that only the higher levels of processing are emphasized, and hence only these result in stable memory traces. One does not usually have much visual, or even linguistic memory, after reading a story, though one certainly can retain such information and some traces of that type are almost always there. The story content, and especially its main events, i.e. its macro-structure, are normally the main concerns of the reader and are remembered best.

When a subject is asked to recall a story he has read, he generates a linguistic output from his memory traces. Whatever remnants of the actual linguistic processing during reading are still available in memory are used for that purpose, but for the most part the text must be reconstructed from the micro- and macro-structure propositions that represent the reader's memory for the meaning of the text.

When the subject is asked to summarize rather than recall the story, his linguistic output is generated directly from the macro-structure propositions, while lower level memory traces tend to be ignored.

5   The role of the macro-structure in comprehension and memory for narratives

5.1   The dominance of the macro-structure in the whole-recall of narratives becomes quite evident when one compares recall protocols with abstracts or summaries for the same narratives. Subjects read the story from Boccaccio's *Decameron* (for its structure, see van Dijk 1975). It is about 1600 words long. Some of the subjects were then asked to recall the whole story in writing, while others were asked to write a summary of the main events in the story. A comparison of the recall protocols and the abstracts revealed some interesting similarities. Recall may be characterized as summary-plus-detail; that is, the statements that subjects make in their summaries tend also to be included in their recall protocols. In addition, recall protocols contain more information about some of the details of the story, which usually does not appear in summaries. These details consist in part of reconstructions (presumably subjects remembered the macro-structure of the story and on that basis reconstructed plausible details of the story at the time of recall), but also genuine reproductions from the story. This was shown by giving subjects who never had read the story the abstract of the story and asking them to reconstruct the story from the abstract: such reconstructions differed from genuine recall protocols in that the latter included many pieces of detailed information derived from the story which do not appear in pure reconstructions. Thus we may conclude, quite in accord with the theoretical expectations outlined earlier, that the subject's memory representation for a narrative consists of the macro-structure plus some micro-structure propositions that are associated with the appropriate superordinated macrostructure propositions. When asked to recall, the subject uses the macro-structure as a retrieval cue, producing both the macro-structure propositions plus whatever micro-structure propositions are still available, and supplementing his recall with plausible reconstructions. When asked to abstract a story, the subjects apparently base their responses directly upon the macro-structure which is stored in memory. It appears, furthermore, that macro-structures are remembered better than micro-structure propositions, for if recall is delayed (for 9 days in one study) most micro-structure information drops out of the recall protocols, which become almost indistinguishable from summaries.

5.2   We have hypothesized that the reader approaches a narrative with a narrative schema in mind, and that part of the process of comprehending the narrative consists in filling in the empty slots in that schema with appropriate information from the text, viz. the macro-structure propositions. So far we have only shown that something like a macro-structure does indeed emerge when one recalls or summarizes a narrative. But is the knowledge of the appropriate narrative schema in fact a necessary condition for understanding the text? We have tried to approach this question by comparing the way readers summarize texts for which they presumably have available the right narrative schema, and texts for which such schemata are lacking. College students are certainly familiar with the narrative schema upon which stories for the Decameron are based (this does not mean of course that they are aware of the schema, or even able to verbalize it: the rules of linguistic processing are no more available to introspection at the text level than they are at the level of syntactic or phonological analyses). On the other hand, the same subjects are unfamiliar with the structure of American Indian tales. Hence they should be able to write significantly better summaries of Decameron stories than of Indian folk tales.

The Indian story which we selected for our experiment is an Apache myth about the origin of corn and deer. It is 1600 words long and contains no difficult sentences or unfamiliar words (complicated names were replaced). Nevertheless, our subjects thought the story to be 'weird', because it does not conform to their expectations about narratives: the person of the hero is not constant, episodes follow each other with no apparent (i.e. causal) connection, the organization of the story is obscure. The story, of course, does follow a well developed schema, but one known only to Indians and anthropologists. For comparison, three stories from the Decameron, each about 1600 words long, were selected. The subject's task was the same in all cases: to read the story, taking as much time as he likes, and then, again without time restrictions, to write an abstract or summary of the story. In order to ensure comparability between the abstracts from different subjects, all abstracts had to be between 60 and 80 words long; furthermore, the abstract had to be written in complete English sentences. To avoid the boring and distracting task of counting and recounting the number of words in the abstract, subjects typed their abstracts on a computer controlled oscilloscope screen, and the computer displayed for them the number of words written.

All statements (corresponding to propositions, as in our earlier work) used in the abstracts were listed, and for each statement the number of subjects using it in their abstract was noted. One would expect that abstracts of stories for which the reader has available a conventional schema would be more or less the same from one subject to the next. If the process of writing a summary is, indeed, directed by the schema, different subjects should agree at least to some extent about what they include in their summaries. Of course, each reader will employ the summarization rules discussed in Section 4.3 differently, and hence there will be some differences among the abstracts they generate, but certainly there should be considerable more differences when no story schema is available to direct the readers' organization of the story. Our results were in good agreement with this prediction: there was significantly more agreement among subjects about the statements used in the summaries of the Decameron stories than about those in the Indian story.

5.3   The strategy of looking at how people summarize or recall stories for which they do not have an appropriate schema available also provides the rationale for a study of how children comprehend stories that was recently undertaken by Dorothy Poulsen and Eileen Kintsch at Colorado. Picture stories without text, comprising about 15–18 pictures, were selected from children's books and shown to four-year olds. After one viewing, the child was asked to describe each picture in his own words. Finally, the child recalled the story as well as he could. The description task was used in addition to the recall task because children at that age typically do not recall stories very well, and the simpler description task provides a better opportunity to study how they comprehend stories.

We were particularly interested in the role that story schemata play in the comprehension processes of four-year olds. For that purpose, the pictures that made up our stories were shown either in their natural order, thus permitting the children to follow the story, or in scrambled order, which made it difficult or impossible for the children to figure out the story. In the one story analyzed so far, much better descriptions of the pictures were obtained when the pictures were shown in their natural order. The total number of correct statements made was about 50% higher for pictures in natural order than in scrambled order. Scrambling the pictures produced a regression to more primitive styles of expression in these children. The simplest descriptions obtained were labeling responses: the child simply points to objects depicted and labels them – "a dog – a wolf – a branch". Such responses were rare in our four-year olds when they were describing the pictures in their natural order (4%), but they became quite frequent when the pictures were presented out of order (28%). However, not all children responded with labeling when they could not comprehend the story that was told by the pictures. Some actively tried to construct a macro-structure, to make some sense of these pictures, even though they were unable to do so. These subjects tended to produce many cognitive statements (the dog *thinks*, the wolf *wants*) or affective statements (the boy is *sad*). Indeed, 20% of all responses were of that nature in the scrambled picture condition, compared with only 8% when the pictures were shown in order.

It is clear that the availability of a story in the natural order condition played a large role in how subjects described these pictures. These four-year olds were responding to the story that the pictures told, not just to each picture separately. When there was no story, they nevertheless tried to make one up – or regressed to an earlier developmental level.

5.4   While the data discussed above indicate that the availability of a macro-structure and a narrative schema may indeed be necessary for the comprehension of a long text, they contain no evidence either for or against the third hypothesis that we made in Section 5, namely that macro-structures are constructed during reading, as an integral part of the comprehension process, rather than at the time of recall or summarizing. The experiment we performed to test this hypothesis is simple, but the argument we make is a little subtle, so we shall first introduce it by means of an analogy to an earlier experiment. One of the studies reported in Kintsch (1974) involves the following argument. From a given text base two texts are constructed, one syntactically simple and one syntactically complex. Subjects read these two versions of the text, and took more time to read the syntactically complex than the simple text. Then subjects were asked some questions (involving inferences) about the text: the way they answered these questions did not depend upon which version they had read, both in terms of percent correct responses and latencies. We concluded from this pattern of results that what these subjects had stored in their memory was independent of the syntactic complexity of the input, i.e. that subjects had stored the meaning of each paragraph in memory in an abstract form, and that the syntactic complexity of the input affected only decoding time, but not what was eventually stored in memory. We now propose to use this type of argument once more, this time not at the syntactic level, but concerning macro-structures. Subjects read the same narrative, but in two versions: some subjects read the story in natural order, with the macro-structure intact, and others read it with the order of the paragraphs randomized. We hypothesized that if readers are indeed constructing macro-structures during reading, those subjects who read the story in natural order should have an easier task than subjects who read the story with the order of paragraphs scrambled; hence reading times should be longer for the scrambled condition. However, after reading both groups of subjects will have constructed the same macro-structures (because, by assumption this is a necessary condition for comprehension) so that if subjects are now asked to summarize the story, there should be no differences in either the quality of the summaries they produce, or in the time they need to write their summaries. The data that we have collected so far confirm these predictions. The average reading time for scrambled stories is 9.85 min., while only 7.45 min. are required to read the same stories in natural order. On the other hand, subjects took on the average 19.33 min. to write abstracts after reading stories in natural order, and 20.04 min., after reading stories in scrambled order. This difference is far from significant statistically. At the same time, subjects agree equally well about what goes into an abstract after reading stories in natural and scrambled order. In fact, it is impossible to tell which abstracts were written by subjects who read natural and scrambled stories. This was confirmed by giving all 24 abstracts to judges, with the instructions to sort them into two piles according to whether the abstract was written from a natural or scrambled story. No judge was able to sort these abstracts with an accuracy significantly better than chance.

5.5   Thus we are left with rather positive evidence regarding all three hypotheses that were suggested in Section 6 about the role of macro-structures in comprehension. Of course, these results are tentative and more systematic experimentation is required before we can be confident about our conclusions. However, the data are certainly suggestive. It seems that the representation of a text that a reader stores in memory indeed includes both micro- and macro-structure components, and that the linguistic work on text bases provides a reasonably accurate idea of the nature of these memory representations. Secondly, we have obtained some evidence for the notion that story comprehension can be compared with filling in the empty slots of conventional text schemata, and that texts for which no specific schemata are available are organized in ideosyncratic ways with little inter-subject agreement. Finally, we found no reason to modify the hypothesis that when subjects are recalling a story, they use the macro-structure as a retrieval cue, supplementing it with whatever detailed information is also available, and that if subjects are asked to summarize a story, the summary is a possible expression of the macro-structure they have stored in memory. We hope that further work along these lines will not only help us to understand better the cognitive processes involved in text comprehension and memory, but will also provide us with some insights about those aspects of text structure that are most relevant for the linguistic analysis of texts.

Note and acknowledgements

This paper is an enlarged version of Walter Kintsch & Teun A. van Dijk, "Recalling and Summarizing Stories", of which a French translation "Comment on se rappelle et on résume des histories" was published in *Langages* 40 (1975) 98–116.

This paper was supported by a grant to Walter Kintsch from the National Institute for Mental Health, MH-15872, and to Teun A. van Dijk from the Netherlands Organization for the Advancement of Pure Research (Z.W.O.) and the Faculty of Letters of the University of Amsterdam. These grants are gratefully acknowledged.

References

Barnard, Philip John *Structure and Content in the Retention of Prose* (Ph.D. Dissertation, University College, London), 1974.

Bartlett, F.C. *Remembering* (London: Cambridge University Press), 1932.

Bobrow, Daniel G., & Allan Collins, eds. *Representation and Understanding* (New York: Academic Press). 1975.

Carroll, John B. & Freedle, Roy, O. eds. *Language Comprehension and the Acquisition of Knowledge* (Washington D.C.: Winston; Wiley Distrib.). 1972.

Charniak, Eugene *Toward a Model of Children's Story Comprehension* (Ph.D. Dissertation, MIT, Artificial Intelligence Lab.), 1972.

Cofer, Charles N. "A Comparison of logical and verbatim learning of prose passages of different lengths", *American Journal of Psychology,* 1941, 54, 1–20.

Crothers, Edward J. "Memory Structure and the Recall of Discourse". In: Freedle & Carroll, eds., 1972, 247–283.

Crothers, Edward J. *Paragraph Structure Description* (University of Colorado, Department of Psychology), 1975.

van Dijk, Teun A. *Some Aspects of Text Grammars* (The Hague: Mouton), 1972.

van Dijk, Teun A. "Recalling and Summarizing Complex Discourse" (University of Amsterdam, mimeo), 1975.

van Dijk, Teun A. "Philosophy of Action and Theory of Narrative", *Poetics,* 1976, 6, 287–338, 1976a.

van Dijk, Teun A. "Complex Semantic Information Processing", Paper contributed to the Workshop on Linguistics and documentation, Stockholm, May 3–5 (University of Amsterdam, mimeo), 1976b.

van Dijk, Teun A. *Text and Context. Explorations in the Semantics and Pragmatics of Discourse* (Longmans, London), 1977a.

van Dijk, Teun A. "Macro-structures, Knowledge Frames and Discourse Comprehension", Paper contributed to the Carnegie-Mellon Symposium on Cognition, May 1976, To appear in: P. Carpenter & M. Just, eds., *Cognitive Processes in Comprehension* (Hillsdale, N.J.: Erlbaum), 1977b.

Dooling, J.L., & R. Lachman "Effects of Comprehension on Retention of Prose", *Journal of Experimental Psychology,* 1971, 88, 216–222.

Freedle, Roy O. "Language users as fallible information processors: implications for measuring and modeling comprehension" In: Freedle & Carroll, eds., 1972, 169–209.

Frederiksen, C.H. "Effects of Task-Induced Cognitive Operations on Comprehension and Memory Processes". In: Carroll and Freedle, eds., 1972, 211–246.

Gomulicki, B.R. "Recall as an Abstractive Process", *Acta Psychologica* 1956, 12, 77–94.

Kintsch, Walter "Notes on the Structures of Semantic Memory". In: Tulving & Donaldson, eds. 1972, 247–308.

Kintsch, Walter *The Representation of Meaning in Memory* (Hillsdale, N.J.: Erlbaum-Wiley), 1974.

Kintsch, Walter *Memory, Language and Thinking,* New York: Wiley, 1977.

Kintsch, Walter, Eli Kozminsky, William J. Streby, Gail McKoon, & Janice M. Keenan, "Comprehension and recall of text as a function of content variables". *Journal of Verbal Learning and Verbal Behavior,* 1975, 14, 196–214.

Lachman, R., & D.J. Dooling "Connected Discourse and Random Strings: Effects of Number of Inputs on Recognition and Recall", *Journal of Experimental Psychology,* 1968, 77, 507–522.

Lee, W. "Supra-paragraph Prose Structures: Its Specification, Perception and Effects of Learning", *Psychological Reports,* 1965, 17, 135–144.

Meyer, Bonnie F. *The Organization of Prose and its Effects on Memory* (Amsterdam: North Holland), 1975.

Minsky, Marvin "A Framework for Representing Knowledge". In: P. Winston, ed., *The Psychology of Computer Vision* (New York: McGraw-Hill), 1975.

Newman, S.E., & E. Saltz "Effects on Learning from Connected Discourse", *American Journal of Psychology,* 1960, 73, 587–592.

Paul, I.H. *Studies in Remembering. The Reproduction of Connected and Extended Verbal Material, Psychological Issues,* Monograph Series, 1959.

Pompi, K.F., & R. Lachman "Surrogate Processes in the Short-Term Retention of Connected Discourse", *Journal of Experimental Psychology,* 1967, 75, 143–150.

Rothkopf, Ernst Z. "Structural text features and the Control of Processes in Learning from Written materials". In: Freedle & Carroll, eds., 1972, 315–335.

Rumelhart, David E. "Notes on a Schema for Stories". In: Bobrow & Collins, eds., 1975, 211–236.

Sachs, Jacqueline "Recognition Memory for Syntactic and Semantic Aspects of Connected Discourse", *Perception and Psychophysics,* 1967, 2, 437–442.

Schank, Roger C. "The Structures of Episodes in Memory". In: Bobrow & Collins, eds., 1975, 237–272.

Slamecka, N.J. "Studies of Retention of Connected Discourse", *American Journal of Psychology,* 1959, 72, 409–416.

Thorndyke, Perry W. *Cognitive Structures in Human Story Comprehension and Memory* (Ph.D. Dissertation, Stanford), 1975.

Tulving, Endel & Wayne Donaldson, eds., *Organization of Memory* (New York: Academic Press), 1972.

On Some Questions and Ambiguities in Conversation*

Emanuel A. Schegloff
University of California, Los Angeles

The datum I am concerned with is the following, in particular the last two exchanges:

```
 1.  B:  An' s- an'(   ) we were discussing, it tur-
 2.      it comes down, he s- he says, I-I-you've talked
 3.      with thi- si- i- about this many times. I said,
 4.      it come down t' this :=
 5.  B:  = Our main difference: I feel that a government,        (1)
 6.      i- the main thing, is- th-the purpose a' the
 7.      government, is, what is best for the country.
 8.  A:  Mmhmm
 9.  B:  He says, governments, an' you know he keeps- he
10.      talks about governments, they sh- the thing that
11.      they sh'd do is what's right or wrong.
12.  A:  For whom.
13.  B:  Well he says- // he-
14.  A:  By what standard
15.  B:  That's what- that's exactly what I mean. he s-
         but he says ...
```

B has been describing to A the differences he (B) has been having with his high school history teacher over the morality of American foreign policy since the time of George Washington. I suppose I should say now that the excerpt is taken from a conversation in a radio call-in show (A being the radio personality), although that will not matter at all to the analysis except in one distant way, in which a formal structural characteristic of the conversation is in this case supplied by that fact; but it is the structural feature that counts, not the fact that in this case it is supplied by the radio setting, the feature being supplied in other conversations by other circumstances of setting.

My initial concern with the sequence 12–15 focused on the interruption in 13. Early work on the sequential organization of turn-taking in conversation (especially that of my colleague, Harvey Sacks) made occurrences of interrup-

* A fuller version will be available in the Pragmatics Microfiche series (ed. S. Levinson, Dept. of Linguistics, Cambridge University, England) and will also be included in the volume 'Studies in the Sequential Organization of Conversation' (ed. H. Sacks et al., Academic Press).

tions and inter-utterance gaps of special interest, as possible violations of the normative organization of the transition from one speaker to a next. Given the recurrent management of that transition with no (or minimal) gap and overlap, and a regular respect for the rights of a speaker, having begun an utterance, to bring it to a point of possible completion,[1] interruptions seemed to warrant examination to find what was involved in departures from that normative practice. In particular, I was attracted by the possibility that interruptions, or some interruptions, might be – so to speak – finely tuned, that is, quite precisely placed by an interruptor.[2] An adequate analysis of what was otherwise going on in the sequence might then yield an understanding of the occurrence, and the precise placement, of the interruption; and some degree of confidence in an analysis of what a sequence was occupied with might be derived if, by reference to it, an otherwise not-particularly-ordered interruption could get seen as "placed".

I

Before turning directly to this datum, let me address a few remarks to the notion "question" in a more or less unlocated way. It is a strong candidate for popularity in a time when some concessions are thought necessary to the "uses of language," or sentences of a language; when, for example, it is argued that some notion of a performative or some type of speech act or some kind of presupposition is involved in the production, and presumably in the comprehension, of a sentence or an utterance. If the mere presence of lexical items such as "I promise," "I bet," "I guarantee" can be taken as invoking the possible membership of the sentence in which they appropriately appear in a class such as "promises" or "bets," with an attached presuppositional structure underlying them, how much more powerful is the appeal of syntactic forms such as "question" or "injunction." A ready bridge is apparently before us to cross from language to social behavior, in which, it might appear, the syntax will bear the load. While it might be conceded that no complete or neat linguistic account of questions is yet available, the relevant attributes being variously apportioned between syntax, prosody, and other resources, still it might appear that linguistic resources will allow the construction and recognition of utterances as questions, and thus as actions of a certain type. Now I think such a view is, or would be, as misleading with regard to "questions" as a way of bridging language and social action at it is in the case of "promises." The general point is that it is misleading to start to account for such categories of action as "questions," "promises," etc., as the analytic objects of interest. They are common-sense, not technical, categories and should be treated accordingly. I cannot

---

[1] Cf. the later statement in Sacks, Schegloff, and Jefferson (1974).
[2] A similar interest animates Jefferson (1973).

pursue that general point here, so let me address it with regard to some particular categories.

Most of the problems derive from treating the categories (such as "questions," "promises"), rather than particular data as problematic. For example, Sacks has noted that for a great many cases (I should hazard a "most" here) of utterances like "I promise" or "I bet," it is not "promising" or "betting" at all that is going on, but rather an attempt at unit-closure, e.g., topic or argument or "making arrangements" closure. The use of the sheer occurrence of the lexical items, without regard to the placement of the utterances in which they occur in the sequential organization of conversation, can be badly misleading, though not implausible.

The same is true where syntax is so used. Consider "injunction." The following is taken from a recent paper on the closing of conversation:[3]

> B has called to invite C, but has been told that C is going out to dinner:
> B: Yeah. Well get on your clothes and get out and collect some of that free food and we'll make it some other time Judy then.
> C: Okay then Jack.   (2)
> B: Bye bye
> C: Bye bye

While B's initial utterance in this excerpt might be grammatically characterized as an imperative or a command, and C's "Okay" then appears to be a submission or accession to it, in no sense but a narrowly syntactic one would those be anything but whimsical characterizations. While B's utterance has certain imperative aspects in its language form, those are not ones that count; his utterance is a closing initiation; and C's utterance agrees not to a command to get dressed (nor would she be inconsistent if she failed to get dressed after the conversation), but to an invitation to close the conversation. The point is that no analysis, grammatical, semantic, pragmatic, etc., of these utterances taken singly and out of sequence, will yield their import in use, will show what co-participants might make of them and do about them. That B's utterance here accomplishes a form of closing initiation, and C's accepts the closing form and not what seems to be proposed in it, turns on the placement of these utterances in the conversation.

And so also with regard to questions. Consider the following:[4]

> B₁: Why don't you *come* and see me some//times.
> A₁: I would like to.
> B₂: I would like you to. Lemme//just-   (3)
> A₂: I don't know just where the-us-this address//*is*.

Where are the questions here? Is there a question here? For a participant whose next utterance or action may be contingent on finding about a current utterance whether it is a "question," because, if it is, an "answer" may be a relevant next thing for him to do, does syntax, or linguistic form, solve his problem? Not only does our intuition suggest that, although no syntactic question (nor question intonation, for that matter) occurs in A's second utterance of the excerpt, a question-answer sequence pair has been initiated, a request for directions if you like; more importantly, it is so heard by B who proceeds to

---

[3] Schegloff and Sacks (1973), p. 313.
[4] Taken from Schegloff (1972), p. 107.

give directions.[5] And while B's first utterance in the excerpt looks syntactically like a question, it is not a "question" that A "answers", but an "invitation" (in question form) that she "accepts."

Now it might do to play with this last point a bit. It might be argued that there is an easy way to provide for not analyzing B_1 above as a question. To wit: consider that the utterance contains in it a component of imperative or injunctive form, "Come and see me sometime." Let us name a construction in English, or American English, an "injunction mitigator". Instances of injunction mitigators are "why don't you," "would you like to," and undoubtedly others. A rule for its use might be that it can front or precede any injunctive form. It might, I suppose, be made a "sociolinguistic" rule, in the narrow sense of that term, by making its use contingent on certain relative statuses between speaker and recipient(s), etc. The rule might be said to transform the syntactic form from "injunctive" to "question," and the action, accordingly, from "command" to "request," "invitation," or "suggestion." And certainly in a wide range of cases that we can imagine or invent, that seems to be what is involved. In such cases, we would have provided for a recipient not hearing in the utterance a question, but a mitigated injunction, or an invitation, etc., though, interestingly enough, a question would still be available to a literal analysis, and so declining the invitation might be done by treating the utterance for the question which it could be proposed to contain. But then we might note that in the present case, B_1, the utterance would be an invitation without the mitigator. And other injunctions do not seem to allow the use of a mitigator, so that if one is used, it does not mitigate an injunction, but rather makes it sarcastic, as in "Why don't you go away and leave me alone." In short, while the forms I have for now named "injunction mitigators" may be operators or particles of a sort, what one of them is doing in any particular case will depend on what it is attached to, and where that is placed. It will not, therefore, serve as a generalized means, or even as a restricted one, for depriving nonquestion question forms of a question-interpretation.

In insisting that the B_1-A_1 sequence involves accepting an invitation rather than answering a question, I may seem to be niggling over details. Still, from the point of view of a recipient of the B_1 utterance, while a "response" of some sort is relevant, important differences turn on whether an answer or an acceptance/rejection is in point. Underlying this theme is the co-membership of question-answer and invitation-acceptance/rejection sequences in the class of sequential units elsewhere called "adjacency pairs."[6]

Adjacency pairs consist of sequences which properly have the following features: 1) Two utterance length; 2) Adjacent positioning of component utterances; 3) Different speakers producing each utterance.

---

[5] *Ibid.*
[6] Schegloff and Sacks, op.cit. pp. 295–296. cf. also Sacks, Schegloff, and Jefferson op.cit. pp. 716–718.

The component utterances of such sequences have an achieved relatedness beyond that which may otherwise obtain between adjacent utterances. That relatedness is partially the product of the operation of a typology in the speakers' production of the sequences. The typology operates in two ways: it partitions utterance types into "first pair parts" (i.e., first parts of pairs) and second pair parts; and it affiliates a first pair part and a second pair part to form a "pair type." "Question-answer," "greeting-greeting", "offer-acceptance/refusal" are instances of pair types. A given sequence will thus be composed of an utterance that is a first pair part produced by one speaker directly followed by the production by a different speaker of an utterance which is a) a second pair part, and b) is from the same pair type as the first utterance in the sequence is a member of. Adjacency pair sequences, then, exhibit the further features (4) relative ordering of parts (i.e., first pair parts precede second pair parts), and 5) discriminative relations (i.e., the pair type of which a first pair part is a member is relevant to the selection among second pair parts).

A basic rule of adjacency pair operation is: given the recognizable production of a first pair part, on its first possible completion its speaker should stop and a next speaker should start and produce a second pair part from the pair type of which the first is recognizably a member.

It is by virtue of the pair organization that a "response" is relevant for either a question or an invitation; it is by virtue of the differing pair types that different second pair parts will be required, depending on which first pair part is found to have been just finished.

Consider, in a similar vein, the following, in which a husband and wife are discussing arrangements for visiting another couple, with whom the previous night's scheduled visit had been cancelled, while their $1^{1}/_{2}$ year old daughter plays on the floor:

W: Why is it that *we* have to go *there*.

H: Because *she* (head-motioning to daughter) can go   (4)
    out more easily than *their* kids can.

Note that H hears and treats W's utterance as a question, and answers it by giving a reason. But also note, as H and W subsequently did, that W's utterance can be heard as a complaint, and a complaint on the part of "us" against "them." In terms of that possible hearing, H's response comes off as a "defense" of them against W's complaint, and some troublesome issues about lines of solidarity might be seen to be raised. Were W's utterance heard and treated as a complaint in the first place, then a quite different response to it might be in order, e.g., joining the complaint, with possibly quite different consequences for the location, and indeed the occurrence, of the visiting. Again, in either case adjacency pairs are involved, in one case question-answer, in the other complaint-echo complaint, or agreement.

One consequence of this discussion, to my mind, is that not only is the path from linguistic questions to interactional ones not a straight line, but that not much may lie at its end. For a substantial part of what we might expect to be available to us as understanding of questions as a category of action is best and most parsimoniously subsumed under the category "adjacency pairs"; much of what is so about questions is so by virtue of the adjacency pair format. And what distinguishes "questions" from first pair parts of other sorts does not seem in any straightforward way to be sought from linguistic resources.

Is there, then, no import at all of linguistic form, such as question form, for the action interpretation of an utterance? Couldn't one say that linguistic form supplies a *prima facie* basis for the analysis of an utterance, which will hold unless superseded by other features; in other words, that it provides a presumption, an "unmarked" interpretation if you will, such that the burden falls elsewhere to make an utterance something else? A likely unparsimoniousness aside, one trouble with such a view is that it treats an utterance's syntactic form as a "first" feature about it, hence "prima facie." And in the traditional practice of linguists, as well as of ordinary language philosophers, in which single sentences are (the) normal units of analysis, this may well be the case. But in the real world of conversation, it is not. Most centrally, an utterance will occur someplace sequentially. Most obviously, except for initial utterances, it will occur after some other utterance or sequence of utterances with which it will have, in some fashion, to deal and which will be relevant to its analysis for co-participants. Less obviously, but more importantly, it (and here initial utterances are not excepted) may occur in a structurally defined place in conversation, in which case its structural location can have attached to its slot a set of features that may overwhelm its syntactic or prosodic structure in primacy. "Well, get on your clothes and get out and collect some of that free food" occurs in such a structurally defined place. Second slots in adjacency pairs are such a structural place.

Even where an utterance is in the linguistic form of a question, and seems to be doing questioning, the latter will not be adequately accounted for by the former. For if the question form can be used for actions other than questioning, and questioning can be accomplished by linguistic forms other than questions, then a relevant problem can be posed not only about how a question does something other than questioning; but how it does questioning; not only about how questioning is done by non-question forms, but how it gets accomplished by a question form.

Let me now try one more line on the theme I have been trying to develop. One thing one might mean by an utterance being interactionally or conversationally a question is that it lays constraints on the next slot in the conversation of a sort special to the QA pair type of adjacency pairs. Leaving aside an explication of what those special constraints might be, we can consider how some of the materials already mentioned and some additional ones look in terms of this notion. There is what I suppose might be called "the clear case"; e.g.,

A: What time is it? B: It's noon.   (5)

in which an adjacency pair is initiated making a second pair part relevant, and the second pair part seems to satisfy whatever formulation of the notion "answer" one uses. There is an earlier considered fragment:

B: Why don't you *come* and see me sometimes.

A: I would like to.   (6)

in which an adjacency pair is initiated, but one whose constraints are not of a QA sort, or whose treatment as of a QA sort, i.e., giving reasons why not, will likely get a hearing as rudeness or teasing rather than answering, as in the similar case of requests, like, "Do you have a cigarette?" "Yes, (pause) would you like one?" There is yet another interesting case which merits extended treatment which it cannot be given here, but which should be mentioned. It is the case in which a QA format is used to package a sequence, such that the initial utterance is indeed used to set answer-relevant constraints on the next slot, but where the sequence is not used to do questioning or answering at all. Here, the format is determined by the linguistic forms, but what is done in that format has nothing to do with questioning. A relevant example is drawn from an earlier point in the conversation from which the initially cited datum comes.

1. B: Because- an' he did the same thing, in
2.   War of- The War of Eighteen Twelve, he said
3.   the fact that we were interested in expansion,
4.   t'carrying farther, was ( ) something *against*.   (7)
5.   Y'know a-argument t'use against. But see the
6.   whole thing is he's against, he's // very- he's
7.   ( )
8. A: Is he teaching history or Divinity.
9. B: I don' kno(h)w. But he's very anti-imperialistic.

Now whatever its appearance when excerpted from the conversation, these last two turns (at lines 8–9) are not respectively a question as to someone's subject matter, and a confession of ignorance, which is the interpretation required if we see them as a QA sequence. The conversation contains early on:

B: ... I'm taking 'merican history this term, I'm a junior. Well I- now the new term began I gotta new teacher, so, we're starting from about you know, Washington's foreign policy (I have omitted interpolations by A)   (8)

"Is he teaching history or divinity" is not asking that, and "I don't know" is not a confession of ignorance. This is not questioning and answering, though a question-answer format is used to "package" the sequence. The distinction is critical to what will be placed in the second slot of the pair, and how what is placed there will be understood.

While in many of these cases, alternative analyses of the first utterance in the sequence are theoretically, or heuristically, conceivable (e.g., the analysis of "why don't you come visit," etc.), they do not appear to be in practice confounded in an ambiguity. The "distinctions" I have been pointing out are quite academic, in the sense that their proper, perhaps only, place is here in the lecture hall. They are not distinctions drawn by the participants, for whom rather it appears that what is being done is quite straightforwardly available or analyzable. Because the constraints on a next utterance for a next speaker can be quite sharply different if a last utterance is seen to be a question or something else, we might do well to examine in some detail a case in which both possibilities, with their attendant constraints are entertained by the participants – a case, that is, of *empirical* ambiguity as to whether an utterance is a question or some determinate alternative. And in examining such an ambiguity, we shall encounter some sequential features of conversation of the sort I suggested before overshadow the contribution made to the understanding of what an utterance is doing of its linguistic form.

II

I now turn to the sequence I put before you at the beginning. My intention is to try to locate the sources of the ambiguity of "For whom" in the sequential structures of the conversation. I further want this to be explication of a real ambiguity rather than a theoretical one, i.e., not one where only one sense is actually operative for the participants, though an analyst can conjure up other senses it might have, under some other circumstances. Therefore, I shall want to support the claim that both analyses of the utterance which I argue compose the ambiguity are available to, and are employed by, the participants, i.e., both analyses will have been dealt with by both parties. Then we can turn to the utterance itself and attempt to explicate the sequential basis for the ambiguity.

The tool I shall use initially is one based on, and fundamental to, a great deal of prior work in conversational analysis. It is that co-participants in conversation operate under the constraint that their utterances be so constructed and so placed as to show attention to, and understanding of, their placement. That means that utterances, or larger units, are constructed to display to co-participants that their speaker has attended a last utterance, or sequence of utterances, or other unit, and that this current utterance, in its construction, is placed with due regard for where it is occurring.

Now that constraint, and what is required to meet it, can vary in power and in detail. Adjacency pairs are especially strong constraints, a first pair part making relevant a particular action, or a restricted set of actions, to be done next. When a next speaker does such an action, he not only complies with the requirements of the particular adjacency pair initiated; he shows in his utterance his understanding of what the prior utterance was doing – a first pair part of that pair type.[7] At the other end of the scale, the constraint of showing attention to sequential context may be satisfied by a speaker's showing that although he may know what is relevant next, what he is about to do is something else. Thus, there is a form we have elsewhere[8] termed "misplacement markers" – "by the way" is a familiar one – which a speaker may use at the beginning of an utterance, which can show, among other things, he knows that something other than what he is about to do is in order, or that what he is about to do is "out of place." While he may then go on to do it, he will have had his utterance display his attention to, and understanding of, the preceding utterance or sequence at least enough to know that what he is doing is not "naturally" or "properly" placed there. There are other such forms, e.g., starting an utterance with an "oh" (sometimes combined with using it to interrupt) when it is not topically

---

[7] cf. Sacks, Schegloff and Jefferson, op.cit. pp. 728–729.

[8] Schegloff and Sacks, op.cit. pp. 319–320.

coherent with what precedes, a show of unplannedness if you like, the way "free association" is accomplished conversationally, a display that what follows has been "touched off," a disjunction marker. Or, the use of "anyway" as a right hand parenthesis, to show that what it precedes is fitted not to prior utterances, but to what preceded them.

Across the range of power and detail, utterances are built to display speakers' understanding; they are thereby made available for co-participants' inspection to see if they display an adequate understanding of that which they claim to understand. This resource we will come back to later. For now, we want to notice that they also thereby make available to the *analyst* a basis in the data for claiming what the co-participants' understanding is of prior utterances, for as they display it to one another, we can see it too.[9] It is this resource that will be used in an initial run-through of the sequence that engages us.

Since the turn at line 12 in this sequence is the one we shall want to focus on, we shall be returning to it in considerable detail. Let it then suffice for now that it appears to be a question. It is, furthermore, a question specifically designed for the place in which it is used. Now the phrase "place in which it is used" is critical, and how we formulate "place" will be central to the later analysis. For now we can note that it is not a fully formed question, but shows its attention to what preceded it, at least in part, by requiring of its hearer attention to what preceded it for its very understanding: it is, so to speak, built off of, or on to, the preceding turn, uses it as a resource for its construction, and requires its use as a resource for its understanding. One thing further needs to be said about its relation to what precedes it at this point, and that is that what it is appended to is a statement of someone else's views; you will note the prior turn starts "*He* says." So a preliminary characterization of 12 might be that it is a question, requesting clarification by B of someone else's views, of which he (B) has just given a (summary) version.

Now "For whom" will sustain a quite different analysis. That is, it can stand as a way for A to show agreement with B. I say "show agreement" to differentiate it from agreeing, or more particularly from claiming or asserting agreement, for agreement, like understanding, is subject to incorrect or manipulative treatment. That is, there can be extrinsic reasons for claiming understanding or agreement, e.g., in the case of agreement, to achieve closure of a topic or argument, a theme to which we will return. In any case, for both understanding and agreement, "claiming" them and "showing" them are different sorts of things, and impose different requirements. In the present case, "For whom" can be seen as an attempt to show understanding of, and agreement with, B. It does this by complaining about, or challenging, a position with which B has just asserted himself to be in disagreement, proferring a possible argument of B's. Under that analysis, it is not an answer to a question that is a relevant next utterance or action, for a question has not been asked (though a question form has been used); rather, an acknowledgement of agreement is relevant.

[9] cf. footnote 7.

It should be noted that neither of these putative "analyses" of "for whom" has yet been provided a basis. They are proposed now as observations, hopefully with some cogency, and I intend next to show that the sequel in the conversation is consistent with first one, and then the other, of these analyses being taken up. But the basis of these understandings of "for whom," either by the parties to the conversation, or for the analyst, remains to be analyzed. Certainly, "for whom" is not a question by virtue of its linguistic form, its inclusion of a "wh-word," alone, for not all utterances with wh-words are questions. And it is not a complaint/agreement in any self-evident way, for no basis has been provided for hearing "for whom" as in someway B's position (which is central to that analysis) rather than A's.

If 12 is a question, then it is a first pair part of an adjacency pair, a pair of the type question-answer, and the one to whom it is addressed should do the second pair part for that pair type, i.e., here he (B) should do an answer. Further, if the question is doing a request for clarification, the answer should do a clarification. And, finally if the clarification requested is of another's views, as was suggested by appending the question that requests it to a statement of those views, then the answer should assign the clarification, i.e., the extension of the views, to their holder. As much of an utterance as B gets to produce at 13 is consistent with all of this. In seeming to undertake a clarification, or further explication, and starting with "he says" where the "he" finds as its referent the same referent as the "he"s in lines 9–11, B can be seen to display his understanding of 12 as a question he is now answering, a request he is now satisfying. Let me emphasize that while for us now he is displaying it too, in the first place he is displaying it to A. And as B is engaged in an analysis of 12 to find what it was doing and what he might then do next, so A is engaged in an analysis of 13. And from the amount of 13 that gets out before A interrupts, what has been suggested above about it is available. "Well he says" is all that is needed to see that B heard 12 as a question, a request for clarification of the other's position, and is starting to do what he should on that analysis, namely, answer the question by giving clarification of the other's position. When enough of the utterance is out to display that, and no more, A interrupts.

It appears that the understanding of 12 "for whom" that B displays himself in 13 to have, is for A, the speaker of that utterance, incorrect. That is, it appears that while B understood that to be a question, requesting clarification of the teacher's position, A did not produce it to be that.

That one party can see that, and how, an utterance of his has been misanalyzed by another from that other's subsequent utterance we have found on quite other materials. For example, someone doing an intendedly terminal greeting who gets back a "yes?", can find that it was heard incorrectly, and, in particular, what wrong thing it was heard as; i.e., his greeting was heard as a summons.[10] In particular, parties can detect such errors by seeing an interlocutor's

---

[10] cf. Schegloff (1968), p. 1082.

utterance as a second pair part, finding the first pair part it would be a proper sequel for, and seeing how the utterance it follows, in many cases their own prior utterance, could have been heard as such a first pair part. Here, I am proposing, A can hear 13 as a possible answer, can locate a question as a prior form of utterance that would have elicited an answer as its proper sequel, and can see how 12, his own prior utterance, while not produced to be a question, could be so analyzed. That much is available from 13, B: "Well he says." By interrupting at that point with an utterance of the type involved, A in effect disallows B's proceeding on that analysis of 12 in this slot.

The utterance with which A interrupts at line 14 is exquisitely designed for its place. While we do not have any equivalence rules for utterances in conversation that I know of, this utterance – "By what *standard*" – is as close to an equivalent for 12 – "for whom" – as I can imagine. In its syntactic form, in its intonational contour, in its stress placement, the two are isomorphic. And, importantly, it is built on to, or off of, attaches itself in exactly the same way as did 12, to line 11. It is more a duplicate of 12 than a repetition of 12 would have been. It is, it appears, *the* way of repeating the turn at line 12.

Its use here is that it invites a reanalysis with a different outcome of the utterance it repeats. It seems to invoke a procedure I will call a "redo invitation": i.e., it invites last speaker to repeat some last operation and come up with a different output. One way the procedure may be invoked is by repeating the element on which the operation is to be redone. Let me cite two quite different sorts of data (in both of which, however, the repetition is done by the recipient of the repeated element, not its speaker):

IDP # 18

S: Do you need any help up there.
D: All we can get.
S: All you can get.   (9)
D: Yes, you have a station wagon or anything
    that can haul injured?

in which a reanalysis of what would be an adequate answer is elicited, more specifics then being produced; and the following which I take from a paper by Gail Jefferson[11]:

Steven: One two three (pause) four five six
        (pause) eleven eight nine ten.
Susan: "Eleven"? – eight nine ten?
Steven: Eleven eight nine ten   (10)
Nancy: "Eleven?"
Steven: Seven eight nine ten.

As this last citation suggests, one way of invoking the procedure involves paralinguistically marked repetition – a special upward intonation pattern, and a special stress placement. Note that neither of these is possible at 14 in the data

---

[11] Gail Jefferson (1972), p. 295.

we are conceerned with. An upward intonation on an utterance of question form with a wh-word makes it into a recipient's repeat of another's question; and the initial version of A's utterance, at 12, already had a heavy stress at the point where the stress would go to invite re-doing. And so A does as close to an equivalent utterance as is perhaps possible, and thereby invites reanalysis of what his utterance was doing. It is worth noting that by building his utterance at 14 to attach to 11 in just the way 12 did, A brings off that the reanalysis he is inviting is what he "intended all along," i.e., it was the correct analysis of 12 too, rather than being only what he is doing now, leaving open what a correct understanding of 12 would have been.[12] That is, the form of his construction here provides for the retroactive, or retrospective relevance of the understanding it is intended to elicit, namely the alternative we suggested earlier for 12, agreement with B via complaint about B's opponent.

That all of this is effective is shown by 15. It was suggested earlier that the alternative analysis of "for whom," under which it is seen as showing agreement with B, makes relevant as a next utterance an acknowledgement of agreement. B, in starting his utterance at 15 with an acknowledgement of agreement, then, displays his understanding of what A has been about as a show of agreement.

This point bears a bit of elaboration, for the form of the utterance at 15 is noteworthy. There is a range of forms through the use of which conversationalists can do the work of bringing off collaboratively that they are in agreement. Some are nearly pre-packaged, e.g., "I agree," "I know," "Right," and the like, which are assertions of agreement; others, unlistable because they are in particulars fitted to the matter being agreed on, show agreement by a variety of techniques, e.g., showing one knows what the other has in mind by saying it for him, as in completing his sentence or his argument. Both of these, concerned with claiming or showing agreement, should be distinguished from a quite different action, namely "acknowledging agreement." The issue of who agrees with whom can be a real one, with sequential consequences, and not as might be thought, one of vanity, in the face of the raw fact of agreement. That issue is: whose "position" is the point of departure, is the thing to be agreed with, and, therefore, who is in a position to be doing "agreeing": the one who does the "base statement" is not one who can do agreement with it (he can do re-assertion of it). Thus if X takes a position, Y may claim or assert agreement. But if X takes a position, and Y then states a position intended to show, rather than claim, agreement with X's position, then X should *acknowledge* agreement to show his appreciation that Y was *showing* agreement. If X should, in that position, agree with Y (rather than acknowledge agreement), it may not be clear to Y that X has understood that he (Y) was showing *his* agreement with X. That is: a first agreement may not take a second, it should get an agreement-acknowledgement. If a second agreement is produced, it may be seen as displaying that

---

[12] An observation for which I am indebted to Katherine Campbell.

the first agreement was not heard or not correctly analyzed.[13] A bit of data to illustrate some of this is taken from a later point in this same conversation:

B: ...... the only difference which is made between
    Mexico 'r United States or Canada or any other
    countries.

A: Mm/hmm   (11)

B: is that if the country has different interest.
    Because of their background, and their al-an'
    history / an'

A: *and* different statures of power. Quite // correct.

B: right

in which A shows agreement by adding a piece of B's argument, then asserts his intention, in doing so, of agreeing – "quite correct" – (relevant here because the stress on the "and" could be taken as modifying it), and B acknowledges the agreement.

Now some forms, e.g., "right," seem to be used both for agreeing and for acknowledgement of agreement. But the one that B uses at 15 is clearly not an agreement, but an understanding not only of A's position, but of A's action. For since shows of agreement (as compared to assertions or claims) are overtly addressed to the matter being agreed on and not to the fact of agreement, which is left to be analyzed by a co-participant, for *them* acknowledgements are specially relevant to show understanding.

Let me note at this point that one of the aims in explicating this sequence may now perhaps be claimed, namely, that the ambiguity I want to address is an empirical one, in that both parties deal with both possible analyses: A both gets his show of agreement understood and recognizes the "question" analysis that the utterance at 13 displays B to have made, so *he* deals with both; 13 displays B to have attended the question analysis of "for whom," and his acknowledgement of agreement at 15 shows him to have employed *that* analysis as well. We have here, then, not merely a theoretically imaginable ambiguity, but an empirically encountered one.

III

At the beginning of the preceding discussion of the sequence from 12–15, I offered initial accounts of two alternative analyses of "For whom," one as a question, requesting clarification of the teacher's position, the other as a show of agreement by A with B byproducing a possible piece of B's argument against the teacher. No basis for either analysis was offered, and it is now time to seek them. By that I mean that no basis for analysing "for whom" as a question has been established, no procedure whereby B could have come to hear it that way.

---

[13] An illuminating, and more empirically worked through, treatment of many of the issues (concerning agreement) may be found in Pomerantz (1975).

I clearly am not suggesting that he did not, or could not, hear it that way, having just finished trying to show that he did; only that *how* he could come to hear it that way has not been shown.

Let me start with the analysis of "for whom" as a question or a request for clarification. I shall need some resources developed on quite different material by Sacks.[14]

Sacks speaks of a story recipient's slot after story completion as a structural, or a structurally defined, "place" in conversation. One line of reasoning that provides for it is this: the basic turn-taking organization of conversation operates on an utterance to utterance basis, an over-simplified version of a transition rule being that any next possible utterance completion point is a point at which a possible next speaker may seek to effect transition. The first application of this rule, clearly, will come at the first possible completion point, which, for now only, let us treat as a first possible sentence completion point.[15] A sequential problem for prospective story tellers, insofar as stories require more than a sentence/utterance to tell, is how to get potential next speakers, who may use a first possible completion point to start talking, to not start talking. There is a variety of techniques for so doing, which I cannot describe here, all of which have the consequence of depriving the sentence/utterance of its transition-to-next-speaker relevance. Extended utterance completion, or speaker turn completion, will then have to be detected by hearers by finding story completion. One reason for story recipient slot upon story completion being a structural place is, then, that in it recipients must display appreciation of story completion. Another is that, not being afforded over the course of a story occasion for displaying their understanding of the story, there is an issue, upon story completion, of story recipients displaying their understanding of the story, and there is a range of ways of doing so. Showing appreciation of completion, and showing understanding of the story are, or can be, linked tasks, one way of showing one sees the completion being to display one's understanding. Since as long as the story is ongoing, other speakers properly hold off, story completion is central to the sequential organization of conversation, and story-recipient's slot after story completion is a specially marked place.

I have gone into all of this because the utterance at 12 "for whom" is, or can be seen by participants as, a story recipient's utterance upon possible story completion. Without going through the whole of the preceding conversation, in which with three exceptions, A does only what we call "continuers" (versions of "mmhmm") which is, among other things, a form for hearers showing they see an extended unit, like a story, is in progress and not yet completed, two features of 1–11 suggest that story completion can be found here: a) B announces it to be a summary ("it came down to this") and summaries or reviews are completion-relevant or closing-relevant (as also in conversational closure,[16] "I just called to

---

[14] cf. Sacks (1972), (1975).
[15] cf. Sacks, Schegloff and Jefferson, op.cit. for details.
[16] Schegloff and Sacks (1972).

find out ..."); and b) the teller has the characters in the story do a closing relevant action, in this case *in the story* summing their positions, that being a way of agreeing to disagree, and agreeing being a way arguments are brought to a close (and thus the use of "I agree" to mean no more than "let's end it," no one believing agreement has been reached). A way of ending stories, as Sacks has nicely shown holds even for children's stories,[17] is by having the characters do a terminal action in a behavior stream, e.g. go to sleep. If I am allowed to omit further elaboration of this claim, then story completion being findable in 1–11, A is talking at 12 in recipient's slot upon story completion, and his utterance is to be scrutinized for its display of appreciation of completion, and for its understanding of the story.

I want now to introduce a small modification in our understanding of this structural place in conversation. It is intended to take account of the fact that in conversation little if anything can be done assuredly unilaterally. Even for utterances, we speak of their "*possible* completion points" because, in part, the speaker may continue or another speaker may build something on to an otherwise seemingly completed utterance, so that its initiator turns out not to control fully what his utterance turns out to be. So also for larger units, like "topics," and so I propose for stories. Rather than speaking of story-completion, then, I shall speak of story-completion proposal. A teller of a story can at some point *propose* story completion, but he cannot by himself *guarantee* it. A story is complete when, its completion having been proposed by teller, it is accepted by recipient by recognition of completion and display of understanding.

But allowing completion and (or by) showing understanding is only one of the tacks a recipient can take upon completion proposal. Another thing he can do is disallow completion. He can do this in effect, but unintentionally, by being wrong when he tries to show understanding; i.e., by producing as his understanding an understanding of the story that is unacceptable to the teller. The story may then be kept open for correction. A recipient can do this intentionally also, that is, he can produce an intentional misunderstanding of the story: for example, B has just reported to A that "Sibbi's sister had a baby boy"; she continues

B: but uh she was long overdue
A: Mm
B: And she-she had gained about forty pounds anyway.
   They said she was tremendous. So   (12)
   I'm sure they're happy about that.
A: Yeah that she's tremendous hh.

But the most regularly used form by which a recipient can keep a story open, one designed in a sense to do that job, is a question about the story. A question about the story, in requiring an answer from teller about the story, may keep the story open. Thus, just as that recipient slot is specially inspected for the possible

---
[17] Sacks (1972b)

appreciation of completion and the understanding of the story it may contain, so it is inspected for the other relevant possibility it may contain, namely, a question about the story to keep the story open. That is a thing for teller to look for, since if it is there he will have to deal with it. And if an utterance in question form appears there, it should be heard, on this account, as a question. It should be heard that way not by virtue of the question form, but by virtue of the relevance of finding a question there if one can, that last condition being satisfiable by a question form. With that, I hope to have shown a basis for the first possible analysis of "for whom," i.e., hearing it as a question, requesting clarification. It is through and through provided by the sequential structure in which it is implicated, and the place it occupies in it. And I hope to have suggested one sort of power linguistic form may have, other that the "action-determining" power rejected in the beginning of this paper. We may call it "constraint-meeting power"; that is, given an independent sequential basis for finding an utterance to be a question "if one can" (the last being the constraint), that constraint can be met by the linguistic form of the utterance – its interrogative form.

Let me now try to provide a basis for the other analysis, according to which A is in the utterance at 12 showing agreement with B by disagreeing with B's announced opponent, or more specifically, by showing he can produce a piece of B's possible argument, and thereby that he understands and is sympathetic. Insofar as this initial gloss is a bit richer than the initial statement of the first alternative, less may be required in the explication. The major point needing development here is the basis for hearing "for whom" as proposedly B's position, or part of it. Certainly we don't want to rely on intuitions about what that position would be if we extrapolated from what is given in the conversation, in order to find "for whom" consistent with it. Let me propose instead that A relies (unsuccessfully at first, as it turns out) on a sequential structure that is operative *within the conversation being reported in the story,* and that is the alternation formula for two party conversation that is conventionally described as "ababab" but ought, for clarities sake here be referred to as BCBCBC, in which C is the teacher.

What I am suggesting is that A produces his utterance not only by reference to the position of his slot as after proposed story completion, but that in constructing an utterance he employs another positioning of that slot, fitted not merely to the fact that he is following *a* story, but fitted to the particular story type and the particular instance of it that his utterance is following. That is: he employs that this is an "opposition-type" story; that it is about a conversation; that it reports the conversation using the BCBC format; that the positions that are in opposition are mapped into that format (that is, that BCBC tracks not only the alternation of turns but also the alternation of positions), and finally that all of this is presented in the proposed story completion, with the BCBC formula turning out to have C's position be the one occupying the last turn. His utterance at 12 – "for whom" – is then, by an extension, produced in a slot *in that conversation* (i.e., the one being reported on) that the formula assigns to B, or if you like B's side, and there is a basis then for hearing it as a contribution to, and thereby an understanding of and agreement with, that side, i.e., with B. It is thus that it can come off as a proposed piece of B's argument, for B eventually to appreciate as "exactly what I mean." In support of this device, which requires for its accomplishment seeing that A is extending the story one slot as his way of showing his appreciation of its completion and his understanding (not to mention his siding with B to which we shall return), and thus that his utterance be seen in terms of the sequencing structure internal to the conversation the story reports, in support of this device A builds his utterance, as we noted before, so that it requires reference to the last utterance in *that* sequence for its understanding. It seeks to make his utterance analyzable as a possible next utterance in the conversation in which the utterance it is appended to occurred. But to no avail, it turns out, the first time around.

If we can appreciate that, on this analysis of "for whom," A is agreeing with B by "siding" with him, joining his side in an oppositional story in which sides are represented by alternating conversational slots, and we can appreciate the relevance, for recipients and tellers, of recipients choosing sides in oppositional stories in which the teller is one of the characters, then perhaps we can briefly re-examine "for whom" under the first analysis – the question analysis – to see how *it* might be understood in terms of A's siding.

Consider: B is presenting an oppositional story in which he is one of the protagonists. One thing A can do is side with one or the other, teller/protagonist or his opponent. Regularly recipients side with tellers, I suppose because that is in part how tellers choose recipients for stories. But recipients don't invariably side with tellers. Is there a way that "For whom" as a question might appear relevant to A's siding with B's opponent? To be sure, a request for clarification can be doing a show of non-understanding, and especially in that structural place; but it can also be examined, when siding is an issue as it may be here, for evidence of siding with an opponent.

Let me suggest that "For whom" can be heard in a way that makes it relevant to siding with "the teacher." That involves hearing "For whom" as a "pre-sequence" question. "Presequence" is a global term for utterances (typically questions) whose relevance is treated by participants as given not so much by what preceded but by what they are foreshadowing. That is, they are treated as specifically preplaced utterances. Dealing with them can then be sensitive to the sequences they are seen to foreshadow. Thus, for example, pre-invitations, such as "Are you doing anything," are heard for their prefactory character. And seeing them as pre-invitations, or pre-requests, can involve that their answers are selected not only, if at all, with an eye to their descriptive adequacy, but with an eye to what is to be done with the anticipatable utterance they preface. And, indeed, a next utterance can inquire for the specifics being prefaced. Thus "Are you doing anything" "Why?" or "What did you have in mind?"

Now the pre-sequence character of an utterance is not linguistically marked; it is a sequential feature. The utterance following A$_2$ in data excerpt
(3) above, following, that is, "I don't know just where the–uh–this address
is," which we earlier suggested is a request for directions, is "Well, what
part of town do *you* live," which is here treated as a pre-sequence to direction
giving; in other sequential contexts it could be a straightforward
question.

I am suggesting that, in the excerpt with which we are concerned, "For
whom" can be heard as a pre-sequence to agreement with the teacher and
disagreement with B, speculatively pro-constructing the putative sequence as A:
For whom, B: Well he says ... A: What's wrong with that. On that hearing, the
question complains not about the position to which it is appended, but about the
presentation the position has been given by another, the "not having done it
justice," and that is a complaint of one who has a possible interest in its being
done justice, one such interest being that it is the complainer's position. In the
present case, that would be, then, a disagreement, or a pre-sequence to disagreement, with B.

Now I want to note that this view of "For whom" places it differently
from the initial analysis as a matter of "strategy" if you will; at a minimum,
it locates it strategically. Nonetheless, it falls within the earlier analysis,
and is but one kind of extension of it, in that it keeps the story
open...

This matter can be approached in a different way, and one that may
elucidate the trouble with using a participants putative "role," e.g., one established at the beginning of the conversation, as of definitive import at any given
place in it, or as governing the production and analysis of utterances rather than
being controlled by them. While those encountering this form of analysis for the
first time regularly feel that the fact this datum occurred on a radio talk show is
of massive and pervasive relevance, the critical fact being the relevance of
"performer" role; or feeling the status of the caller as teenager vis-a-vis an adult
is crucial; or any other of a range of "roles" or identifications of the parties,
none of these are critical here. What seems to be critical to the conversational
phenomenon of telling a story in which the teller is a protagonist, is the
respective relevance of teller vs. protagonist. In the present data the analysis of
"for whom" as a request for clarification is linked to an identification of B as
protagonist in the story, i.e., the particular protagonist he is, vis-a-vis whom
A can align himself.

The "derived" action – showing agreement – is linked to an identification of
B as protagonist, which is how a derived action is possible here, for via B's status
as protagonist the teacher is relevantly available as the target for the "primary"
action of the utterance on that analysis. And the primary action as clarification-
request is linked to B's identification as story-teller, i.e., what he is doing in the
this-conversation.

Let me only note that A eventually allows B to deal with "For whom" and

"By what standard" under both analyses, as long as the "agreement" analysis is dealt with first.

IV

Let me conclude by refocusing on three themes that run through the preceding, in order of increasing generality.

First, *question:* whatever defines the class "questions" as a linguistic form will not do for "questions" as conversational objects, or interactional objects, or social actions. If by "question" we want to mean anything like a sequentially relevant or implicative object, so that in some way it would adumbrate the notion "answer," if, therefore, something like adjacency pair organization is involved, with special constraints on the second pair part of a sort not yet analytically explicated; if, finally, we intend "question" to be able to serve as a form of account of *conversationalists'* behavior, rather than idealized speakers and hearers, or "subjects," then it will not do, for a variety of reasons, to use features of linguistic form as sole, or even invariant though not exhaustive, indicators or embodiments of such objects. Sequential organization is critical. That much given, whether it is useful to discriminate such a class – "question" – as a special object of interest, rather than assimilating it to the class "adjacency pairs" seems to me less clear. But that matter cannot be pursued here.

Second, *ambiguity:* to whatever received accounts we have of sources of ambiguity of utterances, we should add the basis for ambiguity provided by the sequencing structures of conversation. The ambiguity discussed here, concerning the possible question status of an utterance, is certainly not the only sequentially based ambiguity; nor are the sequential organizations implicated in it, and cases like it, the only such ambiguity generating combination. When we get further along in explicating the various sequential organizations of conversation, and interaction, and importantly, their integration, we shall first get a sense of the range of this phenomenon. And then, perhaps, we will be in a position to see not only how surviving ambiguities of the sort here examined may be yielded by sequential organization, but how a range of potential ones are produced and solved before surfacing.

That last clause is produced by an analytic strategy that ought to be made explicit, and perhaps questioned. Most theoretically or heuristically conjurable ambiguities never actually arise. That could be so because of the operations of a so-called "disambiguator," as a component of the brain, as a service of context to syntax, etc. Or it could be that the theoretically depictable ambiguities are derived by procedures that are not relevant to naturally occurring interaction, and therefore in natural contexts the ambiguities are not there to disambiguate.

The problem of ambiguity can be seen as an "overhearer's problem." That is, an overhearer, getting a snatch of conversation, or even all of it without knowing the "what-is-being-talked-about" independently of the talk he is hearing about it, can hear ambiguities in the talk that are not there for the ratified participants (to use Goffman's term) in the conversation. Talk being designed by conversationalists for what the other does and does not know,[18] such design can be expected to avoid in advance much of the potential ambiguity for the co-participants. Hearers for whom it has not been designed will find ambiguities at points at which their knowledge is not isomorphic with that of the party for whom the talk was designed. Of course, an important part of what a co-participant knows is what has already been said in the conversation, and so one getting a snatch of it is almost guaranteed to be able to find an ambiguity.

It is expectable that the problems of ambiguity and indexicality should have had their origin and most pointed interest for logic and science, whose interest is in the evaluation of statements stripped from local context, an evaluation that would hold for any man, anywhere, anytime, and not turning on what anyone in particular knows. That almost defines the conditions in their most extreme form for the discovery of ambiguity empirically. Paradoxically, then, ambiguity as a topic of interest, and the discovery of ambiguities empirically in practice, is a natural consequence of the search for "rational" discourse, under one major sense of rational in this context, i.e., "universalistic." Nor is it, on this view, odd that ambiguity should be treasured by intellectual traditions that are, on the whole, counter-posed to rationalism, e.g., the so-called New Criticism.

A great deal of the ambiguity that has troubled philosophers, logicians, linguists, and some sociologists seems to me characterizable in terms of the overhearer's problem, though the disciplines have not relied on being overhearers in fact. A ready procedure is at hand for generating ambiguities of the appropriate form: one starts with a single sentence, sometimes putting into it a classical source of ambiguity (e.g., an indexical expression like a pronoun), sometimes not, and one imagines a range of settings or scenarios in each of which the sentence, or some component of it would have, or be said to have, a "different meaning" or "different sense." In the finding that the "same sentence" or "same component" can have "different meanings" across the imagined range of scenarios is the kernel of the problem of ambiguity. It is because actual participants in actual conversations do not encounter utterances as isolated sentences, and because they do not encounter them in a range of scenarios, but in actual detailed single scenarios embedded in fine grained context, that I began this discussion with the observation that most theoretically or heuristically depictable ambiguities do not ever arise.

Again, then, a great deal of the ambiguity with which our disciplines have concerned themselves seems to me to be the product of such a procedure. I do not mean to denigrate its status as a problem. I mean only to suggest that the study of such theoretical ambiguity needs to be distinguished from the sort of ambiguity that actual conversationalists actually, empirically encounter as

---

[18] cf. Schegloff (1972); Sacks, Schegloff and Jefferson (1974); Sacks and Schegloff (forthcoming)

ambiguities in the natural course of conversation. There are such empirical ambiguities, and I am proposing that they are a different sort of thing analytically, and should be considered separately.

When we look for the basis of such ambiguities, I think we must recognize a (major) source for them in the sequential organizations of conversation. And that will necessarily differentiate their investigation from that of the more traditional ambiguities, which are precipitated in the first place by depriving them of their sequential placement.

If, finally, these are different classes of ambiguities, with different bases, and different forms of investigation appropriate to them it is not clear to what, in natural interaction, findings about theoretical or heuristic ambiguities and their disambiguation apply. For they are findings about objects that may not, or may not much, appear in the world naturalistically observed nor ones that are models from which natural objects in the world to one degree or another depart. And if this argument turns on the consideration that the sentences are divorced from the contexts in which they might in the "real world" appear, then it goes not only to ambiguities, but to findings such as the claimed greater complexity, syntactically and psychologically, of negatives, passives, questions, etc. The point here is that taking sentences in isolation is not just a matter of taking such sentences that might appear *in* a context *out* of the context; but that the very composition, construction, assemblage of the sentences is predicated by their speakers on the place in which it is being produced, and it is through *that* that a sentence is context-bound, rather than possibly independent sentences being different intact objects in or out of context. The latter is what artificial languages, such as mathematics, are designed to achieve. To treat natural languages in that way is to treat them as *having* the very properties whose absence has motivated the search for artificial formal languages. But it is also to continue to disattend, and indeed to deprecate, the very features that make language, and in particular, its everyday interactional use, the powerful natural object that it is.

References

Baumann, Richard and Joel Sherzer (eds.) (1975) *Explorations in the Ethnography of Speaking* (Cambridge University Press)

Gumperz, John J. and Dell Hymes (eds.) (1972) *Directions in Socio-Linguistics* (New York: Holt, Rinehart, and Winston, Inc.)

Jefferson, Gail (1972) "Side Sequences," in Sudnow (1972)

– (1973) "A Case of Precision Timing in Ordinary Conversation: overlapped tag-positioned address terms in closing sequences," *Semiotica,* 9

Pomerantz, Anita (1975) "Second Assessments: a study of some features of agreements/disagreements," unpublished Ph.D. dissertation, School of Social Sciences, University of California, Irvine

Psathas, George (ed.) (forthcoming) *Papers in the Boston University Conference on Ethnomethodology* (Boston: Goodyear)

Quasthoff, Uta (ed.) (forthcoming) *Sprachstruktur-Sozialstruktur* (Berlin: Scriptor Verlag)

Sacks, Harvey (1972a) "On Some Puns with Some Intimations," in Shuy (1972)

–   (1972b) "On the Analyzability of Stories by Children," in Gumperz and Hymes (1972)

–   (1975) "An Analysis of the Course of a Joke's Telling in Conversation," in Baumann and Sherzer (1975)

–   and Emanuel A. Schegloff (forthcoming) "Two Preferences in the Organization of Reference to Persons in Conversation and Their Interaction," in Quasthoff (forthcoming) and in Psathas (forthcoming)

–   Emanuel A. Schegloff and Gail Jefferson (1974) "A Simplest Systematics for the Organization of Turn-Taking for Conversation," *Language,* 50, 4

Schegloff, Emanuel A. (1968) "Sequencing in Conversational Openings," *American Anthropologist,* 70

–   (1972) "Notes on a Conversational Practice: Formulating Place," in Sudnow (1972)

–   and Harvey Sacks (1973) "Opening Up Closings," *Semiotica,* 8

Shuy, Roger W. (ed.) (1972) *Twenty-Third Annual Round Table Meeting on Linguistics and Language Studies* (Washington: Georgetown University Press)

Sudnow, David N. (ed.) (1972) *Studies in Social Interaction* (New York: Free Press)

Field Analysis of Discourse

Robert Longacre and Stephen Levinsohn
Summer Institute of Linguistics

0   The title of this article is meant to suggest the analysis not of a well-known European language, but of a lesser-known or even little studied language under conditions of field investigation. We summarize here topics for research and study in the field analysis of discourse and suggest in the second section a charting technique for beginning the study of an actual text. The first author is responsible for the form of the first section. Although much of what he includes is from articles involving the second author (and others who have worked with the second author), he takes responsibility for the particular synthesis presented here. The second author has written the methodological section.

1   Topics for Investigation

1.1   Discourse Genre and Type. Different sorts of texts present different sorts of analytical problems. In selecting the beginning text for field analysis, one likes to find as strategic a place to begin as possible. If one sort of text bristles with problems while another is simpler, it is wiser to begin with the latter and gain background for approaching the former. In many parts of the world, it proves useful to use narrative discourse for beginning discourse analysis.

The classification of discourse genre here presented is an interpretation by Longacre of Keith Forster's revision (1977) of the former work of Longacre (1976. 197–206). The system has two primary parameters: ± *chronological linkage;* and ± *agent-orientation;* and two secondary parameters: ± *projected time;* and ± *tension.* The two primary parameters combine to give us four main discourse genre: *narrative* discourse which is + chronological linkage + agent orientation; *procedural* discourse which is + chronological linkage but – agent orientation; *behavioral* discourse (a broad category with many subtypes) is – chronological linkage but + agent orientation while *expository* discourse is

---

[1] The research for this article was performed under National Science Foundation Grant SOC74-04763 and National Endowment for the Humanities Grant RO-20280-75-5. A. A larger version of this paper is in use as a syllabus in sessions of the Summer Institute of Linguistics at Dallas, in linguistic courses at the University of Texas at Arlington, and in field workshops of the Colombia-Panama branch of the S. I. L.

– chronological linkage and – agent orientation. It is assumed that anywhere where minus chronological linkage is indicated, it is replaced by conceptual linkage in the discourse type in question, i.e. the assumption is made that every sort of discourse has some principle of cohesion whether it be chronological or conceptual-logical.

We now add the parameters three and four: In adding parameter 3, ± projected time, we distinguish within the narrative genre, ordinary *stories* which are – projected time from *prophecy* which is + projected time. In procedural discourse, the ordinary *how-to-do-it* text is + projected time (i.e., this is how one would do it whenever he might get around to doing it) but we have *descriptions of past customs* which are clearly procedural and are – projected time. In behavioral discourse, we are most likely to think first of the *hortatory* discourse which is clearly + projected time. We may also, however, have such discourse types as *eulogy* of someone else or apology for one's own behavior which are clearly projected time. In expository discourse, time is not relevant, so we could say that it is – projected time; but there exists a variety of expository discourse which involves explanations of a future stage of events. Such extrapolations are clearly + projected time.

The final parameter ± tension also applies to all the above discourse genre. Narrative discourse is purely *episodic* if it contains essentially no struggle or plot (for example Willa Cather's novel *Shadow on the Rock*). Such discourse is considered to be – tension. Most stories, however, involve some sort of struggle or plot and are clearly + tension. Similarly, in procedural discourse, there are some discourses which are more or less routine, while others involve struggle and alternatives and are therefore + tension. Both behavioral and expository discourse have varieties in which *argumentation* is assumed. These are also + tension. Discourses of these genre which do not have this characteristic are – tension.

A scheme such as the above is essentially a scheme of deep structure. Surface structure discourse genre often involve a skewing of the deep structure intent with a surface structure form (Longacre, 1976. 206–209). Drama, not mentioned above, is essentially a narrative whose surface structure form proceeds by means of dialogue.

1.2   Overall Discourse Structure

1.2.1   Beginning and End of a Discourse. It is not unusual to find formulaic beginnings and endings for discourses in many languages. A formulaic beginning may be termed *aperture*. A formulaic ending may be termed *finis*. If such a formulaic beginning is present, the discourse itself most likely gets going in a section found in the following slot, which can be termed *stage* for narrative discourse, and *introduction* for other types. *Closure,* which precedes finis, is a wrap-up of a discourse in a manner which is specific to the content of that discourse.

1.2.2   In the body of a discourse, we find *episodes* as slots in narrative, and *points* as slots in expository and behavioral discourses. For procedural discourse, we may assume that the main slots of procedural discourse are called *procedures*. In drama we have *acts*.

1.2.3   Characteristically, there is more to a discourse than we have indicated, however. If a discourse is plus tension, there will most likely be some kind of climax of development, some marked surface structure *peak*. In a narrative discourse, there may be a peak to mark the deep structure confrontation (climax) and a *peak'* to mark the deep structure denouement (i.e., a decisive event which loosens up the story and makes resolution possible). There are many ways of marking surface structure peak and peak'. (See below section 1.6). When a story has a peak, it is possible to organize the episodes of the story in reference to that peak. We can speak therefore, of pre-peak episodes, post-peak episodes, and even inter-peak episode (for stories which have bot a peak and a peak'.)

For discourses that are not narrative but still have a climax of development, the peak may mark *target procedure* in a procedural discourse, *climactic exhortation* in a behavioral discourse of the hortatory variety, and a most satisfactory or *culminating explanation* in expository discourse (cf. Longacre 1976, 228–231).

1.2.4   In discussing overall discourse structure, the fundamental task of the author of the discourse should not be lost sight of: to flesh out from the abstract of his discourse its full-bodied structure with all its necessary detail and background. From an abstract of a story, the author generates a whole story. You might say he starts out with a backbone, expands it to a skeleton, and then puts flesh and skin on it. The job of the analyst is to go at this in reverse, to look through the flesh and the skin to the skeletal structure beneath and to perceive the fundamental structure of the whole.

1.3   Discourse Constituents. In approaching the study of a text, one initially attempts to give it some sort of *outline*. This is partly intuitive (based on our sense of how a story or a piece of exposition should go) and partly reflects our growing grasp of the formal signals of the language in which the text is expressed. It should be emphasized, however, that the *discourse constituents* themselves are not equivalent to the points of such an outline. In clarifying our view of the units underlying discourse, we can posit (1) that a discourse consists of such functional slots as described above-for example, in the case of a narrative discourse, aperture, stage, pre-peak episodes, peak, post-peak episodes, closure and finis; and (2) that each of these functional slots is expounded by either a paragraph or by an *embedded discourse*. It is not assumed that embedded discourses have exactly the same structure as unembedded independent discourses- no more than a dependent clause has the structure of an independent clause. One can assume as many layers of embedded discourse as are necessary until one gets down to discourses composed only of paragraphs (which likewise prove to be recursive units).

1.4   Participants

A discourse, whether independent or embedded, has its cast of participants. One of the most useful divisions of the cast of participants of a.discourse is *major* versus *minor* participants. Furthermore, within the major participants there may be a *central character* who is especially singled out. Major participants are relevant to the entire discourse and can become thematic participants of a given paragraph. Discourse level roles assigned to the cast can, perhaps, best be considered to be three (following Levinsohn's current work): *initiator, undergoer,* and *prop.*[2]

At any given part of a discourse, it is sometimes important to know whether two participants are of *equal or unequal rank*. The ranking of participants is often according to an unstated hierarchy. Thus, in a Mixe dialect of Mexico (Shirley Lyons 1967.27) first person outranks second person, second person outranks third person, third person definite (indicated by a proper name) outranks third person indefinite (a man), which in turn outranks animals which in turn outranks inanimate.

Author *viewpoint* can also affect the treatment of discourse reference in a narrative. The author may choose to associate himself with one third person participant as opposed to other third person participants. This may figure in the overt structure of a text in terms of the way in which such participants are referred to pronominally and deictically (Inga, Levinsohn, in press- b), or may even require special morphological marking in the verb (Oksapmin, data from Lawrence, Longacre 1972.153). Author vantage point with a third person participant is not the same thing as *author-sympathy* or identification with such a participant emotionally. Thus, a villain and his deeds may be the vantage point of the author in telling a story (e.g. Catio folklore, Schöttelndreyer and Levinsohn, forthcoming) even though he does not sympathize with the deeds of the villain.

1.5   Strands of Cohesion

1.5.1   It appears that discourse is a cable of several interwoven strands. Thus for narrative discourse, we have to assume that there is an *event-line,* an *agent-line,* and maybe even a *repartee-line.*The event-line indicates successive

---

[2] Cf. Hale's system (1973. 1–27) of role (core) categories: actor, undergoer and a *tertium guid* variously termed referent, site, or scope. Van Dijk (1972. 143–147) in contrast here to both Levinsohn and Hale advocates a full-blown repertoire of case categories a la Fillmore for the analysis of discourse. A further possibility is a set of more traditional roles such as hero, villain, helper to hero, helper to villain, and the like.

events, successive times, or even successive places (trajectory), or a combination of these three (Hale, 1973). Material given in the story may be on the event-line (backbone) or off the eventline. The second author of this paper describes this as progression versus digression (Levinsohn, 1976). Background material, setting, and collateral material (Grimes, 1976) are all digressions from the backbone. On the other hand, not all events, even on the backbone, are of equal importance. A narrative may single out *important events* from more routine and predictable events. This is not merely a classification to be indulged in to humour our taxonomic propensities, but many languages have specific ways to indicate backbone from non-backbone and to mark important events versus more routine events on the backbone.

The agent-line, called the agent-action axis by the second author of this paper, tracks the major participants through the discourse. Minor participants are off this line in the same way that background material and unimportant events are off the main event-line.

If a story has extensive repartee, there is also a line of repartee development.

All the above applies to forms of narrative. Other types of discourse, especially behavioral and expository, have a conceptual or logical development. *Logical development* is primary in behavioral and expository discourses, although secondary logical developments occur all through narrative and procedural discourses as well.

A further cohesive strand in discourse has to do with the *focal intention* (what Hale calls focal content) of a discourse. Why is the discourse told in the first place? How was it elicited? What situation provoked its being given? Clues to the focal intent of a discourse may occur almost exclusively at its beginning and end, (what Hale terms "bundled focal content"), or may crop up here and there throughout the discourse (what Hale calls "scattered focal content"). When such clues occur scattered through the discourse, they provide in effect, a further cohesive strand (Bieri, Schulze, Hale, 1973, esp. p. 403).

1.5.2   Surface structure cohesive devices

(1) The role of *tense* and *aspect*. Significant chunks of the whole verb system of a language can be classified in terms of functions in discourse and paragraph. Thus, each discourse type has its favored tense/aspect for the mainline of its development and other tense/aspects for other functions. The occurrence of a given tense/aspect immediately tells us something about the classification of a text as to discourse type, provides cohesion throughout that text, and may tell us roughly what part of the discourse or paragraph we are looking at.

(2) *Particles* and *affixes*. This overlaps a bit with (1) above insofar as we are speaking of particles and affixes associated with verbs. Particles and affixes associated with nouns or (apparently) floating about somewhat freely in the clause or sentence, provide a very different sort of problem. They may mark the central character as opposed to other major participants, or major as opposed to minor participants, or even the second most important participant as oppos-

ed to the central character. In Cubeo there exists a particle whose occurrence with mainline events is such that if we jot down all the clauses marked by this Cubeo particle we have a viable abstract of the whole discourse. There exists another particle associated with clauses and parts of clauses so that if we compile a compilation of parts of the discourse with which this latter particle occurs, we get a good idea of the focal intent of the whole discourse (J.K. and Neva Salser, 1977). Particles and affixes can mark important events as well as important participants, role reversal, contrastive events or themes, frustration, and some other relations.

(3) Participant *Anaphora.* Participants can be identified by name, by a common noun, by pronoun, by an affix, or just by zero. Such variations in anaphora are never unmotivated. Most commonly, the domain of the participant anaphora chain is the paragraph. Such a chain, however, may continue across several paragraphs if there is nothing to disturb it.

(4) *Deictics.* Such words as "this" and "that" or "that one" or "a certain one" are used in some languages to help keep track of participants. They sometimes have highly specific functions according to central character versus other major participants, or major versus minor participants, or higher-ranking participant versus lower-ranking participant, or newly-introduced participant plus one already in the story.

(5) Lexical ties and *paraphrase.* Such lexical relations as synonymy, antonymy and items of the same semantic domain, are well-known. The serve many functions in giving cohesion to discourse. For example, the verbs which lie on the backbone of a discourse are not a haphazard ensemble. On the contrary, they characteristically come from adjoining semantic domains. Synonyms, negated antonyms, repetitions of predicates, the addition of further accompanying noun phrases, and vocabulary items related in a hierarchy from generic to specific, all make possible varieties of paraphrase. Paraphrase relations give very close ties between sentences in a discourse and characteristically indicate embedded paragraphs. A special kind of lexical tie might be called the *expectancy chain.* Thus, if I say, "He shot him and he …", the hearer is very likely to fill in the word "died". If I say, "He started out in the early morning and …", somebody is likely to supply, "arrived at so and so time". If I say, "He killed it, cooked it, and …", someone is likely to supply, "ate it". Finally, a further sort of lexical tie – often reinforced with specific particles, affixes, and verb modes – is the marking of *frustration,* that is, there is an expectancy chain or a collocation which does not come off. "He started for Paris, but didn't arrive". "She's fat, but not sloppy".

(6) Summary and preview are of considerable importance. Summary is a type of paraphrase which makes use of very generic predicates and substitutes. For example, "That's what they all did". A preview gives in one part of a discourse what is to follow later, or gives in a paragraph setting what is to characterize the course of the entire paragraph.

(7) *Conjunctions* and *introducers.* Some languages have a great wealth of

conjunctions. This is a typical situation in an Indo-European language. Other languages have a considerable dearth of conjunctions – from the one lone conjunction of Pidgin English to the typical handful of conjunctions found in a Philippine language. Conjunctions are usually classifiable as temporal versus logical conjunctions. Some conjunctions, however, are essentially locative as a "from there" in a travelogue (cf. Xenophon's *Anabasis*). As introducers of sentences, conjunctions serve to fit the sentence into paragraph context. They also serve to fit the paragraph into discourse context.

One function of conjunctions in some parts of the world is to mark whether the subject of the clause which follows the conjunction is the same or different from the subject of the clause which precedes. Thus in Paez *sa'* 'and' marks a same subject sequence and *atsa'* 'and' marks a different subject sequence. Dependent verbs may likewise indicate the same distinction via verb affixes. In Papua New Guinea such affixes mark same or different subject relative to whatever clause follows. In the northern part of South America such marking is relative to the independent clause to which the dependent clause is subordinated.

(8) Closely related to conjunctions and introducers is *backreference*. In this device, part or all of the preceding sentence is repeated in the onset of the next sentence. Thus, we may have such a sequence as: "John took off in his Piper Cub for Denver this morning. After taking off in the plane he discovered that he had a faulty engine." The back-reference need not be exact, but can be nominalized, employ a synonym, or vary in other ways.

It is important to scrutinize the function of back-reference. In some languages it is automatic, at least in the oral presentation of discourse, so that every successive sentence which moves the event-line forward in a narrative paragraph, will have such a back-reference. Typically, however, it gives way in some of the successive units to a conjunction such as "and then", or to zero. A delicate question then arises. When is back-reference used, when is a conjunction used to substitute for it, and when is it eliminated? Such variation is never unmotivated (Levinsohn, forthcoming; Gunn, forthcoming).

1.6   Marking of Peak (and Peak')

The high point(s) of a story can be marked by a variety of devices: (1) by rhetorical underlining, i.e., use of paraphrase and repetition; (2) by a concentration of participants (the crowded stage); (3) heightened vividness attained through tense shifts (e.g., from past to historical present), through person shifts (e.g., third person to first person inclusive of second person, or to second person), through transition from narrative to dialogue or to drama (dialogue without formulas of quotation), or through the use of onomatopoetic words; (4) by change of pace through variation in size of units (shorter sentences to longer sentences or vice versa), or through use of fewer conjunctions and other transition signals; and (5) by a change of vantage point or orientation-including role reversal. (cf. Longacre, 1976. 217–231).

1.7   Function of Dialogue in Discourse

First of all, the incidence of dialogue varies according to discourse genre. Thus, while dialogue is common in narrative and serves in some cases to advance the event-line of the narrative, it is quite uncommon in procedural discourse. Whatever the genre there is no doubt that dialogue is a feature which livens up a discourse. Thus, as already stated, often the peak of a discourse contains dialogue while previous sections do not contain dialogue, or the peak may show movement from dialogue to drama. Often all or part of a dialogue lies off the line. In such cases we are simply told what people said while the important events took place.

A further consideration in dialogue is which participant dominates a given exchange. Carol Koontz suggests for Teribe (forthcoming) that participant dominance can be seen in a dialogue by the way that the speaker and hearer are referred to in the formulas of quotation. Levinsohn reports something very similar for Inga.

2   Methodology

This section envisages the analysis of a discourse in four stages: the initial presentation of the discourse in some workable form (2.1); the preparation of displays to facilitate the specific examination of back reference and introducers (2.2); and means of achieving a breakdown of the discourse into its constituents (2.3). It does not follow from this arrangement either that the analysis of a specific discourse should follow the order in which the stages are presented, or that all the stages should be performed. Rather it suggests guidelines.

2.1   The presentation of a discourse in a workable form

Linguistic analysis assumes as a basic premise that at all levels there are patterns which explain the occurrence of any feature. The purpose of displaying a discourse in any way is to make it easier for these patterns to be discerned.

2.1.1   Preparing the discourse to be displayed

We assume that the discourse to be displayed is well-formed, in the sense that it is considered by a native speaker to be grammatically correct and acceptable.[3] It is assumed, therefore, that if recorded, the discourse has been transcribed correctly, and checked by a native speaker. If written, it has been carefully read (preferably both by and to a native speaker). Changes made by the transcriber or proofreader should be noted, since corrections are not always 'correct'!

[3] Thomas Branks (1976) discusses a further aspect of well-formedness, one which selects the most appropriate and aesthetically pleasing of a number of renditions of the same text – all of which are assumed, however, to be grammatically correct and acceptable.

The analyst should also control the facts of the discourse. In other words, in a narrative, he should know who did what to whom, and, as far as possible, what relation one action has to the other actions in its immediate context. To achieve this control, he may have to ask a series of questions about each sentence, such as, "Who hit him?"; "Whom did he hit?"; "When did he hit him?"; "Where did he hit him?";"Why did he hit him?". In addition, the meaning of the individual words and morphemes should be pinned down as exactly as possible. The less variables that have to be taken into account in an analysis, the more quickly the meaning of each remaining variable can be determined.

The initial display separates the discourse into sentences, each sentence into independent clauses, dependent clauses and introducers, and each clause into its phrasal constituents. It is assumed that, whether by grammatical or by phonological criteria,[4] or by both, the analyst has arrived at least at a rough division into the sentences constituting the discourse.

2.1.2   The actual display of the discourse

One simple but practical display is obtained by dividing a long sheet into three basic parts: (i) introducers and pre-nuclear dependent (or nonfinal) clauses; (ii) nuclear/independent (or final) clauses; (iii) postnuclear dependent (or clarification) clauses. The relative size of these parts reflects the relative preference for and complexity of the different clauses in the language. If the nuclear/independent clause is the most complex and carries the most information, then it is given the most space; if, however, sentences characteristically consist of a series of prenuclear dependent (non-final) clauses, and the independent or final clause is relatively simple, then the display of the latter is made more compact. If post-nuclear dependent clauses are virtually non-existent in the language, then that column may be eliminated and the few post-nuclear dependent clauses that are found may be displayed in the independent clause column.

One or more of the above columns is then divided into sub-columns, to enable the basic elements of the clause to be arranged systematically. One sub-column is reserved for the predicate verb phrase, another for the subject of the sentence. The order of sub-columns reflects the most common order of elements in the clause. If, for example, the most common order in a transitive clause is S (subject), O (object), P (predicate), then the first sub-column is reserved for subjects, the third for predicates, and the second for objects and other elements that immediately precede the predicate.

Table 1 displays nine sentences of an Inga (Quechuan) text,[5] whose free translation follows here:

[1]So the mother-in-law went ahead, weeping, to where she had buried the

---

[4] It is the experience of the second author that too few analysts take features of intonation into account in the analysis of oral discourses into sentences.

[5] See Levinsohn, in press-a, for a statement of the phonology and lower-level grammar of Inga. Inga forms are here transcribed in a practical orthography which is based on that of Spanish.

	Intro-ducers	Dependent Clauses	S	Independent Clauses (O)		P	Post-verbal Dependent Clauses
1 $L_0 \to L_1$	Chihora that-time		chi suégraca 1 that mother-in-law		2	ñugpagrinsi went-ahead-of	huacaspa, weeping chilacuán piti A wild-papaya piece (O) pambascamá. (L_1) to-where-had-buried
2 L_1		Chayagríspaca, going-and-arriving	1	Caypimi here	2	ninsi: said	
3 $L_1 \to L_2$		Chasa níspaca, thus saying	3	carumalla to-just-far (L_2)		pambarayá is-buried sipirigrís going-and-strangling-self miticú fled	
4 L_1	Chihora that-time		chi taytaca 2 that father	chi pozótasi that grave		utcú dug	
5 L_1		Alpa sitaspa, earth removing	2	chilacuán wild-papaya pitíllasi A just-piece		tarí found	

6 L₁	Caynórami now	2	Ajay-si oh-no	2	ní. said / yachahuanga. it-will-be- known- to-me
7 L₁→	Chasa níspaca, thus saying	2	rastrótasi footprint	2	catichí followed
8 →L₂	Riscata to-one- who- had- gone (O) 1 / catichíspaca, following	2	fronted 1	2	tarigrinsi. went-and- found
9 L₂	sipiríscasi 1 one-who- had-strangled- self / Timpo already	3			huarcurayá was-suspended

Table I – Initial display of discourse

piece of wild papaya. [2]On arriving, she said, "Here is where he is buried."
[3]Having said that, she fled a little way off and hanged herself.

[4]The father dug into the grave, [5]and, on removing the earth, found just a piece of wild papaya. [6]"Oh, no!" he said. "I'm going to find out what really happened."

[7]So saying, he followed her footprints. [8]and found her; [9]she was hanging, having strangled herself.'

In Table 1, the initial wide column is used for sentence introducers, pre-nuclear dependent clauses and any constituents of the independent clause that precede the subject. The central wide column is divided into three sub-columns for the subject, other pre-predicate constituents, and the predicate respectively. The final wide column is used for post-nuclear dependent clauses, clarifiers, and any constituents of the independent clause that follow the predicate.

The text is displayed in the linear order in which it was spoken or written. If, therefore, an element occurs, not in its most common position in the clause or sentence, but in some other position, its linear position is preserved in the display. In sentence 8, for instance, the object of the independent clause is "fronted" to the beginning of the sentence, so it is placed there in the display. However, it is valuable to record the fronting in the sub-column in which it would most commonly occur (q.v.). Such a presentation enables the analyst to see variations of the order of constituents at a glance, and determine their significance.

The display proceeds from left to right, and from top to bottom. If it is not possible to place an element in its correct column or subcolumn, by moving from left to right, then one moves down the display. For instance, in sentence 1, two post-nuclear dependent clauses occur, so the second one is presented in a new line in the post-nuclear column. Another new line is started, to present sentence 2. Sentence divisions are indicated by an unbroken line across the table.

One important principle in discourse analysis is to distinguish material within a citation from the material in which it is embedded. This is achieved by employing broken underlining as in sentences 2 and 6.

2.1.3   Tracking

The initial display readily lends itself to the tracking of the occurrence of participants and items (2.1.3.1), and of the locations and times of the actions of the discourse (2.1.3.2).

2.1.3.1   Participants and items are tracked throughout the discourse, from their initial introduction, through their continued presence in the story, temporary removals and reappearances, to their final removal from the story. Each participant or item is given a reference number or letter; animate participants are numbered 1, 2, 3, etc., in order of appearance, and items are lettered A, B, C, etc. In Table 1, the mother-in-law is participant 1, the father participant 2, the child participant 3, and the piece of wild papaya item A.

Each time the participant or item has a part in the action of a clause, he is accounted for in the display. For example, in sentence 1, the father is the object of the independent clause (the mother-in-law went ahead of him), so, since no overt reference is made to him in the clause, his presence is accounted for by a long dash and by placing his reference number in the object column (2).

Having indicated the presence of the participants and items in each clause, each occurrence, whether overtly stated or not, is linked together. So, in Table 1, every time the mother-in-law has a part in the action of a clause, her presence is indicated, and these indications are linked by a straight line, if they occur in successive clauses; by a curved line, if not.[6] A circled indication of a participant on an item indicates its initial or final occurrence in the discourse (e.g., in sentence 5, the piece of papaya has a part to play in the story for the last time).

The above tracking of participants forms the basis for analyzing the use of anaphora, deictic and substitutes (1.5.2[3], [4]). The analyst may readily examine the means employed to introduce major and minor participants, significant and incidental items, and the means of further reference to them as they continue in the same role, change role, interact with other participants, are temporally removed or reintroduced to the story, and are removed from the story for the last time.

2.1.3.2.   The far left of Table 1 has been utilized to record continuity or changes in the location and time of the actions of the discourse. These play a significant part in establishing paragraph boundaries (2.3; cf. also 1.5.2 [6]).

Successive locations are given reference numbers L_0 (the "base of operations"), L_1, L_2, etc., and arrows are used to represent a change of location. In sentence 1, '$L_0 \rightarrow L_1$' indicates a change of location from location L_0 (where the mother-in-law and the father had been talking) to Location L_1 (the grave). In sentence 2, 'L_1' indicates that the location of the action was the grave. In sentence 7, '$L_1 \rightarrow$' indicates that the participant left the area of the grave, but that his destination was not specified. In sentence 8, '$\rightarrow L_2$' indicates that the journey was already under way, and that the destination (where the mother-in-law hung herself) was reached.

Short vertical arrows across the unbroken lines separating sentences indicate that the actions of the following sentence follow on naturally, in a chronological sense, from the actions of the previous sentence. Thus, the actions of sentences 1 and 2 are considered to be ordered naturally in a chronological sense. The presence of a number, at the head of an arrow, indicates the sentence whose actions the actions of the new sentence naturally follow. For examples, the actions of sentence 4 follow not from that of 3, but of 2; the father dug in response to the mother-in-law's words, not her hanging herself. Cf. also sentence 9.

Discontinuities in locations or in the chronology of the actions of successive

---

[6] The analyst must decide whether the linkage line should be traced through all the dependent clauses, as well as the independent ones; in Inga, tracing the linkage line through dependent clauses would only obscure the pattern of participant reference.

sentences commonly correspond with special features of the structure of the discourse. Between sentences 3 and 4, for instance, both a locational and chronological discontinuity occur (the mother-in-law arrives at L_2, while the father is still at L_1; the activity of the father is not linked chronologically with the activity of the mother-in-law). This corresponds with a paragraph break in Inga, as other features confirm. Between sentences 8 and 9, the discontinuity is only chronological; sentence 9 gives the content of what the father found (sentence 8).

Successive temporal horizons, where relevant to a discourse, can likewise be given reference numbers beginning with T_0 (time assumed at onset of discourse) and proceeding through T_1, T_2, etc.

2.2   Conjunctions, introducers, and back reference

The importance of these has been discussed in 1.5.2. (7), (8); this section considers some methodological steps that may be taken in one's analysis of the significance of each. The deep structure relationships represented by each of the above forms of linkage are considered in 2.3.2; we concentrate here on the surface structure forms employed

2.2.1   Displaying the forms of linkage employed

The display of Table 1 spreads most discourses out over too many pages to facilitate the examination of the forms of linkage employed. Table II takes the three wide columns: introducers and pre-nuclear dependent (or non-final) clauses; nuclear/independent (or final) clauses; and post-nuclear dependent (or clarification) clauses, and represents their contents by a box in which the forms relevant to the type of linkage being studied are inserted. To distinguish dependent verbs from introducers, the latter are placed in the dependent verb column, but a box is not drawn around them. Such a display may be used to consider in turn different forms of cohesion. For example, parallelism in structure or the repetition of the same nouns or verbs may be recorded in such a display (e.g. the use of forms of the verb *siriri* 'strangle oneself' in sentences 3 and 9). (See also 1.5.2 [5].) The display of Table II, however, concentrates specifically on the introducers (e.g. *Chihora* 'that time' [sentences 1 and 4]), and on forms of back reference using pre-verbal dependent clauses (sentences 2, 3, 5, 7, and 8). The specific morphemes used to indicate, in the surface structure, the relationship between the sentences linked are also recorded, cf. 2.3.2.

2.2.2   Tracking.

Having displayed the forms of linkage found in the discourse in a way comparable to that of Table II, one must indicate the point of reference of each link, and the type of linkage employed. The link is joined to the point of reference by means of an arrow. So, for instance, the dependent form 'arrive' (sentence 2) is joined by an arrow to its point of reference 'went-ahead' (sentence 1); 'arrive' refers to the completion of the action of going ahead.

The form of the arrow used reflects a classification of the type of linkage employed. The form of an introducer (e.g. *Chihora*) automatically makes it distinct from the dependent verb forms employed in back-reference. The latter however, are usefully classified into at least three groups: those that refer back to the immediately preceding sentence by means of repetition of the independent verb in a dependent form (marked by an unbroken arrow in Table II); those that refer back to a sentence which does not immediately precede (i.e. those that "flash back") (not represented in Table II), and those that refer back to the immediately preceding sentence, by means of a dependent verb which is related to the independent verb (marked by a broken arrow in Table II). The relation between the two actions may be construed as one of expectancy ("go" expects "arrive" as the next action), or, as one of reference to distinct aspects of a single action: going and arriving are parts of one movement in Inga (sentences 1 and 2); digging and removing earth likewise refer to the same action (sentences 4 and 5).

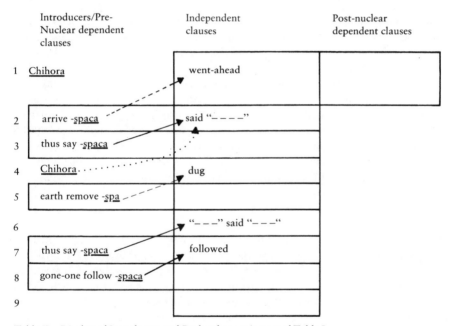

Table II – Display of Introducers and Back reference in text of Table I

Key:

Back reference by means of repetition of independent
        verb in dependent form.

– – – – – → Back reference by means of use of dependent verb
        related to independent form.

· · · · · · · · ·› Point of reference of introducer.

The use of one form of linkage over another often corresponds with divisions or other features of the paragraph or discourse. As paragraph breaks are proposed, for instance, the correlation of the break with one or another form of linkage should be examined. For example, in Inga, the use of a dependent clause referring to a different aspect of the action of the previous sentence corresponds with a (paragraph) break representing a change of scene (sentence 2) or tempo (sentence 5). Back-reference involving repetition of the verb of the immediately preceding sentence is used to introduce climactic actions in a paragraph, e.g. the final response in a set of actions (sentence 3), the carrying out of a decision (sentence 7), or the achievement of a goal (sentence 8). (See Levinsohn, forthcoming-a).

2.3   The breakdown of the discourse into its constituents

The meaning and distribution of many elements in a discourse do not become clear until the structure of the discourse, in terms of the paragraphs that comprise it, the embedded paragraphs that comprise them, etc., is determined, and the relationship between each of the constituents is established. When the complete jig-saw has been assembled, many confirmations of the divisions proposed are found (e.g., the distribution of the different forms of back-reference – cf. 2.2.2; and the use of one form of participant reference over another). However, to arrive at the correct division into constituents, the analyst must first make intuitive breaks and groupings, then seek features that confirm or deny their correctness. This section considers one means of making an initial intuitive display of the breaks and groupings (2.3.1), and of arriving at the relationships between them (2.3.2). The types of features that may be taken into account, to establish these divisions on a less subjective basis, are discussed in 2.3.3.

2.3.1   Displaying the constituents of a discourse

The steps in arriving at an intuitive division of a discourse into its constituents are threefold: (i) group together those sentences that seem to naturally belong together; (ii) divide the discourse at those points at which it seems to naturally separate; (iii) take the groupings or divisions so far established and consider them as established, as a basis for further grouping or division.

Two principles, which can be applied from the tables already made, help in these divisions: (i) in discourses (except possibly travelogues), a change of location or temporal discontinuity usually corresponds with a paragraph break. (ii) The absence of a link element usually signifies one of two opposite possibilities: either two elements are associated very closely together (cf. 1.5.2 [5]), or else a major (paragraph) break in the discourse occurs. The difference between the two should be obvious.

Table III below displays a possible first step in an intuitive division of the Inga text of Table I. The sentence numbers are listed vertically. Horizontal lines are drawn to represent the initial divisions (based on principle [i] above). Boxes are drawn to enclose those sentences that seem to be associated together most closely (confirmed by principle [ii] above).

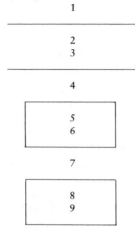

Table III

	1	
End of action 1	2	Temporal succession
	3	from 2
Temporal succession from/result of 2	4	
End of action 4	5	
	6	Response to 5
Temporal succession from 5–6	7	
Temporal succession from 7	8	
	9	Content of 8

Table IV

Each of these divisions is then considered in turn, treating the groupings as single units. For example, considering sentences 4–9 as four units (4; 5–6; 7; 8–9), is there any point at which they naturally separate?; are any of them especially closely associated together? (See Table IV (2.3.2), for a full display of the divisions and groupings.)

2.3.2 The relationships between the constituents

Relationships between constituents will eventually be expressed more or less formally, based on the catalogues prepared by Longacre (1976. 99–164), Beekman (Beekman and Callow 1974. 267–312), Grimes (1976, Chap. 14) et. al. They will be tied in also with the description of the structure of paragraph types. However, an initial informal statement of the relationship between constituents is useful, in arriving at initial conclusions concerning the functions of each of the forms of linkage, etc. One means of presenting such relationships is displayed in Table IV.

The relationship between the previous larger constituent and the beginning of the following corresponding constituent is given in the left of Table IV. The relationships between more embedded constituents are given to the right of the table. In charting a whole discourse in this way, several tables are necessary – some for displaying the structure and relationships of the larger constituents of the discourse; others for displaying the structure and relationships of the more embedded paragraphs.

2.3.3 Following the establishment of intuitive divisions of the discourse into constituents, and an informal expression of the relationships between them, a comparison of these divisions and relationships is made. This section outlines some of the possible comparisons.

One of the first comparisons to be made is with the display of introducers and back reference (Table II). The function of the different forms of linkage in Inga has already been sketched out (2.2.2). Assuming that one's intuitive divisions are reasonably accurate, a general correlation of certain forms of linkage with the divisions proposed will emerge. Once a hypothesis has been formed, apparent exceptions to it are examined, resulting either in the modification or rejection of the hypothesis, or in the modification of the initial division of the discourse into constituents.

A second comparison can be made between Tables II and IV, focussing on the relationships between the constituents, and the surface markers found on the linkage elements. For example, the form *-spa(ca)* would immediately be associated with the idea of temporal succession (in fact, *-spa* is a succession marker, indicating that the subject of the action of the dependent verb and of the following independent verb is the same).

A comparison of the constituents displayed in Table IV with various features displayed in Table I can also be made. Foremost among these might be the introduction and forms of reference to participants. Does the initial introduction of a major participant occur at the beginning of a new paragraph? Is there any correlation between certain forms of overt reference to a participant and the beginning of a paragraph? (For example, the use of the demonstrative *chi* 'that' in Inga, to modify references to participants, partially corresponds with a new paragraph (sentence 4; cf. Levinsohn, forthcoming-a). Other features to be examined include shifts in the tense or aspect of the independent verbs (cf. 1.5.2 [1]), and the use of unidentified particles (cf. 1.5.2 [2]). As hypotheses concerning each feature are formed and tested, the initial constituent analysis is modified as necessary, until all the pieces of the jigsaw fit together naturally.

In conclusion, the basic principles of the above methodology can be seen to be (i) to display the material in a systematic and revealing way; (ii) to have a check-list of features to consider with respect to the display. Some areas of the check-list are sketched out in 1. The successful analyst creates his own displays, according to his areas of interest, and the particular problems encountered. It is hoped that the above presentation contributes enough ideas on how and what to display, that the analyst can see how to create the displays he needs, to analyze the problems which he faces.

Bibliography

Beekman, John and John Callow. 1974. *Translating the Word of God,* Grand Rapids: Zondervan.

Bieri, Dora, Marlene Schulzer, and Austin Hale. 1973. "An Approach to Sunwar Discourse" in Hale: *Clause, Sentence, and Discourse Patterns in Selected Languages of Nepal* 401–462, Norman: SIL Publications 40:I.

Branks, Thomas. 1976. "An Approach to the Discovery of Spoken Style", *Notes on Translation* #59 (March, 1976), Huntington Beach, Calif.; Summer Institute of Linguistics.

Forster, Keith. 1977. "Narrative Folklore Discourse in Border Cuna". Longacre and Woods 2.1–23.

Gerdel, Florence E. and Marianna Slocum. 1976. "Paez Paragraph and Sentence Structure." Longacre and Woods 1.259–443.

Grimes, Joseph. 1976. "*The Thread of Discourse*", The Hague: Mouton.

Gunn, Robert D. 1976. "Some Aspects of Linking in Bocata Narrative Discourse". *Lingua* 48.131–150.

Hale, Austin. 1973. "Toward the Systematization of display grammar" in Hale: *Clause, Sentence and Discourse Patterns in Selected Languages of Nepal* 1–27, Norman: SIL Publications 40:I.

Howard, Linda. 1977. "Camsá: Certain Features of Verb inflection as Related to Paragraph Types". Longacre and Woods 2.273–299.

Kondo, Victor. 1977. "Participant Reference in Guahibo Narrative Discourse". Longacre and Woods 3.25–44.

Koontz, Carol. 1977. "Features of Dialogue within Narrative Discourse in Teribe". Longacre and Woods 3.111–132.

Levinsohn, Stephen H. 1976. "Progression and Digression in Inga (Quechuan) Discourse". *Forum Linguisticum* 1.122–147.

Levinsohn, Stephen H. in press-a. *The Inga (Quechuan) Language,* Janua Linguarum (Series practica) 188, The Hague: Mouton.

Levinsohn, Stephen H. in press-b. "Participant Reference in Inga Narrative Discourse", *Anaphora in Discourse,* ed. by John Hinds. Dordrecht: D. Reidel Publishing Co.

Longacre, Robert E. 1972. *Hierarchy and Universality of Discourse Constituents in New Guinea Languages: Discussion,* Washington: Georgetown University Press.

Longacre, Robert E. 1976. *An Anatomy of Speech Notions,* Lisse: Peter de Ridder Publishing Co.

Longacre, Robert E. and Frances Woods, ed. 1976–77. *Discourse Grammar: Studies in Indigenous Languages of Colombia, Panama, and Ecuador, Part 1* (1976), *Parts 2* and *3* (1977). Summer Institute of Linguistics Publications 52. Dallas: SIL.

Lyon, Shirley. 1967. "Tlahuitoltepec Mixe Clause Structure", IJAL 33.25–33.

Mansen, Richard and Karls. 1976. "The Structure of Sentence and Paragraph in Guajiro Narrative Discourse". Longacre and Woods 1.147–258.

Salser, J.K. and Neva. 1977. "Some Features of Cubeo Discourse and Sentence Structure". Longacre and Woods 2.253–272.

Schöttelndreyer, A. Mareike and Stephen H. Levinsohn. Forthcoming. "Catio Folklore as a Play in Acts and Scenes".

van Dijk, Teun A. 1972. *Some Aspects of Text Grammar,* The Hague: Mouton.

Waltz, Nathan E. 1976. "Discourse Functions of Guanano Sentence and Paragraph". Longacre and Woods 1.21–145.

Narrative Studies in Oral Texts

Joseph E. Grimes
Cornell University and
Summer Institute of Linguistics

Studies of narrative patterns in oral texts have been made in over a hundred languages and in at least twenty-five countries.[1] Taken together, these studies put a strain on general linguistic theory that seems likely to force us soon to broaden the theory, though not necessarily to change its essential character.

Three themes recur in this body of work on narrative, themes so persistent in overview that I take them to reflect three partially independent subsystems of language. I call the three content, cohesion, and staging (Grimes, 1975 b). They subsume phenomena not only in narrative discourse but in hortatory, expository, and expressive discourse as well.

The first, content, refers to what we normally think of as semantics. The second, cohesion, has to do with redundancies in text: how the things one is saying now relate back to all that has gone before. The third, staging or topic or thematic structure, deals with the way the speaker controls the perspective from which he presents everything he says.

Content

One part of content that has been reviewed fairly thoroughly is the realm of *lexical* relationships. These involve a small, possibly universal set of roles or cases of the kind associated with Charles Fillmore's name (1968), or equivalent relationships established by subcategorization (Winograd, Mel'chuk). Much of what can be said about meaning revolves around these relationships.

Lexical relationships are an important part of content, but they do not show up in the analysis of narratives in as fundamental a way as *rhetorical* relationships like result or attribution. These organize discourses by relating lexical complexes to each other, and recursively by relating rhetorical complexes to each other. The constraints on their arguments, unlike the constraints on the arguments of lexical relationships, do not involve role categories. The work of

[1] I wish to thank the National Science Foundation of the United States government, which through its grant GS-3180 made possible much of my own work on discourse, as well as the field seminars in which many of the empirical studies I refer to were undertaken.

Beekman, Callow, and Callow on Biblical texts (1974) is an example of high level rhetorical analysis, which again is not strictly limited to narrative.

In thinking about these lexical and rhetorical relationships, it is significant that scholars from approaches as diverse as those of Quillian, Schank, or Simmons in artificial intelligence, the stratificational grammarians in ordinary linguistics, and Mel'chuk and Zholkovsky in lexicography have settled on networks that are not trees as a representation of content. The tree, though familiar to linguists and a perfectly adequate representation of much of what we want to say about grammar, may simple be too restricted for some kinds of study including the study of narrative.

One consequence of looking at content structure separately from cohesion and staging is that we find fairly regular ways in which different kinds of content in discourse map to different surface grammatical patterns, each in its own way. Robert C. Thurman has developed a chart format from a display originally proposed by H. A. Gleason, Jr., for separating out different kinds of information. Applied to narrative, the Thurman chart is a useful analytical tool because it highlights the distinction between event information on the one hand and the identification of participants, setting, explanation, evaluation, and collateral information on the other. The events in a narrative constitute its backbone, from which other kinds of information depend. Other kinds of information are the backbone of other kinds of discourse; we find especially that explanatory information is at the core of logical-sounding discourses.

Distinct grammatical forms go with different kinds of information. For example, in Xavante of Brazil Ruth McLeod finds that the aspect system for events operates quite differently from the aspect system for explanations, even though the two systems share some of the same affixes (1974).

Situational factors permeate content. 'I', 'you', 'here', and 'now' are given in a typical act of speaking. Because they are given, they can be used as a frame of reference against which all other frames of reference, including embedded acts of speaking, are calibrated.

The first situational factor to consider is time – not the time of stopwatch or calendar, but linguistic time. Litteral has called attention to how time is handled topologically rather than metrically by language (1972). Linguistic time is concerned with relations like 'before' and 'after' and with bounded or unbounded blocks of time, and only incidentally with measures of time. Often the sequence in which events happen and the sequence in which they are told are deliberately put out of kilter with each other. In languages that permit this, special linguistic features typified by the interplay between simple past and perfect in English are used to keep the hearer oriented to the time line.

A second area where situational factors influence content is in the identification of participants in discourse. Kenneth L. Pike and Ivan Lowe have shown how person categories always relate systematically to the ones that are implicit in the situation of speaking itself. This holds even in complex situations, such as when direct quotations are embedded. If A says to B, *You said to me, "I'll see you at ten"*, the word *you* refers to B the first time it is used and to A the second time. This reassignment, however, is completely consistent with Lowe's Theorem of pronominal reference.

Space is also a situational factor, beginning with the place where the speaking is being done and relating other places to it. The situational layout influences lexical choices, for example, in motion and position expressions. The same action may be called *go* or *come* depending on where it happens in relation to the one who carries the first person label at the moment. Elaborate schemes of spatial reference, such as the one used in Oksapmin of Papua New Guinea that establishes a primary location and relates secondary locations to it by means of motion verbs (H. Lawrence, 1972), have also been described in Maxakali of Brazil and Huichol of Mexico (Popovich, 1967; Grimes, 1966).

Cohesion

In a sense, content gives us the bare bones of what we are saying, while cohesion, the second major system, tells us how we relate what we are saying to the hearer. The speaker has to decide as he goes along how the things he is saying relate to what he thinks his hearer already knows. As Halliday has shown (1967), the speaker decides what quantity of information he thinks the hearer can assimilate, and within the expression of that quantity, what part of it is likely to be the least predictable to the hearer. His judgment of redundancy may go back to situational factors, as in certain uses of pronouns. It may also go back to information already given or implied by the preceding part of the same text.

The speaker's judgments about redundancy influence his intonation in English. In Bacairi of Brazil, however, Wheatley cites cases where similar decisions influence word order instead; and in the highlands of Papua New Guinea, these same judgments are expressed in the medial and final inflections of the verb (M. Lawrence, 1972).

Anaphoric or backward pointing reference is based on the same kind of judgment by the speaker: he assumes that the hearer already knows some of what he is talking about. Not only do we base pronominalization on situational and textual reference; we also use inclusive vocabulary items like *animal* to refer back to what was originally named more specifically as *horse*. From the point of view of discourse studies the significant question is not 'how do we pronominalize?' but rather 'under what circumstances do we not pronominalize?'

A special kind of cohesion system is discussed by Thurman and others. It is found in the *linkage* patterns of many languages. In linkage a portion of text is repeated to give a starting point for what follows. The extreme case of linkage encountered so far is that of Kayapó of Brazil (Stout and Thomson, 1971). In Kayapó one repeats an entire paragraph nearly verbatim as a lead into a paragraph that describes a new course of events. In most other languages a single clause is repeated or paraphrased as a link, or a conventional consequence (like 'leave'/'arrive') is given.

Cataphoric systems represent a different kind of cohesion, one that alerts the hearer to something that is yet to come. Within single sentences Langacker has discussed the special set of conditions he labels 'command' that permit a pronoun to appear before its antecedent.

Cataphoric relationships also hold between sentences. In a number of languages of the Eastern Highlands of Papua New Guinea, though not in as many as use anaphoric linkage, there is a type of forward reference which McCarthy has labeled *chaining*. It is like a promise either to continue with the same subject as the present sentence or to change to a different subject. It operates sequentially, from one sentence to the next, rather than between a main clause and its subordinate clauses like the Huichol conjunct system and some Greek participles, or between a matrix clause and a complement clause as in English.

A still higher level of cataphora has been found in Kham of western Nepal. David Watters finds twin morphological paradigms for each verb; the one says that the information is being given because it will be needed later in order to understand something that is to come later, the other that the information is to be responded to directly in the light of all else that has been said.

Staging

We have seen how the speaker decides what he is going to say and how he will relate it to what has gone before. He also decides on a perspective from which he wishes to stage what he says.

To a remark like *Sally bought it in the market* there are several natural comebacks, including *How much did she buy it for?* and *How much did they sell it to her for?* Both take the same answer. The first, however, continues on the line of what Sally was doing, while the second shifts the perspective to that of the market people.

Sometimes we announce with a fanfare what it is we are talking about, as when we say *Our lecture this afternoon is about discourse.* Many languages including English also have more subtle ways of announcing a topic. The most common appears to be fronting, as in *Fleas my dog has.* Wheatley, however, also finds a pronoun system in Bacairi of Brazil that distinguishes between the topic of a stretch of discourse and everything else that may be referred to in the third person. As a result, when pronouns are used, order is free to signal other things, so initial position is reserved for the least predictable part of the sentence in cohesive terms. John Newman finds a similar system of topic pronouns in Longuda of Nigeria.

Besides the major topic of a discourse there are usually subsidiary topics. These less inclusive topics may be introduced by special subordinators as in

Koine Greek and probably in most other languages, or by special verb forms as in Nambiquara of Brazil (Kroeker, 1975). English treats a topic that is informationally new as subsidiary in level (Clements, 1975). Grammatical subordination and relativization provide low level subsidiary topics; in effect, they tuck the things they are about into corners of the picture outside the main center of attention.

English pronominalization is a cohesion oriented process for keeping track of who is who. What about languages that delete instead of pronominalizing? Mary Ruth Wise and Ivan Lowe have uncovered one mechanism that appears to keep track of reference through long term expectations about regular shifts in staging. They call it *participant orientation.*

Suppose we rank the participants in an event on a scale that runs from relatively high involvement in the action to zero involvement: in terms of lexical roles, for example, agent outranks patient, which in turn outranks instrument. Suppose then that we choose three characters, A, B, and C, and express their ranking by listing them in descending order from left to right. The sequence ABC would match something like 'A harmed B using C' or 'A spoke to B about C'. The other five possible configurations are ACB, CAB, CBA, BCA, and BAC.

By defining two operations we can relate any one of these rankings of participants to any other ranking. Both operations are order permutations. The first, symbolized *r,* is *reversal,* the interchange of the first two elements in a ranking: r (ABC) = BAC. The second, symbolized *s,* is *switch,* the interchange of the second two: s(ABC) = ACB. Composite changes of state lead to all six possibilities.

In an Ayore text from Bolivia reported by Janet Briggs we can call the narrator A, a jaguar he hunts B, and a third character C. The sequence of events begins with 'I speared a jaguar', which has the shape ABC if we consider C, off stage, to be in the lowest possible rank. The response, 'he lunged at me', BAC, is reached by reversal of A and B. A series of events, with reversals back and forth between ABC and BAC, follows, until 'I was about to kill him', ABC, is reached. These repeated reversals in the early part of a narrative may be the key to the ways speakers of some languages keep their reference straight without pronouns.

At this point the third character steps out of the jungle and finishes off the jaguar while A stands by helplessly. The configuration is CBA, in which the roles are completely backwards from those of the original state. This role configuration by itself identifies the tension point of stories in a number of languages. Furthermore, the composite sequence of operations *rsr* or *srs* that is required to get from ABC to CBA signals a surprise action any any language that uses regular staging sequences in this patterned way.

The story ends blandly with 'The place where I killed the jaguar is not far from here', ABC. The mental process of getting back to ABC from the CBA configuration carries its own surprise for the hearer, and again involves the composite *rsr* or *srs* operation.

The different levels of staging or perspective formation that I have already referred to show a kind of stage management in selecting linguistic forms. The speaker puts certain things up front where the hearer cannot help but take them as the most important. He relates other things to the central ones but puts them upstage, and attaches additional details and embellishments around the edges. This stage management seems to be the real reason why languages need devices like embedding and subordination, and so may be behind the common observation that the form of language is organized hierarchically. We set up our speech around focal points or themes at many levels at once.

Bonnie Meyer and Paul Clements have tested psycholinguistic reactions to discourse structure by plotting which elementary propositions in the content of a text are recalled most readily. Meyer has compared these propositions with the ones that careful readers feel are the most relevant to the text. Both investigators find that hearers tend to recall points that are placed high in the staging hierarchy, and not to recall points that are buried farther down; this is true even when the really important points are the ones that are buried. In one text the only time an important point was recalled was in a proposition that was a word for word repetition of the title, and hence was related to the topmost level of all. The implications of these tests for rhetoric are obvious; I am trying to follow them even in this article.

The relation between high levels of content and high levels of staging is far from worked out; but it does appear that either can be varied independently of the other. For example, the rhetorical relationship of cause or covariance (Frederiksen, 1975) can be expressed with the antecedent first or with the consequent first, depending on how the speaker wants the hearer to view the situation. Even the elements of a narrative sequence can be permuted out of temporal order in some languages, always at the cost of adding words that preserve the time framework, like *after* and *before* in English.

Manipulating large blocks of content like this for staging purposes may be no different in its theoretical implications than moving smaller blocks around inside a sentence. Just as a lexical predicate within the grammatical framework of a clause can have one of its arguments fronted as theme, so a high level rhetorical predicate can have one of its arguments fronted.

The idea of writing generative transformational grammars that apply to complete narratives and that reflect the factors I have mentioned has a curious consequence from the point of view of the development of that theory from its Chomskyan basis, although it is completely consistent with the meaning/text model of generative grammar worked out by I.A. Mel'chuk and A.K. Zholkovsky. We are trying to do three things: (1) express the content structure of the whole narrative, (2) order its parts in a way that expresses the staging dimension, and (3) calibrate relative redundancy and newness with reference to this partially linearized structure. Where does the sentence fit in all this?

It seems reasonable now, in the light of both the Russian work and Robert F. Simmon's studies in the simulation of productions, to take the sentence as one of the smallest in a hierarchy of units by means of which we arrive at the final linearization of the content. It is much like a packaging unit in which a certain portion of the content can be arranged for export via sound to the hearer.

Or to use another metaphor, we do not expect the hearer to drink our whole kettle of semantic soup at one gigantic gulp; we give it to him a spoonful at a time. Part of the content fits the framework of one sentence, another part the next, and so on. Thus part of the grammar must concern itself with the way in which the content, staged and made cohesive, is blocked into sentences as well as into higher units.

In the development of transformational grammar this is paradoxical. Even though something corresponding to the sentence can probably be kept as a primitive unit of the theory, the idea of a root or independent sentence within which other sentences are embedded has to be made to depend on broader factors such as rhetorical structure, staging, and cohesion. There are probably still other factors at work; and if there are, this affects linguistic theory by making root sentences a phenomenon defined ultimately in terms of performance.

Bibliography

This bibliography combines the references to works cited in this paper with an illustrative but not exhaustive list of works on narrative in a variety of languages.

Allen, Janice D. 1972. 'Halia sentences'. Pacific Linguistics, Series A, 34:1–15.

Allen, Jerry. 1971. 'Tense/aspect and conjunctions in Halia narratives'. Oceanic Linguistics 10:1.63–77.

Andrews, Henrietta. 1972. 'Rhetorical questions in Otomí of the State of Mexico'. Notes on Translation 44:25–28.

Austing, John. in press. 'Semantic relationships in Ömie'. Language Data.

Ballard, Jr., D. Lee. 1974. 'The semantics of Inibaloi verbal affixes'. Lingua 34:2/3.181–218.

Bearth, Thomas. 1969. 'Phrase et discours en Toura', Cahiers Ferdinand de Saussure 25:29–45.

Beekman, John, and John Callow. 1974. Translating the Word of God. Grand Rapids: Zondervan.

Bishop, Ruth, Ella Marie Button, Aileen Reid, and Robert E. Longacre. 1968. Totonac: from clause to discourse (Summer Institute of Linguistics Publications in Linguistics and Related Fields, No. 17). Norman OK: Summer Institute of Linguistics.

Bradley, Virginia M. 1971. 'Jibu narrative discourse structure'. Anthropological Linguistics 13:1.1–15.

Brennan, P. W. 1969. The structure of Koine Greek narrative. Hartford Seminary Foundation Ph. D. thesis.

Bridgeman, Loraine Irene. 1966. Oral paragraphs in Kaiwa (Guarani). Indiana University Ph. D. thesis.

Briggs, Janet R. 1973. Ayoré narrative analysis. International Journal of American Linguistics 39:3.155–163.

Callow, Kathleen. 1974. Discourse considerations in translating the Word of God. Grand Rapids: Zondervan.

Clements, Paul. 1975. The effects of staging on recall from prose. Cornell University Ph. D. thesis.

Cromack, Robert E. 1968. Language systems and discourse structure in Cashinawa (Hartford Studies in Linguistics, No. 23). Hartford, Connecticut: Hartford Seminary Foundation.

Crowell, Thomas H. 1973. 'Cohesion in Bororo discourse'. Linguistics 104:15–27.

Daneš, František, ed. 1974. Papers on functional sentence perspective. The Hague: Mouton & Co.

Daswani, Tilottama C. 1975. Locative systems in Marathi and Hindi discourse. Cornell University Ph.D. thesis.

Davis, Donald R. 1973. 'Wantoat paragraph structure'. Linguistics 110:5–16.

Dorfmann, Eugene. 1969. The narreme in the medieval Romance epic. Toronto: University of Toronto Press.

DuBois, Carl. 1973. 'Connectives in Sarangani Manobo discourse'. Linguistics 110:17–28.

Fillmore, Charles J. 1968. 'The case for case'. In Emmon Bach and Robert Harms, eds. Universals in linguistic theory. New York: Holt, Rinehart and Winston, 1–88.

Frederiksen, Carl. 1975. 'Representing logical and semantic structure of knowledge acquired from discourse'. Cognitive Psychology 7:3.371–458.

Gieser, Richard. 1972. 'Kalinga sequential discourse'. Philippine Journal of Linguistics 3:1.15–34.

Gleason, Jr., H.A. 1968. 'Contrastive analysis in discourse structure'. Georgetown University Monograph Series in Languages and Linguistics 21:39–64.

Glover, Jessie. 1971. 'Paragraph structure in Gurung discourse'. Mimeo. Kathmandu: Tribhuvan University.

Glover, Warren William. 1973. Sememic and grammatical structures in Gurung (Nepal). Australian National University Ph.D. thesis.

Grimes, Joseph E. 1966. 'Some inter-sentence relationships in Huichol'. In Summa Anthropológica en homenaje a Roberto J. Weitlaner. México, D.F.: Instituto Nacional de Antropología e Historia, 465–470.

–.   1971a. 'Kinds of information in discourse'. Kivung 4:2.64–74.

–.   1971b. 'Participant orientation'. Philippine Journal of Linguistics 2:2.93–100.

–.   1972. 'Outlines and overlays'. Language 48:3.513–524.

–.   1975a. 'Signals of discourse structure in Koine'. In George MacRae, ed. Society of Biblical Literature 1975 seminar papers, Vol. 1. Missoula, Montana: Scholars Press, 151–164.

–.   1975b. The thread of discourse. The Hague: Mouton & Co.

–.   ed. in press. Papers on discourse (Summer Institute of Linguistics Publications in Linguistics and Related Fields). Norman OK: Summer Institute of Linguistics.

–.   and Naomi Glock. 1970. 'A Saramaccan narrative pattern'. Language 46:2.408–425.

Hale, Austin, ed. 1973. Clause, sentence, and discourse patterns in selected languages of Nepal (Summer Institute of Linguistics Publications in Linguistics and Related Fields, No. 40). Norman OK: Summer Institute of Linguistics, 4 vols.

Halliday, Michael A.K. 1967. 'Notes on transitivity and theme in English'. Journal of Linguistics 3:37–81; 3:199–244; 4:179–215 (1968).

Hewer, Philip L. in press. 'A lexical approach to clause series in Kasem'. Linguistics.

Hohulin, Lou. 1971. 'Complex predicates in Keley-i Kallahan'. Pacific Linguistics, Series A 32:19–32.

Hohulin, Richard. 1971. 'Cohesive organization in Keley-i Kallahan'. Pacific Linguistics, Series A 32:1–17.

Holzhausen, Andreas. 1974. 'Narratives in the New Testament'. Notes on Translation 53:22–33.

Hooker, Betty. 1972. 'Cohesion in Ivatan'. Asian Studies 10:1.33–43.

Huisman, Roberta. 1973. 'Angaataha narrative discourse'. Linguistics 110:29–42.

Huisman, Ronald. 1973. 'Angaataha verb morphology'. Linguistics 110:43–54.

Kilham, Christine. 1974. Thematic organization of Wik-Munkan discourse. Australian National University Ph.D. thesis.

Kroeker, Menno H. 1975. 'Thematic linkage in Nambiquara narrative'. In Grimes, The thread of discourse, 361–368.

Labov, William, and Joshua Waletzky. 1967. 'Narrative analysis: oral versions of personal experience'. In June Helm, ed. Essays on the verbal and visual arts. Seattle: University of Washington Press, 12–44.

Langacker, Ronald. 1969. 'On pronominalization and the chain of command'. In David A. Reibel and Sanford A. Schane, eds. Modern studies in English. Englewood Cliffs, NJ: Prentice-Hall, Inc., 160–186.

Larson, Virginia. 1972. 'Pronominal reference in the Ivatan narrative'. Philippine Journal of Linguistics 3:2.37–42.

Lawrence, Helen. 1972. 'Viewpoint and location in Oksapmin'. Anthropological Linguistics 8:311–316.

Lawrence, Marshall. 1972. 'Oksapmin sentence structure'. Pacific Lingṵ

Litteral, Robert. 1972a. 'Rhetorical predicates and time topology in Anggor'. Foundations of Language 8:391–410.

–. 1972b. 'Time in Anggor discourse'. Kivung 5:1.49–55.

Litteral, Shirley. 1972. 'Orientation shifts in Anggor'. Pacific Linguistics, Series A 31:23–44.

Longacre, Robert E. 1968. Discourse, paragraph, and sentence structure in selected Philippine languages. Santa Ana: Summer Institute of Linguistics, 2 vols.

–. 1970. 'Paragraph and sentence structure in New Guinea Highlands languages'. Kivung 3:3.150–163.

–. 1971. Philippine discourse and paragraph studies in memory of Betty McLachlin (Pacific Linguistics Series C, No. 22).

–. 1972. Hierarchy and universality of discourse constituents in New Guinea languages. Washington, D.C.: Georgetown University Press, 2 vols.

Loos, Eugene. 1963. 'Capanahua narration structure'. University of Texas Studies in Literature and Language 4, supplement, 697–742.

Loriot, James, and Barbara Hollenbach. 1970. 'Shipibo paragraph structure'. Foundations of Language 6:1.43–66.

Lowe, Ivan. 1969. 'An algebraic theory of English pronominal reference'. Semiotica 1:2.397–421; 5:43–73 (1974); 5:233–254 (1974).

Mel'chuk, I.A. 1973. 'Towards a linguistic "meaning $\langle == \rangle$ text" model'. In Ferenc Kiefer, ed. Trends in Soviet theoretical linguistics. Dordrecht: D. Reidel, 33–57.

– and A.K. Zholkovsky. 1970. 'Towards a functioning "meaning-text" model of language'. Linguistics 51:10–47.

Meyer, Bonnie J.F. 1974. The organization of prose and its effects on recall. Cornell University Ph.D. thesis.

Miller, Helen. 1973. 'Thematization in Mamanwa'. Linguistics 110:55–73.

McCarthy, Joy. 1965. 'Clause chaining in Kanite'. Anthropological Linguistics 7:5.59–70.

McLeod, Ruth. 1974. 'Paragraph, aspect, and participant in Xavante'. Linguistics 132:51–74.

Newman, John. in press. 'Participant orientation in Longuda folktales'. In Grimes, ed. Papers on discourse.

Perrin, Mona. 1974. 'Direct and indirect speech in Mambila'. Journal of Linguistics 10:1.27–38.

Pike, Kenneth L. and Burkhard Schoettelndreyer. 1972. 'Paired sentence reversals in the discovery of underlying and surface structures in Sherpa discourse'. Indian Linguistics 33:1.72–83, reprinted in Hale 1973.

– and Ivan Lowe. 1969. 'Pronominal reference in English conversation and discourse – a group theoretical treatment'. Folia Linguistica 3:68–106.

Popovich, Harold. 1967. 'Large grammatical units and the space-time setting in Maxakalí'. Atas do Simpósio sôbre a Biota Amazônica 2:195–199.

Quillian, M. Ross. 1968. 'Semantic memory'. In Marvin Minsky, ed. Semantic information processing. Cambridge, Massachusetts: The MIT Press, 227–270.

–. 1969. 'The teachable language comprehender: a simulation program and theory of language'. Communications of the Association for Computing Machinery 12:8.459–476.

Rowan, Orland. 1972. 'Some features of Paressi discourse structure'. Anthropological Linguistics 14:1.19–22.

Schank, Roger C., Neil M. Goldman, Charles J. Rieger III, and Christopher K. Riesbeck. 'Inference and paraphrase by computer'. Journal of the Association for Computing Machinery 22:3.309–328.

Simmons, Robert F., and J. Slocum. 1972. 'Generating English discourse from semantic networks'. Communications of the Association for Computing Machinery 15:10.891–905.

Stennes, Leslie. 1969. Participant identification in Adamawa Fulani (Hartford Studies in Linguistics, No. 24). Hartford, Connecticut: Hartford Seminary Foundation.

Stout, Mickey, and Ruth Thomson. 1971. 'Kayapo narrative'. International Journal of American Linguistics 37:4.250–256.

Taber, Charler R. 1966. The structure of Sango narrative (Hartford Studies in Linguistics, No. 17). Hartford, Connecticut: Hartford Seminary Foundation.

Thurman, Robert C. 1975. 'Chuave medial verbs'. Anthropological Linguistics 17:7.342–352.

Trail, Ronald L., ed. 1973. Patterns in clause, sentence, and discourse in selected languages of India and Nepal (Summer Institute of Linguistics Publications in Linguistics and Related Fields, No. 41). Norman OK: Summer Institute of Linguistics, 4 vols.

van Dijk, Teun A. 1972. Some aspects of text grammars. The Hague: Mouton & Co.

Watters, David. in press. 'Speaker-hearer involvement in Kham'. In Grimes, ed. Papers on discourse.

West, Anne. 1973. 'The semantics of focus in Amganad Ifugao'. Linguistics 110:98–121.

Wheatley, James. 1973. 'Pronouns and nominal elements in Bacairi discourse'. Linguistics 104:105–115.

Wheeler, Alva. 1967. 'Grammatical structure in Siona discourse'. Lingua 19:60–77.

Winograd, Terry. 1972. Understanding natural language. New York: Academic Press.

Wise, Mary Ruth. 1968. Identification of participants in discourse. University of Michigan Ph. D. thesis.

–   and Ivan Lowe. 1972. 'Permutation groups in discourse' (Languages and Linguistics Working Papers, No. 4). Washington, D. C.: Georgetown University Press, 12–34.

Textlinguistic Approaches to Written Works of Art

Götz Wienold
Universität Konstanz

0 Statement of Intent

I take the principal aim of textlinguistics to be *the study of the production of meaning in texts*. With the advent of new sentence linguistics in generative grammars one insisted on the essential newness of every sentence uttered and understood by a language participant. Yet, it is actually in what we call texts that we find the novelty of language as it occurs. Texts, in this as in many other respects, are much less abstract objects of linguistic study than sentences. So, one may also say that the aim of textlinguistics is *the study of the production of new meaning in texts*. And this, I submit, is the main reason for selecting written works of art as a special area of interest in textlinguistics. Art often is considered as an activity where creativity acts with increased momentum and with a quality more strongly vibrating than in everyday use of the materials of the human world. Written works of art, then, are an area where textlinguistics may study linguistic creativity in some particularly distinct manifestations. That is not at all to say that linguistic creativity is limited to so-called works of art. Therefore we will say that one major aim of textlinguistic analysis of written works of art is to contribute towards the understanding of linguistic creativity.

Considering the linguistic creativity of mankind as well as the linguistic creativity of every language participant we are inclined to say that language is new in every new creative moment. And an understanding of what enables man to be creative in his language is what linguistics, for some time, has taken as a main objective. Regarding texts, particularly those texts called 'works of art', 'literature' or 'poetry', it is an insight of Russian formalism, which is still valid, that such linguistic creativity takes place with respect to a received body of texts and received ways or devices of formulating texts (cf. Striedter 1969; Stempel 1972; Ihwe 1973). In a more general sense, one may use the concept of text processing (cf. Wienold 1972, 26f., 146ff.) to characterize the basis of the production of new meaning in texts: In formulating and understanding texts, language participants make use of socially codified and/or individually ac-quired texts; but, in addition to this, a large amount of text production and reception actually takes place in processing texts into new texts, particularly in the realm of literature with all the activities of rewriting, reworking, criticizing, interpreting, commenting, evaluating, translating and transposing into new media. It is these activities which form much of 'literary life'.

In presenting the following assessment of research, therefore, I will use the concept of text processing as a frame of reference (Wienold-Rieser 1976, Wienold 1976a, 1976b). I will attempt to sketch main lines in the study of the production of meaning in a body of texts referred to as 'written works of art'. Space and time do not permit more than a rather selective presentation of the enormous amount of research done in this field. So it seems advisable to concentrate on reporting important developments of thought rather than on the work of individual researchers. This means, we will be interested in special notions or instruments developed within linguistics for the study of the production of meaning in texts. We take "production of meaning" to refer to the activities of both producers and receivers of texts, if for lack of space we are allowed to stick to this rather elementary and somewhat disturbing façon de parler rather than attempting to introduce a pragmatic terminology more appropriate to our subject. We do not overlook the important contributions to the study of meaning in literary texts as developed in literary scholarship, literary criticism or *Literaturwissenschaft* (see, e.g., Hirsch 1967, Hobsbaum 1970, Foulkes 1975). But linguistics really set out to get closer towards what makes language participants assign meanings to linguistic utterances and so, at its best and ideally, linguistics considered itself to be on the other side of interpretation, that is – in one way of formulating this objective – to understand understanding (a research program on this line has been most stringently developed by Koch (e.g. 1971, 1976; cf. also Schmidt 1974).

Before we draw an outline of this area in greater detail it seems advisable to comment on the notions of 'written' and 'work of art'.

1   Some Comments on 'Written' and on 'Work of Art'

'Written' linguistic utterances have attracted growing interest in their "writtenness" since linguistics became more aware of the mostly double modality of the representation of language. Yet, it took a long time until linguistics really turned to spoken language; even today syntactic and semantic studies often do not pay attention at all to the fact that the sentences of Western European natural languages which they discuss are sentences of the written modality of language most of the time (cf. Abercrombie 1965). Nevertheless, the growing awareness of the specific properties of the spoken variety of language made linguists also aware of the fact that there are properties specific to the written manifestation and that there is a need for descriptive instruments to deal with them. With the advent of pragmatics and paralinguistics higher-level properties of the spoken and written modalities of language came to the fore. That is, a textlinguistic approach to 'written' works of art, ideally, is required to spell out specific representational and pragmatic properties that concern the modality of these texts. More specifically, one also has to take account of the distinction between 'written' and 'printed' language, as most of the texts called 'works of art' are nowadays published and distributed in a printed or print-like form (e.g., typed). Vachek takes the lack – I would say: the relative lack – of Bühler's function of 'Ausdruck' (Vachek translates it by 'air') in printed language as one of the differentiating factors between written and printed language. Vachek remarks that "most of the features characteristic of written language have been pushed to the extreme" in printed language (Vachek 1948, 71). Common methods of reproduction of spoken language and written language differ considerably as to the conservation of features pertaining to the individual which produces the utterance, as Vachek points out. These differences do not exist by historical accident but, rather, reflect the different functions that spoken, written or printed language serves.

Besides general studies on writing and written language (cf. Kavanagh and Mattingly 1972; Vachek 1973) one may consult here a study of Ihwe (1972b) that deals with the pragmatics of narratives. Furthermore, one will be interested in specific formulational devices provided by the 'technology of writing'. Like spoken language written texts have properties that obviously have demarcative functions (cf. Coquet 1973, 52). The suprasegmentals of spoken language can be replaced by syntactic formulational devices (Smith 1971, 215). There are suprasegmentals specific to written texts, which are based on typographical devices, for instance, based on the arrangement of the printed text on a page or a sequence of pages (as exploited, e.g. in *poésie concrète*) or based on possibilities of indicating higher units by paragraphs and the like. Textually, spoken and written language differ in the use of certain properties, e.g., deictics (cf. Harweg 1968b; 1974, 94, 103 f.).

The 'writtenness' of a text also is in need of a sociolinguistic comment. 'Written language', in many societies, is a special standard reserved for specific purposes of language use and communication. The written language often rivals with the spoken language in a diglossia – or sometimes triglossia – situation as characterized by Ferguson 1959 (cf. Cadora 1965). An implication of this is that what in a given society is considered a written work of art – a comment on this notion will follow presently – is, to some degree, dependent on constraints on the overall practice of written language, its teaching and appreciation. There is a further aspect of writtenness which should at least be touched upon, and this is a diachronic one. The medium of written (and printed or typed) language offers the language participants specific uses. These uses are distinguished by greater degrees of permanency and accessibility over the space and time limits characteristic of the oral varieties. Especially the directive influences on language use and standard which go along with these functions influence the development of a language. On the other hand the written medium offers a reservoir of texts to be drawn upon when formulating a new text, so that "older" language can influence via written texts "less old" language.

It is these properties of writtenness that allow for special procedures followed in the processing of written texts, especially written works of art. With written texts, there are considerably less constraints placed on time and space limits. And this fact allows for quite complicated relationships between texts to be established in their processing (cf. Hertzler 1965, 441 ff.; Wienold 1972a, 171 ff.).

A second initial comment concerns the expression 'work of art'. We do not subscribe to the view that there are inherent properties of objects which determine their assignment to the group of objects which are called "works of art". Rather, we maintain that there is a process of selection related to societal or group norms which determines which objects are classified as "works of art". This process of selection operates with arguments which refer to properties of the objects considered "works of art". But it is an abstraction from this process of justifying of calling an object a work of art which forms the apparent foundation of the view of inherent properties of works of art. In textlinguistic studies, the artfulness of a linguistic text has been construed particularly as its 'poeticalness': one outcome of these studies was that there are no intensional criteria that demarcate strictly between texts traditionally considered 'poetical' or 'literary' (that is 'being a work of art in the medium of language'). Details will be reported in a later section of this paper. Russian formalism which for the first time studied the literariness or poeticalness of texts which are considered 'works of art' also pointed out that there is a change (or evolution) of evaluation of works of art taking place in time; the criteria chosen for evaluating works of art change with time according to some statable regularity (Tynjanov; cf. the reformulation in Ihwe 1973). Another formulation of regularities of change of evaluation of works of art is owed to Abraham A. Moles (1966). 'Aesthetic' is a special focus of a participant applied to the processing of a text ('focus': cf. Koch 1968), evaluation is an aggregate of objects and participant activities (Krause 1971). This activity – like any activity of text processing – is embedded in the evolution of processes of assigning structures to linguistic (more generally: semiotic) objects. (Wienold 1971, 1972a). Schmidt 1972 considers 'fictionality' as a basic property that distinguishes literary texts from other texts; but, 'fictionality' in his analysis, is not a semantic property of such texts, but a property of their place in a communication system (cf. Lüthe 1974).

Within the framework of the concept of text processing we will regard expressions like 'literature', 'literary', 'poetic' and so on as pragmatic predicates which designate relations between a group of users of texts and a body of texts. We do no longer attempt to define these texts by intrinsic criteria pertaining to all of them which explicate what is meant by the users of the words 'literature' in a meaningful way. Adopting this point of view, one, then, can use the highly interesting work done in establishing criteria which a certain group of texts considered 'poetic' satisfy in order to deal with matters of text processing.

One may ask questions like: Given a group of people in a society and a group of texts called 'literature' by this group, what common characteristics do this special group of texts or subgroups of it show? If among this group of people there happens to be a division about whether a given text should be counted as belonging to the group of texts called 'literature': what criteria are being used in this discussion? Does the text under discussion satisfy these criteria? Do the texts already codified as literature satisfy the criteria? When one embarks upon such questions soon one will find oneself immersed in the most intricate problems of a sociological nature which may reveal why such a discussion is of importance to that group and why the group uses the specific criteria advanced in the given case.

Artfulness in this approach, then, is relative to the participants and evaluative standards employed by the participants with regard to specific uses made of by participants (the groups of evaluators and users need not be identical).

With this understanding of the expression 'written works of art' in mind, I propose the following classification of the research to be reviewed. In the study of linguistic artfulness of written works three main areas of research seem to be of special importance:

(1) the analysis of written works of art in the framework of grammars
(2) the analysis of specific textual structures of written works of art
(3) the analysis of processes in participating in written works of art.

The first area is mainly covered by the study of poeticalness, the second area comprises work on structural properties of genres, on socalled macro-structure and so on, the third area comprises considerations of pragmatics and may also comprise sociolinguistic and psycholinguistic research as well as studies in structural change with regard to written works of art.

2 Analysis of Written Works of Art in the Framework of Grammars

Interestingly enough, it was within a renewed effort to improve upon grammatical descriptions that linguists became involved in the analysis of the language of written works of art. With the development of generative grammars following Chomsky's early work and with the general interest in the notion of grammaticalness the use of language in written works of art appeared in need of a special grammatical dicussion, as this use often did not conform to what was considered grammatical in (some) other uses of language. Deviation from grammaticalness, then, served as an indicator of the language of written works of art or of its 'poeticalness'. There were even attempts to develop a generative poetics in the format of generative grammars (Bierwisch 1965). That is, the driving force behind the sudden rise in the study of poeticalness within the framework of generative grammars was the renewed interest in linguistic creativity. Soon, other indicators of poeticalness were suggested: ambiguity, complexity, equivalence constructions. Formation of equivalent structures was an indicator suggested already in earlier work by Jakobson, and parallelism was considered the foremost exponent of such equivalent formation in poetic texts. Studies of particular interest with regard to indicators of poeticalness are: Baumgärtner

1965, 1969, Bierwisch 1965, Greimas 1967, Jakobson 1960, 1965, Koch 1966, 1968, Leech 1966, Levin 1962, 1963 (cf. also Stempel 1972). There are several volumes of conferences or collections of articles that either touch on the subject or even survey it in great detail. Of those I mention: Chatman 1971, Davie et al. 1961, Fowler 1966, Garvin 1964, Greimas 1970, 1972, Koch 1972a, Sebeok 1960. Ihwe produced the most thorough survey of theoretical and methodological questions of a study of literature from the point of view of linguistics, particularly from the point of view of generative grammars (Ihwe 1972a) and edited two collections of articles to survey the prospects of a study of literature either based on or at least inspired by linguistics: Ihwe 1971/2, 1972/3.

In Jakobson's discussion the features proposed as indicators of poeticalness served to highlight one of six functions of language which was particularly prominent in poetical uses of language. Jakobson calls it the "poetic function which focuses" on the message for its own sake and which "projects the principle of equivalence from the axis of selection into the axis of combination" (Jakobson 1960, 356 ff.). Jakobson locates the poetic function in a general model of linguistic communication which distinguishes six elements: addresser, addressee, context, code, message and contact. The concentration on the message, the poetic function, is then characterizable by the linguistic indicators of poeticalness. Poeticalness, then, is assumed to explicate what is the artfulness of written works of art (see also Posner 1969). If one considers the distribution of the indicators of poeticalness, however, one finds that these indicators are also found in many texts that are not considered poetical or literary and that there are texts which are considered literary or poetical and do not display indicators of poeticalness at all or only to a low degree.

The framework of generative grammars also was used to define the goals of linguistic stylistics. As the notion of poeticalness, particularly poeticalness by deviation from grammaticalness, was linked to Chomsky's notion of the native speaker's competence, stylistics was linked to notion of the speaker's performance (Ohmann 1964, 1968, Thorne 1965, 1969, Hayes 1966, Leech 1966, Doležel 1969, Smith 1971; cf. Hendricks 1975.) Besides this, attempts towards the definition and description of style markers have continued, which would allow for insights into the effect of a particularly modelled use of language on a hearer or reader. I limit my references to Enkvist et al. 1964, Enkvist 1973, Chatman 1967, Mitchell 1974, Colson 1975, Riffaterre 1959, 1960, 1964, 1970, 1971.

Some studies of poeticalness of literary texts sometimes give the impression of isolating individual features of the creative use of language in texts rather than of actually approaching a study of textual properties. There are, however, more than a few studies which attempt an analysis of the functions of poetical properties in texts. Such studies aim at bringing to the attention the complicated interrelations of such features in a text. Again, this kind of study is very much connected with the name of Jakobson, (see e.g. Jakobson-Lévi Strauss 1962, Jakobson 1967, 1973, Jakobson-Jones 1970, Levin 1962, Feinberg 1973) but also reflects tendencies of linguistic structuralism in general, as one of the earliest studies of this genre shows (Hill 1955, cf. Hill 1951). In a sense, such studies are instances of a more general description of poetic structures that the ambition of generative poetics aimed at. As Jiři Lévy puts it: "Das theoretische Anliegen der generativen Poetik ist es, ein ästhetisches Gebilde derart in Elemente und Kombinationsregeln zu zerlegen, daß es möglich ist, es zu rekonstruieren und zu generieren, indem die Regeln auf das Elementarinventar angewendet werden" (1971, 563). Jakobson's criteria for poeticalness, particularly parallelism, are critically analyzed in Werth 1976.

Problems of developing text grammars have been most rigidly connected with aspects of describing poetic texts by Petöfi (e.g. 1967, 1968, 1969, 1971, 1972). Petöfi's aim is to analyze the relationships between "compositional units" and the semantic interpretation of a poetic text.

Such detailed analyses also take us to a more important level than the discussion of problems of grammaticalness and poeticalness intimates, that is the analysis of meaning in poetical texts, or the understanding of linguistic creativity in production of meaning in poetical texts.

As descriptive semantics in linguistics is still in a rather infant stage there is little of general knowledge to be reported on here. A survey of various positions and objectives with regard to the study of meaning of written works of art or of literature can be found in Foulkes 1975. Eaton 1970 distinguishes between "semantics of literature" studying "the totality of the relevant references in the mind of the author during the composition of the work and all referents to which these references were adapted" and "semics" (of literature) studying "the totality of the relevant references in the mind of the reader during the reading of the work and all referents to which these references are adapted" (cf. Eaton 1972). A French school of thought, on the other hand, proclaims to study the "production du sens" independent of references in the mind of authors or readers or their manifestations. In spite of his criticism of procedural steps noticeable in the studies of the "production du sens" in a literary text by Kristeva (1972) or Meschonnic (1970), Coquet (1973, 17ff.) insists on the relevance of such endeavours to the study of the production or organisation of meaning in texts. In so doing, Coquet is following the tenet to analyse a text independently of its relations to author or recipient: "Selons nous, le linguiste doit laisser au message son statement d'infrastructure qui lui confère une relative autonomie et admettre en conséquence que la signification ne se détermine pas seulement en deux points (émission et réception) mais en trois; et que ce troisième point, le message, n'est pas situé au même niveau que les deux autres." What it concerned is "l'intelligibilité du texte", for the description of which one is in need of models (Coquet 1973, 27f.).

Methodologically, the most far reaching attempt in a linguistic study of the production of meaning in literary texts seems to me to be the analysis of interpretations assigned to literary texts by participants and relating these interpretations to the original text in order to understand how initiant and resultant texts of such text processing are related semantically (for the concepts of initiant and resultant texts cf. Wienold 1976 a, 1976 b, Wienold-Rieser 1976). I submit this view for two reasons.

(1) This approach provides the analysis with a vast body of material in the semantic study of literary texts: The material can, in many cases, be enlarged by asking informants for additional interpretations and even by eliciting particular responses in more formally structured procedures of data gathering (cf. Wienold 1972 a, 180 ff., 193 ff., 1973).

(2) In studying interpretations of literary texts and the relationships between initiant and resultant texts of such text processing we may be able to get hold of the role which such meaning relationships play in what participants do with literary texts in space and over time as they experience it. (This point will be enlarged upon in section 4).

The first study of an intent of this general direction, to my knowledge, comes from the glossematic school of Copenhague: Johansen 1949 (For the contributions of this school to the study of literary texts within a general framework of semiotics and of their impact in later thought cf. Trabant 1970, Busse 1971, Ihwe 1972 a, 160 ff.). Johansen proposed to analyse texts which are offered as interpretations of literary texts as formulations of the reception of literary texts by their readers. In tune with Hjelmslev's glossematic model, Johansen construed such formulations as manifestations of the level of content.

Other studies of the semantics of literature in this vein are: Lehmann 1965, who proposes to introduce principles of linguistic methodology into the assignment of meaning to symbolist poetry; Koch 1972 b, who analyzes strategies in determining how meaning is assigned to literary texts by participants; Wienold 1972 c, who discusses possibilities of defining levels of information which are introduced in assigning meaning and investigates how the use of different levels may influence interpretation (cf. also Wienold 1972 d).

More on empirical studies which are related to such endeavours in section 4. A study of the logics of interpretation is Göttner 1973.

Conceding such an approach, one may realize that production of new meaning in literature is not limited to the production of new texts but can also be found and fruitfully studied in the production of derived texts that purport to interpret a given literary text. Novelty of literary meaning, thus, is a feature of literary life.

3   The Analysis of Specific Textual Structures of Written Works of Art

Linguistic discussion of literary texts within the framework of grammatical descriptions mainly centers on poetry, whereas the studies to be dealt with in this section concentrate on narrative texts with a few structural studies of dramatic texts. There are studies of this nature which also appeal to the framework of generative grammars, but as such structures are not generally thought of as belonging to the realm of grammatical description proper and as there are actually serious difficulties of discussing such structures within this framework I prefer to discuss them in a separate section.

One of the important discoveries in the research of Russian formalism was Vladimir Propp's finding that Russian fairy tales could be described structurally by regularities of sequences of elements which he called functions (Propp 1928). Attempts at greater generality of structural descriptions by folklorists like Dundes (1962, 1963) and Colby (1970) and by French semiologists, particularly Bremond (1964, 1966, 1968, 1970; but cf. also Barthes 1966; Eco 1966; Greimas 1966; Todorov 1966, 1967; Kristeva 1968) led to models of narrative structure which separated general traits of the portrayal of the development of action in a narrative, which takes place by constellations of persons in sequences of states of development, from their descriptive components. Thus, one attempted to separate between narration as general procedures of structuring the telling of a tale and their implementation by theme (cf. Ihwe 1972 a, 402 ff.). Studies in narrative composition in Russian and German poetics linked up with these developments (cf. the survey in Doležel 1973 a). The general concern of such studies is to explore the creative expressiveness of man in using language in textual structures; and narrative structures besides others (games, proverbs, myths etc., even 'ritualized' gossip) offered ample material for this study. This is best formulated in Colby's words: "The structures of narrative are part of the vast and little understood cultural system which influences all human behavior... A science of narrative culture... should be directed toward finding, describing, and explaining regularities and patterns in the varieties of narrative concern shown by man" (Colby 1970, 177).

Within the general link-up between developments of linguistic theory and descriptive apparatuses on the one hand and theory of literature and search for its structures and functions in the various structuralist and semiotic schools on the other hand there developed approaches of supporting the structural analyses of the textual properties of narratives by linguistics. Dundes 1962, e.g., referred to Pike's linguistic framework, Taber 1966 based his study of Sango narratives on Hjelmslevian glossematics as recast in the framework of Lamb's stratificational grammar. And thus also an attempt was made to base narrative analysis on the developing theory of generative grammars and its approaches to the description of linguistic properties of sentences, particularly in its use of transformational rules.

Bierwisch, in his discussion of poetic competence, pointed out that there was little known about the link between higher-order textual structures and the lower-order ones as studied in generative grammars proper. But he also maintained that it was a point worth while of research whether there were systems of rules which govern higher-order textual structures or, as is often said, "macrostructure" (Bierwisch 1965, 63 f.). A hypothesis, which one may call the macrostructure hypothesis, was proposed that macro-structure properties of texts could be derived within a generative system of rules. This hypothesis was proposed and substantiated, among others, by Teun A. van Dijk (particularly 1972a, 130ff., 273ff., cf. also van Dijk et al. 1972, van Dijk 1972b), another approach on similar lines was developed by Žolkovskij and Ščeglov 1972 and Ihwe 1972a, 424ff. Rule systems of this kind have been suggested for some corpora of texts (cf., e.g., Dorfman 1969, Tusseau-Wittmann 1975). A proposal which also aligned itself with generative grammars but approached some higher-order textual properties in a different way was made by Wienold 1972e, 1972a, 65ff.). It seems to me that is has not been established that macro-structure properties of texts can be derived constructively from underlying structures in the same strict way in which syntactic sentential properties can be derived from underlying structures in the generative-transformational grammars hitherto available. It may even be questioned whether it is a promising approach to the description of specific textual properties to attempt to generate them in a generative-grammar-like fashion (cf. Wienold 1972b, 319f.; Harweg 1974, 94ff.). The stimulating discussion that van Dijk provoked with his presentation of the macro-structure hypothesis (Rieser-Wirrer 1974, Dascal-Margalit 1974, J. and Ö. Dahl 1974) seems to indicate that specific textual properties of the macro-structure type have to be dealt with in a way different from sentence grammars.

On a level of observation and elicitation of data rather than on that of theorizing, some tentative proposals have been made for the organization of some specific textual properties of the macro-structure type, e.g. Labov-Waletzky 1967, Labov 1972, 354ff., Maranda-Maranda 1971, 83ff.) Textual aspects of phenomena, that engage the interest of the participant in reading a narrative text (e.g., suspense, horror, emotional participation) have been, among others, suggested by Koch (1973, 195ff.), Fónagy (1971), Wienold (1972a, 74ff., 1972e, 1975).

Some aspects of telling have also been integrated into textlinguistic or textlinguistically oriented studies: the narrator (Doležel 1967), the presentation of time in narratives (Doležel 1973b; Stempel 1971, 1973) and the speech varieties of direct speech, indirect speech and "free indirect speech" or "nonreportive style" (Banfield 1973; Kuroda 1974). After Kuroda's analysis of the hypersentence hypothesis for narrative sentences, narration is best considered as one special type of language-use (or one special 'language-game' in the game-theory approach to describing pragmatic conventions) besides conversation, recitation, learning and inscription (cf. also Nierlich 1973, 20ff., on "Äußerungsakte").

This work on speech types, which we have just referred to, also touches the question of coherence of texts which, in a discussion of the artfulness of written texts, has some bearing on the analysis of poeticalness) cf. van Dijk 1972a, 277ff.). In narrative texts one finds uses of anaphoric pronouns and the definitivizing article which deviate from the regularities in other texts (Backus 1965; Harweg 1968a, 1968b). In reconstructing the relationship between story-teller and listener in a story by Thomas Mann – on the basis of the use of deictic pronouns, personal names and presuppositions – Harweg 1975 elaborates some deviations from textgrammatical usage with regard to a typology of relationships between story-teller and listener/recipient. These properties might be further indicators for the hypothesis that telling is a special type of language use for which not the same conventions hold as for conversation. Harweg, implicitly, seems to reject this hypothesis.

Another approach concerned with questions of coherence investigates semantic relationships between sentences and lexical items in the sequential structure of a text, cf. e.g. Rastier 1972. Stempel 1973 investigates constraints of coherence in reporting events.

There is not much research on thematics which provides insights into specific textual properties. Content-analysis research (cf. Saporta-Sebeok 1959) seldom reaches a point where it allows for generalization beyond the treatment of specific topics. It seems promising for such a venture, though, to study thematic properties in relation to macro-structure properties (cf. Pêcheux 1967, Doležel 1971, de Lillo 1971, Wienold 1972 a, 106 ff.). A thematic study of a dramatic text one finds in Ehrmann 1970, thematic studies of poetry in van Dijk 1969 and Assmann 1973, the latter being of special interest because it attempts such an analysis for a reconstructed historical culture. There is some interesting work in content analysis applied to the sequence of a text, cf. Martindale 1974.

The study of drama with an orientation towards textlinguistics has not been as prolific as research on narrative texts. With drama, of course, there is the added problem of how to deal with aspects of the presentation of dramatic texts on the stage and the question of analyzing plurimedial texts. The proposals of structural analyses of dramas by Jansen 1968, Pagnini 1970, among others, accordingly distinguish between the textual and the scenical level (cf. also Nierlich 1973 on the specific type of language use in dramatic presentation from a pragmatic point of view and Hein 1976 on analyzing the communication situation of dramatic presentation.) Next to Souriaus well-known system of classifying basic dramatic situations according to the roles of the participating agents, one finds categorizations of actions reminding him of Bremonds triadic functions in narrative analysis (cf. Wienold 1972 a, 120 ff.), and one finds structurally richer descriptions along the lines of French semiological studies, e.g., Coquet 1973, 147 ff. A more generalized classification of dramatic situations on the basis of Koch 1971 is presented in Hein 1976, 122 ff. I would like to mention also a few studies in structural analysis of dramatic texts which fall really into the realm of structuralist literary research which will have to be considered as avenues of approach: Levitt 1971, Schmid 1973, van Kesteren-Schmid 1975. A mathematical model of dramatic structures has been proposed by Marcus 1971 and further worked out, particularly with the due consideration given to thematics for the model to be of interest, by Brainerd-Neufeldt 1974.

Hein 1976 is a highly valuable study in developing a descriptive model for the analysis of dramatic texts and their presentation. Hein integrates various sociological and communication-theoretical approaches to human behavior in interpersonal interaction and its perception in order to analyse dramatic situations with respect to their perception by the onlooker. And he develops a structurally rich model of describing elements, sequences and higher – order relations of dramatic texts in presentation. A predominantly sociological study is Goodlad 1971.

It is not possible within this article to go into descriptions of specific properties of various other types or kinds of texts that one would want to differentiate. The question how to classify texts seems to me to be still at an elementary stage, particularly with regard to written works of art (cf. Gülich-Raible 1972; Harweg 1974, 107 ff.). Also, I exclude any questions of metrics from my report, although there is a rather intimate connection to the development of the use of linguistic descriptions for specific properties of texts in the area of metrics, particularly within 'generative metrics' (see Beaver-Ihwe 1974).

Types or kinds of texts have special pragmatic conditions associated with them. Of special interest in this area are anthropological studies which consider texts as parts of "communicative events" (cf., e.g., Abrahams 1970, Hymes 1971) and attempts to reconstruct genre-types for a historical culture (cf., e.g., Seibert 1967). Such considerations of specific properties lead to the next section.

4   The Analysis of Processes in Participating in Written Works of Art

The development of textlinguistics is intimately connected with the development of pragmatics, and this is also true of the development of textlinguistic approaches to written works of art (cf., e.g., van Dijk 1972 a, pp. 313 ff.). Within the report on the description of specific properties of narrative and dramatic texts it seemed appropriate to point towards a theoretical approach which distinguished types of uses of language from a pragmatic point-of-view (in one specific approach: a game-theoretical development within pragmatics.) The general pragmatic issues cannot be followed up here. However, I do want to point out that as soon as one seriously embarks upon considering the roles of participants with regard to written works of art, this becomes an issue concerning the kind of analysis that a linguist would want to give to written works of art or to their artfulness.

The framework of the concept of text-processing, which I proposed as a useful framework for discussing developments within textlinguistic approaches to written works of art, is a framework which, at least potentially, allows for discussing the description of properties of written works of art as a description which should provide indicators for what participants do with regard to written works of art. The question of poeticalness then becomes a question of what in the linguistic use which participants make of text it is which the proposed indicators of poeticalness actually characterize. The question of describing specific properties of texts then becomes a question of what kind of properties can be surmised as having an influence on what a recipient does with a text and also on what a producer of a text does within the process of producing it.

Thus, it is the relation of any structural description of a text to processes involved in receiving it and processing it onwards into new texts which even within the realm of structural descriptions presents the question of how such structural descriptions relate to sequential properties of texts that are perceived and processed by participants in a dynamic way. As Lotman puts it: "One of the most wide-spread cases of a dual approach to a description of a text is such: We can, having examined a work, extract from it some sort of structure – a hierarchical organization of elements of various levels. However, examining the structure obtained in this manner, we cannot say what was new and unexpected for the reader in the text and what was easily predictable from the very beginning. In this fashion, the problem of the semantic significance of the various elements of the text remains unexplained" (Lotman 1974, 59). Hendricks 1973 also points to the problem of analysing the sequence of sentences in narrative texts. A content-analytical treatment of sequential properties of texts is illustrated in Martindale 1974. Petöfi (1969) distinguishes between "hierarchical" and "linear patterning".

Any approach to view literature or written works of art as a means of communication in a society (most recently, Corti 1976) has to discuss what properties of texts play what role within what is regarded communication via literature (for some basic problems involved see Wienold 1972b, 1973, 1974). Ferrara 1973, for instance, bases his approach to structural descriptions of fiction on the premise that fiction, being part of cultural communication, is "persuasive communication (i.e., of norms for social living)" (Ferrara 1973, 247). Characterizations of literature as "Kommunikatives Handlungsspiel" (Schmidt 1972, 1973, 43 ff.) or "öffentlich-mediale Gemeinschaftshandlung" (Nierlich 1974) point into related directions, however differently elaborated schemes of categorizing the field of study such proposals present.

Time and again, the point has been argued whether and to what extent linguistic analyses can (or should) contribute to interpretation and criticism of written works of art (see, e.g., recently Leventson 1974 and Hendricks 1974). In this paper, it is argued that there is a much more fundamental point to be considered. And this point is what properties of written works of art are involved in the coming about of interpretations of texts, of criticism, of any kind of reworking a given text (initiant text) into a new text (resultant text). This is, of course, mainly a semantic and a pragmatic question. The concept of text processing, then, approaches structural properties of texts within a specific pragmatic framework which aims at describing factors which play a role in what participants do with a literary text. It was pointed out above, that promising approaches to the semantics of literature have taken this approach.

Established procedures of text processing like criticism, interpretation, codification in literary history, didactic uses of texts, then, themselves become an object of study in the study of written works of art, because they can be considered to provide one type of empirical evidence for what participants do with regard to written works of art under specific conditions of text processing (Wienold 1972a, 26f., 146ff.; Wienold 1976a, 1976b, Wienold-Rieser 1976).

In this report, we will be concerned with properties of texts which can be either shown or tentatively suggested to have some bearing on what participants do with regard to texts. There are some empirical studies which enquired into the reactions of participants to texts particularly when a text was presented to them in segments. Also judgments of participants on what they believed the reaction to a text should be were investigated (Smith 1971, Squire 1964, Wilson 1966, Purves 1971, 708ff.). Except for Smith 1971, this research is hardly of a structuralist or linguistic kind.

Phenomena of the participation in a text by a participant like suspense, horror, emotional engagement have been hypothetically related to certain structural properties of texts. These phenomena of an engagement of the participant were structurally related to activities of the recipient in rearranging a narrative text. The sequential text is hypothesized to be rearranged by the recipient according to the order of events related by the sequential text (Wienold 1972a, 82ff., 1972e, 1975). The general need for methodological reflection in this area (Wienold 1972b, 1973, 1974) led to the proposal that one way of studying phenomena of participation in texts was to study relationships between texts which stand in text processing relationship to each other.

An important notion in this context seems to be the notion of condensation. Condensation of a narrative text seems to presuppose a rearrangement as postulated above. Resultant texts of text processing in many cases compress the content of the text in condensates. This has also been assumed in memory research, and van Dijk in discussing his macro-structure hypothesis, interestingly enough, develops a second approach in searching for correlates of macro-structures in condensates (van Dijk 1972a, 133f.; cf. Rieser-Wirrer 1974, 21f., Hendricks 1975, 67f.). In later work, van Dijk has followed the connections between text structures and memory (van Dijk-Kintsch 1975). Hendricks 1973 raised the methodological point of "synopsizing" a narrative text for a *in toto* analysis vs. "structurizing" it for a sequential analysis. Koch and students of his have proposed analyses of what they call "text kernels" with high-degree semantic reduction of texts and which, ideally, are thought of as hypotheses about a high-degree level of a reduction (condensation) of a text by a participant (cf. eg., Koch 1971b, 149ff., Nöth 1976, Hein 1976, 185ff.).

Harweg considers the organisation of higher-order sequence structures like paragraphs and chapters of narrative texts as related to text kernels (Harweg 1974, 102). There is some work on linguistic properties of paragraphs of narrative texts (cf., e.g., Davis 1973, Padučeva 1974). Such phenomena may also be of interest to a theory of text production.

A general conceptual discussion of the problems involved in this area is Koch 1976 b. He presents a categorization of levels and loci of structuring a given text in relationship to structurizations of texts or behaviors which can be related to this text. Research strategies of interest when considering empirical work are also discussed in Koch 1976 b.

Development of empirical methods in this area has been largely dependent on instruments developed in sociology, psychology and educational research (cf., e.g., Groeben 1972; Heuermann et al. 1975). Theoretical developments have also profited from related approaches in literary theory and mass communication research (cf., e.g., Hohendahl 1974; Warning 1975; McQuail 1972).

The concept of text processing assumes that changes of literature in history are related to text processing of higher-order complexity. Structural changes cannot be ascribed just to a collection of texts arranged in some order of periods, but have to be connected to the text processing relationships which process the new meaning of texts into new meaning. A preliminary survey of studies of literary history on this line can be found in Wienold 1971 a, 163 ff., and Wienold 1972 a, 149 ff., 173 ff. Certain properties of formulation of literary texts have been followed as to changes in time affecting them, cf., among others, Kroeber 1971 and Hankiss 1972. Content aspects of change have been experimentally simulated by Martindale 1973 (cf. 1974, 59 f.).

Koch 1976 b also takes the view that what takes places in literary history can only be explained within a very rich model of how participants assign structures to texts and reflect this in other behavior. 'Literature' as a body of texts existing at some time in some society is a product of historical processes over textual structures assigned by participants (see also Lotman 1976).

It is the speakers participating in texts – be it participating as producers or as recipients in a very simplified model – who bring about new meaning. Textlinguistic approaches to written works will be best able to gain insight into the production of new meaning in texts if they elaborate models of participation in texts.

Bibliography

Abercrombie, David. 1965. "Conversation and Spoken Prose," in: id., *Studies in Phonetics and Linguistics* (London: Oxford University Press), pp. 1–19

Abrahams, Roger D. 1970. "A Performance-Centered Approach to Gossip," Man, N.S., V, 290–301

Asmann, Jan. 1973. "Wort und Text: Entwurf einer semantischen Textanalyse," *Göttinger Miszellen,* VI, 9–31

Backus, Joseph M. 1965. "'He Came Into Her Line of Vision Walking Backward': Nonsequential Sequence-Signals in Short Story Openings," *Language Learning,* XV, 67–83

Banfield, Ann. 1973. "Narrative Style and the Grammar of Direct and Indirect Speech," *Foundations of Language,* X, 1–39

148   G. Wienold

Barthes, Roland. 1966. "Introduction à l'analyse structurale des récits," *Communications*, 8, 1–27
Baumgärtner, Klaus. 1965. "Formale Erklärung poetischer Texte", in: Kreuzer, 67–84
Baumgärtner, Klaus. 1969. "Der methodische Stand einer linguistischen Poetik," *Jahrbuch für Internationale Germanistik* I, 15–43
Beaver, J.C. and Ihwe, J.F. (Eds.). 1974. *Generative Metrics = Poetics*, 12
Bierwisch, Manfred. 1965. "Poetik und Linguistik", in: Kreuzer, 49–65
Brainerd, Barron and Neufeldt, Victoria. 1974. "'On Marcus' Methods for the Analysis of the Strategy of the Play," *Poetics*, X, 31–74
Bremond, Claude. 1964. "Le Message narratif", *Communications*, 4, 4–32
Bremond, Claude. 1966. "La logique des possibles narratifs", *Communications*, 8, 60–76
Bremond, Claude. 1968. "Postérité américaine de Propp," *Communications*, 11, 148–164
Bremond, Claude. 1970. "Combinaisons syntaxiques entre fonctions et sequences narratives", in: Greimas, 585–590
Busse, Winfried. 1971/72. "Das literarische Zeichen: Zur glossematischen Theorie der Literatur," in: Ihwe, II, 437–454
Cadora, Frederic J. 1965. "The Teaching of Spoken and Written Arabic," *Language Learning*, XV, 133–136
Chatman, Seymour. 1967. "The Semantics of Style," *Social Science Information*, VI
Chatman, Seymour (Ed.). 1971. *Literary Style: A Symposium* (London and New York: Oxford University Press)
Colby, Benjamin N. 1970. "The Description of Narrative Structures," in: Paul L. Garvin (Ed.), *Cognition: A Multiple View* (New York and Washington: Spartan Books), p. 177–192
Colson, Jacques. 1975. "Contribution to the Description of Style," *Folia Linguistica*, VII, 339–356
Coquet, Jean-Claude. 1973. *Sémiotique littéraire: Contribution à l'analyse sémantique du discours*. (Tours: Mame)
Corti, Maria. 1976. *Principi della communicazione letteraria* (Milan: Bompiani)
Dahl, Jelena and Östen. 1974. "Teun A. van Dijk: Some Aspects of Text Grammars," in: Projektgruppe Textlinguistik Konstanz, pp. 121–134
Dascal, Marcelo and Margalit, Avishai. 1974. "Text Grammars: A Critical View," in: Projektgruppe Textlinguistik Konstanz, pp. 81–120
Davie, D. et al. (Eds.). 1961. *Poétics – Poetyka – Poétika* (The Hague and Warsaw: Mouton)
Davis, Donald R. 1973. "Wantoat Paragraph Structure," *Linguistics*, 110, 5–16
van Dijk, Teun A. 1969. "Sémantique structurale et analyse thématique," *Lingua*, XXIII, 28–53
van Dijk, Teun A., Ihwe, Jens, Petöfi, János S. and Rieser, Hannes. 1972. *Zur Bestimmung narrativer Strukturen auf der Grundlage von Textgrammatiken* (Hamburg: Buske)
van Dijk, Teun A. 1972 a. *Some Aspects of Text Grammars: A Study in Theoretical Linguistics and Poetics* (The Hague and Paris: Mouton)
van Dijk, Teun A. 1972 b. "Aspects d'une théorie générative du texte poétique," in: Greimas, pp. 180–206
van Dijk, Teun A. 1974. "Action, Action Description and Narrative", *New Literary History*, VI, 273–294
Doležel, Lubomír. 1967. "The Typology of the Narrator: Point of View in Fiction," in: *To Honor Roman Jakobson* (The Hague and Paris: Mouton), I, 541–552
Doležel, Lubomír. 1969. "A Framework for the Statistical Analysis of Style," in: Lubomír Doležel and Richard W. Bailey (Eds.), *Statistics and Style* (New York: American Elsevier), pp. 10–25
Doležel, Lubomír. 1971. "Toward a Structural Theory of Content in Prose Fiction," in: Chatman, 95–110
Doležel, Lubomír. 1973 a. "Narrative Composition: A Link Between German and Russian Poetics," in: Stephen Bann and John E. Bowlt (Eds.), *Russian Formalism* (Edinburgh: University Press), pp. 73–84
Doležel, Lubomír. 1973 b. "A Scheme of Narrative Time," in: Roman Jakobson et al. (Eds.), *Slavic Poetics: Essays in Honor of Kyril Taranovsky* (The Hague and Paris: Mouton), pp. 91–98
Dorfman, Eugène. 1969. *The Narreme in the Medieval Romance Epic: An Introduction to Narrative Structures* (Toronto: University Press)

Dundes, Alan. 1962. "From Etic to Emic Units in the Structural Study of Folktales," *Journal of American Folklore,* LXXV, 95–105

Dundes, Alan. 1963. "Structural Typology in Northwestern American Folktales," *Southwestern Journal of Anthropology,* XIX, 121–130

Eaton, Trevor. 1970. "The Foundations of Literary Semantics," *Linguistics,* 62

Eaton, Trevor. 1972. *Theoretical Semics* (The Hague: Mouton)

Eco, Umberto. 1966. "James Bond: Une combinatoire narrative," *Communications,* 8, 77–93

Ehrmann, Jacques. 1970. "Structures of Exchange in Cinna," in: Michael Lane (Ed.), *Structuralism: A Reader* (London: Cape), pp. 222–247

Enkvist, Nils Erik, et al. 1964. *Linguistics and Style* (London: Oxford University Press)

Enkvist, Nils Erik. 1973. *Linguistic Stylistics* (The Hague and Paris: Mouton)

Feinberg, Lawrence E. 1973. "The Grammatical Structure of Boris Pasternak's *Gamlet,*" in: Roman Jakobson et al. (Eds.), *Slavic Poetics: Essays in Honor of Kiril Taranovsky* (The Hague and Paris: Mouton), pp. 98–124

Ferguson, Charles C. 1959. "Diglossia," *Word,* XV, 325–340

Ferrara, Fernando. 1973. "Theory and Model for the Structural Analysis of Fiction," *New Literary History,* V, 245–268

Fónagy, Ivan and Judith. 1971. "Ein Meßwert der dramatischen Spannung," *Zeitschrift für Linguistik und Literaturwissenschaft,* I, 4, 71–98

Foulkes, Peter A. 1975. *The Search for Literary Meanning: A Semiotic Approach to the Problem of Interpretation in Education* (Bern: Lang)

Fowler, Roger (Ed.). 1966. *Essays on Style and Language* (London: Routledge and Kegan Paul)

Garvin, Paul L. (Ed.). 1964. *A Prague School Reader on Esthetics, Literary Structure and Style* (Washington, D.C.: Georgetown University Press)

Göttner, Heide. 1973. *Logik der Interpretation* (München: Fink)

Goodlad, J.S.R. 1971. *A Sociology of Popular Drama* (London: Heinemann)

Greimas, A.J. 1966. "Eléments pour une théorie de l'interprétation du récit mythique," *Communications,* 8, 28–59

Greimas, A.J. 1967. "The Relationship Between Structural Linguistics and Poetics," *International Social Science Journal,* XIX, 8–16

Greimas, A.J. et al. (Eds.). 1970. *Sign, Language, Culture* (The Hague and Paris: Mouton)

Greimas, A.J. (Ed.). 1972. *Essais de sémiotique poétique* (Paris: Larousse)

Groeben, Norbert. 1972. *Literaturpsychologie* (Stuttgart [etc.]: Kohlhammer)

Gülich, Elisabeth and Raible, Wolfgang (Eds.). 1972. *Textsorten: Differenzierungskriterien aus linguistischer Sicht* (Frankfurt/M.: Athenäum)

Hankiss, Elemér. 1972. "The Structure of Literary Evolution," *Poetics,* 5, 40–66

Harweg, Roland. 1968a. *Pronomina und Textkonstitution* (München: Fink)

Harweg, Roland. 1968b. "Textanfänge in geschriebener und in gesprochener Sprache," *Orbis* XVII, 343–388

Harweg, Roland. 1974. "Textlinguistik", in: Walter A. Koch (Hrsg.), *Perspektiven der Linguistik* II (Stuttgart: Kröner), pp. 88–116

Harweg, Roland. 1975. "Präsupposition und Textrekonstruktion: Zur Erzählsituation in Thomas Mann *Tristan* aus textlinguistischer Sicht," in: Michael Schecker und Peter Wunderli (Hrsg.) *Textgrammatik: Beiträge zum Problem der Textualität* (Tübingen: Niemeyer), pp. 166–185

Hayes, Curtis W. 1966. "A Study in Prose Style: Edward Gibbon and Ernest Hemingway," *Texas Studies in Literature and Language,* VII, 371–386

Hein, Norbert. 1976a. "Ansatz zur strukturellen Dramenanalyse," in: Koch, 119–213

Hendricks, William O. 1973. "Methodology of Narrative Structural Analysis," *Semiotics,* VII, 163–184

Hendricks, William O. 1974. "The Relation between Linguistics and Literary Studies," *Poetics,* 11, 5–22

Hendricks, William O. 1975. "Style and the Structure of Literary Discourse" in: *Style and Text: Studies Presented to Nils Erik Enkvist* (Stockholm: Språkförlaget Skriptor, 1975)), pp. 63–74

Hertzler, Joyce O. 1965. *A Sociology of Language* (New York: Random House)

Heuermann, Hartmut, Hühn, Peter and Röttger, Brigitte (Eds.). 1975. *Literarische Rezeption: Beiträge zur Theorie des Text-Leser-Verhältnisses und seiner empirischen Erforschung* (Paderborn: Schöningh)

Hill, Archibald A. 1951. "Towards a Literary Analysis," in: *English Studies in Honor of James Southall Wilson* (Charlottesville, Va.), pp. 147–165

Hill, Archibald A. 1955. "An Analysis of *The Windhover:* An Experiment in Structural Method," *Publications of the Modern Language Association,* LXX, 968–978

Hirsch, Jr., E.D. 1967. *Validity in Interpretation* (New Haven: Yale University Press)

Hobsbaum, Philip. 1970. *A Theory of Communication* (London: Macmillan)

Hohendahl, Peter Uwe (Ed.). 1974. *Sozialgeschichte und Wirkungsästhetik* (Frankfurt a.M.: Fischer-Athenäum)

Hymes, Dell. 1971. "The Contribution of Folklore to Sociolinguistic Research," *Journal of American Folklore,* LXXXIV, 42–50

Ihwe, Jens. (Ed.). 1971/72. *Literaturwissenschaft und Linguistik: Ergebnisse und Perspektiven,* 3 vols., (Frankfurt a.M.: Athenäum)

Ihwe, Jens. 1972a. *Linguistik in der Literaturwissenschaft: Zur Entwicklung einer modernen Theorie der Literaturwissenschaft* (München: Bayerischer Schulbuchverlag)

Ihwe, Jens. 1972b. "On the Foundation of a General Theory of Narrative Structure," *Poetics,* 3, 5–14

Ihwe, Jens (Ed.). 1972/73. *Literaturwissenschaft und Linguistik: Eine Auswahl. Texte zur Theorie der Literaturwissenschaft,* 2 vols. (Frankfurt a.M.: Fischer-Athenäum)

Ihwe, Jens. 1973. "Aspects empiriques et aspects théoretiques d'un modèle de littérarité basé sur un modèle de la communication verbale," in: Charles Bouazis et al., *Essais de la théorie du texte* (Paris: Larousse), pp. 51–78

Jakobson, Roman. 1960. "Linguistics and Poetics," in: Sebeok, 350–377

Jakobson, Roman. 1965. "Poesie der Grammatik und Grammatik der Poesie," in: Kreuzer, 21–32

Jakobson, Roman. 1967. *"Vocabulorum constructio in Dante's sonnet Se vedi li occhi miei,"* Studi Danteschi XLIII

Jakobson, Roman. 1973. "Letter to Haroldo de Campos on Martin Codax's Poetic Texture," in: Stephen Bann and John E. Bowlt (Eds.), *Russian Formalism* (Edinburgh: University Press), pp. 20–25

Jakobson, Roman and Jones, L.G. 1970. *Shakespeare's Verbal Art in 'Th'expense of spirit'* (The Hague: Mouton)

Jakobson, Roman and Lévi-Strauss, Claude. 1962. "'Les Chats' de Charles Baudelaire," *L'Homme,* II, 5–21

Jansen, Steen. 1968. "Esquisse d'une théorie de la forme dramatique," *Langages,* 12, 71–93

Johansen, Svend. 1949. "La notion de signe dans la glossématique et dans l'esthétique," *Recherches structurales* (= Travaux du Cercle linguistique de Copenhague V) (Copenhagen), pp. 288–303

Kavanagh, James F. and Mattingly, G. (Eds.). 1972. *Language by Ear and Eye: The Relationships between Speech and Reading* (Cambridge, Mass., and London: M.I.T. Press)

van Kesteren, Aloysius und Schmid, Herta (Eds.). 1975. *Moderne Dramentheorie* (Kronberg/Ts.: Scriptor)

Kintsch, Walter and van Dijk, Teun A. 1975. "Comment on se rappelle et on résume des histoires," *Langages,* 40, 98–116

Kloepfer, Rolf. 1975. *Poetik und Linguistik: Semiotische Instrumente* (München: Fink)

Koch, Walter A. 1966. *Recurrence and a Three-Modal Approach to Poetry* (The Hague: Mouton)

Koch, Walter A. 1968. "Linguistische Analyse und Strukturen der Poetizität," *Orbis,* XVII, 5–22

Koch, Walter A. 1971. *Taxologie des Englischen* (München: Fink)

Koch, Walter A. (Ed.). 1972a. *Strukturelle Textanalyse – Analyse du récit – Discourse Analysis* (Hildesheim und New York: Olms)

Koch, Walter A. 1972b. "He explained his couldn't, he rhymed his could," in: Koch 1972a, 429–461

Koch, Walter A. 1973. *Das Textem. Gesammelte Aufsätze zur Semantik des Texts* (Hildesheim und New York: Olms)

Koch, Walter A. (Hrsg.). 1976a. *Textsemiotik und strukturelle Rezeptionstheorie: Soziosemiotische Ansätze zur Beschreibung verschiedener Zeichensysteme innerhalb der Literatur* (Hildesheim und New York: Olms)

Koch, Walter A. 1976b. "Ontologiethese und Relativitätsthese für eine Textlinguistik," in: Koch 1976a, 1–38

Krause, Ulrich. 1971. "Ästhetische Wertung als Aggregation," *Zeitschrift für Linguistik und Literaturwissenschaft*, 4, 99–114

Kreuzer, Helmut (Ed.). 1965; ²1967. *Mathematik und Dichtung: Versuche zur Frage einer exakten Literaturwissenschaft* (München: Nymphenburger)

Kristeva, Julia. 1968. "La productivité dite texte," *Communications*, 11

Kristeva, Julia. 1972. "Quelques problèmes de sémiotique littéraire à propos d'un texte de Mallarmé: *Un coup de dés*", in: Greimas 1972, pp. 208–234

Kroeber, Karl. 1971. *Styles in Fictional Structure. The Art of Jane Austin, Charlotte Bronte, George Eliot* (Princeton, N. J.: Princeton University Press)

Kuroda, S.-Y. 1974. "On Grammar and Narration," in: Christian Rohrer and Nicolas Ruwet (Eds.), *Actes du Colloque Franco-Allemand de Grammaire Transformationelle*, 2 vols. (Tübingen: Niemeyer), II, 165–173

Labov, William and Waletzky, Joshua. 1967. "Narrative Analysis: Oral Versions of Personal Experience," in: June Helm (Ed.). *Essays in the Verbal and Visual Arts* (Seattle and London: American Ethnological Society/University of Washington Press), pp. 12–44

Labov, William. 1972. *Language in the Inner City: Studies in the Black English Vernacular* (Philadelphia: University of Pennsylvania Press)

Leech, G. N. 1966. "Linguistics and the Figures of Rhetoric," In: Fowler, 135–156

Leventson, E. A. 1974. "A Scheme for the Interrelation of Linguistic Analysis and Poetry Criticism," *Linguistics*, 129, 29–47

Levin, Samuel R. 1962; ²1964. *Linguistic Structures in Poetry* (The Hague: Mouton)

Levin, Samuel R. 1963. "On Automatic Production of Poetic Sequences," *Texas Studies in Literature and Language*, V, 138–146

Levitt, Paul M. 1971. *A Structural Approach to the Analysis of Drama* (The Hague and Paris: Mouton)

Levý Jiři. 1971/72. "Generative Poetik", in: Ihwe, II, 554–567

de Lillo, A. 1971. "L'analisi del contenuto qualitativa," in: A. de Lillo (Ed.). *L'Analisi de contenuto: Dalla teoria dell'informazione allo strutturalismo* (Bologna: Il Mulino), pp. 123–192

Lotman, Jurij M. 1974. "On Some Principal Difficulties in the Structural Description of a Text," *Linguistics*, 121, 57–93

Lotman, Jurij M. 1976. "The Content and Structure of the Concept of 'Literature'", *PTL*, I, 339–356

Lüthe, Rudolf. 1974. "Fiktionalität als konstitutives Element literarischer Rezeption," *Orbis Litterarum*, XXIX, 1–15

Maranda, Elli Köngäs and Maranda, Pierre. 1971. *Structural Models in Folklore and Transformational Essays* (den Haag und Paris: Mouton)

Marcus, Solomon. 1971. "Ein mathematisch-linguistisches Dramenmodell," *Zeitschrift für Literaturwissenschaft und Linguistik* 1/2, 139–152

Markiewicz, Henryk. 1972. "The Limits of Literature," *New Literary History*, IV, 5–14

Martindale, C. 1973. "An experimental simulation of literary change," *Journal of Personality and Social Psychology*, XXV, 319–326

Martindale, C. 1974. "The semantic significance of spatial movement in narrative verse: patterns of regressive imagery in the *Divine Comedy*," in: Mitchell, 57–64

McQuail, Denis (Ed.). 1972. *Sociology of Mass Communication Selected Readings* (Harmondsworth: Penguin)

Meschonnic, H. 1970. *Pour la poétique* (Paris: Gallimard)

Mitchell, J. L. (Ed.). 1974. *Computers in the Humanities* (Edinburgh: University Press)

Moles, Abraham A. 1966. "Aspect temporel de la perception de l'œuvre picturale," *Sciences de l'art: Annales de l'Institut d'Esthéthique et de Sciences de l'Art*, III, 136–145

152   G. Wienold

Nierlich, Edmund. 1973. "Pragmatik in der Literaturwissenschaft?", *Zeitschrift für Literaturwissenschaft und Linguistik,* III, 9/10, 9–32
Nierlich, Edmund. 1974. "Beschreibung der Kompetenz zur öffentlich-medialen Gemeinschaftshandlung: Ein Lehrziel für die literaturwissenschaftliche Ausbildung der Fremdsprachenlehrer," *Linguistik und Didaktik V,* 83–97
Nöth, Winfried. 1976. "Zur Textkernstruktur in englischen Gedichten," in: Koch, 39–118
Ohmann, Richard. 1964. "Generative Grammar and the Concept of Literary Style," *Word,* XX, 423–439
Ohmann, Richard. 1968. "A Linguistic Appraisal of Victorian Style," in: George Leviné and William Madden (Eds.). *The Art of Victorian Prose* (New York: Oxford University Press), pp. 289–313
Padučeva, E. V. 1974. "On the Structure of the Paragraph," *Linguistics,* 131, 49–58
Pagnini, Marcello. 1970. "Per una semiologia del teatro classico," *Strumenti Critici,* 12, 121–140
Pêcheux, Michel. 1967. "Analyse de contenu et théorie du discours," *Bulletin du Centre d'études et de recherches en psychotechnique,* XVI, 211–227
Petöfi, János S. 1967. "On the Structural Linguistic Analysis of Poetic Works of Art," *Computational Linguistics,* VI, 53–82; also in Koch 1972 a, 400–428
Petöfi, János S. 1968. "Notes on the Semantic Interpretation of Verbal Works of Art," *Computational Linguistics,* VII, 79–105
Petöfi, János S. 1969. "On the Linear Patterning of Verbal Works of Art," *Computational Linguistics,* VIII, 37–63
Petöfi, János S. 1971. *Transformationsgrammatiken und eine ko-textuelle Texttheorie: Grundfragen und Konzeptionen* (Frankfurt a. M.: Athenäum)
Petöfi, János S. 1972. "On the Syntactico-Semantic Organization of Text-Structures," *Poetics,* 3, 56–99
Posner, Roland. 1969. "Strukturalismus in der Gedichtinterpretation: Textdeskription und Rezeptionsanalyse am Beispiel von Baudelaires 'Les Chats'", in: Ihwe 1972/73, I, 136–178 (first in: *Sprache im technischen Zeitalter,* 29 (1969), 27–58)
Projektgruppe Textlinguistik Konstanz (Hrsg.). 1974. *Probleme und Perspektiven der neueren textgrammatischen Forschung* I (Hamburg: Buske)
Propp, Vladimir. 1928. *Morphology of the Folktale* (Philadelphia: American Folklore Society 1958; original Russian edition, 1928)
Purves, Alan C. "Evaluation of Learning in Literature," in: Benjamin S. Bloom et al. (Eds.). 1971. *Handbook of Formative and Summative Evaluation of Student Learning* (New York [etc.]: McGraw-Hill)
Rastier, François. 1972. "Systématique des isotopies," in: Greimas, 80–106
Rieser, Hannes und Wirrer, Jan. 1974. "Zu Teun van Dijks 'Some Aspects of Text Grammars': Ein Beitrag zur Textgrammatik- und Literaturdiskussion" in: Projektgruppe Textlinguistik Konstanz, pp. 1–80
Riffaterre, Michael. 1959. "Criteria for Style Analysis," *Word,* XVI, 154–174
Riffaterre, Michael. 1960. "Stylistic Context," *Word,* XVI, 207–218
Riffaterre, Michael. 1964. "L'étude stylistique des formes littéraires conventionelles," *The French Review,* XXXVIII, 3–14
Riffaterre, Michael. 1970/71. "The Stylistic Approach to Literary History," *New Literary History,* II, 39–55
Riffaterre, Michael. 1971. *Essais de stylistiques structurale* (Paris: Flammarion)
Saporta, Sol and Sebeok, Thomas A. 1959. "Linguistics and Content-Analysis," in: Ithiel de Sola Pool (Ed.), *Trends in Content Analysis* (Urbana, Ill.: University of Illinois Press), pp. 131–150
Schmid, Herta. 1973. *Strukturalistische Dramentheorie:* Semantische Analyse von Čechov's 'Ivanov' und 'Der Kirschgarten'. (Kronberg/Ts.: Scriptor)
Schmidt, Siegfried J. 1972. "Ist 'Fiktionalität' eine linguistische oder eine texttheoretische Kategorie?", in: Gülich-Raible, 59–80
Schmidt, Siegfried J. 1973. *Texttheorie: Probleme einer Linguistik der sprachlichen Kommunikation* (München: Fink)

Schmidt, Siegfried J. 1974. *Wissenschaftstheoretische Probleme einer theoretisch-empirischen Literaturwissenschaft,* Bielefelder Papiere zur Linguistik und Literaturwissenschaft 2.

Sebeok, Thomas A. (Ed.). 1960. *Style in Language.* (Cambridge, Mass.: M. I. T, Press)

Seibert, Peter. 1967. *Die Charakteristik: Untersuchungen zu einer altägyptischen Sprechsitte und ihren Ausprägungen in Folklore und Literatur* I (Wiesbaden: Harassowitz)

Smith, Carlota S. 1971. "Sentences in Discourse: An Analysis of a Discourse by Bertrand Russell," *Journal of Linguistics,* VII, 213–235

Smith, Robert Jerome. 1971. "The Structure of Esthetic Response," *Journal of American Folklore,* LXXXIV

Souriau, Etienne. 1950. *Les deux cent milles situations dramatiques* (Paris: Flammarion)

Squire, James R. 1964. *The Responses of Adolescents While Reading Four Short Stories,* NCTE Research No. 2 (Champaign, Ill.: National Council of Teachers of English)

Stempel, Wolf-Dieter. 1971. "Möglichkeiten einer Darstellung der Diachronie in narrativen Texten," in: id. (Ed.), *Beiträge zur Textlinguistik* (München: Fink), pp. 53–78

Stempel, Wolf-Dieter. 1972. "Zur formalistischen Theorie der poetischen Sprache," in: id. (Ed.), *Texte der russischen Formalisten* II (München: Fink), pp. IX–LIII

Stempel, Wolf-Dieter. 1973. "Erzählung, Beschreibung und der historische Diskurs", in: Reinhart Koselleck and Wolf-Dieter Stempel (Eds.), *Geschichte: Ereignis und Erzählung* (München: Fink), pp. 325–346

Striedter, Jurij. 1969. "Zur formalistischen Theorie der Prosa und der literarischen Evolution," in: id. (Ed.), *Texte der russischen Formalisten* I (München: Fink), pp. IX–LXXXIII

Taber, Ch. Russel. 1966. *The Structure of Sango Narrative* (Hartford Studies in Linguistics 17), 2 parts (Hartford, Conn.)

Thorne, James Peter. 1965. "Stylistics and Generative Grammars," *Journal of Linguistics,* I, 49–59

Todorov, Tzvetan. 1966. "Les catégories du récit littéraire," *Communications,* 8, 125–131

Todorov, Tzvetan. 1967. *Littérature et signification* (Paris: Larousse)

Trabant, Jürgen. 1970. Zur Semiotik des literarischen Kunstwerkes: Glossematik und Literaturtheorie (München: Fink)

Tusseau, Jean-Pierre and Wittmann, Henri. 1975. "Règles de narration dans les chansons de geste et le roman courtois," *Folia Linguistica,* VII, 401–412

Vachek, Josef. 1948. "Written Language and Printed Language," *Recueil de linguistique de Bratislava,* I, 67–75

Vachek, Josef. 1973. *Written Language: General Problems* and Problems of English (The Hague and Paris: Mouton)

Warning, Rainer (Ed.). 1975. *Rezeptionsästhetik: Theorie und Praxis* (München: Fink)

Werth, Paul. 1976. "Roman Jakobson's Verbal Analysis of Poetry," *Journal of Linguistics,* XII, 21–73

Wienold, Götz. 1971. *Formulierungstheorie – Poetik – Strukturelle Literaturgeschichte: Am Beispiel der altenglischen Dichtung* (Frankfurt a. M.: Athenäum)

Wienold, Götz. 1972a. *Semiotik der Literatur* (Frankfurt a. M.: Athenäum)

Wienold, Götz. 1972b. "Empirie in der Erforschung literarischer Kommunikation," in: Ihwe 1972/73, I, 311–322

Wienold, Götz. 1972c. "Die Konstruktion der poetischen Formulierung in Gedichten Paul Celans," in: Koch 1972a, 208–225

Wienold, Götz. 1972d. "*Deor:* Über Offenheit und Auffüllung von Texten," *Sprachkunst,* III (1972), 285–297

Wienold, Götz. 1972e. "On Deriving Models of Narrative Analysis from Models of Discourse Analysis," *Poetics,* 3 (1972), 15–28

Wienold, Götz. 1973. "Experimental Research on Literature: Its Need and Appropriateness," *Poetics,* 7, 22–85

Wienold, Götz. 1974. "Ein Konzept für die Erforschung literarischer Kommunikation," in: Peter Hartmann and Hannes Rieser (Eds.), *Angewandte Textlinguistik I* (Hamburg: Buske), pp. 180–196

Wienold, Götz. 1975. "Aufgaben der Textsortenspezifikation und Möglichkeiten der experimen-

154   G. Wienold

tellen Überprüfung," in: Heuermann et al. 1975, 50–71 (earlier Version in: Gülich-Raible 1972)

Wienold, Götz. 1976 a. "The Concept of Text Processing, the Criticism of Literature and Some Uses of Literature in Education," in: A. Peter Foulkes (Ed.), The Uses of Criticism (Bern: Lang), pp. 111–131

Wienold, Götz. 1976 b. "Semantic Relations Between Sentences and Between Texts," *Folia Linguistica*, IX, 37–44

Wienold, Götz and Rieser, Hannes. 1976. "Vorüberlegungen zur Rolle des Konzepts der Textverarbeitung beim Aufbau einer empirischen Sprachtheorie," Kolloquium on "Die Rolle der Grammatik in den automatisierten und nichtautomatisierten textverarbeitenden Disziplinen" ed. János S. Petöfi (to appear)

Wilson, James R. 1966. *Responses of College Freshmen to Three Novels,* NCTE Research Report No. 7 (Champaign, Ill.: National Council of Teachers of English)

Žolkovskij, Aleksandr K. and Ščeglov, Jurij. 1972/73. "Die strukturelle Poetik ist eine generative Poetik," in: Ihwe I, 245–270.

French Structuralist Views on Narrative Grammar

Ernst Ulrich Grosse
Universität Freiburg

1 Introduction

This study will be limited to narrative research, for it is here that the most important contributions of French structuralism to textlinguistics are to be found. The continued prevalence of interest in the narrative has historical reasons:

1° the reception of Propp in France,
2° Lévi-Strauss' pioneer work,
3° the supposition – inspired principally by Benveniste[1] – that the universe beyond the sentence limit consists only of either narrative (Fr. récit, Benveniste: histoire) or discourse (Fr. discours) or transitional phenomena, so that, according to the last criterion, narrative research was looked upon as if it were an exploration of half of the textual world.

But two reasons should also be mentioned which seem "inherent" to narrative texts as research objects, at least from the point of view of French structuralists: First, in all ideologies, there are always oppositions of values, just as in human reality where non-verbal and verbal behaviour are directed by unconscious or conscious ideologies. These oppositions of values can easily become a kind of pre-story, a kind of non-elaborated story (Nef 1976: 58–66). Thus many non-narrative text types or even many proverbs may be regarded as *precursors* of narrative texts (Greimas 1970: 164)[2]. Secondly, and in connexion with the above conception, narrative texts appear as the only complete realization of all the tendencies to "narrativization". Therefore, the narrative system is regarded by French semiologists as the most *complex* one among the semiotic systems, and this point of view stimulates special interest (Stierle 1973: 113).

Remark: There has been much superficial discussion of French structuralism, especially in the field of narrative research. It has been my aim to investigate the interrelations of the more fundamental arguments made by the above mentioned authors. The real background of research interests must be reconstructed in the case of many French structuralists (cf. Stierle 1973: 127). I have tried to show that the concentration on narrative texts has conceptual reasons in addition to the historical ones of research development. So the greater complexity of, e.g., lyrical poetry – a greater complexity from another point of view – need not be discussed here.

---

[1] See Communications 8, 1966, 20 (Barthes), 126 (Todorov), 159 (Genette), with some modifications of Benveniste's conception, and Adam/Goldenstein 1976: 302–313.
[2] Consequently, Greimas points out the "polemic" character of narrative.

1.1   Macro-structures and text grammar

Up to now, the main interest of French structuralism concerning the narrative has been in macro-structural research. No doubt, this domain is intermediate between textlinguistics and general semiotics. But one could also emphasize along with van Dijk (1972: 17) that a *text grammar* must contain both "the rules for the derivation of textual macro-structures", which have "an abstract semantic character" and specified rules for textual "micro-structures" (or "surface structures"). From this point of view, macro-structural rules form a necessary part of textlinguistics.

1.2   Extension of the conceptual framework

Whereas van Dijk first tended to identify macro-structure with deep structure, micro-structure with surface structure, the following distinctions seem to be more adequate for French semiological conceptions (cf. 1° and 2° below) and, thus, more adequate for my exposé on French contributions to a comprehensive narrative grammar:

1° macro-deep-structure, containing, e.g., a series, provided with a least one actant, of 'eventuality' + 'performance' + 'result' (cf. 2.2 and 3.1),

2° macro-surface-structure, with, e.g., extinction of the second element (cf. Bremond 1973: 332 and also van Dijk's own reflection in Chabrol 1973: 205),

3° in an intermediate level: micro-deep-structure, e.g. presence (and in description: representation) of the "acteurs" on a level before pronominalization in what Harweg called an "emic text", i.e. on a level where the actants which belong to the series 'eventuality' ± 'performance' + 'result' have already been transformed into "acteurs" (see 2.3), yet without pronominalization,

4° micro-surface-structure, e.g., in an "etic text" according to Harweg (opposition "emic" vs "etic": cf. phonemic vs phonetic, etc., see Harweg's contribution in this volume).

Without a doubt still more intermediate levels between textual deep structure (= 1°), macro-surface-structure (= 2°) and micro-surface-structure (= 4°, in the so-called "macro-syntactical" succession of pronominalization, tenses etc.) would have to be introduced into such a conception.

1.3   Necessary restrictions

Wishing to inform the reader about current trends in French narrative research, I had to choose between an encyclopedian style with a large number of terms and references and a "selective" style in which the essentials are stressed and supplemented by examples. I have chosen the latter procedure.

1.4   Todorov, Kristeva, Genette

Because of my choice concerning the procedure, I shall refer only briefly to these authors. General references: As to Todorov, Kristeva and Genette, cf. Lange 1975: 279–325, where, in addition to general information, a good bibliography for each author can be found. Furthermore, cf. Coquet 1976 and also (probably, for the book is not yet published and thus unknown to me) Gülich/Raible 1977. Bremond 1973: 103–127 contains a very informative discussion of Todorov's "Grammaire du Décaméron" (1969). Todorov and Genette are editors of the literary review "Poétiques" (Paris, Seuil). Julia Kristeva is one of the editors of the "avant-garde" review "Tel quel"(Paris, Seuil).

1.5   Reviews

There are many other reviews where structuralist or semiological contributions are being published, among them "Communications" (Paris, Seuil), "Langages" (Paris, Didier/Larousse), "Langue française" (Paris, Larousse), "Littérature" (Paris, Larousse), "Pratiques" (2 bis, rue des Bénédictins, F 57000 Metz), which has become important. But nearly all French linguistic, literary or "semiotical" reviews could be enumerated here. Outside France, "Poetics", "Semiotica" (both: The Hague, Mouton) and the various series of the "Documents de travail et pré-publications" (Centro internazionale di Semiotica e di Linguistica, Università di Urbino, Italia), with studies in French or English, many of them inspired by Greimas' work, are particularly important. Finally, with two volumes p.a., there is an interesting newcomer: "Linguistique et sémiologie" (U.E.R.Sciences du Langage, Université Lyon II, 86 rue Pasteur, F 69007 Lyon).

1.6   "Semiology" and "semiotics"

In France, there are quite a few linguists who – referring to the term "semiology" – claim to be de Saussure's true successors and the faithful trustees of his heritage (cf., e.g., George Mounin's "Introduction à la sémiologie", Paris, Editions de Minuit, 1970). Other semiologists claim to represent a more independent development, though partly founded on de Saussure's program, by using the term "semiotics" (Benveniste, Lévi-Strauss, Greimas and Barthes founded the "Cercle sémiotique de Paris" in 1969). For example, Coquet (in Arrivé/Coquet 1973: 3) attributes the area of "signification systems" to "semiotics" and the domain of "sign systems" to the Saussurean "semiology". However, this is only an inclination, and I shall use "semiology" as a cover word, as many French linguists do.

2   Common hypotheses in French narrative macro-structure research

In French narrative research, there is still a great diversity of conceptions, procedures and terms. Different methods have been worked out by Greimas, Bremond, Barthes and Todorov, to mention only the most important "initiators". However some fundamental common traits may be discerned:
(1) the distinction between an *immanent,* "pre-linguistic" level and an *exterior* level in narrative texts,
(2) the concepts of *actants* and of *function*-types; these concepts form a pair in models of the immanent (or an intermediate) level,
(3) the attention paid to *sequences* (consisting of more than one actant-function-group) and to the syntagmatic linking of sequences. Besides these three traits indicated in a very general manner by Bremond (1973: 102), there is still another one:

(4) a slowly increasing affinity to generative linguistics; thus a designation like"structural-generative semiology" would now become more suitable than, say, "structuralism" (see 2.1)

2.1 Distinction between "immanent" and "exterior" level

Generally, this distinction corresponds to the pair "deep structure" – "surface structure" in generative linguistics (see restrictions in 1.2). However, as the latter distinction concerns the syntactic domain, there is a decisive difference. From the French structural-generative point of view the different models for deep structure bases worked out by generative linguists can all be situated in a stage of development which is quite near the actual manifestation on the surface-level. Surely this stage must be passed through in the process of "signifiance" (Kristeva)[3] if the use of a "verbal" language as an instrument (and not a non-verbal one) is made in this activity of sense-imprinting. But this stage is so close to the surface-level that it is considered less important. Actual narrative texts (manifestations on the exterior level – linguistic, non-linguistic or mixed ones such as films and comics) are generated by single or repeated selections of rules and units belonging to the immanent level.

The following terms correspond more or less to this distinction between an immanent and an exterior level:

Greimas: "niveau immanent" (immanent in all narrative and also some non-narrative manifestations) vs "niveau apparent" (where "apparent" has two meanings, not only the denotative one of phenomenon, but also the connotative one of deceptive appearance, cf. Greimas 1970: 158 and cover text; also Bremond 1973: 89–90),

Bremond: "logique du récit" (behind the "raconté") vs "racontant", see Bremond 1973, passim,

Barthes: "fonctions" (and other terms) vs "narration", already mentioned in Barthes 1966: 6[4].

2.1.1 Immanent level

This level is postulated as containing not only universal structures of the narrative, but also universal virtual structures of human thinking (Greimas 1970: 160–164, cf. also 137–138, Greimas' formulations in this respect, however, are always cautiously expressed) or of human behaviour (Bremond 1973: 331, though Bremond emphasizes the freedom of the author: narrative mimesis

---

[3] See Coquet 1976 § 3.1.

[4] To avoid confusion, Todorov and Kristeva will be referred to here. *Todorov's* distinction between "histoire" and "discours" is close to the opposition "plot" (fable) vs "sujet" in Russian formalism. But there is no clear conceptual background corresponding to Greimas' "niveau immanent" or to Bremond's "logique du récit" (see the reasons in Bremond 1973: 126–128). As to *Kristeva,* surely, "phéno-texte" more or less corresponds to the second terms in Greimas, Bremond, Barthes and Todorov. But "géno-texte" is quite another concept (see the discussion in J. C. Coquet: "Sémiotiques", in Langages 31, sept. 1973, 6–8).

"regenerates" and does not "imitate"). Thus, in 1966, Bremond (p. 76) had already pointed out that "la sémiologie du récit tire sa possibilité et sa fécondité de son enracinement dans une anthropologie"[5]. In literary critiques the project of a universal narrative grammar is generally considered an illusion (e.g., in Hardt 1976: 65–90). This is a matter of opinion in the present stage of research. What I have tried to emphasize is that some French semiologists even lean towards anthropological universals which are not limited to elements within a supposed human *narrative* competence.

2.1.2 An intermediate stratum

Between the "immanent level" and the external one, there is a less abstract, thus an already more concrete stratum, which I here refer to as the stratum of archimodels[6] (cover-models, to be compared with cover words). These archimodels are the results of the research of invariants[7] in a corpus of narrative texts, e.g., a corpus constituted by some variants of the myth of Oedipus (Lévi-Strauss, cf. Greimas 1970: 118 and Hardt 1976: 71–74). However, in the last few years "archimodels" have become rare. French semiologists often refer now directly to the immanent level.

2.1.3 Exterior level

There is no well-elaborated theory pertaining to the passage from the immanent and the archimodel level to the exterior level of manifestation. Actants appear now as "acteurs" (cf. 2.3), function-types as functions (cf. 2.4), and indices are common to both, although it is not clear where they come from (see 4).

Whereas the "exterior" level was considered less important in the beginning stages of French semiology, a counter-current is now appearing. For instance, in 1966, Barthes (p. 2) proclaimed and firmly defended a *deductive* procedure in structural analysis of the narrative. It was, however, not a deductive procedure but a long phase of prevailing theoretical work that followed. But now, decisive steps in model construction have been made. A "return to the sources" (and, thus to the textual exterior level) can be ascertained. Barthes himself was a

---

[5] Todorov, too, tends towards a universal narrative grammar, but without any suppositions to a correspondent non-narrativized human reality. See Bremond 1973: 127–128.

[6] In Greimas 1970: 163, the archimodels are called "constitutional" or "taxonomic" models. They are considered here to be common value structures of an ideological and cultural "micro-universe" which is incarnated, on the exterior level, in all the texts (or "textual variants") of a coherent corpus. Cf. also 5.1–5.4. Actants and function-types were always regarded as elements of the immanent level. Yet, according to Greimas 1970: 135–230, they should be looked upon as elements of a second intermediate level, emerging from a first intermediate level, that of archimodels.

[7] Here, the concept of invariants does not include the notion that each "invariant" element is to be found in each text of the corpus. If some oppositions are discernible in nearly every text, these oppositions will be regarded as pertinent and as basic for the archimodel. Thus, the fact that one term of an opposition is lacking in, say, text D, is not regarded as a decisive obstacle. – In Greimas' "school", the general trend is towards two oppositions which form a correlation. Cf. 5.1–5.4.

predecessor here (e.g., in a personal lecture and "re-writing" of Balzac's short novel "Sarrasine", Barthes 1970). Others – including Greimas 1976 – have followed. But theoretical studies also continue (e.g., in Greimas 1976 a). Thus French semiologists of the present day are proving the adequacy of their models and adjusting or transforming them (see 2.3.1–2.3.3. as an example).

2.2   Actants and functions

2.2.1   Different linguistic bases

Although Propp pointed out seven action domains besides his list of functions, neither a structured function system nor a structured actant system could be found in Propp's work. Greimas, generally considered as a pioneer of French systematisations of *functions* and *actants,* was also the first to "provide" this distinction with a linguistic base. With some modifications he transferred Tesnière's (micro-structural) valence grammar to (macro-structural) narrative grammar[8]. Thus, Greimas' distinction between function and actants corresponds to Tesnière's distinction – and also hierarchical relation – between verb and actants. Good examples of this may be found in Coquet 1974: 107.

For Bremond, the distinction between actants and functions in narrative grammar is based on the relation subject-predicate, not only in his own works, but in all works of French semiologists (Bremond 1973: 102). However, he later on departs from the ternary model "agent"-"processus"-"patient" (1973: 134). His linguistic sources are evident, despite the fact that they are not indicated and discussed: the Indo-European agens-actio-schema and the particular sentence type: subject-verb-object.

2.2.2   Actantial continuity

Thus, as far as theoretical bases are concerned, contradictions and even semi-conscious linguistic conditionings in model construction must be ascertained[9]. But let us not forget that Bremond's assertion of an underlying subject-predicate-relation seems to be basically correct. A *continuity* of at least one actant, say, a "topic actant" instead of a "subject" (according to Mathieu 1974: 365–367: either an "agent" or a "patient"), must exist in a story, whereas the "predicates" may (and must) change. (Cf. 3.3). If there is no such continuity or coherence, there will be no story. This is one reason why Adam/Goldenstein (1976: 211) consider Caesar's well-known formula, "Veni, vidi, vici", to be a real story. "Raconter, pour le redire une dernière fois, ne sera jamais que dire ce

---

[8] This transfer presupposes the existence of a real correspondance between sentence level and text level, micro-structure and macro-structure. The general philosophical background of this presupposition has not yet been investigated. But I think that the foundations could be traced back to Neoplatonic philosophies in the Renaissance and in Antiquity.

[9] All these schemata might be useful for narrative grammars. But French semiologists should take into consideration that these schemata stem from Indo-European clause structures. Narrative grammars cannot be founded on an Indo-European linguistic basis and at the same time be regarded as "universal" ones.

qu'il advient d'une personne où d'une chose, énoncer la succession des prédicats que son devenir lui confère." (Bremond 1973: 332, for further arguments see this work).

It is clear that different levels of narrativity would have to be distinguished here in order to solve the contradictions. Other distinctions[10] would then have to follow.

2.2.3   Roles

The same trend (towards a conception of textual coherence originating from the idea of actant continuity) is apparent when the history of the term "role" in French semiology is considered. The cover word "actions" in Barthes 1966: 6 and 15–18 is still quite close to Propp's conception. Then, "role" became the cover word for a set of functions asserted for the same actant. Thus, according to Greimas (in Chabrol 1973: 164–166), one actant may assume several "actantial roles" (specific function sets) during the course of a text, in opposition to other roles held by other actants. Bremond 1973 has presented the best elaborated French model for narrative roles and emphasized their importance for textual coherence. Cf. also 2.3.3.

2.3   Actants and "acteurs"

The narrative actants are abstract elements in a structural pattern of interrelations, whereas the narrative "acteurs" are mostly individual persons, animals or non-human anthropomorphous beings (angels, devils, allegories, etc.) in the external or surface structure of a text. An actant might also be represented by "acteurs" like "history", "world", "matter", "spirit" (Greimas 1966: 181). Different "acteurs" in a corpus or in a text can represent the same actant. On the other hand, during the syntagmatic succession within a text, one single "acteur" may also assume the tasks of two or even three actants (cf. Greimas' formalization in Chabrol 1973: 161).

2.3.1   Greimas' actantial model

Greimas (1966: 180) first proposed a model with six actants: destinator (he who gives an order to a subject, to a "hero"), object, beneficiary (addressee) on one axis and adjuvant (helper), subject, opponent on the other. This model already provided a certain order: a subject wants an object (relation of desire), gets a helper and/or on opponent, reaches or gains the object and finally gives it to the beneficiary (or to himself as beneficiary).

---

[10] E.g., between "object-actant narrative topicalisation" and "subject -actant narrative topicalisation" (e.g. in a simple short story about what happened to a person). See also Mathieu 1974: 358–367, especially p. 366, based on the minimal condition of "one-actant-continuity" according to Bremond.

2.3.2   Modifications

Greimas' first modification of the actantial model (in Chabrol 1973: 162–164) is based only on two sentence types: a type with a bivalent verb or "function" (function, subject, object) and a type with a trivalent one (function, destinator, object, adressee). Furthermore, a negative series of actants is correlated to the "positive" one. This revision leads to the following model:

Positive subject	vs Negative subject (Anti-subject)
Positive object	vs Negative object
Positive destinator	vs Negative destinator (Anti-destinator)
Positive addressee	vs Negative addressee (Anti-addressee)

In narrative texts, "positive" and "negative" *can* appear as "good" and "bad", i.e. with moral and ideological values.

Greimas has now augmented this structural inventory of actants. A "non-destinator" (an apparent and illusory destinator) corresponds to the (positive) "destinator", and a "non-anti-destinator" to the "anti-destinator" (Greimas 1976: 63, cf. also 89, 95, 111). Likewise, corresponding to the subject is (and remains) an anti-subject, but the parallelism to the destinator is not extended further.

As long as no new model of actants is presented, this might take on the appearance of a scholastical exercice. But in effect Greimas has realized that *two points of view* must be taken into consideration: that of a subject-actant and that of his adversary (and vice versa). Thus there is no longer an "opponent" but an "anti-subject". Both subjects have their own respective destinators and strategies of interaction, including their strategies in speaking (Greimas 1976: 192–214, here, Greimas has not only reached the niveau of recent developments in speech-act theory, but seems to have gone beyond them).

The modifications mentioned above are also Greimas' first attempt – without explicitly saying it – to integrate Bremond's conception of two corresponding points of view (cf. 2.3.3 and 3.2.3) into his own theory. These correspondencies do not exist in all narrative texts, but they can be discovered in many.

2.3.3   Bremond's actantial model

This model also contains six actants: three main types of "agents" called "the influencer", "the improver" (special case: the protector) and "the deteriorater" (special case: the obstructor) and three corresponding main types of "patients": "the influenced", the beneficiary and the victim (Bremond 1973: 137–309). It is impossible to point out here their stemmatic development or the convergences and divergences with Greimas.

2.4   Functions

A terminological distinction corresponding to "actants" vs "acteurs" does not exist in French semiology. Thus there are only "functions", as in Propp's often –

quoted work, but no "functemes"[11] or "function-types. But generally these narrative units are meant as parts or terms of a system structured by oppositions and correlations. In Greimas 1966: 192–221, for example, a "pact" group of functions corresponds to a "(pact) performance" group of functions. The "pact group" is now divided into an "injunctive pact" ('prescription' vs 'interdiction', 'acceptance' vs 'refusal') and a "permissive pact" ('demand' and either 'permission' or 'prevention', Greimas 1976: 95). The "performance group" contains functions like 'struggle', 'victory' vs 'defeat' and also subsequent functions arranged in forms of oppositions and correlations. Greimas was the first semiologist to apply the "idea" of phonemic systems to the domain of functions. The difference is evident: phonemic systems are exclusively paradigmatic, whereas 'functemic' systems also contain a virtual syntagmatic dimension.

As this example shows, the idea that a macro-structural model of functions must contain *alternatives* (e.g. 'victory' vs 'defeat') is already outlined in Greimas 1966, a book which goes back to earlier lectures. This idea of alternatives was then developed in Bremond's conception. According to Bremond 1966 and 1973, a decisional logic generates the development of the plot in narrative texts.

2.5   Sequences

The actions which correspond to each other in the plot of a narrative text are called functions. On a more abstract level of reflection about narrative texts, French semiologists have become aware that these functions are basically always the same (cf. Propp). In the narrative, a system of function types (I called them "functemes") is at work, although the author may not know it – as in the case of native speakers who do not know that their speech acts, prior to manifestation in all its details and diversities, have to go through the instances of sentence-type, morpheme and phoneme "selection".

There are pre-formed larger units in natural languages[12] (e.g. pre-formed morphemes, as determinated phonematic successions – with or without variants) which serve to manifest a semantic unit. The relation between sequence[13] and functions (functemes) is similarly conceived. *The functions are only able to manifest a "sense" within the framework of a sequence.*

"Sense" means 'direction' (Greimas 1970: 15–16). According to Greimas, this is not only true in the macro-structural field (it is crucial to be aware of it here), but on all levels which are explored by semiology (thus the sentence level, etc., is included).

---

[11] Cf. the concept of emic motifs or "motifemes", opposed to "allomotifs", in Alan *Dundes*: The Morphology of North American Indian Folktale (FFC 195), 1964: 101.

[12] This is the fundamental argument in Pottier's critique of linguistic generative transformation models. See B. Pottier: "La grammaire générative et la linguistique", in: Travaux de linguistique et de littérature VI/1, 1968, 7–26. Though he does not exclude transformations at all, Pottier would use the same argument today against generative semantics, emphasizing the "memorized" syntactical patterns called syntaxies and the "memorized" lexical units called lexies.

[13] As to the concept of sequence in Propp and Dundes, see Güttgemanns 1973: 12–23.

This is the common hypothesis concerning sequences. The particular conceptions of *sequences* are dependent upon the respective conceptions of *functions*. As the latter vary with the authors, so do the former.

The most advanced conception of sequences in French semiology has been elaborated by *Bremond*. Now I wish to leave the domain of common trends. Particular narrative grammars – though wide-spread in French narrative research today (with the exception of Barthes' model[14]) – will be presented (in selected aspects).

3   Bremond's decisional grammar

In current French narrative research and discussion, Bremond's conception of a narrative grammar has become as important as Greimas' theory. The main reason for this is to be seen in its importance for the *syntagmatic* dimension of narrative macro-structures. This dimension is present in the "elementary narrative sequence" (cf. 3.1) and in the "sequence combination types" (cf. 3.2). Furthermore, the elementary narrative sequence provides *two* kinds of possibilities for an author: not only his possibilities while writing a *part* of a plot, but also his choices in the construction of the *whole* plot. Similarly, according to Larivaille (1974: 387), the interpreter may not only discover underlying elementary sequences in the different *parts* of a story, but may also become aware that the *whole* story, the essence of a plot, is a single elementary sequence in reality.

3.1   The elementary narrative sequence

According to Bremond, the elementary narrative sequence is a triadic[15] succession of functions:

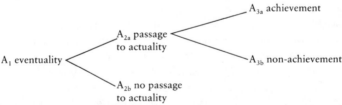

Each function (with the exception of the terminal ones, i.e., there is no unlimited game tree[16]) opens an alternative which, according to Bremond

---

[14]   Barthes' model, however, is still of certain interest today, for it is able to fill an important gap in the theory of narrative, in spite of its deficiencies. See 4 and also Hardt 1976: 82–90.

[15]   In his discussion of Dundes' "Morphology of the North American Indian Folktale", Bremond (1973: 59–80) considers Dundes' binary model as still too close to Propp's schema and proposes to substitute it with a more adequate ternary model.

[16]   There is a misunderstanding in Güttgemanns 1973: 47 which unfortunately ruins his estimation of the practicability of Bremond's model.

(1966: 60–61; 1973: 131), can only be dyadic. For example: At the beginning of a story, a character called Sam feels he is in a dangerous situation (= eventuality). He takes measures to defend himself (= passage to actuality) or does not (= no passage to actuality, no complete elementary sequence in this case). Eventually, his defensive measures prove successful (= achievement, also called "objective attained") or ineffective (= non-a., "objective missed"): Thus it is basically either a story with a happy end or a tragic story (a "story" could be a "novel", "ballad", "drama" or even "historiographical passage", "diary", "news" in some cases). By introducing alternatives into his narrative grammar, Bremond has linked together two fundamental ideas: narrative necessity (according to Propp) and narrative liberty (according to Bremond's principal reservations about Propp's conception).

3.2   Sequence combination types

Let us suppose that an author has chosen the succession A_1-A_{2a}-A_{3b}, which will now be called A_1-A_2-A_3. According to Bremond, this is the most simple case of a plot. But an author can also "extend" the plot. He has three basic possibilities or sequence combination types at his disposal.

3.2.1   Concatenation

The end of one elementary sequence – the new situation (A_3) – is at the same time the starting point of another elementary sequence, and so on (cf. Bremond 1966: 61). This is the "enchaînement bout-à-bout", the overlapping of end and beginning, which we will call, according to the French term, "concatenation". Using J. Giovanni's novel "Le deuxième souffle" as an example: malevolence (a project of a hold-up, A_1) – misdeed (action according to the project, A_2) – success of the action (A_3), which is at the same time a crime to be investigated by the police (B_1) – police investigations (B_2) – identification and punishment of the evil=doers (B_3). See Dupuy 1974: 175. This is quite a "materialistic" conception: the "sense" of a plot could thus be compared to the direction of an electric current, flowing through cables with plugs and sockets at their ends, which can be installed and connected. However, this conception seems to provide an adequate explanation for the macrostructure of many stories. The concatenation concept shows that there is no simple chronological succession of functions, but a kind of "double function" (e.g., A_3/B_1, B_3/C_1), which serves to connect two sequences.

3.2.2   Insertion

Before the end of one elementary sequence, another one may be inserted. Van Dijk's interpretation (1972: 286) of Bremond is not correct here. Bremond's concept of "enclave" (insertion) contains not only embedded sequences like, e.g., A_1 – (embedded: B_1 – B_2 – B_3) – A_2 – A_3 or A_1 – (embedded: B_1 – B_2 –

$B_3) - A_2 -$ (embedded: $C_1 - C_2 - C_3) - A_3$, but he (1966: 61) starts from another possibility, which is fundamental for a narrative grammar:

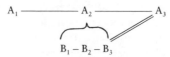

The inserted sequence *is identical with* A_2. A_2 is elaborated as the succession $B_1 - B_2 - B_3$; B_3 in this succession is identical with A_3. Thus the inserted sequence has instrumental power (cf. Bremond 1966: 61, Dupuy 1974: 175–177): by defeating "Vercingetorix" in the "Alesia episode" ($A_2 = B_1 - B_2 - B_3$), "Caesar" attained his objective of dominating Gaul (A_3). This example shows that Bremond's concept of insertion contains the idea of *hierarchical interrelations* between the functions (cf. also Pavel 1973: 21–23).

3.2.3 "Bracketing"

If there are different points of view held by the participants (basically, those of one "agent" and one "anti-agent"), the same "action" can mean different functions for different participants:

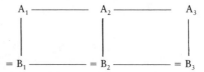

This is the "accolement", a term which could be literally translated as "bracketing" and which denotes a parallel and interdependent plot development. To shorten a textual example, which illustrates all of Bremond's sequence combination types, Macbeth's defeat and death (A_3) is at the same time the definitive success of the action of his adversaries (B_3).

This example is also typical of the double perspective as a governing principle for the functions in many narrative texts: there are two fundamental "senses" of functions within elementary sequences: *amelioration* and *deterioration*. What is deterioration for one actant is amelioration for the other, and vice versa. Thus the "bracketing" structure is actually the basic type for all more complex narrative texts. Bremond (1966, 1973, 1976) has developed an elaborate logic of narrative possibilities, which originates from the very double perspective contained in the type of "bracketing".

3.3 Minimal conditions

Where is the starting point of narrativity? Is it possible to formulate some minimal conditions? As early as 1966 (p. 62), Bremond re-discussed this problem, and, later on, Hamon (1972: 200–221) and van Dijk (1972, cf. especially 288–309), cp. now Bremond (1973: 93, 100, 332).

3.4   Applications

Bibliographical references. Cf. especially Hamon 1972: 204 (influence on Todorov), Bremond 1973: 141–308 (examples and "plot interpretations" from Homer till Poe), Bremond in Chabrol 1973: 96–121 (French fairy-tales), Pavel 1973: 22–24(*generative* representation by rewrite rules), Dupuy 1974: 173–186 (detective stories and novels, also with application to a typological distinction), Mathieu 1974: 357–367, Larivaille 1974: 368–388, see esp. 374–387, Scheerer/Winkler 1976: 1–24 (review, application to Maupassant), Bremond/Paulme 1976 (African tales of deceivers, index of deceits – Fr. "ruses"), Adam/Goldenstein 1976: 213–222, 246–248, 285–287 (essay-writing in school, a French folk tale, stories in advertising and criticism of ideology), Adam 1976: 63 (Maupassant), Goldenstein 1976: 69–79 (more explicit about essay-writing). Mutual influences between Greimas and Bremond: see 2.3.2, 2.4 and Bremond 1973: 101.

4   Barthes' most important contributions

Whereas Greimas, Bremond and Larivaille used mainly Propp's results as a starting point for their elaboration of narrative grammars[17], Barthes has never really been influenced by Propp. From his first works on, he has predominately observed the "external level" of signs. However, he has also observed these signs as telltale carriers which direct the attentive reader to ideological, social and psychological backgrounds[18]. Therefore, his concept of *indices* (already present in his well-known attempt at a first synthesis in 1966: 8–11, an introductory essay which, though now rather antiquated, has become a landmark) and the transfer of Hjelmslev's *connotation* concept to general semiology[19] are his main contributions to French narrative research.

Barthes' concept of indices has been developed mainly by Greimas (1976: 53), who distinguishes between circumstantial, spatio-temporal and aspectual indices and assigns to each class specific roles within narrative texts.

Barthes extends and elaborates his "own" connotation concept first in 1970 (lecture of Balzac's "Sarrasine", cf. Gallas 1973: 385–386), then in 1972: 145–155 (study of J. Verne) and in 1973 (in Chabrol 1973: 29–54, on a story of E. A. Poe). Other influential applications to narrative texts, with further elaboration of the conception, are to be found in Arrivé 1969: 7–10, in Greimas 1970: 93–102, 118, in Alexadrescu's study of Maupassant (in Chabrol 1973: 85–95) and in Greimas' work on the same author (Greimas 1976: 54–62, 139–150, 226–239).

We can try to give a preliminary, still rudimentary synthesis of this evolution in the following model:

---

[17]   Cf. also the retrospective in Greimas 1976: 7–8.

[18]   Cf. Theis in Lange 1975: 252–278.

[19]   Cf. Barthes 1967: 89–94, Lange 1975: 267, Adam/Goldenstein 1976: 18–20, 84–97.

This model describes a development of figurative indices (= i) and of corresponding symbolic values (= s) which is *concomitant* with the plot development (e.g., functions $A_1 - B_5$). The imagery of day, hiding of light, black night, thunderstorm and flashes of light etc. in Shakespeare's "Macbeth" has an evident symbolic value (reign of good, transition to evil, reign of evil, and inversion, within the all encompassing metaphysical struggle and "dualism"[20] in Shakespeare's tragedy) and serves, like other indicial concatenations in this text, as a visual-symbolic and "ideological" background to the plot development.[21]

A concomitance of this kind has already been alluded to in Barthes 1972: 148 and in the other works mentioned above. In the case of Shakespeare's "Macbeth", the omission of an initial stage (now A_1, with i_1 'day' and s_1 'reign of good') is necessary if a model of five-phase-sequences is used. Deletion transformations of "index positions" as well as doublings and triplings of indices and more complicated bracketing types (cf. 3.2.3) are possible. The model furthermore suggests the possibility of indicial and symbolic *isotopies* in narrative texts, and the existence of such isotopies has in fact already been demonstrated by Alexandrescu and by Greimas 1976 (cf. above). The conclusion is evident: at least a part of the indices in narrative texts belongs not only to the "surface phenomena" but can also stem from a deeper level of narrativity as does the plot.

The model, despite its imperfections[22], may also illustrate another current trend in French semiology: Many contributions to French narrative grammar now provide indicial and symbolic markers which are often connected with the pure functions[23]. That is to say, not only the "skeleton", but also the "flesh" and the "blood" are now considered. Stories and dramas of high semantic complexity (far more complex than Propp's fairy tales) can thus be examined. The chief merit of this evolution is doubtlessly due to Barthes' somewhat scattered, yet stimulating studies. (There is a growing trend to declare a study of this kind a mere personal "lecture" and to emphasize the "reception" and the possibility of many other interpretations. With regard to French semiology, this trend can be seen in close connexion with the increasing interest in more complex texts).

---

[20] Though the drama has a monotheistic background, not a Manichean one, there is a clear tendency to dualism (hell vs. heaven and corresponding indices, actants and functions). Cf. note 24.

[21] Cf. J. Wain (Editor): Shakespeare, Macbeth, a casebook, London (Macmillan) 1968, 25–26, 64–76, 99–103, 166, 225–239.

[22] It must be added that poetic narrative texts often contain not only concomitant indices, but also "cataphorical" ones (e.g., the frequent indicial premonition in Shakespeare's and Lorca's tragedies) and even counter-indices (intented, e.g., to mislead the reader of detective stories; cf. the "leurres" in Hamon 1974: 145–146).

[23] However, various and different terminologies are at present used in this field, i.e. the terminology is still fluid.

5 Greimas' grammar, founded on the "semiotic square"

Some principles and constituents of Greimas' narrative grammar have already been presented in 2.1, 2.2, 2.3.1, 2.4 and 4, where they served as examples for common trends. The new and more specific framework, however, will now be dealt with in its most essential traits.

5.1 The "semiotic square"

Greimas' "Sémantique structurale" (1966) was founded on the notions of (overlapping) *axis* and (binary) *opposition*[24]. Greimas (1966: 196, 201, 204–256) extended this conception to a quaternary one, when he applied it to narrative texts: Two other terms were *correlated* with a fundamental binary opposition. A further elaboration led Greimas and Rastier[25] to the *"semiotic square"*[26]:

S

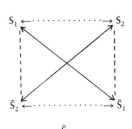

S̄

The points mark a relation between opposites. The perforated lines show a relation of implication (which is, however, considered subject to debate[27] in Greimas 1970: 136, note). The solid intersecting lines indicate relations between contradictory terms. As this square model is clearly influenced by Aristotelian "semiology", I shall first take an example from de Libéra's discussion (in Nef 1976: 29):

S_1 'This solid is hot' (Fr. chaud)
S_2 'This solid is cold' (Fr. froid)
$\overline{S_1}$ 'This solid is cool' (Fr. frais)
$\overline{S_2}$ 'This solid is lukewarm' (Fr. tiède)

The axis S could be called 'fundamental temperature assertions' and its negation 'non-fundamental temperature assertions'. The example can be sustained as far as it regards the relations between opposites and between contradictory terms. The "implications", however, are difficult to detect in

---

[24] Cf. the discussion in Grosse 1971 and, for a surprising parallel in Baudelaire, cf. Pachet in Poétique n° 20, 1974, 445 (without comparison to Greimas' theory).

[25] Greimas 1970: 137, 160. Cf. "The interaction of semiotic constraints" in Yale French Studies 41, 1968, 86–105 and Hendricks 1972: 109–117.

[26] It is also called "elementary structure of signification" or "constitutional model" (since the model is considered fundamental for each organized manifest signification), or "semiological square" or "logical square in canonical form" (see Nef 1976: 5–66).

[27] Cf. Bremond 1973: 93. My conclusion is that "implication" should be substituted by "contiguity" (relation totum: pars or pars: pars). Relations of the type pars: pars exist, e.g., in cases of gradual oppositions (see the following example) and of temporal contiguity (see Greimas 1976: 88, 95).

the case of propositions with "scale words". According to Blanché, the four propositions within the square can be substituted by four terms only. The restriction to propositions has thus been given up (cf. Güttgemanns 1973: 9), and the model is generalized.

5.2   The taxonomic model

Greimas regards the semiotic square as a universal abstract model, which is to say a form of thinking and of structuring, like the circle or the spiral in certain philosophies. The four "empty" positions within the square can also be filled by four more or less evaluative and ideological terms (cf. examples in Greimas 1970: 118, 141). This is now a taxonomic model. It is a specific "semantic micro-universe", which is dependent upon a philosophy of life, a kind of ideology with its corresponding value system. (For further distinctions, cf. p. 163). Such a taxonomy can be fundamental for "static" non-narrative discourses (cf. 5.4), as well as for "dynamic" narrative discourses, more precisely the essential event-processes which will constitute the basis of a (narrative) plot. For Shakespeare's "Macbeth", the underlying taxonomic model would be:

order   disorder[28]
loyalty   disloyalty[29]
(with the same relations as in 5.1).

The four interdependent terms constitute, according to Greimas, the *morphology* within the "fundamental grammar". The first part of its *syntax* is constituted by four possible operations, which are always *directed:*

$$S_1 \Rightarrow \overline{S_1}, \quad \overline{S_1} \Rightarrow S_1, \quad S_2 \Rightarrow \overline{S_2}, \quad \overline{S_2} \Rightarrow S_2.$$

These are operations of *contradiction*. For example, in the first case, S_1 is denied and $\overline{S_1}$ is affirmed. As the second part of the syntax, by an operation of "presupposition" or *"implication"* (I would call it conceptual contiguity), S_2 will appear and will be joined to $\overline{S_1}$ (Greimas 1970: 165).

Similar subsequent operations as well as *other* movements in the diagram (e.g., beginning from $\overline{S_1}$) are possible[30].

The four terms are arranged according to the semiotic square. Therefore, 'disloyalty' (and not 'disorder') is considered as $\overline{S_1}$. – The semiotic square, the corresponding "syntactic" operations and the taxonomic model belong to the immanent level or to the level of archimodels, respectively (cf. 2.1.1, 2.1.2). Greimas (1970: 162–166) uses "fundamental grammar" as a global term for the structures and rules of these levels.

---

[28] The first and fundamental opposition can also be subdivided into different correlated pairs. This has been demonstrated by Rastier (1974: 138, see also 72, 149, 157).
[29] The second opposition is practically always subordinate to the first. Cf. the studies mentioned in 5.4 and also Bremond 1973: 95.
[30] Greimas 1970: 165, Bremond 1973: 95–96, Chabrol 1973: 20.

5.3   Anthropomorphic representation and transfer of object values

Since 1969, Greimas has placed a "narrative surface grammar" (which, in reality, serves to describe an intermediate state of transformations) in opposition to the "fundamental grammar". As Greimas' most important text (1970: 157–183) is very difficult and has seldom been adequately explained, I shall try to present briefly the principles of the conception. Firstly, the "surface grammar" shows how a narration (Fr. récit) can arise out of movements within the taxonomic model[31] (cf. the "syntactic operations" in 5.2). Secondly, some characteristics of narrative texts are basic, according to Greimas; however, in his exposition only one of them (the first) is given real axiomatic status. Narrative texts are *anthropomorphic*[32], *polemic* (and thus the operations of contradiction lead to narrative disputes, struggles or fights) and they contain *transfers of values*[33] which may in part be objects of these disputes or struggles.

According to this conception, the four abstract *values* within the semiotic (and logical) square are now changed into anthropomorphic *"positions"*, mainly positions of actants (cf. 2.3.1, 2.3.2), to name the most important change. All these "positions" can be carriers of a disputed object-value, e.g. 'power' or 'princess'. Similarly, the "logical" syntactic *operations* are now transformed into anthropomorphic "functions" (cf. 2.4), more generally: into an anthropomorphic *"activity"* (Fr. "faire")[34]. For example, by an operation of contradiction ("negation") of S_1, carrier of an object-value like 'power', this value will be transferred to $\overline{S_1}$. Later on, on the exterior level of manifestation, this operation will be represented in figurative forms like murder, robbery or victory after a struggle.

Further operations, which also become "functions" (and "simple narrative utterances" if actants are connected to them), may tend to bring about similar changes [35] or even a complete circuit of the object=value[36].

5.4   Discussions and applications

The most important discussions of Greimas' narrative grammar are to be found in Bremond 1973: 81–102[37], Stierle 1973: 110–128, Chabrol 1973: 20–22 and Nef 1976. In Nef's book, various authors deal with the history of the "semiotic square" and with Greimas' narrative grammar and

---

[31] Greimas 1970: 164, Hamon 1974: 150–151, "récit".

[32] See critical statements in Bremond 1973: 91–92.

[33] This concept stems from economic theories. It is interesting that Greimas was director of post-graduate studies within the section of *economic and social sciences* of the "Ecole pratique des hautes études" at Paris, like Barthes and Ducrot. (Now "Ecole des Hautes Etudes en Sciences Sociales", Groupe de recherches semio-linguistiques). Cf. also Greimas 1966: 182–183, 1976a: 9–42, 79–128 and Greimas in Chabrol 1973: 162.

[34] Bremond (1973: 91–92) maintains that these transformations are quite frequent, but not necessary in the genesis of narrative texts.

[35] Greimas 1970: 94, Coquet 1976: 2.1.2, 3.2.3.

[36] See the formulae in Greimas 1970: 177. The symbol s is now changed into d (deixis, according to the transformations into "local" positions).

[37] Particularly important are p. 89, 99–101.

apply it to narrative and even non-narrative texts. There has been a veritable boom of applications of this narrative grammar since 1970. They can be found, with further bibliographical references, in the Urbino series (cf. 1.5), in Chabrol/Marin 1971 (passim), Greimas 1972: 98, 140–154, Chabrol 1973: 14–28, 55–95, 122–136, 161–176, Arrivé/Coquet 1973 (passim), Rastier 1974 (passim), Coquet 1974: 93–118 and 1976: 2.1.2, 3.2–3.2.3, Greimas 1976 (passim) and 1976a: 79–157.

A more detailed version of § 5, together with an additional § 6 'Trends toward micro-structural research' will appear in Linguistica Biblica 40, May 1977.

Bibliography

Adam, Jean-Michel, 1976. Langue et texte: imparfait/passé simple. In: Pratiques 10, 49–68

Adam, Jean-Michel/Goldenstein, Jean-Pierre, 1976. Linguistique et discours littéraire. Paris, Larousse

Arrivé, Michel, 1969. Postulats pour la description linguistique des textes littéraires. In: Langue française 3, 3–13

Arrivé, Michel/Coquet, Jean-Claude (Ed.), 1973. Sémiotiques textuelles. Langages 31

Barthes, Roland, 1966. Introduction à l'analyse structurale des récits. In: Communications 8, 1–27

Barthes, Roland, 1967. Elements of Semiology. London, Cape

Barthes, Roland, 1970. L'Empire des signes. Genève, Skira

Barthes, Roland, 1972. Le degré zéro de l'écriture, suivi de Nouveaux essais critiques. Paris, Seuil

Bremond, Claude, 1966. La logique des possibles narratifs. In: Communications 8, 60–76

Bremond, Claude, 1973. Logique du récit. Paris, Seuil

Bremond, Claude/Paulme, Denise, 1976. Typologie des Contes Africains du Décepteur. Principes d'un Index des Ruses. Documents de Travail 50–51, Urbino (see 1.5)

Chabrol, Claude/Marin, Louis (Ed.), 1971. Sémiotique narrative: récits bibliques. Langages 22

Chabrol, Claude (Ed.), 1973. Sémiotique narrative et textuelle. Paris, Larousse

Coquet, Jean-Claude, 1974. Sémantique du discours et analyse du contenu. In: Connexions 11, 93–118 (EPI, 68 rue de Babylone, F 75007 Paris)

Coquet, Jean-Claude, 1976. Sémiotique. Provided for publication in the collections "Creusets", Brussels, Ed. Complexe and "Hachette Université", Paris

van Djik, Teun A., 1972. Some Aspects of Text Grammars. The Hague, Mouton. – Cf. also Chabrol 1973

Dupuy, Josée, 1974. Le roman policier. Paris, Larousse

Gallas, Helga, 1973. Strukturalismus in der Literaturwissenschaft. In: Arnold, H. L./Sinemus, V. (Ed.), Grundzüge der Sprach- und Literaturwissenschaft Vol. I, München, dtv, 374–388

Genette, Gérard: cf. 1.4

Goldenstein, Jean-Pierre, 1976. Une grammaire de texte pour la composition française. In: Pratiques 10, 69–79

Greimas, Algirdas Julien, 1966. Sémantique structurale. Paris, Larousse

Greimas, Algirdas Julien, 1970. Du sens. Essais sémiotiques. Paris, Seuil

Greimas, Algirdas Julien (Ed.), 1972. Essais de sémiotique poétique. Paris, Larousse

Greimas, Algirdas Julien, 1976. Maupassant. La sémiotique du texte: exercices pratiques. Paris, Seuil

Greimas, Algirdas Julien, 1976a. Sémiotique et sciences sociales. Paris, Seuil

Grosse, Ernst Ulrich, 1971. Zur Neuorientierung der Semantik bei Greimas. In: ZrP 87, 359–393

Grosse, Ernst Ulrich, 1976. Text und Kommunikation. Eine linguistische Einführung in die Funktionen der Texte. Stuttgart, Kohlhammer

Gülich, Elisabeth/Raible, Wolfgang, 1977. Linguistische Textmodelle. München, Fink

Güttgemanns, Erhardt, 1973. Einleitende Bemerkungen zur strukturalen Erzählforschung. In: Linguistica Biblica 23/24, 2–47. (Address: Kirchweg 15, D 5300 Bonn-Röttgen 1)

Hamon, Philippe, 1972. Mise au point sur les problèmes de l'analyse du récit. In: Le français moderne 40, 200–221

Hamon, Philippe, 1974. Analyse du récit: éléments pour un lexique. In: Le français moderne 42, 133–154

Hardt, Manfred, 1976. Poetik und Semiotik. Tübingen, Niemeyer

Hendricks, William O., 1972. The Structural Study of Narration: Sample Analyses. In: Poetics 3, 100–123

Kristeva, Julia: cf. 1.4

Lange, Wolf-Dieter (Ed.), 1975. Französische Literaturkritik der Gegenwart in Einzeldarstellungen. Stuttgart, Kröner

Larivaille, Paul, 1974. L'analyse (morpho)logique (sic) du récit. In: Poétique 19, 368–388

Mathieu, Michel, 1974. Les acteurs du récit. In: Poétique 19, 357–367

Nef, Frédéric (Ed.), 1976. Structures élémentaires de la signification. Brussels, Ed. Complexe

Pavel, Thomas G., 1973. Some Remarks on Narrative Grammars. In: Poetics 8,5–30

Rastier, François, 1974. Essais de sémiotique discursive. Tours, Mame

Scheerer, Thomas M./Winkler, Markus, 1976. Zum Versuch einer universalen Erzählgrammatik bei Claude Bremond. In: Poetica 8, 1–24

Stierle, Karlheinz, 1973. Semiotik als Kulturwissenschaft. A. J. Greimas, Du sens, Essais sémantiques. In: ZFSL 83, 99–128

Todorov, Tzvetan: see 1.4

Stylistics and Text Linguistics

Nils Erik Enkvist
Åbo Akademi

1.1 The four words of my title may look innocuous enough; still they juxtapose two many-faced terms, *stylistics* and *text linguistics*. A brief explanation will be given of the sense in which these terms should be interpreted here.

1.2 In a book offering a score of separate papers on a wide range of overlapping questions it seems wise to define one's subject narrowly rather than comprehensively.[1] A wide approach might even flood the present essay under a wave of material both from linguistics and from literary theory and criticism. Some scholars have expressly identified stylistics with the study of textual spans beyond the sentence. Taken in this way, the scope of the present essay would at once expand indefinitely: text linguistics would become stylistics, and vice versa. To others, style is a variety of language which correlates with context, including situation, much as regional dialects correlate with place, sociolects with social groups and historical forms of language with time. But as all texts too correlate with context and situation, this avenue also leads us far afield. To keep from embarking upon such global missions, to avoid the responsibility for writing about all of stylistics and to minimize overlaps with matters dealt with elsewhere in this volume, I shall define the central concerns of my essay more narrowly as

> the isolation, definition and study of such style markers as require description in text-linguistic terms, that is, in terms referring to intersentential phenomena and not merely to features within individual sentences.

After such a definition, which drastically reduces the scope of my paper, my next obligation will be to explain what I mean by 'style markers'.

2.1 As I have argued elsewhere at length (Enkvist 1973a, 1973b), that which is customarily called 'style' is fundamentally an impression arrived at through comparison. This is no less true of styles in language. A text is compared with a

---

[1] Those wishing for more comprehensive information on available studies will be served not only by general linguistic bibliographies and a wide range of literary ones, but also by the stylistic bibliographies in the journal *Style,* which contain headings such as 'theoretical orientations', 'syntax', and 'beyond the sentence: discourse and rhetoric'.

network of other texts or text types which are regarded as significantly related to the original text, and therefore worth the comparison. Out of this process, the impression of 'style' arises as a result of the sum total of those features that make a text similar to, as well as different from, the features in the network used for comparison. Style is thus a relation, a differential. Which particular texts or text types should furnish the background and yardstick for the comparison is determined by what we are after. To pin down characteristics of an individual style we must obviously compare a text produced by the relevant individual with a network of comparable texts – a 'norm' for short, if the term can be shorn of its evaluative connotations – produced by others. To arrive at genre styles texts from one genre must be compared with texts from other genres. To describe period styles texts from one period will be related to texts from another period. And to describe styles used in a particular speech situation it must be seen how texts emanating from this situation differ from texts emanating from other situations. The total impression of the style of a text may often arise from a complex network of such comparisons, which are performed by matching a text against a whole set of experiences of other texts, similar and different, that emanate from a spectrum of contexts, situations and backgrounds.

2.2   This matching is often done routinely and subconsciously. An analysis of conspicuous stylistic features is presumably part of the decoding of a text, because style can contribute to the total meaning of a message, for instance by revealing a speaker's attitudes through his choice of levels of politeness. But the stylistic comparison may also be carried out consciously and explicitly if there is some reason to pay particular attention to an individual's language (for instance when choosing between applicants for a certain job) or when doing linguistic or literary research. Often it is enough to note that the text either conforms to or departs from the expected norm (that is, from what we have learned to expect after long experience of language in context). Literary critics customarily express their impressions in subjective, even metaphorical language, where pithy elegance and suggestiveness are at a premium. But stylolinguists are professionally committed to more explicit procedures. Their work usually involves studies of frequencies and computations of densities (that is, occurrences of linguistic features per some measure of text length) for sets of explicitly defined linguistic units or features such as sound patterns, words, syntactic structures, and so on.

2.3   The central point is that for both the critic and the linguist, the text and the 'norm' must have a contextually significant relationship. Sonnets are worth comparing with other sonnets, with other poems and with certain kinds of prose; comparing them with, say, textbooks of anatomy or with laundry lists would be more far-fetched and perhaps even futile. But the insistence on a contextually relevant relation between text and norm brings with it an important corollary. Styles are at the same time examples of context-bound language.

Let us assume that a text differs from another text, and that it is possible to define how the contexts of these two texts differ. Then the differences between the two texts can at once be correlated with those contextual differences that distinguish the context of one text from that of the other. Styles, then, are at the same time both context-bound varieties of language and sums of differences between text and norm. Which of the two views we opt for depends on which approach happens to be more expedient for our particular purpose. As such, these two views are perfectly compatible: they are two sides of the same coin.

2.4   This leads us to a definition of 'style markers': A style marker is any linguistic feature whose density in the text is significantly different from its density in the contextually relevant norm. Thus the occurrence of a given feature in the text becomes a style marker if that feature does not occur in the norm. The absence of a feature in the text becomes a style marker (but a 'negative' or 'minus' one) if that feature does occur in the norm. And if the same feature occurs both in the text and in the norm, it can still be a style marker if its density in the text is significantly different from its density in the norm. This is why linguistic stylistics often turns into a quantitative discipline. It involves counts of potentially interesting features and assessments of the significance of differences in their occurrence in text and norm. This also explains why many linguists regard stylistics as the statistical level of language.

3.1   Any linguistic features, including those whose function is to link sentences into texts, are in principle capable of working as style markers. Thus any textual mechanism can yield potential style markers. Indeed styles are not characterized only by what happens within the sentence. A text may acquire its characteristic style and 'texture' from the ways in which its sentences are strung together. To describe such textual style markers, stylistics needs the support of grammars capable of describing intersentential phenomena. Whether such grammars arise through the expansion of sentence grammars to cover textual phenomena, or by the setting-up of special text grammars, is here irrelevant, though in itself a highly interesting question. The important point is that stylistics can use a machinery for the description of all potential and actual style markers, including textual ones. But conversely, text linguistics also needs stylistics. Text theories and models may have to explain how different discoursal features correlate with functions and styles of language, how they give rise to stylistic impressions and to stylistic judgments and evaluations.

3.2   In the most restricted sense of all, a text-linguistic style marker would be a marker which is definable only within a text-linguistic frame of reference, and which therefore remains beyond the reach of grammars designed for the study of isolated sentences one at a time. But sentence grammars can themselves produce cumulative data which illustrate textual qualities. Sentence length and complexity for instance exist in a text as cumulative discriminants of style. Styles can be characterized, not by the length of any single sentence but by the mean sentence length and the standard deviation or some other appropriate statistical measure. Thus though basic data are provided for one sentence at a time, the cumulative statistics all the same illustrate qualities of the text as a whole. Similarly, cumulative data on types and densities of conjunctions in a text may reflect text structure, but are nevertheless accessible to investigations without a special text-grammatical apparatus. Richard Ohmann's classic paper applying the densities of certain transformations to the description of stylistic differences between Hemingway, D. H. Lawrence and others (Ohmann 1964) is another example of how concepts of sentence grammar could illuminate text structure. Ohmann's method was possible because the sentence grammar he worked with was Chomsky's model of 1957: it operated with 'kernel sentences' and their combinations into larger units, which is a procedure comparable to the building of texts out of text atoms (see below under 3.3).

3.3   But there are also features that can be best, or only, defined in terms of text-based grammars and not sentence grammars. Let us list a few at once. Many text linguists view texts as having been generated out of a set of underlying units: text atoms, predications, propositions, underlying sentences, or whatever we wish to call them. If so, the manner in which the text (as against its sentences one by one) has been put together out of such units can contain stylistic characteristics. The same set of text atoms could have been combined into many different texts ('allotexts' of the same 'texteme' to speak with Koch 1969), and the manner chosen (the text strategy) is in itself a style marker with many components. Among them are the marking of temporal, causal and other relations between text atoms; their grouping and ordering into clauses and sentences, and the grouping and ordering of sentences into larger units of discourse; the flow of information within each clause and sentence, for instance in terms of old versus new information; the ways and patterns by which sentences are linked to each other; and the manner in which the argument is made to proceed from general principles to particulars or from particulars to general principles. How such matters should be modelled depends on the theory the grammarian wishes to adopt, and also to some extent on the structure of the particular language he is working with. Most grammarians have started out from syntactic arrangements or from a semantic base, but some (notably Sgall et al. 1973) have given primacy to thematic principles ('topic-comment articulation') which are actually part of the strategy of text composition. As to models for text grammars, one relevant distinction is between fixed-linearity models and models without fixed linearity; in the latter, linearization takes place within the grammar on the basis of rules and parameters governing linearization (Petöfi in Petöfi & Rieser 1973: 9ff). Models without fixed linearity will thus contain parameters for linearization, and such parameters may in theory offer important style markers.

3.4   To capture some types of covert intersentential cross-reference we shall need the support of pragmatics as well. If we hear a text such as

"Out of the window I saw a traffic warden in Queen's Lane. I had to rush to put in another coin."

the first sentence activates a network of pragmatic knowledge (which some linguists explicate in terms of presuppositions): traffic wardens mean trouble for those who break parking regulations. The second sentence coheres perfectly with the first if we provide the missing link: the speaker had parked his car in Queen's Lane, and the parking meter was about to expire. Should the character and density of such covert but pragmatically motivated cross-references turn out to be relevant for the style of the text, the investigator must enlarge his apparatus to cover, not only formal matters present on the textual surface but also pragmatic matters underlying the text.

3.5   In this light we can now assess the importance of text grammars for stylistics. A radical view has been expressed by Roland Harweg in a simple and coherent argument. Harweg begins by identifying a good style with a fluent style. He also considers the explication of what constitutes good style to be a primary task for stylistics. But stylistic excellence is the same thing as fluency, and fluency is obviously a textual feature including intersentential linkage, rather than a characteristic of an individual sentence. Therefore, says Harweg, to capture the essence of fluency, stylistics must abandon sentence grammar and rest squarely on text grammar (Harweg 1972: 75). Harweg has also advocated a method 're-generating' literary or other texts. This involves 'correcting' the text by rewriting it and thus bringing it more closely into line with a set of ideal principles of text grammar (Harweg 1973). A text is thus 'good' to the extent that it conforms to a set of text-grammatical rules and thus becomes text-grammatically 'correct'. The comparison between the original text and its re-generated form is of course likely to bring out relevant style markers as well: in fact a count of the operations of re-generation can be regarded as a step in stylistic analysis. The argument of the present paper has been somewhat less radical in suggesting that textual style markers can be of two kinds, or that the term 'textual' can have two senses. One category of textual style markers consist of cumulative data provided by analyses of one sentence at a time. Here sentence grammars, or modified sentence grammars, will be helpful. But another category of textual style markers which consist of truly intersentential patterns cannot be analysed cumulatively with sentence grammars. They must be approached in terms of text-based grammars.

3.6   We have, then, set the lower border for text linguistics: text grammars, or at least such sentence grammars as are enlarged with an apparatus capable of describing intersentential phenomena, are needed as soon as sentence grammars cease to be helpful. But those working with linguistic stylistics – as opposed to literary stylistics and literary criticism – are often also concerned about defining a ceiling for their endeavours. The present writer's policy would be to leave the upper limits of linguistic stylistics open and undefined, because linguistics seems to be expanding in those directions – for instance towards logic and towards pragmatics – which are likely to raise the ceiling of text linguistics. But those who yearn for firmer policies might contemplate solutions such as that suggested by Cesare Segre (1975). Here the textual level of 'discourse' correlates with the cultural contexts of language, style, rhetoric and metrics, and is properly a subject for linguistic investigation (in the wide sense of the term). But the higher textual levels of plot, fable and narrative model correlate with the cultural contexts of technique of exposition, anthropological materials and key concepts and logic of action, and are thus less accessible to the methods and approaches of linguistics proper.

4.1   Even with such restrictions, contacts between stylistics and text linguistics, or the forerunners of text linguistics, have a long history. I shall attempt a summary catalogue of some important points in such developments, hoping that it will be useful to those who read this paper without having had the support of more thorough recapitulations of these matters.

4.2   A number of features qualifying as textual style markers – patterns of organizing texts ('dispositio'), argument patterns, the explicit marking of certain types of cohesion, transitions between text units, paragraph structure, and so forth – have been discussed by rhetoricians and by teachers of composition ever since the ancients. This tradition of course goes on, as seen in modern textbooks on composition, for instance on paragraph structure (Christensen 1967, Chaplen 1970). Literary critics and theorists have often dealt with such matters too, though usually with the aid of an apparatus more impressionistic and even metaphorical than strictly descriptive or linguistic. Traditional philologists have often concerned themselves with relevant phenomena. The Russian formalists and their followers, including particularly the Soviet semioticists, the Italian semioticists and the French neo-structuralists, have shown an active interest in approaches that unite stylistics and the study of textual spans beyond the sentence.
Within linguistics proper in a more restricted sense, at least three schools require special mention. These are the Prague school, the Tagmemic school, and Text Linguistics proper, as I shall call them for short.

4.3   The hallmark of Prague-School structuralism, as opposed to other brands of structuralism, was a determination not to impose any preconceived limitations on the subjects and materials studied. One manifestation of this catholicity of approach was the emphasis on the correlation of language with extralinguistic factors. Whereas American structuralists had achieved their finest results in the narrowly restricted fields of phonemics and morphemics (if we exclude the ethnolinguists, who perforce had to look at language in context), Prague-school linguists dealt with a wider spectrum of problems. Often they crossed over from the study of linguistic form into the study of the organization of texts, including literary ones. Some scholars indeed defy traditional pigeonholing into literary scholars or linguists: they qualify as both. One of the most concrete contributions of Prague-school thought to text linguistics has been the study of theme, rheme and focus, initiated by Vilém Mathesius and developed by a large group of Czechoslovak linguists: P. Adamec, Jan Firbas, František Daneš, Petr Sgall, and many others (see Tyl 1970, Daneš 1974 and Firbas 1964 and 1974). Though the students of theme and rheme, like the Russian analysts of theme, rheme and *aktual'noe členenie predloženija,* originally did not stress the textual functions of their units, it has now become increasingly obvious that theme, rheme and focus are integral parts of the cohesive mechanisms integrating sentences into a text. They are devices which help to signal the progression of the argument and the difference between given or known and new information. In stylistics, a prominent Prague-school concept has been 'functional style', that is, a variant of language used for a specific function. This principle has been fertile also in the Soviet Union, the DDR and other socialist countries in Marxist frames of reference. A social theory readily makes functions of language primary to forms. Such a view leads to an emphasis on functional variation and on connections between social and economic forces and functional categories, which appears in a host of works of style theory as well as in many individual investigations. (Two East-German examples are Gläser 1969 and Fleischer et al. 1975).

4.4   Ever since the 1940's and 50's, Kenneth Pike, the founder and leader of the Tagmemic school, has shown an interest in relating linguistic structures to larger patterns of human behaviour. More recently, the work of Pike and his group has been increasingly anchored in descriptions of discourse, largely in 'exotic' languages. This emphasis on language in context and on speech acts, in addition to linguistic units, has made the tagmemicists pay special attention to discoursal phenomena. Thus in the 1960's, Pike, Robert Longacre and several others were systematically relating grammatical features to discourse structure and situational roles. They were also beginning to develop stringent, even algorithmic, models for the description of discourse structure. Studies of narrative patterns in Philippine and other languages have been another focus of their interest. Though tagmemicists have not made much explicit use of the term 'style' in their writings, their work has rich implications for students of style and text. (Brend 1974 is a useful introduction to tagmemic linguistics.)

4.5   Text linguistics proper – a term *faute de mieux* – is a very general label for that many-facetted movement in linguistics which professedly deals with text theory and discourse analysis. Its supporters claim that sentence grammars are incapable of describing all the relevant aspects and mechanisms of language. Many of them (see e.g. van Dijk 1972, Petöfi and Rieser 1973) prefer special text grammars to grammars that merely add textual components to treatments of the sentence.

4.6   It would be misleading to draw precise borders between text linguistics and formalism in various literary and narratological theories, French neo-structuralism, Italian and Soviet semiotics, Soviet stylistics, various currents in recent German linguistics such as stylistics and pragmalinguistics, and the like. There is a great deal of overlap and even deliberate synthesis between these currents; if borders must be drawn, their course will depend on the scholars' own labels for their work, and on the classifications and cross-classifications of various bibliographers. Nevertheless it is obvious enough that, in the 1960's, a host of scholars began emphasizing that intersentential, textual and discoursal phenomena were insufficiently catered for in current linguistic theory and practice. (A good bibliography of such studies is available in van Dijk 1972 and in Dressler and Schmidt 1973.) Sometimes there were attempts to deal with discoursal phenomena in terms of sentence grammar. Texts were even commuted into one sentence to bring them within the scope of existing grammars. Often, aspects of textual and intersentential context were brought into the structure of the individual sentence through devices such as performatives, presuppositions, conversational implicatures, referential indices, and the like. But many linguists went further in emphasizing that text linguistics was in fact a new kind of linguistics rather than an attempt at patching up sentence grammar with the introduction of new features. In Germany, under the stimulus of Peter Hartmann and a host of others, theories were set up to cater for expressly textual problems; they have also found resonance in Austria. At the same time in England, grammarians such as M. A. K. Halliday (e.g. 1967, 1968, 1976) and Ruqaiya Hasan (1968) did pioneering work in integrating textual considerations into a holistic approach to language. Their ideas and grammatical models of textual functions as one systemic level of language have been further applied to stylistics and sociolinguistics. An example of such applications is Robinson and Rackstraw (1972), which reports on question-and-answer sequences within a sociolinguistic frame. Also the grammarians who work with large bodies of texts, for instance those associated with Randolph Quirk's Survey of Contemporary English, have come to observe discoursal features. In the Soviet Union, the growing interest in text linguistics was symbolized by the conference at the Thorez Language Institute in Moscow in 1974 whose papers appeared under the title *Lingvistika teksta*. Several of them combine an interest in text linguistics with a concern for style. And in a number of countries, individual linguists have contributed to text linguistics. Scholars such as Teun van Dijk in Amsterdam (e.g. 1972) and Bengt Sigurd in Stockholm (1974) have written on, and stimulated research into, text linguistics in ways relevant to students of style.

4.7 A far longer and more detailed catalogue could be drawn of various matters of interest to students of style in the works of text linguists. But many students of style have also become increasingly aware of the potential contributions of text linguistics to stylistics. This trend can be amply illustrated in a number of textbooks on stylistics and style theory. Thus Bernd Spillner's *Linguistik und Literaturwissenschaft. Stilforschung, Rhetorik, Textlinguistik* (1974) expressly comments on connections between stylistics, text linguistics and narratology, and gives useful bibliographies of these areas. Willy Sander's little *Linguistische Stiltheorie* (1973) also has a chapter on cohesion and text types. *Deutsche Stilistik* by Elise Riesel and E. Schendels (1975) has a section on 'macrostylistics' containing various textual and narratological considerations. I. R. Gal'perin's Moscow textbook *Stylistics* (1971) contains the useful concept 'gap-sentence link' for instances where the reader must fill in implied, covert connections between two seemingly disjoint sentences (pp. 231–3). A thorough overall treatment of 'Satzübergreifende Konstruktionen' is available in the recent *Stilistik der deutschen Gegenwartssprache* by Wolfgang Fleischer, Georg Michel and their collaborators (1975). These authors begin with an exposition of intersentential crossreference, and go on to discuss paragraph structure, reported speech, interior monologue, indirect speech and *erlebte Rede*. Thus the relevance of text linguistics to stylistics here appears in two areas: first, crossreference, and, secondly, different strategies of embedding one text in another. The latter area of course borders on narratology. Intersentential style markers were also discussed in special sections in the two textbooks written by the present writer: *Linguistic Stylistics* (1973a) and *Stilforskning och stilteori* (1973b). Such examples – which could no doubt be multiplied, and from areas other than the English, German or Scandinavian – show that theorists and teachers of stylistics have come to regard textual considerations and text linguistics as highly relevant to their own concerns.

5.1 Such major historical trends provide a backdrop against which to view individual contributions applying textual views to the study of style. In the following I shall cite a small selection of contributions which examplify text-linguistic approaches to stylistics, that is, investigations which make use, or are relevant to the definition, of such textual style markers as are inaccessible to sentence grammar. And I shall start with some examples of studies concerned with patterns of composition of a text out of text atoms. In this area, the problems consist of the grouping of text atoms into sentences; the ordering of text atoms, clauses, sentences, and text units; and the marking of semantic relations and conjunctions between text atoms, clauses, sentences, and larger units. All this involves text strategies and that part of text linguistics which borders on narratology, and which can be approached with the aid of Hendricks (1973), Koch (1969, 1972), and a host of French neo-structuralist textbooks and studies such as Chabrol (1973).

5.2   One interesting attempt to describe narrative structure is that of Labov and Waletzky (1967). Their materials consisted of oral versions of personal experience, tape-recorded from two kinds of context: face-to-face interviews, and interaction within a group. One of the investigation's prime concerns was the way in which a narrative matched the sequence of actual events with the verbal sequence of clauses. Each clause was tested for potential range of displacement by finding out into what other positions in the text it could be moved without changing the original interpretation of the text. Thus some clauses cannot be moved at all: they are narrative clauses whose sequence is essential. Other clauses are free and can be placed anywhere in the text; others are restricted in that they have some, but not perfect, liberty of movement. The displacement range of each clause can be measured, and the result can be manipulated mathematically to yield stylistically relevant data. In the light of possibilities of displacement, the story itself can also be adjusted and rewritten according to certain 'idealized' patterns. A related approach characterized the paper of Kenneth L. Pike and Evelyn G. Pike of 1972. This paper has the practical aim of introducing elementary students to the practical analysis of discourse. There are seven exercises: story replacement, flipping sentence order, reversing total order, replacement of sentences within the story, replacing the reporter, replacement of neutral reporting with emotional colouring, and rewriting the story with phonological constraints (for instance, into metrical form). Neither paper operates with an expressly stylistic framework. Obviously, however, the principles of these papers are relevant to students of style. The displacement patterns of the sentences of a given text are potential style markers. And some of the Pikes' exercises are in a sense stylistic: they can be said to produce stylistically different variants of the same underlying text.

5.3   Another type of stylistically relevant approach is the study of sequencing in dialogue. In the study of face-to-face communication and in literary representations of such communication, sequencing, turn-taking, methods of opening and of closing discussion, of changing the subject and generally of interaction are of potential stylistic relevance. Students of style may here profit from the methods developed in the work done on sequencing with the aid of corpus materials (e.g. Schenkein 1972, Wise and Lowe 1972, Sacks et al. 1974) and from more theoretical considerations related to sequencing in discourse (Duncan 1973, Banfield 1973, Klammer 1973, Mohan 1974). Conversational roles and strategies and interactive relationships have, according to Sinclair and Coulthard (1975: 150), been analyzed by M. H. Short in a Birmingham thesis on the style of Steinbeck's *Of Mice and Men*.

5.4   Closely related to such studies of dialogue are the investigations of question-answer sequences, of which two recent ones – Fries (1975) and Wikberg (1975) – both concern themselves with the stylistic implications of their materials. Fries works with a corpus drawn from recent British drama, Wikberg with yes-no-questions and their answers in Shakespeare's plays. Wikberg's book in fact contains a chapter devoted to stylistic implications. Thus Shakespeare's comedies proved to contain a far higher average of question-answer units than did the history plays, though with the conspicuous exception of *A Midsummer Night's Dream,* which has fewer such units. This is obviously related to this play's unique combination of romance and low comedy. The distribution of answer types also suggests a certain stylistic development: in the romances and late plays, less stereotype answers consisting of elements other than fixed items or repetitions of part of the question grow increasingly frequent. Thus not only the number of question-answer units but also the correlation between types of question and types of answer may provide the investigator with style markers.

6.1   In text linguistics, problems of co-reference and cross-reference have of course loomed large; in stylistics too, attention has been paid to such matters. Lybbert and Cummings (1969) are among those numerous students of style who have discussed the conceptual apparatus relevant to cohesion studies. Their paper began by reminding its reader of the rhetorical contrast between economy and elaboration. Handbooks of rhetoric have often advised writers to prefer 'economical' sentences such as

"Jim had the spirit of cooperation which is necessary if one wishes to get along with people."

to 'uneconomical' ones such as

"This spirit of cooperation is essential and necessary for anyone to have in order to get along with people, and this is a quality Jim had."

However, the difference between such sentences is not merely a matter of economy, but of 'rhetorical syntax', that is, theme-rheme structure. Indeed there are contexts where the 'uneconomical' arrangement of the sentence is preferable: the text strategy and the cohesive principle may motivate reasons for the sentence to begin with *this spirit of cooperation* rather than with *Jim.* The text strategy and the theme-rheme structure of the text need to be taken into consideration. It would be wrong to advise students to observe very general and sweeping rules such as 'always avoid passives' unless the textual function of such rules is made clear.

6.2   This paper was followed up by another by Cummings, Herum and Lybbert (1971) giving a taxonomy of types of co-referential and cross-referential links between sentences. The categories presented were systematic substitution (through pronouns and pro-verbs), themic recurrence ('near-reiteration'), semi-systematic substitution (reference by general hyperonymic terms: *Charlie – guy, London – city*), parallel substitution (postcedent abbreviates antecedent), derived substitution (postcedent is of a syntactic class different from antecedent), and different types of nonreferential recurrence: specification (*parents – fa-*

ther), expansion(*father – man*), inclusion (which others have called paronymy or co-hyponymy, for instance the relation between *father* and *mother,* which are co-hyponyms of *parent*), and a range of different connotative and associative links (*washing dishes – wife, snake on the patio – scream*). These papers summarize a number of concepts familiar to text linguists and students of cross-reference. Here, however, the aim is to suggest avenues towards a 'rhetorical syntax', or theory of style, which can be applied to discourses to show how different kinds and patterns of cross-reference produce different stylistic effects. Such an apparatus can of course also be normatively applied to help students to gain fluency in discourse. Language teachers and compilers of teaching materials will profit from these conceptual frames.

6.3   A qualitative inventory of devices of co-reference and cross-reference between sentences is an indispensable first stage. It permits an attempt to trace and chart intersentential cohesion devices in actual texts. And after this has been done, the results may be used for the stylistic description of the text. Thus Valerian Swieczkowski has studied types of co-reference and cross-reference as style markers distinguishing between Kipling, Priestley, Virginia Woolf, and a grammar book (Swieczkowski 1961). Another example of an attempt at describing sentence attachments of a text in quantitative terms is John Newton Winburne's analysis of the *Gettysburg Address* (Winburne 1964). And the intersentential structures studied by Myrna Gopnik in scientific texts (Gopnik 1972) for purposes of information processing are of obvious stylistic relevance.

6.4   Figures on frequencies and densities of intersentential cross-reference can also be used as the basis for statistical parameters measuring text connectivity. Three such parameters have been suggested by the Soviet linguists Buxbinder and Rozanov (1975). A 'local coefficient' K_1 can be determined for any sentence pair according to the formula $K_1 = R/N$, where R = the number of cross-references between the two sentences and N = the number of full words (as opposed to form-words) in the two sentences. The 'coefficient of regressive linkage' is computed as $K_r = K / (M-1)$, where K is the number of cross-referential links between words in a string of sentences, and M the number of sentences in this particular string. The third coefficient is one of 'semantic load', $K_S = L/N$, where L is the number of cross-references between the full words of the sentence studied and other full words in the text, and N is the total number of full words in all the sentences that are cross-referentially linked to the sentence studied, plus the full linking words of the sentence itself. Obviously such statistical parameters can illustrate the breakdown of a text into units of discourse. But they can also be regarded as potential parameters of style: their means as well as their deviations within the text may be stylistically significant.

6.5   It is then possible to classify and count intersentential links and even devise statistical parameters and 'coefficients' characterizing the cohesion of a text. However, in addition to such counts of degrees of cohesion and densities of cohesion devices it is also relevant to study the patterns according to which co-references and cross-references link sentences into texts. These patterns in fact give better indications of text strategies than do mere figures on densities of cohesion devices. Thus the difference between texts such as

(a) *John* came into the room. *He* walked across the carpet. *He* went to the cupboard, *0* opened the door and *0* took out *his* gun.
(b) Temperatures are measured with *thermometers*. *A thermometer* consists of a glass tube containing mercury, and a *scale*. *The scale* is divided into *degrees*. *Zero* is, on the centigrade scale, set at the freezing point of water...

will not appear merely through counts and statistical parameters: we must also observe what positions and functions the linking constituents have in their respective sentences. In two papers (1970a, 1970b), František Daneš has set up a taxonomy for patterns of thematic progression: his terms are 'simple linear progression', 'progression with a continuous theme', 'exposition of a split theme', 'thematic progression with derived themes', and 'thematic progression with an omitted link'. These 'abstract principles' then appear in various combinations, whose densities and proportions may turn out to be style markers. The present writer has tried to apply somewhat simpler principles to a comparison of texts of different kinds, giving his procedure the working label 'theme dynamics' (Enkvist 1973c). Thus texts such as Boswell's *London Journal* and Hemingway proved to have a high incidence of cross-referential links from theme to theme within the text. On the contrary, certain scholarly articles were characterized by high proportions of cross-reference from the rheme of one sentence to the theme of the next. Thus the patterns of cross-reference, beside the densities of cross-references as such, may also be stylistic discriminants.

6.6   For those evaluating such studies or contemplating the use of such methods, it is important to note that, however accurate the emerging figures may seem, the results can never be more reliable than the input. And the input into the calculations must consist of informant judgments of the existence and type of cross-referential links between constituents of different sentences. Anybody who has analysed texts for cross-reference knows that such judgments often contain a subjective element. This is particularly striking in texts whose links involve subtle allusions – poetry or literary prose, for instance – and not only unambiguous references of the kind writers of scientific prose struggle to achieve. In practice, then, common sense is needed to decide what data on intersentential connections are sufficiently firm for meaningful quantification, and what data are better expressed as, say, literary explication, 'close reading' of a poem and the like. The problem is a familiar one indeed to all those who have contemplated lines of demarcation between linguistic stylistics in the strict sense, and the literary stylistics that merges into criticism.

7.1   The study of cohesion devices and intersentential cohesion patterns provides the basis for yet another branch of textual stylistics, namely that studying suprasentential text units at different levels and their structure. Sometimes such studies are known as investigations into 'paragraph structure'; a less traditional term such as 'discourse unit' would be preferable as a reminder that linguistically definable units may, but need not, coincide with conventional typographical paragraphs (in fact the extent to which they do so coincide might also be a style marker). The psychological reality of discourse units has been investigated by psycholinguists (for example Koen et al. 1969); the clustering of sentence types (Streeter 1973) may also provide stylistically relevant evidence for the existence of discourse units.

7.2   As Soviet linguists have been particularly interested in the ontological status and characteristics of suprasentential units (sverhfraznoe edinstvo, slož-noe sintaksičeskoe celoe) as well as in stylistics, it is not surprising that these two interests have been combined to produce some works making use of textual features as style markers. Two of the longer studies characterized by such an approach are T. I. Sil'man's *Problemy sintaksičeskoj stilistiki* (1967) and G. Ja. Solganik's *Sintaksičeskaja stilistika* (1973). Silman devoted the three major chapters of her book to syntactic and lexicosyntactic links between sentences and to paragraph structure in the prose of Winckelmann, Lessing, Herder and Goethe. Solganik deals first with mechanisms of cross-reference and then with textual units held together by cross-reference. His term for units of discourse is *prozaičeskie strofy;* these 'proze stanzas' are then classified and their characteristics used as style markers. Ol'ga Akhmanova and her pupils, as well as S. I. Gindin, E. V. Padučeva, N. S. Pospelov, A. L. Pumpjanskij, N. I. Serkova and V. N. Skibo are among those numerous Soviet linguists who have dealt with thematic characteristics of texts and with suprasentential features as style markers. L. Friedmann's papers on paragraph structure are more rhetorical than linguistic in their frames of reference (Friedmann 1972). At the stylistics conference at the Thorez Language Institute in Moscow in 1969, out of 75 papers at least three dealt with intersentential connections and paragraph structure; at the conference of text linguistics at the same place in 1974, several contributions dealt with, or touched upon, stylistic and literary problems of texts.

7.3   Of course discourse units can be used in any distribution studies. To mention just one example: Jan Svartvik and Bengt Törjas have studied the distribution of time references by paragraph in James D. Watson's *The Double Helix* and noted a certain amount of patterned variation, which apparently reflects alternation between narrative passages (having many time references) and descriptive passages (with low densities of time references) (Svartvik and Törjas 1975).

8.1   Two concluding remarks are in order. First, this essay has been concerned with the application of text grammar and discourse analysis to the stylistic description of texts. But it is worth noting that the current can run in the opposite direction as well. The stylistic description of texts is bound to throw light on textual variation and thus provide data and materials for text grammarians and text theorists. In fact it can be said that an approach which uses style and textual variation as an input to validate various points of text theory has appeared in a number of studies, for instance in several of those collected into recent anthologies of text linguistics (for instance Gülich and Raible 1972 and Grivel and Kibedi Varga 1974). These papers are concerned with text typologies and distinctive characteristics of text types, but the brunt of their argument seems to run from text types and text variants towards text grammar and text theory rather than from text theory and text grammar towards style.

8.2   Finally, to gain perspective we might recall that as late as 1968, Dwight Bolinger wrote: "We have not begun to scratch the surface of textual dynamics." (Bolinger 1968: 39.) Today we can say that a certain amount of mining has been done. Indeed some linguists have a feeling that text theory has been comparatively well developed and that further empirical work with the discoursal analysis of corpora of texts will now be in order to test the theories. Stylistic studies are bound to play an important role in this process, and they can draw some support from recent contributions to theories of linguistic variation. There is, to all appearances, plenty of room for intensive work. Some methods and approaches have been mentioned in this essay. But we can still use new, and perhaps more imaginative, applications of textual concepts in the comparison and stylistic analysis of texts.

References

Akhmanova, Ol'ga, & M.M. Gluško, ed. 1974. *Funkcional'nyj stil' obščenaučnogo jazyka i metody ego issledovanija.* Izdatel'stvo Moskovskogo universiteta.

Banfield, Ann. 1973. "Narrative Style and the Grammar of Direct and Indirect Speech." *Foundations of Language* 10, 1–39.

Bolinger, Dwight. 1968. "Judgments of Grammaticality." *Lingua* 21, 31–40.

Brend, Ruth M., ed. 1974. *Advances in Tagmemics.* North Holland Publishing Company, Amsterdam & London; American Elsevier Publishing Company, Inc., New York.

Buxbinder, V.A., & E.D. Rozanov. 1975. "O celostnosti i strukture teksta." *Voprosy Jazykoznanija* 1975:6, 73–86.

Chabrol, Claude, ed. 1973. *Sémiotique narrative et textuelle.* Larousse, Paris.

Chaplen, Frank. 1970. *Paragraph Writing.* Oxford University Press, London.

Christensen, Francis. 1967. "A Generative Rhetoric of the Paragraph" in *Notes Towards a New Rhetoric.* Harper & Row, New York, Evanston, London, pp. 52–81.

Cummings, D.W., John Herum & E.K. Lybbert. 1971. "Semantic Recurrence and Rhetorical Form." *Language and Style* 4:3, 195–207.

Daneš, František. 1970a "Zur linguistischen Analyse der Textstruktur." *Folia Linguistica* 4, 72–78.

- 1970 b. "One Instance of Prague School Methodology: Functional Analysis of Utterance and Text" in Paul Garvin, ed., *Method and Theory in Linguistics*. Mouton, The Hague & Paris.
- ed. 1974. *Papers on Functional Sentence Perspective*. Academia, Prague & Mouton, The Hague & Paris.

Dressler, Wolfgang U., & Siegfried J. Schmidt, edd. 1973. *Textlinguistik. Kommentierte Bibliographie*. Fink, Munich.

Duncan, Starkey, Jr. 1973. "Toward a Grammar for Dyadic Conversation." *Semiotica* 9:1, 29–46.

Enkvist, Nils Erik. 1973a. *Linguistic Stylistics*. Mouton, The Hague & Paris.
- 1973b. *Stilforskning och stilteori*. Gleerup, Lund.
- 1973c. "'Theme Dynamics' and Style." *Studia Anglica Posnaniensia* 5:1/2, 127–135.

Firbas, Jan. 1964. "From Comparative Word Order Studies." *Brno Studies in English* 4, 111–127.
- 1974. "Some Aspects of the Czechoslovak Approach to Problems of Functional Sentence Perspective" in F. Daneš, ed., *Papers on Functional Sentence Perspective*. Academia, Prague & Mouton, The Hague & Paris, pp. 11–37.

Fleischer, Wolfgang, Georg Michel et al. 1975. *Stilistik der deutschen Gegenwartssprache*. VEB Bibliographisches Institut, Leipzig.

Friedmann, L. 1972. "Einige Besonderheiten polythematischer Absätze und ihrer Komponenten in der deutschen Gegenwartssprache." *Zeitschrift für Phon., Sprachwissensch. und Komm. forschung* 25:4/5, 281–288.

Fries, Udo. 1975. *Studien zur Textlinguistik. Frage- und Antwortsätze. Eine Analyse an neuenglischen Dramentexten*. Wilhelm Braumüller, Wien & Stuttgart.

Gal'perin, I. R., ed. 1969. *Naučnaja konferencija problemy lingvističeskoj stilistiki*. 1–j Moskovskij gosudarstvennyj pedagogičeskij institut inostrannyx jazykov imeni M. Toreza. Moskva.
- 1971. *Stylistics*. Higher School Publishing House, Moscow.

Gläser, Rosemarie. 1969. *Linguistische Kriterien der Stilbeschreibung*. Typescript of Habilitationsschrift, Karl-Marx-Universität, Leipzig.

Gopnik, Myrna. 1972. *Linguistic Structures in Scientific Texts*. Mouton, The Hague & Paris.

Grivel, Ch., & A. Kibedi Varga. 1974. *Du linguistique au textuel*. Van Gorcum, Assen & Amsterdam.

Gülich, Elisabeth, & Wolfgang Raible. 1972. *Textsorten. Differenzierungskriterien aus linguistischer Sicht*. Athenäum, Frankfurt.

Halliday, M. A. K. 1967, 1968. "Notes on Transitivity and Theme in English." *Journal of Linguistics* 3, 37–81, 199–244; 4, 179–216.
- & Ruqaiya Hasan. 1976. *Cohesion in English*. Longmans, London.

Harweg, Roland. 1972. "Stilistik und Textgrammatik." *LiLi* 2:5, 71–81.
- 1973. "Text Grammar and Literary Texts." *Poetics* 9, 65–91.

Hasan, Ruqaiya. 1968. *Grammatical Cohesion in Spoken and Written English*. Longmans, London.

Hendricks, William O. 1973. *Essays on Semiolinguistics and Verbal Art*. Mouton, The Hague & Paris.

Kallmeyer, W., W. Klein, R. Meyer-Hermann, K. Netzer & H. J. Siebert, Hrsg. 1974. *Lektürekolleg zur Textlinguistik*. Athenäum Verlag, Frankfurt am Main.

Klammer, Thomas P. 1973. "Foundations for a Theory of Dialogue Structure." *Poetics* 9, 27–64.

Koch, W. A. 1969. *Vom Morphem zum Textem*. Olms, Hildesheim.
- 1972. *Strukturelle Textanalyse. Discourse Analysis. Analyse du Récit*. Olms, Hildesheim & New York.

Koen, Frank, Alton Becker & Richard Young. 1969. "The Psychological Reality of the Paragraph," *Journal of Verbal Learning and Verbal Behavior* 8, 49–53.

Labov, William, & Joshua Waletzky. 1967. "Narrative Analysis: Oral Versions of Personal Experience" in June Helm, ed., *Essays on the Verbal and Visual Arts*. University of Washington Press, Seattle & London, pp. 12–44.

Lingvistika teksta. 1974. Materialy naučnoj konferencii. I–II. Moskovskij gosudarstvennyj pedagogičeskij institut inostrannyx jazykov imeni Morisa Toreza. Moskva.

Lybbert, E.K., & D.W. Cummings. 1969. "Rhetorical Syntax, Economy, and the Theme-Rheme Distinction." *Language and Style* 2:3, 244-256.

Mohan, Bernard A. 1974. "Do Sequencing Rules Exist?" *Semiotica* 12:1, 75–96.

Ohmann, Richard. 1964. "Generative Grammars and the Concept of Literary Style." *Word* 20, 423–439.

Petöfi, Janos S., & Hannes Rieser. 1973. *Studies in Text Grammar*. Dordrecht & Boston.

Pike, Kenneth L., & Evelyn G. Pike. 1972. "Seven Substitution Exercises for Studying the Structure of Discourse." *Linguistics* 94, 43–52.

Riesel, Elise, & E. Schendels. 1975. *Deutsche Stilistik*. Verlag Hochschule, Moskau.

Robinson, W.P., & Susan J. Rackstraw. 1972. *A Question of Answers, I–II*. Routledge and Kegan Paul, London.

Sacks, Harvey, Emanuel A. Schegloff & Gail Jefferson. 1974. "A Simplest Systematics for the Organization of Turn-Taking for Conversation." *Language* 50:4, 696–735.

Sanders, Willy. 1973. *Linguistische Stiltheorie*. Vandenhoeck & Ruprecht, Göttingen.

Schenkein, James N. 1972. "Towards an Analysis of Natural Conversation and the Sense of *Heheh*." *Semiotica* 6:4, 344–377.

Schmidt, Siegfried J. 1973. *Texttheorie*. München.

Segre, Cesare. 1975. "Le strutture narrative e la storia." *Strumenti critici* 27, 198–207.

Sigurd, Bengt. 1974. *Experiment med text*. Papers from the Institute of Linguistics, University of Stockholm.

Sil'man, T.I. 1967. *Problemy sintaksičeskoj stilistiki (na materiale nemeckoj prozy)*. Prosveščenie, Leningrad.

Sinclair, J.McH., & R.M. Coulthard. 1975. *Towards an Analysis of Discourse. The English Used by Teachers and Pupils*. Oxford University Press, London.

Solganik, G. Ja. 1973. *Sintaksičeskaja stilistika*. (Složnoe sintaksičeskoe celoe.) "Vysšaja škola", Moskva.

Spillner, Bernd. 1974. *Linguistik und Literaturwissenschaft. Stilforschung, Rhetorik, Textlinguistik*. Kohlhammer, Stuttgart.

Stempel, Wolf-Dieter, ed. 1971. *Beiträge zur Textlinguistik*. Fink München.

Streeter, Victor J. 1973. "A Look at Sentence-Type Cohesion." *Language and Style* 6:2, 109–116.

Svartvik, Jan & Bengt Törjas. 1975. "Rhythmic Variation in the Use of Time Reference" in Håkan Ringbom et al., eds., *Style and Text. Studies Presented to Nils Erik Enkvist*. Skriptor, Stockholm, pp. 416–432.

Swieczkowski, Valerian. 1961. "On the Margin of Syntax and Style" in Donald Davie et al., eds., *Poetics. Poetyka. Poetika*. Warszawa & The Hague.

Tyl, Zdenek, ed. 1970. *A Tentative Bibliography of Studies in Functional Sentence Perspective*. Ceskoslovenská akademie ved, Ustav pro jazyk česky, Praha.

Vachek, Josef, ed. 1964. *A Prague School Reader in Linguistics*. Indiana University Press, Bloomington.

Van Dijk, Teun A. 1972. *Some Aspects of Text Grammars*. Mouton, The Hague & Paris.

– 1973. "Text Grammar and Text Logic" in J.S. Petöfi & H. Rieser, eds., *Studies in Text Grammar*, Reidel, Dordrecht & Boston, pp. 17–78.

Wikberg, Kay. 1975. *Yes-No Questions and Answers in Shakespeare's Plays. A Study in Text Linguistics*. Acta Academiae Aboensis, A. Humaniora 51:1, Åbo Akademi.

Winburne, John Newton. 1964. "Sentence Sequence in Discourse" in Horace G. Lunt, ed., *Proceedings of the Ninth International Congress of Linguists*. Mouton, The Hague & Paris, pp. 1094–1099.

Wise, Mary Ruth, & Ivan Lowe. 1972. "Permutation Groups in Discourse," *Language and Linguistics Working Papers* 4, Georgetown University Press, Washington D.C., pp. 12–34.

Discourse Analysis in the Framework of Zellig S. Harris

Ellen F. Prince
University of Pennsylvania

1 Introduction

For some linguists, particularly in the United States, there exists a dichotomy between the grammatical analysis of sentences and the grammatical analysis of discourse; indeed it is to this apparent dichotomy that the present volume is addressed.[1]

In the framework of Zellig Harris, as it has evolved over the past quarter of a century in particular, no such dichotomy is observable. That is not to say that, for Harris, the sentence has not figured as an important piece of data. It in fact was all that was apparently required for the study of phonology and morphology, the domain of descriptive linguistics:

"... Descriptive linguistics generally stops at sentence boundaries. This is not due to any prior decision. The techniques of linguistics were constructed to study any stretch of speech, of whatever length. But in every language it turns out that almost all the results lie within a relatively short stretch, which we may call a sentence. That is, when we can state a restriction on the occurrence of element A in respect to the occurrence of element B, it will almost always be the case that A and B are regarded as occurring within the same sentence." (1952a: 1f.)

For example, the conditioning environments of the various allophones of English /p/, as in *pot, spot, top,* or of the various allomorphs of *be,* as in *am, is, are,* are always intrasentential and the sentence is therefore an appropriate datum.

However, phonological and morphological analyses did not account for all that is of interest to the linguist. The next step was *immediate constituent analysis* (see Harris 1946, Wells 1947), whereby utterances were parsed following the criterion of substitutability; this was the descriptive linguist's rigorous, formal response to the impressionistic, semantically-based parsing of traditional grammarians. However, it was soon apparent that IC analysis did not reveal all of language structure. It was at this stage that Harris embarked on what he called *discourse analysis,* the 'analysis of connected speech (or writing)'

---

[1] I wish to acknowledge my deepest gratitude to Zellig S. Harris for his most patient explanations and to Danuṭa Hiz and Gerald Prince for their very helpful comments and criticisms. Errors are, of course, my own.

(1952 a:1), for which purpose sentences per se were no longer useful objects of study:

"Although we cannot state the distribution of sentences (or, in general, any inter-sentence relation) when we are given an arbitrary conglomeration of sentences in a language, we can get quite definite results about certain relations across sentence boundaries when we consider just the sentences of a particular discourse – that is, the sentences spoken or written in succession by one or more persons in a single situation... Language does not occur in stray words or sentences, but in connected discourse – from a one-word utterance to a ten-volume work, from a monolog to a Union Square argument. Arbitrary conglomerations of sentences are indeed of no interest except as a check on grammatical description." (1952 a:3)

Below, we shall first examine the model of discourse analysis as originally posited by Harris in the 1950s (section 2). Then we shall trace the development of transformational theory as a tool for discourse analysis (section 3), and we shall examine various applications of this theory to discourse analysis (section 4). Lastly, we shall study the two-systems model of grammar and its development as a model of transformational grammar based directly on discourse.

2   Discourse analysis: the early model

As first presented in 1952 a, b, 1963, discourse analysis was an attempt to analyze in a strictly formal manner concrete samples of connected speech or writing. *Formal* is taken to mean 'according to form', that is, not according to meaning. 'The method [depends] only on the occurrence of morphemes as distinguished elements; it does not depend on the analyst's knowledge of the particular meaning of each morpheme' (1952 a:1). The only prior knowledge of which the analyst is at liberty to make use is knowledge of what the morphemes of the language are. He/she, therefore, can segment the text or stream of speech into sequences of morphemes.

2.1   The method

Once the morphemes and morpheme boundaries have been identified, the text is ready for discourse analysis. The method is distributional: we begin by isolating occurrences of words (morphemes) or sequences thereof that have identical environments, where the environment is the rest of the sentence. Those words or morphemes having identical environments are then said to be *equivalent*. It is important to note that for two items to be equivalent does not require that they be equal to each other in any general sense and certainly not that they be synonymous or equivalent in any semantic way; see 1952 a: 7. Equivalence means simply 'occurrence in like environments' or, put differently, substitutability preserving acceptability (though not necessarily meaning). This is a central notion in Harris' work, as will be seen in later sections.

To return to the method of discourse analysis, consider the following text:
(1) Andy toured Moscow; Bill toured Moscow;
    Carol visited New York; Bill visited New York.
The sentences of the text may be segmented and numbered as follows:
(1) 1. $(Andy)_1$ $(toured\ Moscow)_1$, 2. $(Bill)_2$ $(toured\ Moscow)_2$,
    3. $(Carol)_3$ $(visited\ New\ York)_3$, 4. $(Bill)_4$ $(visited\ New\ York)_4$,
where the subscripts indicate the number of the sentence in the text in which
each morpheme(-sequence) occurs. To analyze the text, we make use of the
following relations:
i. $a =_0 b$ iff a is the same morpheme-sequence as b and occupies the same
    grammatical position in a sentence.[2]
ii. $a =_n b$ iff env $a =_{n-1}$ env b, where a, b, ... are morphemes or sequences
    thereof and env a is the sentential complement of a, itself a morpheme or
    (perhaps discontinuous) sequence thereof (1963: 8, 42f.).
Thus, by (i):
    $(toured\ Moscow)_1 =_0 (toured\ Moscow)_2$,
    $(visited\ New\ York)_3 =_0 (visited\ New\ York)_4$, $(Bill)_2 =_0 (Bill)_4$
We may now drop the subscripts, as $=_0$ indicates identity. By (ii), one then
obtains the following equivalences:
    Andy $=_1$ Bill, Bill $=_1$ Carol, toured Moscow $=_1$ visited New York
There are now two ways of establishing a relation between *Bill* and *Carol*. One,
making use of symmetry and transitivity, yields:
    Bill $=_1$ Andy $=_0$ Andy $=_1$ Carol,
    Bill $=_1$ Andy $=_1$ Carol, Bill $=_2$ Carol
The other makes use of (ii):
    Bill $=_2$ Carol iff toured Moscow $=_1$ visited New York
    In addition, the theory posits certain 'ad hoc equivalences' (1963: 9f.). The
first concerns *grammatical parallelism:*
iii. If *a* is in the same grammatical relation to *f* as *b* is to *g,* then, if af = bg, then a
    = b, f = g.
Reconsidering our text, preliminary parsing tells us that *toured* (1, 2) is a verb
whose direct object is *Moscow*. Likewise, *visited* (3,4) with respect to *New
York*. Therefore,
    visited = toured, Moscow = New York
    The text may now be represented as a *double array,* where the columns
show the equivalence classes and the rows the sentences (actually, the periods;
see below) of the text:

	A	T	M
1.	Andy	toured	Moscow
2.	Bill	toured	Moscow
3.	Carol	visited	New York
4.	Bill	visited	New York

---

[2] This will be revised below.

(Other ad hoc equivalences, not needed for this text, are:

iv. If *d* does not occur except with *a* and if *d* is an adjunct of *a*, i.e. *ad* is a phrase of the category *a* (*a* therefore being the *center* of *ad*), then ad = a or da = a.

v. *asserted equivalence:* if the text includes some sentence or transform thereof like *a is b* or *a includes b*, then a = b.)

The above equivalence relations are more than adequate for texts like the exceedingly simple one given above for illustration. For more complex texts, however, these relations alone are inadequate, since the equivalences are based on environments within the sentence, which, in actual discourse, appear quite dissimilar. It was for this reason that Harris invented (discovered?) linguistic transformations:

"The method of linguistic transformations makes it possible to reduce some of these dissimilarities. We want in this way to eliminate stylistic variations among the sentences of the discourse, to align these sentences grammatically." (1963: 11)

Linguistic transformations had actually been introduced by Harris as early as 1952 for this very purpose: to regularize or normalize the text so that the distributional methods of discourse analysis could be employed:

"... It is useful to combine [the] method of [discourse analysis] with descriptive linguistics. To this end we would use only those statements of the grammar of the language which are true for any sentence of a given form. For example, given any English sentence of the form $N_1 V N_2$ (e.g. *The boss fired Jim*), we can get a sentence with the noun phrases in the reverse order ... by changing the suffixes around the verb: *Jim was fired by the boss*. The justification for using such grammatical information in the analysis of a text is that since it is applicable to any $N_1 V N_2$ sentence in English it must also be applicable to any $N_1 V N_2$ sentence in the particular text before us, provided only that this is written in English ... It merely transforms certain sentences of the text into grammatically equivalent sentences ..., in such a way that the application of the discourse analysis method becomes more convenient, or that it becomes possible in particular sections of the text where it was not possible to apply it before." (1952a: 4)

Making use of transformations, we proceed with an analysis as follows: We apply the transformations to the sentences of a discourse D, obtaining a transform TS of the sentences, making up a transform TD of D. Since the transformations are varied and optional, we actually obtain various transforms T_iD of D. One of these transforms, T_0D, will be optimal for the applicability of the above equivalences. Call this, the optimal transform, D'. The sentences of D', S', are the *periods* of D. Insofar as the transformations are paraphrastic, D' will be a paraphrase of D. The periods of D', together with the connectors between them, necessarily make up the whole discourse. That is, there is no item in the discourse that neither is within a period nor is a connector between periods. (Tabular material, mathematical expressions, etc. are reduced to linear form and are expressed as a succession of periods.)

By way of illustration, let us consider the following text:

(2) The *Mona Lisa* and *Waterlilies* are priceless. The great *Mona Lisa* is on exhibit in Paris and *Waterlilies* in New York. I guess that the world has been enriched by the *Mona Lisa,* but I know that *Waterlilies* has enriched my life.

If we try immediately to look for equivalences, we find that there are none, for, in spite of repeated occurrences of the same morphemes, no two occurrences have identical environments. Therefore, the text must first be regularized by means of transformations, for example:[3]

a. N_1 and $N_2 V_i \Omega_i \rightarrow N_1 V_i \Omega_i$ and $N_2 V_i \Omega_i$
b. $N_1 V_i \Omega_1$ and $N_2 \Omega_2 \rightarrow N_1 V_i \Omega_1$ and $N_2 V_i \Omega_2$
c. N_2 be $V_i$en by $N_1 \rightarrow N_1 V_i N_2$

If these transformations are applied to the sentences of discourse (2), the following transform of the discourse obtains:

(3) (i) The *Mona Lisa* is priceless (ii) and *Waterlilies* is priceless. (iii) The great *Mona Lisa* is on exhibit in Paris (iv) and *Waterlilies* is on exhibit in New York. (v) I guess that the *Mona Lisa* has enriched the world, (vi) but I know that *Waterlilies* has enriched my life.

Obviously, many other transforms of discourse (2) are possible, if we apply different transformations, e.g.

(4) The *Mona Lisa* is priceless and *Waterlilies* is, too. It is in Paris and New York that the great *Mona Lisa* and *Waterlilies* are on exhibit, respectively. What I guess is that the *Mona Lisa* has enriched the world, but what it is that I know is that my life has been enriched by *Waterlilies.*

It is clear that the greater number of equivalences are statable if we take (3), and, therefore, (3), rather than (4), will serve as the optimal transform. The numbering in (3) thus marks off the periods of (2). Having obtained the optimal transform of the text, one finds little difficulty in setting up the equivalence classes, which may be represented by the following double array:

	A	I	G	M	P
(i)				the *Mona Lisa*	is priceless
(ii)	and			*Waterlilies*	is priceless
(iii)				the great *ML*	is on exhibit in Paris
(iv)	and			*Waterlilies*	is on exhibit in NY
(v)		I	guess that	the *Mona Lisa*	has enriched the world
(vi)	but	I	know that	*Waterlilies*	has enriched my life

In a double array, as was mentioned above, each period is assigned a row and each relevant morpheme or sequence of morphemes a column, labeled arbitrarily. 'Then each column is an equivalence class, each row shows the composition of equivalence classes into a period, and the sequence of all the rows is the transformed discourse itself' (1963: 17).

---

[3] The notation used here and below is as follows: N = noun(-phrase), V = verb, Ω = object phrase (including prepositional phrase, adverb, etc.), Ven = past participle, t = tense, P = preposition, A = adjective, A_{1y} = manner adverb, D = time/place adverb, φ = operator.

Even such a simple text suggests interesting facts. For example, there are some morphemes, e.g. those appearing in column G, that introduce into the discourse a following MP, which, had it occurred alone, would have constituted a sentence. Upon analyzing many discourses, one finds that the syntactic classes set up according to distributional criteria often seem to coincide with semantic classes. ('. . . Differences in meaning correlate highly with differences in linguistic distribution' (1952a: 25).) In this case, G will turn out to be a 'metadiscourse' morpheme class, including as well *except, find,* etc. I, that is, the subject of G, are, in this discourse and in general, human nouns. Although such facts are often beclouded in an ordinary discourse, they emerge clearly following the methods of regularization and analysis into equivalence classes. (In complex texts, the regularization and analysis are far more involved and interesting, but the resulting patterns are no less clear. See for example the analysis of a scientific text in 1963: 44ff.)

3   Linguistic transformations

3.1   Motivation in discourse analysis

It is clear from the above that linguistic transformations are the sine qua non of discourse analysis. In the early presentations, those transformations that are needed are simply posited (1952a: 18ff., 1952b: 477ff.), which Harris himself recognizes as being a 'cavalier treatment of horizontal order' (1952a: 9). Obviously, this situation had to be remedied: transformational analysis – the act of normalizing a text – has to be as rigorously formal and precise as any subsequent partitioning into equivalence classes. Thus, in the mid to late 1950s, with this goal in mind, Harris embarked on a study of linguistic transformations. What follows is a brief and simplified examination of the development of Harris' transformational theory.

3.2   Criteria for transformations

It is an empirical fact of language that utterances are composed of, or may be analyzed as being composed of (e.g. as in writing), discrete elements which are linearly ordered. Likewise, it is a fact that not all combinations of the elements of a language, i.e. linear orderings, occur as utterances or sentences of that language. This is not, of course, peculiar to the level of word/morpheme: the same is true at the phonological and morphological levels. At the level of the sentence, for example, we find the following:

(5) a. John visited Paris.   d. *John Paris visited.
    b. *Visited John Paris.   e. *Visited Paris John.
    c. Paris John visited.   f. *Paris visited John.

Of the six possible permutations of *John, visited, Paris,* only two, (a) and (c), occur as utterances of English. In case this is an isolated fact of these particular morphemes, we test other triplets of morphemes of the same grammatical categories, e.g.

(6) a. Mary loves pancakes.

and so on. Consider the (a) form of (5) and of (6) to be of the form $N_1 V N_2$ and label the (b-f) sentences accordingly. $N_1 V N_2$ is then a *sentence-form*. If we realize this form with an arbitrary sample of appropriate morphemes, some of the resultant strings will occur as sentences of English, while others will not, e.g.

(7) a. Mary loves pancakes.   c. John visited Paris.

    b. *Osmosis understands Jane.

    d. *Ice misses jealousy.

Now consider the same morphemes in a different sequence of morpheme-classes, e.g. $N_2 N_1 V$:

(8) a. Pancakes Mary loves.   c. Paris Sam visited.

    b. *Jane osmosis understands.   d. *Jealousy ice misses.

The two sets of sentences display the same facts of co-occurrence, i.e. what co-occurs as a sentence in (7) co-occurs as a sentence in (8), and, conversely, what is not a sentence in (7) is not a sentence in (8). We then conclude that there exists a transformation which maps sentences of the form of (7), $N_1 V N_2$, onto sentences of the form of (8), $N_2 N_1 V$, *transformation* being defined as a mapping of a set of sentences of a given form$_i$ onto a set of sentences of a given form$_j$, *preserving co-occurrence*[4] (1957 c: section 1.3). Compare with word-sequences of the form $N_2 V N_1$:

(9) a. *Pancakes love(s) Mary.   c. *Paris visited Sam.

    b. Jane understands osmosis.   d. *Jealousy misses ice.

Since the relative acceptability-ordering of (7) and that of (8) differs from that of (9), there is no transformation mapping sentences of the form $N_1 V N_2$ or $N_2 N_1 V$ onto those of the form $N_2 V N_1$. If we revise our thinking to take into account the division of the vocabulary into lexical items and grammatical items and permit the sentence-forms to include specific grammatical items as constants, then we obtain transformations like the following:

(10) a. $N_1 t V N_2 \leftrightarrow N_2 t \text{Ven by } N_1$

    John saw the movie $\leftrightarrow$ The movie was seen by John.

    b. $N t V \Omega \leftrightarrow$ It is N that/who/which $t V \Omega$

    John left $\leftrightarrow$ It is John who left.

    c. $N_1 t \text{ have } N_2 (\text{wh-}N_2 V \Omega) \leftrightarrow N_1{}'s N_2 (V \Omega)$

    Mary has a friend (who is here) $\leftrightarrow$ Mary's friend (is here)

The notion of *preservation of co-occurrence* turns out to be insufficiently supple, as co-occurrence is a yes/no question, whereas strings may be neither in nor out but also in between. Thus Harris refines this notion to *preservation of relative acceptability-ordering* (1957: section 1.44, 1964b: 475, 1965: section 2, and elsewhere). Thus the informant need merely evaluate the relative accept-

---

[4] If i = j, the relation is an identity relation.

ability of any two sentences; he/she need not say for any individual sentence whether it is 'good' or 'bad'.[5]

3.3   The elementary sentence-forms

It has already been shown that, given a list of all the morpheme-classes of the language, for some (most) of the possible sequences of those classes, there is no word-choice satisfying that sequence and occurring as a sentence of that language, e.g. $V N_1 N_2$ for English. Call those sequences that do occur *sentence-forms*. Once the transformations have been determined, it turns out that certain sentence-forms can be obtained by applying one or more transformations to certain other sentence-forms. For example, if our list of sentence-forms includes:

$N_1 t V N_2$, $N_2 N_1 t V$, $N_2 t$ be Ven by N_1,

and if we have determined that the following transformations exist in the language:

$N_1 t V N_2 \leftrightarrow N_2 N_1 t V$ (Asyntactic Permutation)

$N_1 t V N_2 \leftrightarrow N_2 t$ be Ven by N_1 (Passive),

then we may take $N_1 t V N_2$ to be an *elementary sentence-form* or a *kernel sentence-form* and the other two to be derivable from it (or decomposable into it). The word-choices which satisfy elementary sentence-forms produce the *elementary* or *kernel sentences*.

3.4   The paraphrastic transformations and the increments

Harris distinguishes between two types of operations on sentences: paraphrastic transformations and incremental operations, which may be considered separately.

3.4.1   The paraphrastic transformations

As illustrated above, if two sets of sentences, each set composed of sentences of a particular sentence-form but containing the same word-choices, display identical relative acceptability-orderings, then there is a paraphrastic transformation which maps the sentences of one set onto those of the other. These transformations consist of a small number of operations: permutation (φ_p), morphophonemic or shape change (φ_m), including addition of constants, and zeroing (φ_z) (1964a: 483, 1965: 372f., 1968: 121f.). For example, (10a) above involves permutation and addition of constants, (10c) above zeroing and morphophonemic change. When a transformational operation operates on a sentence, it leaves a *trace* (1964a: section 7.1, 1966: 605, 1968: 61ff. et passim), which may be a unique sentence-form, e.g. $N_2 N_1 t V$, or a particular constant, e.g. *be* + past participle + *by,* or an occurrence of a particular

---

[5] Such constraints on the type and amount of knowledge that the informant is asked to verbalize has been characteristic of Harris' work from the outset; see 1951.

morpheme without its usually required co-occurrents, e.g. *John read all night* ←
John read something/things all night (Zeroing of indefinite objects). The notion
of trace insures that the transformations can be 'undone'; in particular, it
guarantees that material may be zeroed only if it is redundant and, therefore,
retrievable. A particular morpheme may be redundant in a given context for
linguistic reasons, as in the zeroing of repeated material, e.g. *We hope (that) we
win, We hope for us to win* → *We hope to win,* or it may be redundant for
nonlinguistic reasons. For example, in *My dog has been found by someone,* it is
selection (co-occurrence) and not arbitrary grammar that makes *by someone*
redundant and hence zeroable.

The fact that transformations leave traces and are therefore 'undoable' does
not imply that they are uniquely so. In fact, two different transformations, each
operating on different sentences, may leave homonymous traces, resulting in
degeneracy and hence ambiguity. However, the resulting sentence can still be
analyzed; it will simply have two analyses (if it is two-ways ambiguous), e.g.
Frost reads smoothly ← *Frost reads things smoothly* and also ← *Someone/Pe-
ople read(s) Frost smoothly* (1965: fn. 31, 1966: 607, 1968: 120).

The bulk of the paraphrastic transformations are defined on elementary
(kernel) sentences. Except for Asyntactic Permutation, they have resultant
sentences which are kernel-like in form, in which case they themselves may be
operated on by other paraphrastic transformations (1965: 374). For example,
given the transformations Passive and It-Extraction (10 a, b), the elementary
sentence (11 a) may be transformed into (11 b) and then into (11 c):

(11) a. John saw Mary. → b. Mary was seen by John. → c. It is Mary who was
seen by John.[6]

3.4.2   The incremental operations

At this stage, we have kernel sentences and paraphrastic transformations
which operate on them. In addition, there are the incremental operations, which
Harris describes as follows (1965: 374):

"The incremental operations add to a sentence-form a whole category of
words. These naturally alter the meaning of the sentence, but the added meanings are not like the concrete meanings of the words in the elementary
sentence; rather, they are metasentential (in the sense of talking about meanings
in the sentence), or relational, or aspectual, or they refer to conditions of time,
place, and manner, and so on. The addition of any of these increments yields
again a sentence, and the resultant ... has an elementary sentence-form (with
new items satisfying some of the symbols) plus, possibly, adjuncts. It is therefore
possible to consider the addition of these increments to be ... transformations."[7]

---

[6] There are also paraphrastic transformations which apply on the resultants of incremental
operations, e.g. *I want for me to leave* → *I want to leave, John left and Mary left* → *John and Mary
left.*

[7] In the hope of avoiding unnecessary confusion, I shall continue to restrict the term *transformation*
to paraphrastic transformations.

The increments may be divided into unaries and binaries, the former operating on single sentences (plus, in some cases, additional nouns) and the latter on sentence-pairs (plus, occasionally, additional nouns). Of course, in both cases, the resultant is a single sentence. The unaries include:

Inserts: almost, however, can, ...

Verb-operators (φ_v):

 i. Bring in a new V, making the old V its object, predicate N or A (V_n, V_a): He walked → He took a walk, This helps us → This is helpful/a help to us.

 ii. *be -ing, have -en*

Sentence-operators (φ_s): Verbs (including *is (P) N, is A*) which take deformed sentences as their subject or object:

(That John left) is a fact.

(John's leaving) surprises me.

I appreciate (John's having left).

The binaries (φ_c) include:

Coordinate conjunctions: and, or, but

Subordinate conjunctions:

i. *because, due to, ...* (I am here) because (John is sick).

ii. *comparatives* (John speaks) more (loudly) than (Mary sings)

iii. *wh-* between two sentences each containing a particular N_i

 (I read the book) wh(ich you bought)

← (I read the book) wh- (you bought the book)

Sentence-operators: imply, be before, ...

 (John's leaving) implies (that he was angry).

Some of the subordinate conjunctions and all of the binary sentence-operators produce K-like sentences, which may then be operated on by the paraphrastic transformations, e.g. *That John was angry is implied by his leaving.* Like the paraphrastic transformations, the incremental operators may also be considered to leave a trace, which may simply be their physical presence. In addition, those increments which produce K-like structures do so because they impose one of a small number of nominalizing (morphophonemic) deformations on the sentences on which they operate. This set of operators may then be called *containers* and the sentences on which they operate *contained sentences*. The deformations for English include (1964a: 489ff. 1965: 376ff., 1968: 73f.):

 i. that/whether S, ii. for N to V (Ω),

 iii. N's Ving (Ω), iv. N's Ving/Vn (of Ω)

In a study of the sentence deformations of English, Vendler (1968) finds that their nominalizing effect is non-uniform; in particular, (i–iv) above are listed in order of increasing strength of nominalization, with (i) the weakest and (iv) the strongest.

We may now briefly illustrate how these operations interact in the building up (inverse decomposition) of a sentence:

(11)   a. John saw the criminal.

$\xrightarrow{\varphi_p, \varphi_m}$ b. The criminal was seen by John.

$\xrightarrow{\varphi_s}$ c. That the criminal was seen by John is a fact.

$\xrightarrow{\varphi_p,\ \varphi_m}$ d. It is a fact that the criminal was seen by John.

$\xrightarrow{\varphi_s}$ e. Everyone assumes that it is a fact that the criminal was seen by John.

$\xrightarrow{\varphi_p}$ f. That it is a fact that the criminal was seen by John everyone assumes.

4   Text decomposition and decomposition lattices

Following the transformational theory outlined above, one may decompose any text into its kernels, incremental operations, and paraphrastic transformations. Let us illustrate with an actual text, the opening lines of Edward T. Hall, *The Silent Language* (Greenwich, CN: Fawcett):

(12) "Time talks. It speaks more plainly than words. The message it conveys comes through loud and clear. Because it is manipulated less consciously, it is subject to less distortion than the spoken language. It can shout the truth where words lie."

Note that the methods of the early model of discourse analysis yield nothing if applied directly to this text. That is, there are no two morphemes or sequences thereof which have identical environments. Now consider the following transformational decomposition:

1. K: *Time talks*
2. K: *Time speaks*
3. φ_s *(is plain)* operating on 2 gives: *Time's speaking is plain*
4. φ_p, φ_m on 3: *Time speaks plainly*
5. K: *Words speak*
6. φ_s *(is plain)* on 5: *Words' speaking is plain*
7. φ_p, φ_m on 6: *Words speak plainly*
8. φ_c *(more than)* on 4, 7: *Time speaks plainly more than words speak plainly*
9. φ_z on 8: *Time speaks plainly more than words*
10. φ_p on 9: *Time speaks more plainly than words*
11. φ_c *(;)* on 1, 10: *Time talks; time speaks more plainly than words*
12. φ_m on 11: *Time talks; it speaks more plainly than words*
13. K: *A message comes through*
14. φ_s *(is loud and clear)* on 13: *A message's coming through is loud and clear*
15. φ_p on 14: *A message comes through loud and clear*
16. K: *Time conveys a message*
17. φ_c *(wh-)* on 15, 16: *A message comes through loud and clear wh- time conveys a message*
18. φ_m, φ_p, φ_z on 17: *The message time conveys comes through loud and clear*
19. φ_c *(;)* on 12, 18: *Time talks; it speaks more plainly than words; the message time conveys comes through loud and clear*

20. φ_m on 19: ... *the message it conveys* ...
21. K: *People distort time*
22. φ_v on 21: *People make a distortion of time*
23. φ_s *(is subject to)* on *time*, 22: *Time is subject to people's making a distortion of time*
24. φ_z on 23: *Time is subject to distortion*
25. K: *People distort the language*
26. φ_v on 25: *People make a distortion of the language*
27. K: *People speak the language*
28. φ_m, φ_p, φ_z on 27: *The language is spoken*
29. φ_c *(wh-)* on 26, 28: *People make a distortion of the language wh- the language is spoken*
30. φ_m, φ_z, φ_p on 29: *People make a distortion of the spoken language*
31. φ_s *(is subject to)* on *the language*, 30: *The language is subject to people's making a distortion of the spoken language*
32. K: *People speak the language*
33. φ_m, φ_p, φ_z on 32: *The language is spoken*
34. φ_c *(wh-)* on 31, 33: *The language is subject to people's making a distortion of the spoken language wh- the language is spoken*
35. φ_m, φ_z, φ_p on 34: *The spoken language is subject to people's making a distortion of the spoken language*
36. φ_z on 35: *The spoken language is subject to distortion*
37. φ_c *(less than)* on 24, 36: *Time is subject to distortion less than the spoken language is subject to distortion*
38. φ_z on 37: *Time is subject to distortion less than the spoken language*
39. φ_p on 38: *Time is subject to less distortion than the spoken language*
40. K: *People manipulate time*
41. φ_m, φ_p, φ_z on 40: *Time is manipulated*
42. φ_s *(is conscious)* on 41: *Time's being manipulated is conscious*
43. φ_p, φ_m on 42: *Time is manipulated consciously*
44. K: *People manipulate the language*
45. K: *People speak the language*
46. φ_m, φ_p, φ_z on 45: *The language is spoken*
47. φ_c *(wh-)* on 44, 46: *People manipulate the language wh- the language is spoken*
48. φ_m, φ_z, φ_p on 47: *People manipulate the spoken language*
49. φ_m, φ_p, φ_z on 48: *The spoken language is manipulated*
50. φ_s *(is conscious)* on 49: *The spoken language's being manipulated is conscious*
51. φ_p, φ_m on 50: *The spoken language is manipulated consciously*
52. φ_c *(less than)* on 43, 51: *Time is manipulated consciously less than the spoken language is manipulated consciously*
53. φ_z on 52: *Time is manipulated consciously less than the spoken language*
54. φ_p on 53: *Time is manipulated less consciously than the spoken language*

55. φ_c *(because)* on 39, 54: *Time is subject to less distortion than the spoken language because time is manipulated less consciously than the spoken language*

56. φ_z on 55: *Time is subject to less distortion than the spoken language because time is manipulated less consciously*

57. φ_p, φ_m on 56: *Because time is manipulated less consciously, it is subject to less distortion than the spoken language*

58. φ_c *(;)* on 20, 57: *Time talks; it speaks more plainly than words; the message it conveys comes through loud and clear; because time is manipulated less consciously, it is subject to less distortion than the spoken language*

59. φ_m on 58: *... because it is manipulated ...*

60. K: *Time shouts something*

61. K: *Something is true*

62. φ_v on 61: *Something is the truth*

63. φ_c *(wh-)* on 60, 62: *Time shouts something wh- something is the truth*

64. φ_m, φ_z on 63: *Time shouts the truth*

65. φ_s *(is at a place)* on 64: *Time's shouting the truth is at a place*

66. φ_p, φ_m on 65: *Time shouts the truth at a place*

67. φ_v *(can)* on 66: *Time can shout the truth at a place*

68. K: *Words lie*

69. φ_s *(is at a place)* on 68: *Words' lying is at a place*

70. φ_p, φ_m on 69: *Words lie at a place*

71. φ_c *(wh-)* on 67, 70: *Time can shout the truth at a place wh- words lie at a place*

72. φ_m, φ_p, φ_z on 71: *Time can shout the truth where words lie*

73. φ_c *(;)* on 59, 72: *Time talks; it speaks more plainly than words; the message it conveys comes through loud and clear; because it is manipulated less consciously, it is subject to less distortion than the spoken language; time can shout the truth where words lie*

74. φ_m on 73: *... it can shout ...*

75. φ_m on 74: *... where words lie.*

The text may now be represented as a double array, as in Figure 1.

Further compactness is easily attainable. First is is clear that T must be identical with L and may, therefore, be dropped as a separate equivalence class. Second, if (f)-(l) are transformed into the passive, then L is equivalent to W and $D^{-1}P$ is equivalent to S. (We note also that CE is equivalent to S and that $C^{-1}E$ is equivalent to O, but the gain from collapsing these classes is somewhat dubious.) Thus, we have a compact double array in Figure 2.

M	T	I	P	D	L	W	S	A	C	E	O	N
(1) a.						time	talks					
(3) b.						time	speaks					plainly
(8) c. more than						words	speak					plainly
(13) d.										a message	comes thru	loud and clear
(17) e. wh-	time					time			conveys	a message		
(23) f.	time	is subject to	people	distort	time			make				
(37) g. less than	language	is subject to	people	distort	language			make				
('') h. wh-			people	speak	language							
('') i. wh-			people	speak	language							
(56) j. because			people	manipulate	time							consciously
('') k. less than			people	manipulate	language							consciously
('') l. wh-			people	speak	language							
(67) m.						time		can	shout	the truth		at a place
(71) n. wh-						words	lie					at a place

Figure 1.

	M	I	W'	S'	A	C	E	O	N
(1) a.			time	talks					
(3) b.	more than		time	speaks					plainly
(8) c.	more than		words	speak					plainly
(13) d.							a message	comes through	loud and clear
(17) e.	wh-		time			conveys	a message		
(23) f.		is subject to	time	is distorted by people	make				
(37) g.	less than	is subject to	language	is distorted by people	make				
('') h.	wh-		language	is spoken by people					
('') i.	wh-		language	is spoken by people					
(56) j.	because		time	is manipulated by people					consciously
('') k.	less than		language	is manipulated by people					consciously
('') l.	wh-		language	is spoken by people					
(67) m.			time		can	shout	the truth		at a place
(71) n.	wh-		words	lie					at a place

Figure 2.

The more detailed double array might be the more appropriate for a purely structural analysis of the text; for example, it shows clearly that $W \cup T \cup L$ *(time, words, . . .)* functions as subject in the first part of the text, then as (underlying) subject and object, then as (underlying) object, and finally again as subject at the end of the text. It shows also that *a message* is unique distributionally (although not semantically) and, in fact, it is the case that it is an important word in the text and receives heavy stress.[8]

On the other hand, the more compact version would be more relevant if one were interested in the text for its information-content, as it clearly shows what is predicated of the members of W'.

I should like now to reconsider the original decomposition in an effort to clarify the individual transformational operations. The kernel sentences, (1), (2), (5), (13), (16), (21), (25), (27), (32), (40), (44), (45), (60), (61), and (68), can be said to be operated on by a variety of increments and transformations which map them onto the sentences of the text. The increments and transformations are the following (the numbers in parentheses refer to the sentences of the decomposition):

φ_v: a. *aspectual verb*
  i. $Nt V_i (\Omega) \rightarrow Nt V_{asp}$ a $V_i n (P\Omega)$,
     where V_{asp} = *take, make, give, have, . . .* (22)
     John walked $\rightarrow$ John took a walk
  ii. N's Ving Ω is $A_i \rightarrow$ N's Ving Ω is a $A_i n$ (62)
      John's leaving is possible $\rightarrow$ John's leaving is a possibility (These are 'restricted' operators, due to their idiosyncratic nature. When they do operate, however, their semantic increment is uniform: they perfectivize or 'bound' their operand.)
  iii. *can* (65)

φ_s: a. __is plain (3, 6)
  b. __is loud and clear (14)
  c. __is conscious (42, 50)
  d. __is at a place (66, 69)
  e. *(N_i)* is subject to *(N_j's Ving of N_i)* (23, 31)
     (*Is subject to* is one of a small class of φ_s whose subject [first argument] must be coreferential with the object of its object verb [with the second argument of its second argument]. Others in this class are *undergo, submit to, suffer*.)

φ_c: a. __more than__ (8)
  b. __less than__ (37, 52)
  c. __wh-__ (17, 29, 34, 47, 63, 71)

---

[8] It is 'more' unique than this double array suggests: I have fudged on classifying the two occurrences as equivalent. They are actually equivalent only if (e) is passivized, in which case *is conveyed by time* is a member of O. As is obvious, one has many options in setting up equivalence classes.

d. __because__ (55)

e. __;__ (11, 19, 58, 73)

φ_p: a. *Tense-transplacing:*

N's Ving Ω t be A/PN/D $\rightarrow$ N t V Ω A$_{1y}$/PN/D (4, 7, 15, 43, 51, 67, 70)

b. *Comparative-permuting:* The first part of the comparative morpheme *(-er, more, less)* permutes to the left of the preceding constituent. (10, 39, 54)

c. *Passive* (Also φ_m) (28, 33, 41, 46, 49)

d. *Wh- permuting:* Proworded item under *wh-* moves to immediate right of *wh-*. (18, 72)

e. *Adjective-permuting:* After zeroing of *wh- t be,* remaining adjective permutes to left of head noun (30, 35, 48)

f. *Subordinate-clause-permuting* (57)

φ_m: a. *Prowording of repeated material:* If two nouns are the same but are not in the same K or K-like sentence, the second is proworded. (12, 20, 57, 59, 74)

b. *Wh-prowording:* A noun which is in the sentence to the right of *wh-* is proworded *(-o(m), -ich, -at, -ere, ...)* if it is the same as a noun in the sentence to the left of *wh-*. (18, 30, 35, 48, 64, 72)

c. *Passive* (Also φ_p)

d. *Sentence-intonation* (75)

φ_z: a. *Zeroing of repeated material:* A noun which refers to the same individual as another noun in the same sentence may be zeroed when both nouns are in certain specifiable positions. (The details are complex, as is also the case with many of the other transformations listed here.) (9, 24, 36, 38, 53, 56)

b. *Zeroing of constants:*

i. *Wh- word* is zeroed if it is in a restrictive relative clause and is not the subject of its sentence. (18)

ii. *Indefinites* are zeroed in certain specifiable positions (24, 28, 33, 36, 41, 46, 49)

iii. *Wh- t be* (30, 35, 48)

iv. *that which t be* (before N) (64)

v. *at the place* (before *where*) (72)

Such a decomposition can be represented also as a semi-lattice (plus left-right distinction), where the kernels are the null points at the bottom and the entire text the universal element at the upper right. The operations, both incremental and paraphrastic, are the nodes. If an operation φ_1 operates on the resultant of some other operations on the resultant of φ_2, then φ_1 is an upper bound of φ_2. If there is no φ_3 such that φ_1 is an upper bound of φ_3 and φ_3 is an upper bound of φ_2, then φ_1 is the least upper bound (1.u.b.) of φ_2. Any node which is the 1.u.b. of K$_i$, K$_j$, where i $\neq$ j, will be a φ_c. The above decomposition may then be respresented as in Figure 3. (See 1967, 1968 for a thorough discussion of this mode of representation.)

5   Recent developments: the two-systems model

The transformational model outlined above seems to work quite well for decomposing texts, especially scientific texts. (See Hiż 1975 for a discussion of science sublanguages and transformational grammar.) At the same time, the model leaves something to be desired on the level of capturing generalizations about the structure of (the) language. In particular, as shown by Figure 3, such a grammar makes a sharp distinction only between kernel sentences and operators. However, as we have seen, the operators fall into two clearly divergent categories: paraphrastic transformations T (φ_m, φ_z, φ_p) and increments I (φ_v, φ_s, φ_c). First, they differ functionally in that the members of I add objective information to the text, whereas the members of T have a very different type of semantic value, still poorly understood, but clearly subjective (topic/comment, point of view, etc.). Second, T and I affect relative acceptability-orderings differently: the T (ideally) preserve such orderings while the I alter them for reasons having to do with selection (i.e. semantic compatibility). Compare:

(13) a. John saw Mary. b. ?Rocks need grammar. c. *The sofa ate concentration.

(14) a. Mary was seen by John. b. ?Grammar is needed by rocks. c. *Concentration was eaten by the sofa.

(15) a. John didn't see Mary. b. Rocks don't need grammar. c. *The sofa didn't eat concentration.

The sentences of (13) and (14), which are related by a T (Passive), have identical relative acceptability-orderings, whereas those of (13) and (15), which are related by an I (Negative) do not. In particular, sentences like (13 b), which are judged marginal due to blatant falseness, will become normal if negated. Similar reorderings can be demonstrated for all I. This brings us to the third difference between T and I: the qualitative difference in the restrictions on their application. Briefly, the restrictions on I are selectional: a particular I_i may operate on a string S_j just in case I_i and S_j are semantically compatible. Selectional restrictions are not hard and fast rules of language that a grammarian can (or should) predict but have more to do with the speaker's (purported) view of the world and are, therefore, subject to change. For example, whether a given speaker finds (16a) or (16b) anomalous has to do with his/her beliefs about the shape of our planet, not with his/her grammar:

(16) a. John doesn't realize that the world is flat.

   b. John is pretending that the world is flat.

Further, whichever one a speaker rejects would be perfectly acceptable to that speaker in the context of a fairytale.

The restrictions on T, on the other hand, have to do with morpheme classes and subclasses and seem to be describable without reference to semantics. We shall return to the matter of restrictions below.

As set forth in Harris 1969, a two-systems model incorporates transformational grammar in a more comprehensive theory of language and language structure. Its primary goal is to remove restrictions, a goal which is not unique to this model.

The two-systems model divides all sentences (i.e. sentence-types) into two sets, thereby creating two sublanguages. One sublanguage, called the *report-* or *information-language,* is characterized by the fact that the sentences in it are free of arbitrary grammatical restrictions. The other sublanguage, the *paraphrase-language,* is its complement in the whole language and is derivable from the report-language by means of transformations. Thus all arbitrary grammatical restrictions are contained in the paraphrase-language. For example, the fact that

(17) *I am owning a house

is unacceptable is apparently due to arbitrary grammar: *own,* like *know, owe,* etc. does not 'take the progressive'. One can do no more than simply list such verbs. On the other hand,

(18) ?I am in the process of owning a house

I am (engaged) in a process wh- ?My owning a house is a process

is questionable or marginal rather than non-occurring, its marginality being due to a selectional infringement – owning a house is not normally seen as a process – and not a rule of grammar. Thus (17) will be in the paraphrase-language, derivable from something like (18), which will be in the report-language.

It turns out that the report-language, in addition to being grammatically restrictionless, has the following properties: (i) No two sentences in it are paraphrases of each other (except, perhaps, due to local lexical synonymy, and this may possibly be avoided if sets of lexical items are used, rather than individual lexical items), (ii) No sentence in it is structurally ambiguous, and (iii) Everything sayable in the language as a whole is sayable in it. The structure of the report-language is comparatively very simple, as would be expected from the restriction-removal, and the practical implications for information-storage and retrieval are great:

"Moving the restrictions is ... not merely a matter of structural compactness or elegance, but a gain for the interpretation and utilization of language-information, because the restrictions have ... been moved out of a distinguished part of [the language], leaving that distinguished part as a far simpler system which is nevertheless capable of doing all the objective informational work." (1969: 667)

The sentences of the report-language are composed of the members of a primitive alphabet of nouns and operators:

N: concrete nouns, e.g. *a lamp, a house, a cigarette*

V_n: operators which take one N as argument, e.g. *sleep, (is) a mammal, (is) here*

V_{nn}: operators which take two N as arguments, e.g. *see, (is) a father of, (is) similar to*

V_{nnn}: operators which take three N, e.g. *sell, give*

V_v: operators which take as argument one V (which, in turn, has its arguments), e.g. *(is) a fact, begin, (is) likely*

V_{nv}: take N as subject (first argument) and V as object (second argument), e.g.
    believe, regret, (be) eager
V_{nnv}: e.g. *say, tell, ask*
V_{vn}: e.g. *surprise, shock, dismay*
V_{vv}: e.g. *precede, is after, mean*
and
or

Sentences, or discourses (as in Harris, forthcoming a), are built up by a primitive V (V_n, V_{nn}, V_{nnn}) selecting as arguments the number of N that satisfy it. Further operators may then enter the discourse. The one process of discourse-formation is concatenation, and the one rule of string-structure is that an operator stands in second position with respect to its arguments. The transformations, which are similar in kind to those discussed in 3.4, are responsible for all structural ambiguity and paraphrase, as well as for focus and brevity. (The report-language sentences/discourses are generally highly repetitive although not redundant.)

In this necessarily sketchy outline of Harris' framework, two further points deserve mention: the metalanguage, which is in the (report-)language, and an addressing technique, by which discourses may refer to distinguished parts of themselves. For example, sameness of reference, necessary for certain types of prowording and for relative clause formation, may be expressed by something like:

(19) a. I like the book which you read
← b. I like a book wh- you read a book and *a book* in sentence 1 refers to the same individual as *a book* in sentence 2

Analogously, tense is derived from zeroed metastatements which chronologically order the first non-performative operator plus arguments with respect to the saying, or, more precisely, to the time of the performative operator of saying, which is always *now*, and subsequent operators are ordered with respect to preceding ones, as in:

(20) a. John left
← b. I announce to you that John left
← c. I announce to you John's leaving wh- John's leaving is before my announcing

In conclusion, we see that discourse analysis is no longer even ostensibly separable from transformational grammar: the latter is simply a means of doing the former. The areas that remain to be worked on all indicate this bond: one must re-examine the transformations to see what are the conditions on their application within a discourse, e.g. when may or must Passive be applied, in what kind of discourse and in what stage is It-Extraction (*It was a dress that Jean bought in New York ← Jean bought a dress in New York*) appropriate, etc. Such questions, at the heart of transformational grammar, cannot even be formulated (nor their existence noticed) unless discourse is seen as the object of study.

References

Fodor, Jerry, and Jerrold Katz, eds. 1964. *The Structure of Language: Readings in the Philosophy of Language*. Englewood Cliffs, NJ: Prentice-Hall. [FK]

Harris, Zellig S. 1946. 'From Morpheme to Utterance'. *Language* 22. 161–83. Also in PSTL, pp. 100–25; RIL, pp. 142–53.

–. 1951. *Methods in Structural Linguistics*. Chicago: Univ. of Chicago Press.

–. 1952a. 'Discourse Analysis'. *Language* 28. 1–30. Also in PSTL, pp. 313–48; FK, pp. 355–83.

–. 1952b. 'Discourse Analysis: A Sample Text'. *Language* 28. 474–94. Also in PSTL, pp. 349–72.

–. 1957. 'Co-occurrence and Transformation in Linguistic Structure'. *Language* 33. 283–340. Also in PSTL, pp. 390–457; FK, pp.155–210.

–. 1963. *Discourse Analysis Reprints*. (Papers on Formal Linguistics, No. 2) The Hague: Mouton.

–. 1964a. 'The Elementary Transformations'. T. D. A. P. 54, Department of Linguistics, Univ. of Pennsylvania. Also in PSTL, pp. 482–532. (Page numbers in text refer to PSTL.)

–. 1964b. 'Transformations in Linguistic Structure'. *Proceedings of the American Philosophical Society* 108, No. 5, pp. 418–22. Also in PSTL, pp. 472–81. (Page numbers in text refer to PSTL.)

–. 1965. 'Transformational Theory'. *Language* 41. 363–401. Also in PSTL, pp. 533–77.

–. 1966. 'Algebraic Operations in Linguistic Structure'. Read to the International Congress of Mathematicians, Moscow. Published in PSTL, pp. 603–11.

–. 1967. 'Decomposition Lattices'. T. D. A. P. 70, Department of Linguistics, Univ. of Pennsylvania. Also in PSTL, pp. 578–602.

–. 1968. *Mathematical Structures of Language*. New York: Interscience Publishers, Wiley & Sons.

–. 1969. 'The Two Systems of Grammar: Report and Paraphrase'. T. D. A. P. 79, Department of Linguistics, Univ. of Pennsylvania. Also in PSTL, pp. 612–92. (Page numbers in text refer to PSTL.)

–. 1970. *Papers in Structural and Transformational Linguistics*. Dordrecht: Reidel. [PSTL]

–. Forthcoming a. A Theory of Language Structure.

–. Forthcoming b. A Transformational Grammar of English.

Hiż, Henry. 1975. 'Specialized Languages of Biology, Medicine, and Science, and Connections between them'. *Communication of Scientific Information*, pp. 37–43.

Joos, Martin, ed. 1957. *Readings in Linguistics I*. Chicago: University of Chicago Press. [RIL]

Plötz, Senta, ed. 1972. *Transformationelle Analyse. Die Transformationstheorie von Zellig Harris und ihre Entwicklung*. Frankfurt/Main: Athenäum.

Vendler, Zeno. 1968. *Adjectives and Nominalizations*. (Papers on Formal Linguistics, No. 5) The Hague: Mouton.

Wells, Rulon. 1947. 'Immediate Constituents'. *Language* 23. 81–117. Also in RIL, pp. 186–207.

Functional Sentence Perspective and Textlinguistics

Zdena Palková and Bohumil Palek
Charles University, Prague

1   The starting point of our deliberations is the assumption that text-grammar and the theory of FSP (under which concept we for the time being subsume all related approaches) are in part concerned with the same phenomena. This assumption is implicitly, and sometimes explicitly, contained in several works devoted to the problems of text-grammar (TG) or to those of FSP, and it constitutes the prime reason why the present paper was included in this collection. The degree to which it is indeed justified will be more apparent from the argument itself.

It is indisputable from a historical standpoint that the FSP theory (under whatever name it may go) is older (cf. Daneš 1974b) than the interest of linguists in text-grammar[1]. This renders comparison of the two approaches on the one hand more problematic but at the same time a pressing requirement. We do not intend to question to what extent the FSP theory stimulated the development of that of TG nor to assess the relative status of these two trends of research in the framework of linguistic disciplines. Worthy of consideration are in our view those points where the objects of the two investigations coincide and, in these instances, whether the methods of analysis employed agree or diverge. The value of such comparison is to be found in the possible application of the results and experience of one method of analysis to the other. It is particularly to be expected that TG might gain something from the longer experience of linguists who have concerned themselves with FSP.

Very generally it can be said that the theories of FSP are directed to the description of the sentence from the point of view of its (potential) use in a message (framed in a text or a situation) while TG aims to describe the structure

---

[1]   The history of FSP, linked in its beginnings, at least as far as Czech linguistics is concerned, with the name of V. Mathesius (cf. the new edition [Mathesius 1975]), has been outlined in numerous works (Daneš 1974b), (Firbas 1974a), (Dressler 1973) and others. Recent years have seen an increase in the interest shown in this problem (esp. in works on transformational grammar (cf. [Chomsky 1971], [Akmajian 1970], [Dahl 1969], [Yang 1974], [Kuno 1972], [Jackendoff 1972], [Kuroda 1972] and many others). One manifestation of this interest was the 1st Conference on FSP, held in Marienbad in 1970 (cf. [Daneš ed. 1974]). An extensive bibliography of works published up to that date was prepared for the Conference by Tyl (Tyl 1970), cf. also (Firbas, Golková 1976). Our article concerns itself chiefly with newer works which appear to be most representative of current developments (the reader will find further bibliographies in these works).

of texts in all its aspects. Ignoring all other aspects of TG, we note that one possible description of the text as a sequence of sentences (cf. Palek 1974) obviously treats matters common to the FSP approach. Whereas it may be supposed from this that some of the findings of FSP are of importance for TG, it must also be noted that there is a fundamental distinction between the two approaches: from the point of view of FSP theory, the sentence is the unit of the highest order, while in TG it is principally a fundamental component in a unit differently conceived.

From a multitude of relevant problems two major aspects have been selected for consideration in this article. TG must inevitably question what it is that binds sentences together as units of a coherent text. In view of this,

1) We shall consider the extent to which phenomena described by FSP are an acceptable part of the answer to this question.
2) We shall attempt at the same time to ascertain at least some of the methodological requirements which must be fulfilled if the findings of FSP are to be applicable to TG.

2   The terms employed in the various conceptions of FSP are not standardized; some of them are divergent and some correspond only partially. So as to avoid undesirable terminological associations, the symbol DEN (FSP) is used in this article to designate what the basic concepts of FSP denote.

In accordance with the maximum differentiation of co-ranking elements in the individual conceptions, DEN (FSP) is used to designate the following:

a) The idea that it is possible to draw a distinction between segments in a sentence which present information already known (from the context or the situation) and segments conveying new information which cannot be inferred by the listener.
b) The idea that it is possible to distinguish segments which are context dependent, i.e. which are connected with segments of another sentence of the same text.
c) The idea that it is possible to distinguish in a sentence segments which are of greater or lesser communicative importance; this importance is first and foremost a question of the speaker's purpose.
d) The idea that in communication there is a certain favoured order for saying something(y) about something(x), which is mapped in the sentence and wherein x usually precedes y.
e) The idea of one element of the sentence being emphasized by contrast with all other elements; this aspect is usually connected with the question of the motivation of contrasts and that of marked phonic realisation.

The individual DEN (FSP) (further DEN a-e) are presented in the conceptions in the form of dichotomous, trichotomous or n-tomous schemes which are applied to sentences.

DEN a-d formulated in this way reveal various degrees of compatibility in an intuitive judgment, yet at the same time they differ to such a degree that anyone of them employed as a criterion on its own may produce a different result in the analysis of utterances. Taken together, DEN a-e represent in a certain sense the range of problems embraced by FSP analysis; (in actual works the range of phenomena to which FSP theory is applicable is rarely cited).

It should now be evident at first glance that findings in the framework of DEN-b in all cases contribute information useful to TG, and one may consider to what extent examination of text structure is furthered by DEN-d or possibly by DEN-c (which is usually presented as a certain arrangement of the sentence). To apply this in practice is not, however, as simple as it may appear. Individual conceptions do not distinguish DEN a-d finely and often do not even account for them all.

Generally speaking, it is normal for authors to treat one or two aspects of FSP explicitly, and in so doing they sometimes comprehend more than one DEN under a single aspect (if not in definition then in the interpretation of examples). The fundamental range of problems is sought in the area covered by DEN-a to DEN-d.

DEN-e is usually referred to as a special case of FSP; it tends to be seen in the context of phonic realisation, sometimes exclusively in this context, or to be linked with sentences of the so-called second instance (cf. Firbas 1974a). Regularly, however, it enters these conceptions only at the periphery. It is also left aside in the present article, whose scope does not allow of a sufficiently detailed analysis of means for expressing FSP.

3   We shall now illustrate how DEN a-d appear in some contemporary conceptions.

3.1   J. Firbas uses the concept 'communicative dynamism' (CD) as a single complex DEN (FSP). The manner in which the concept is presented is based on the notion of degrees of communicative importance (DEN-c): "The concept of CD is based on the fact that communication is not a static, but a dynamic phenomenon: By CD I understand a quality displayed by communication in its development (unfolding) of the information to be conveyed and consisting in advancing this development. By the degree of CD carried by a sentence element, I understand the extent to which the sentence element contributes to the further development of the communication." (Firbas 1974c: 3)

CD indirectly reflects the idea of DEN-a, as the mainstay of "communicative importance", and at first sight also the idea of DEN-b: "The concept of CD can be established empirically and inductively. Adopting this approach, we find that elements conveying known information (context dependent elements) contribute less to the further development of communication than elements conveying unknown information (context independent elements). Context dependent elements carry a lower degree of CD than context independent elements." (3) (Firbas then assumes along with Bolinger that "semantic contents increase their communicative importance – in my terms, their degree of CD – if the elements conveying them are shifted toward the end of the sentence" [3].)

The idea of context and context dependence acquires, however, in Firbas's theory a character somewhat different from the usual meaning of the terms. Firbas discovers a hierarchy involving several layers of context. The most general is 'context of experience' which "is provided by the common knowledge (experience) shared by the speaker and listener" (4). "The ad-hoc context of immediate experience", which "is contributed by the situation at the moment of utterance" constitutes a degree of greater restriction as, even more so, does "ad-hoc verbal context of preceding the sentence". The smallest unit is the sentence itself, and this is the very unit (not indeed the ad-hoc verbal context) from which Firbas derives the concept of 'context dependence' or 'independence' as the expression of the goal or purpose of the speaker: "But the contextual conditioning at the very moment of communication cannot be determined without due regard to the immediate communicative concern (purpose) of the speaker. It is this communicative concern of the speaker that sets what can be termed the narrow scene. By the narrow scene I consequently mean the contextual conditioning obtaining at the very moment of utterance. It is the narrow scene that ultimately determines context dependence or independence." (5) It is seen that even though the term 'context dependent/independent' occur frequently in Firbas's conception it would not be correct to assume that this conception of DEN (FSP) assigns an important place to DEN-b as one of its components. This thought-orientated concept of 'context-dependence' presents itself more obviously as a concept comprised by DEN-c, specifying communicative importance as *importance from the speaker's standpoint.*

3.2 M. A. K. Halliday elaborates his conception principally with the aid of two terms which he defines by reference to various dichotomies.

a) His sentence-parsing into 'theme' and 'rheme' corresponds in its definition to DEN-d: "The speaker assigns to the clause a two-part structure of theme-rheme, the theme taking initial position in the sequence ... The theme may be an item which is recoverable from the preceding discourse but is not necessarily so; the selection is independent of the context." (Halliday 1967: 242) ... "theme ... is the FSP element that is realized by first position, and has nothing to do with previous mention." (Halliday 1974: 53)

b) Halliday's definition of the second dichotomy, 'given' – 'new', is arrived at via the concepts information unit and information focus, a procedure in which awareness of the phonic realisation is presupposed: "Each information unit is realised as one tone group ... (Halliday 1967: 202) "Each information unit has either one primary point of information focus or one primary followed by one secondary" (203). "Information focus is one kind of emphasis, that whereby the speaker marks out a part (which may be the whole) of a message block as that which he wishes to be interpreted as informative. What is focal is 'new' information; ... If we use ... the term 'given' to label what is not 'new', we can say that the system of information focus assigns to the information unit a structure in terms of the two functions 'given' and 'new' (204).

The essence of the definition of 'new' is thereby the communicative purpose of the speaker. 'Given' is defined primarily in reference to the preceding context. For example, 'given' and 'theme' are distinguished as follows: "'given' means 'what you were talking about' (or 'what I was talking about before'), 'theme' means what I am talking about' (or 'What I am talking about now')" (212), and on p. 206, where he cites anaphoric items and substitutes as inherently 'given' elements.

When viewed in the perspective of our scheme of concepts, this second dichotomy is seen to embrace more than one DEN: 'given' covers the area where DEN-a and DEN-b overlap, and comprises in the first instance what is known from the context. 'New' evidently contains DEN-c, which never becomes clearly differentiated from DEN-e. (The differentiation of the two is more closely reflected in the distinction of 'marked' and 'unmarked' focus.)

Although each dichotomy is formulated independently of the other, their mutual relationship and interaction in particular units of language is naturally presupposed. "While therefore the given – new structure is not itself realized by the sequence of elements, and the focus of information may fall anywhere in the information unit, the partial congruence between this variable and the one which is in fact realized by the sequence of elements, that of theme – rheme, together with the partial congruence between clause and information unit, results in a tendency towards a left to right form of organization in the information unit with given, if present, preceding new" (205).

In view of the list of themes which Halliday incorporates in the text component (cf. Halliday 1974: 52), we can infer that Halliday himself considers only the first dichotomy ('theme' – 'rheme') to be a part of FSP, while the second ('given' – 'new') is assigned to "relations of presupposition".

3.3   Östen Dahl works with the dichotomy 'topic' – 'comment', which in practice directly corresponds to DEN-d: "If we want to present the concept of topic and comment very loosely, we might say that in general every sentence can be divided into two parts, the topic, in which we name something that we want to make a statement about and the comment, where we make this statement." (Dahl 1969: 5)

The main subject of interest is revealed to be the question of how various modifications to a sentence which continue to carry one and the same semantic interpretation are to be expressed in accordance with the requirements of a particular grammar (in this case transformational grammar – e.g. "We shall see later on that what seems to be permutations in the surface structure in the reality is a reflection of the order of elements in the base structure" (6).

3.4   P. Sgall, whose underlying aim is to expand and remodel Firbas's conception of FSP for the purposes of description in the framework of a generative grammar, distinguishes three hierarchically ordered layers in FSP: "... in the basic unmarked layer the location of individual words on the scale from theme to rheme is conditioned by their position in the semantic structure of sentence, in the second layer this location is additionally affected by the context or the situation ("contextual boundness") and the third layer is constitued by emphasis on one element of the sentence in cases of what is called the second instance" (Sgall 1973 b: 203).

The concept fundamental to the first layer is 'communicative importance' (CI), more especially the grading of this, which is more or less comprehended by DEN-c.

The fundamental term applied to the second layer is 'communicative dynamism' (CD): "the term communicative dynamism will be reserved for the actual hierarchy of elements of a sentence, be it in accordance with the scale of communicative importance ... or affected by deviating influence of context or situation" (Sgall 1973 a: 45). DEN-b and DEN-a are hereby taken as interfusing (as with Halliday's "known from the context"), even though the concept 'contextual boundness' is itself defined somewhat loosely: "Contextually bound are, in our understanding ... such elements that the speaker only reminds of, as elements known to the hearer, either known from the context, from the situation or from general conditions of the given utterance. This broader understanding of contextual boundness comprises also the elements called local and temporal setting" (47–48)[2].

3.5   F. Daneš distinguishes two basic aspects considered under the heading of FSP, namely: 1) the dichotomy 'given' – 'new', which he also treats as a 'context-dependent' dichotomy (Daneš 1964, 1970, 1974a: 106ff.), 2) the dichotomy of 'theme' – 'rheme' in the sense of Halliday's "thematization", i.e. DEN-d. He does not, however, hold it necessary or perhaps meaningful to maintain a strict distinction between these two aspects, a point manifest particularly in his own analysis and most obviously explicable by reference to his doubts as to the total lack of dependence of the "thematic aspect" (the second dichotomy) on the context. He himself principally employs one dichotomy, that of 'theme' – 'rheme', which embraces both DEN-a and DEN-d, drawing mainly on the area of overlap of the two DEN. We quote from Daneš's commentary on the delimitation of 'themes', to which he devotes great attention – especially in (Daneš 1974: 112): "The amount (or the potential) of successively accumulated information is mostly so extensive that the speaker, carrying on the discourse, must necessarily make a choice from this mass. And we may rightly assume that he selects the utterance theme from it (unless he has some special reason to choose something that is not comprised in it). In any case, the portions (ele-

---

[2] The use of the concepts "theme" and "rheme" (in Czech literature also called "základ" and "jádro") in the description of CD or employment of the concept "topic-comment articulation" alongside FSP would seem to be no more than multiplication of terms in a way which does not imply further differentiation of DEN.

ments) of "known" information occurring in an utterance are exactly those elements that are closely connected with the selected theme (and indirectly with rheme) ... it is evidently necessary to distinguish between the mass of information accumulated up to a certain point of text, and the portion of this mass contained (occurring) in the particular utterance following this point. This distinction involves the selection from the mass of known information for every utterance. We assume that this selection is determined, directly or indirectly, by the choice of the utterance theme ..." DEN-b, however, is itself also implied in the dichotomy 'theme' – 'rheme' since it is treated as an inherent component of DEN-a, i.e. Daneš relies on context in determining DEN-a. The fact is highlighted when the author uses the dichotomy 'theme' – 'rheme' as the main component of thematic sequences in the description of coherent texts.

4   The varying degrees of compatibility of the individual DEN (FSP), which were mentioned at the outset, are traceable in their concurrent exploitation in the different conceptions. In point of fact this concurrence is characterized by its assymmetric nature: for example, from the pair constituting DEN-a ('known' – 'new') 'known' is markedly similar to context dependent, which is contained in the idea of DEN-b, whereas the second element of the DEN-a pair, 'new', may well be linked in the mind of the language user to the DEN-c element, communicatively more important. Notwithstanding, we shall not always be inclined to relate the idea of context dependent with that of communicatively less important, for the user's attention may be focused on an indication of textual coherence as such[3]. A straightforward relation of the elements of the DEN-c pair to those of DEN-d is likewise far from proven[4].

It must now be pointed out that the DEN (FSP) exhibit as a group a certain degree of incongruity from at least two standpoints. Incongruous are:

1) The interpretations of the different DEN (FSP). In some DEN (FSP) the language user's evaluation constitutes an inherent component and in this sense they are mentally orientated (as with DEN-c and in some conceptions with DEN-a); the other DEN (FSP) refer to the structure of the utterance and are founded on the relationship between its elements (as with DEN-b and DEN-d).

2) The fundamental attitudes to communication which the DEN imply. Some DEN imply an approach to the text (or the speech situation) which is orientated primarily from the standpoint of the speaker, others one in which the listener's standpoint is paramount, while in some further cases no orientation is

---

[3] Were we, for example, to interpret sentences of the "second instance" on this basis, it would be possible to include DEN-e within the sphere of DEN-b.

[4] Diverging evaluations of the importance of the individual parts of sentences are found, amongst others, in (Firbas 1974a: 20) and in (Quirk et al. 1972: 945). In the sentence *A/the girl broke a vase* Firbas establishes the order of importance to be $0 - V - S$ (descending order). Quirk considers as most important "the last stressed element of clause structure", the theme coming next by importance and then the remainder. In the above sentence this gives $0 - S - V$, of. (Quirk, et al. 1972: 945).

clearly discernible. For example, in the case of DEN-c it is necessarily presupposed that the speaker chooses a certain form of expression because he considers a certain part of the sentence as most important. On the other hand, in the case of DEN-a, the distinction between known and new is significant mainly for the listener. With DEN-d the analysis is directed towards the structure of the utterance itself, whereby no consideration is paid to the language user.

This situation amounts to a severe obstacle, should one wish to apply findings made in one approach as fundamental data in another approach which is independent of the first, especially if one's aim is to set a partial description (FSP) in relationship to a more comprehensive one (TG). For instance, in producing an adequate description of a text, one can hardly ignore the difference which often becomes apparent between analyses from the point of view of the speaker and those from that of the listener.

How should one understand the statements of individual authors about the DEN (FSP) in relation to their overall conceptions? Two possibilities present themselves.

1) These statements may be taken as an explanation of the concepts of a theory which are in correspondence to them and which may at the same time be congruous and yet impossible to define more specifically. A closer understanding of these statements remains to be acquired from the way the concepts are used in the various approaches, especially in practical application.

If this attitude is to be acceptable – leaving aside the question of its vagueness – the minimum precondition that a given phenomenon (i.e. a given DEN (FSP)) should be evaluated in an incontestably similar fashion by different users of the given language must be fulfilled. In view of the fact that even the carefully selected examples interpreted in the individual conceptions for the purpose of demonstration give rise, on occasion, to debate amongst linguists themselves, it is to be feared that FSP, however defined, is not a phenomenon for which this condition can be met.

2) These statements are to be considered as an intuitive characterization and are calculated to evoke an approximate idea of DEN (FSP). They presuppose the existence in some form of a further explanation determining the domain of the given DEN and guaranteeing an unambiguous interpretation of the object under investigation. If it is to be possible for the results of one employed conception to be transferred into another conception it is consequently necessary that an explanation of this kind should be such as to iron out the inherent incongruity of the stated concepts. This means that in a conception in which more than one DEN may be identified, it is obviously essential to determine their mutual relationships, their hierarchy or order of preference etc., and this not only in the explication of the concepts but above all by demonstration of the analysis of actual examples.

In view of the foregoing it would be worthwhile to examine the manner of this explication more closely.

a) The explication is determined in accordance with some operative rule of a particular grammar (e.g. in Halliday DEN-d becomes attached to the initial position in the sentence as, in comparable fashion, does Chomsky's concept of 'topic' (Chomsky 1965: 221). It is symptomatic of these cases that only one DEN is usually chosen and its foundation in the relevant operative rule is often quite free.

b) The explication is determined in accordance with the procedure whereby the basic concepts of a given approach are to be applied to actual examples (e.g. the so-called question test used by Daneš (Daneš, 1974a), Sgall (Sgall 1973b) and many other Czech authors (cf. also (Dressler 1974), Posner's test by comment (Posner 1972) etc.). The demand for a precise statement of the mutual relationships of the DEN employed transfers itself to this procedure.

Fulfilment of this demand would evidently contribute towards a more consistent use of the concepts involved, even where the author hesitates as to whether he should analyze them further. This can be exemplified on Daneš's concept of 'theme' – 'theme', where the distinction between DEN-a and DEN-b is clearly presented at the beginning but the author consciously discards it in his own analysis, and, as is apparent from his examples, henceforth takes into account only that which is common to both DEN.

5   Having in mind the prominent interest of TG in the cohesion of sentences in texts, we shall now take a more detailed look at that DEN (FSP) which has the clearest relevance to this cohesion, namely DEN-b, and shall formulate our stated requirement more explicitly.

The concept DEN-b has been characterized hitherto as "context dependence". In some conceptions of FSP it appears directly under this name as a term in the explication of basic concepts, in others it is recogniable as a tacit criterion in the analysis of actual examples. Even our quotations thus far suffice to distinguish the following:

a) The term 'context dependence' comes into its own above all in defining the 'theme' in its close connection with the idea of known in Den-a (cf. the above remarks on the intersection of the two DEN in Daneš (3.5), Halliday (3.2) and others).

b) The idea of context dependence is not formulated in any precise way, and where the authors approach a closer definition of the term they do so in order to broaden this concept or their concept of text so as to cover "general conditions" or "context of experience". In a different approach, the device of the so-called "narrow scene" (e.g. in Firbas [3.1]) implies transposition of the concept of context into the realm of the private intention of the speaker, i.e. into a sphere equally difficult for the investigator to penetrate. This approach – again thought-orientated – makes it possible to accommodate under one concept both the interpretation of DEN-b on the basis of verbal context and its interpretation by reference to the speaker. Judged in the light of the serviceability of the findings of such conceptions for other conceptions in particular from the standpoint of textlinguistics, this is more of a disadvantage than a benefit, because it at the same time prevents any differentiation of the two interpretations.

In (Palek 1968: 128) a tentative distinction was drawn between two ways of describing relationships between sentences which were designated as the textual and contextual approaches[5]. To avoid confusion of this meaning of "contextual" with that of "context" as used in the present article, we shall here refer to the contextual approach as a sentential approach.

FSP theories naturally employ the sentential approach, for the sentence is the largest unit they admit. We have already seen that even the concept of context dependence (or 'boundness') is defined entirely within the limits of the sentence. A brief inspection from the textual standpoint is enough to reveal certain relationships between the segments of a text which are evidently the same as the phenomena described by FSP. Due to this fact it would seem useful, even essential, on the one hand to specify the concept of 'context dependence' considered as DEN-b and on the other hand to differentiate between manners of its expression.

a) In some cases it is apparent from the form of the given sentence (without any further information being required) that it is taken out of context, it may even be apparent from what kind of context. In so far as a sentence fails to tally with its context, i.e. if the context does not correspond to what is implied in the form of the sentence, this last is felt as being incorrectly composed. For example, the sentence *The old man was revered by everyone in the village* presupposes that the preceding context has already introduced both the old man and the village. In the sentence *The old man was revered by his whole family* it is plain that at least the notion of the old man must have already occurred in the text.

b) The form of the given sentence does not in itself always furnish any information as to its context (as it does in a) and contextual dependence becomes apparent only when the surroundings of the sentence are known. This state of affairs has a number of variants.

ba) In some sentences there is found a segment (or segments) which may be contextually determined (i.e. contextually dependent). For example, from the standpoint of DEN-b the following sentences can be considered neutral:

(i) Arthur set out in his best suit on the road to his sister's early in the evening.
(ii) Arthur set out on the road to his sister's early in the evening in his best suit.
(iii) Early in the evening Arthur set out on the road to his sister's in his best suit.
(iv) Early in the evening Arthur set out in his best suit on the road to his sister's.

Any of these could legitimately appear in the context:

(v) It was a wet March day and most of the villagers were indoors by the fireside
  ... (i) (ii) (iii) (iv) ... He aimed to arrive by six.

---

[5] As a simple explanation: the textual approach proceeds from the idea of the text as an entire unit in which smaller units are somehow connected; the contextual – here sentential – approach describes the sentence and notes phenomena in it whose complete description requires reference to the context.

However, if (i) – (iv) are coupled with the sentence

(vi) It was impossible to get the sports-jacket clean in time.

as their preceding context variants (ii) and (iii) make the train of thought clear by the order of their segments whereas (i) and (iv) make it unclear under the conditions of neutral phonic realization.

On the other hand, if they are to be coupled with

(vii) She was expecting the whole family.

or

(viii) In some places the drains were blocked and there were huge puddles.

as their succeeding context, it is most unlikely that either of (ii) or (iii) would be used at all, and (iv) is more likely than (i).

It may be noted as a special instance of contextual dependence that what is, in isolation, the most awkward ordering of the segments of sentences (i) – (iv), namely

(ix) Arthur set out on the road to his sister's in his best suit early in the evening.

becomes perfectly natural when attention is directed to the last two phrases by the preceding context (vi).

It is clear that use of the contexts (vi) and (vii), i.e. preceding and succeeding (i) – (iv), demands such an ordering of the segments in the second sentence that (vi, iv, vii) is the sole admissible sequence. In this sequence the succeeding context is more restrictive than the preceding, which would seem to suggest that it is the dominant factor in the ordering of the sentence.

Under ba) we must also mention the type presented by the sentence *Bob went to the window* (or by Czech *Bob přistoupil k oknu)*, which is required in many contexts because all modifications (e.g. *It was Bob who went to the window* – cf. Czech *K oknu přistoupil Bob* etc.) belong to type a) and cannot be used where the preceding context does not justify them.

bb) In other sentences no formal expression of cohesion with their surroundings is to be found, DEN-b originating simply in the immediate concatenation of sentences whose contents are compatible.

(x) There was an uproar in the next room. A girl broke a vase.

The context would have to be extended in order for it to be clear whether the second sentence is the explanation of the first or its consequence.

Within the space of this article a detailed analysis of possible individual types is not practicable. Those outlined above are intended to show how DEN-b, as treated in the sentential approach, appears in the light of the requirements of the textual approach.

1) Our viewpoint clearly requires that the concept of context dependence should be defined as a relation, i.e. not as a one-place predicate ("x is context dependent"), as assumed in FSP, but as an at least binary relation CON (x, y), where x is a segment of a given sentence and y is a segment or segments of its verbal context. Any extension of the concept of context outside the confines of verbal context (cf. 3.1) makes this relation appear vaguer than it really is.

2) From the examples given in ba) it is equally apparent that a definite and formally statable role is played not merely by the preceding context but still more so by what follows. Through the definition of CON one arrives at a way of explaining the not infrequent cases where the sentence-final position (reserved in the FSP approach for rhemes in the sense of DEN-c) is filled by expressions known from the context.

One conception which deals with verbal context and involves per se the understanding of DEN (FSP) as a relation appears in Daneš's analysis into "thematic progressions" (cf. Daneš 1968, 1974a, c). Even though his explication of basic concepts is formulated in the perspective of a purely sentential approach (cf. 3.5), it follows from his analysis of examples that the fundamental criterion for determining the thematic part of the sentence was in fact the concrete verbal context coupled with the awareness of inter-sentence cohesion.

6   The confrontation of the sentence-orientated theories of FSP with the requirements of TG brings to light a whole range of further questions, which may be of interest for both sides. It must suffice if only one of these problems is expanded here, one which concerns methodology.

In any conception of linguistic description it is salutary to bear in mind the distinction between two basic kinds of concept. Concepts may be formed for a certain purpose (which should always be explicit) in a given grammar, and here their formulation is accompanied by a statement of the procedure whereby they may be applied to any unit subjected to description. In this case there is no need to raise the question of whether the particular concept corresponds to anything that exists in the linguistic awareness of the ordinary speaker. Such concepts may be referred to as perception non-motivated concepts (PnC). Alternatively, concepts are sometimes formulated to pin-point a phenomenon which manifests itself in the functioning of the language sufficiently prominently for one to enquire as to how it is interpreted by the language-user, particularly, where applicable, in respect of its communicative function. These cases may be called perception-motivated concepts (PC), and they require the support of experimental evidence of the nature of the perception concerned.

The character of phenomena treated by TG very often requires employment of the PC-approach. This is also plainly required by the problems which were made the starting point for the contrast with the FSP standpoint, namely problems of the linking of sentences as units of a coherent text. It is necessary to know to what extent the concepts evolved to deal with these problems can be identified with PC, for this kind admit of less modification in different conceptions.

The question as to what TG should assimilate from the theories of FSP is for the most part not simple to solve. The dichotomies of 'theme' – 'rheme' in Halliday (3.2) or 'topic' – 'comment' in Chomsky (Chomsky 1965: 221), which correspond to DEN-d, are evident examples of PnC. In other cases the reader stumbles on a certain contradiction between the nature of the explication and the application of the concepts to actual examples. Theoretical considerations which introduce the basic concepts of FSP usually have recourse to the "feeling" of the language-user and testify to the fact that the authors really intend these concepts as PC. In fact it usually happens in the analysis of examples that these concepts are handled as though they were PnC. By way of example one may recall the method by which basic concepts are specified for the purposes of analysis. The question of what communicative functions the language-user (verifiably and indisputably) acknowledges as the foundation for these concepts is disregarded in favour of the search for a procedure enabling the linguist to identify a given dichotomy (or some of its exponents) in concrete sentences. It is also typical of the discussions that they revert again and again to the definition of basic concepts, and when they come to the forms by which a particular natural language expresses them the treatment is unsystematic.

If we scrutinize the sentences of a text, or even only the examples analysed within individual conceptions of FSP, from the standpoint of the lay user of the language in question, we certainly come across sentences to which the stated concepts can be applied without difficulty, yet there remain some sentences which do not admit of their application and run counter to the proposed explanation.

Clearly, the sentence

(xi) The girl broke the vase.

presents no serious problems of analysis for the language-user from the point of view DEN-d. However, doubts could arise as to its evaluation from the standpoint of DEN-c, because the language-user can hardly determine the relative importance of the segments without recourse to the context. The lay user is likely to encounter substantially greater difficulties in applying DEN a–d to sentences such as

(xii) All at once fire broke out in a large hay-stack on the skyline.

There is reason to assume that, faced with the analysis of this kind of sentence, the lay language-user would admit defeat. The linguist has two possibilities. He can define his conception as being valid for a certain type of material, i.e. admit that some types of sentences are neutral with respect to FSP and attempt to specify these types as accurately as he can. Alternatively, he will try according to a fixed procedure to extrapolate his FSP analysis to cover neutral sentences, at the same time stating what aim the extrapolation is designed to fulfil (cf. Quine 1960: 19–21). In this event his FSP concepts necessarily become PnC. Both are justifiable solutions. In the second case, however, the possibility of applying findings obtained by FSP theory within the framework of TG is conditional upon an explicit statement of the confines beyond which the concepts are extrapolated. This condition is all the more important because the phenomena corresponding to DEN (FSP) are seldom in the nature of rules: their infringement or neglect is not often felt by the language user as a "mistake", it is more usually a question of tendencies or habits which need not always be realized.

7   Obviously it has not been possible in this article to treat more than a small selection of the problems which might be subsumed under its title. Our main concern was with the basic concepts of FSP, since we consider their elucidation to be a prerequisite of the solution of further problems (cf. [Novák 1974] and similar problems in [Friedman 1975]). For this reason we did not touch on the important question of whether the bearer of inter-sentence cohesion is the sentence as a whole or the organisation of certain segments within it. The question of the means by which DEN (FSP) may be realised was likewise left aside: the material for a rich discussion is to be found particularly in the relations between grammatical and semantic means on the one hand and phonetic means on the other. Another aspect not accounted for in this article is the possible exploitation of the individual conceptions in text-analysis, and we unfortunately did not have room for a detailed discussion of Daneš's thematic progressions, which contain many valuable observations.

Notwithstanding the somewhat fragmentary nature of our observations, they bring to light at least one step towards the improvement of methods of text-analysis, which would well be taken as soon as possible: linguistic science should develop an interpretation and classification of context dependence as an *n*-ary relation, founding this interpretation in the first place on the analysis of its members and their domains. Whether this step should be taken by FSP or by textlinguistics is of little meaning.

References

(The works marked by an asterisk are directly relevant to FSP)

*Adamec P., 1966: Poryadok slov v sovvemennom russkom yazyke, Prague
*Akmajian, A., 1970: *Aspects of the Grammar of Focus in English,* unpublished doct. diss., MIT
*Benešová E., 1971: *Some Questions of Topic/Comment Articulation and Word Order in Czech* (in Czech), AUC, Slavica Pragensia XIII, Prague
*Benešová E., Sgall P., 1973: *Remarks on the Topic/Comment Articulation* I, II (with E. Hajičová), PBML 19, pp. 29–58, 20, pp. 3–42
Chomsky N., 1965: *Aspects of the Theory of Syntax,* MIT
Chomsky N., 1971: *Deep Structure, Surface Structure, and Semantic Interpretation,* in *Semantics* (ed. D. Steinberg, L. Jacobovits), Cambridge University Press, pp. 183–216
*Dahl Ö., 1969: *Topic and Comment: A Study in Russian and General Transformational Grammar,* Acta Universitatis Gothoburgensis, Uppsala
*Dahl Ö. (ed.), 1974: *Topic and Comment, Contextual Boundness and Focus.* Papiere zur Textlinguistik 6, H. Buske, Hamburg
*Dahl Ö., 1975: rev. of (Sgall et al. 1973) JL 11, pp. 347–354

*Daneš F., 1968: *Types of Thematic Progressions in Texts* (in Czech), Slovo a slovesnost 29, 1968

*Daneš F., 1974a: *Functional Sentence Perspective and the Organization of the Text*, in Daneš (ed.), pp. 106–128

*Daneš F., 1974b: *Zur Terminologie der FSP*, in (Daneš (ed.)), pp. 217–222

*Daneš F., 1974c: *Semantic and Thematic Structure of Sentence and Text* (in Polish), in *Tekst i język (Problemy semantyczne)*, Wrocław-Warszawa (ed. M.R. Mayenowa), pp. 23–40

*Daneš F., 1976: Czech Terminology of FSP (in Czech), in Jazykovedné Štúdie, Bratislava (in press)

*Daneš F. (ed.), 1974: *Papers on Functional Sentence Perspective*, Academia, Prague

*van Dijk Teun A., 1975: *Issues in the Pragmatics of Discourse*, Amsterdam (mimeo)

Dressler W., 1973: *Einführung in die Textlinguistik*, Niemeyer, Tübingen

*Dressler W., 1974: *Funktionalle Satzperspektive und Texttheorie*, in (Daneš [ed.] pp. 87–105)

*Enkvist N.E., 1973: *Linguistic Stylistics*, Mouton, The Hague

*Enkvist E.N., 1974: *Style and Types of Context*, in *Reports on Text Linguistics: Four Papers on Text, Style and Syntax* 1 (ed. by N. Enkvist), Åbo

*Firbas J., 1971: *On the Concept of Communicative Dynamism in the Theory of Functional Sentence Perspective*, SPFFBU, pp. 135–144

*Firbas J., 1974: *Some Aspects of the Czechoslovak Approach to Problems of Functional Sentences Perspective*, in (Daneš [ed.]), pp. 11–37

*Firbas J., 1974b: *Two Chapters on the Function of the Question in the Act of Communication*, Wassenaar (mimeo)

*Firbas J., 1974c: *A Functional View of 'Ordo Naturalis'*, Wassenaar, The Netherlands (mimeo)

*Firbas J., 1975: *On the Thematic and the Non-thematic Section of the Sentence*, in *Style and Text* (Studies presented to Nils Erik Enkvist), Spragforlaget, Skriptor AB, Stockholm, pp. 317–334

*Firbas J., Golková E., 1976: An Analytical Bibliography of Czechoslovak Studies in Functional Sentence Perspective.Brno (mimeo)

*Firbas J., Pala K., 1971: rev. of (Dahl 1969), JL 7, pp. 91–101

Friedman H.B., 1975: *The Ontic Status of Linguistic Entities*, F. of L. 13, pp. 73–94

Hajičová E., 1975: *Negation and Presupposition in the Semantic Structure of the Sentence* (in Czech, English summary), Academia, Prague

*Halliday M.A.K., 1967: *Notes on Transitivity and Theme in English*, JL 3, Part 1: 37–81, Part 2: 199–244

*Halliday M.A.K., 1974: *The Place of "Functional Sentence Perspective" in the System of Linguistic Description*, in (Daneš [ed.]) pp. 43–53

Hausenblas K., 1971: *Der Aufbau der Verbalen Kommunikate und ihr Stil* (in Czech, German Summary), AUC-Monographia XXXV, Prague

Hlavsa Z., 1975: *Denoting of Objects and its Means in Contemporary Czech* (in Czech, English Summary), Academia, Prague

Jackendoff R.S., 1972: *Semantic Interpretation in Generative Grammar*, MIT

*Kuno S., 1972: *Functional Sentence Perspective*, LI, 3, pp. 269–320

*Kuroda S., 1972: *The Categorical and Thetic Judgment: Evidence from Japanese Syntax*, F. of L. 9, pp. 153–185

*Lapteva O.A., 1972: *Unsolved Problems of the Functional Sentence Perspective* (in Russian), Voprosy jazykoznaniya, No. 2, pp. 35–47

*Mathesius V., 1975: *A Functional Analysis of Present Day English on a General Linguistic Basis*, Academia, Prague (edited by J. Vachek)

*Nikolayeva T.M., 1972: *The Functional Sentence Perspective as a Category of Text Grammar* (in Russian), Voprosy yazykoznaniya, No. 2, pp. 48–54

*Novák, P., 1974: *Remarks on Devices of Functional Sentence Perspective*, in (Daneš [ed.]), pp. 175–178

Palek, B., 1968: *Cross-Reference, A Study from Hyper-Syntax*, AUC. Monographia XXI

Palek B., 1974: *On the Nature of Hyper-Syntactic Relations*, in Proc. of the XIth Int. Congress of Linguists, Bologna, pp. 881–893

Posner R., 1972: *Theorie des Kommentierens*, Linguistische Forschungen 9, Athenäum Verlag

Quine W.O., 1960: *Word and Object*, MIT

Quirk R., Greenbaum S., Leech G., 1972: *A Grammar of Contemporary English,* Longman London

*Sgall P., et al., 1973: *Topic, Focus and Generative Semantics,* Scriptor, Kronberg

*Sgall P., 1973 b: *Contextual Boundness and the Question Test* (in Czech), Slovo a slovesnost 34, pp. 202–211

*Tyl Z. (ed.), 1970: *A Tentative Bibliography of Studies in Functional Sentence Perspective,* Prague

*Uhlířová L., 1974: *Semantics of Adverbials and their Roles in Functional Sentence Perspective* (in Czech), SaS 35, pp. 99–106

*Warburton I., 1975: *The Passive in English and Greek,* F. of L. 13, pp. 563–578

*Yang, In-Seok, 1974: *Semantics of Delimiters,* IULC – mimeo

Text in the Systemic-Functional Model

Ruqaiya Hasan
Macquarie University

1 Introduction

In examining the development of the systemic-functional model (SF model), one soon becomes aware of the fact that, here, from the very earliest stages, text has been viewed as a linguistic entity, the description of which is as legitimate a concern of linguistics as the description of the traditionally recognized units in the grammar and lexicon of a language. The questionable opposition between 'sentence-centred' and 'text-centred' theories of language (Petöfi: 1975) is regarded as a distortion of the nature of human language. In this, as in many other respects, the SF model is very close to the Firthian view of language; according to Firth, a major part of the semantics of a sentence could be stated only if the sentence were studied as a part of a text, occurring within a context (Firth: 1956; Mitchell: 1975). It is all the more interesting that at no stage does this model view the text as a 'super-sentence'. By implication, it also rejects a taxonomic hierarchy with an unbroken constituency chain from morpheme to text – a view implied in Harris (1952; 1963) Pike (1963), van Dijk (1972) and others. Instead, the question of text study has been approached from two seemingly distinct and unrelated directions, which, on closer examination, can be seen to derive from the two notions most fundamental to the text-ness of text: *texture* and *structure*.

1.1 Texture

A random string of sentences differs from a set of sentences representing a (part of a) text, precisely in that the latter possesses the property of texture. Texture is the technical term used to refer to the fact that the lexicogrammatical units representing a text hang together – that there exists linguistic cohesion within the passage. This cohesion is effected by the use of such linguistic devices as those of reference, substitution, ellipsis, conjunction and lexical organization (Halliday and Hasan: 1976; Hasan: 1971). The semantics of these cohesive devices ranges from absolute identity of meaning (eg the identity of meaning between *John* and *he,* where *he* coheres with *John*) to simply certain kinds of contiguities of meaning (such as exist between the members of the pairs *children-boys; boy-lad; big-small; buy-sell; blue-pink; hand-thumb* etc.).

1.2   Structure

The property of structure is what allows us to distinguish between complete and incomplete texts on the one hand, and between different generic forms on the other. With some oversimplification, the assumptions here can be stated as follows: associated with each genre of text – ie type of discourse – is a generalized structural formula, which permits an array of actual structures. Each complete text must be a realization of a structure from such an array. The generic membership of the text is determined by reference to the structural formula to which the actual structure can be shown to belong. A text will be perceived as incomplete if only a part of some recognizable actual structure is realized in it; and the generic provenance of the text will remain undetermined, if the part so realized is not even recognizable as belonging to some distinct actual structure.

Because the term *structural formula* is so basic to the discussion of text structure as developed in this paper, it is important to clarify the notion. A well-known example of structural formula would be the Aristotelian one for texts belonging to the genre of Greek tragedy; they must consist of three elements: *Beginning, Middle* and *End,* the elements occurring in that order. The formula could be presented as B^M^E where the symbol $\hat{}$ denotes fixed order. A structural formula is any well-defined configuration of the elements of the structure of a text.

Each such element is realized by some combination of lexicogrammatical units; the relationship between these and the text is that of realization (Halliday: 1961a; Lamb: 1964; Lockwood: 1972; Hjelmslev: 1943) not of constituency. The elements of text structure cannot be defined by reference to the rank status or sequential ordering of the lexicogrammatical units which have the function of realizing these elements. To be at all viable, the definition will have to be functional (Sinclair and Coulthard: 1975), the functions themselves being determined by the semiotics of the text genre (Hasan: 1972; Halliday: 1974; 1975; 1976a). It seems quite irrefutable that the controls upon the structural make-up of a text are not linguistic in origin, in that language as a formal system does not enable one to predict what generalized structural formula could be associated with which genre. Instead, the control is contextual: the nearest non-Linguistic analogue of a text is not a logico-mathematical formula, but a non-verbal social event. A text is a social event whose primary mode of unfolding is linguistic. If text can be seen as a bridge between the verbal symbolic system and the culture, this is because of the relationship between text and social context: text is 'in language' as well as 'in culture'. It follows from this relationship between text and context, that the specification of structural formulae for distinct genres requires a model of language in which context is a well-defined category, not just an ad hoc stand-by to which appeal can be made in analysing sentences which might otherwise prove recalcitrant.

2   Context, genre and text-structure

In the SF model the concept of register is a ready-made link between context and generic structure, since for most material purposes register and genre are synonymous. Linguists have long paid tribute to the difficulty of systematizing context (Katz and Fodor: 1964; Leech: 1974; Lyons: 1968). Indeed, it has been seriously maintained that an appeal to the notion of context would render our analysis of language less valid (Leech: op. cit). Yet, at the same time, no linguist has managed to demonstrate that the facts of language can be satisfactorily described without the systematization of context of situation (Palmer: 1976).

2.1   Context and register

There is no doubt that the notion of context of situation is difficult to handle except through some such category as that of text genre or register. However, register itself cannot be recognized legitimately in a model which insists either upon the absolute autonomy or on the homogeneity of language. The very definition of register depends upon the recognition of systematic variation – variation in language form in correlation with variation in the context of situation (Halliday et al: 1964; Gregory: 1967; Ellis: 1966; etc.). Such a definition makes the weak claim of simple co-occurrence of particular values of certain linguistic and extralinguistic variables. Recently a stronger claim has been made in the SF model (Hasan: 1973; 1975; Halliday: 1974; 1975; 1976a) that the correlation is causally determined, with certain contextual variables functioning as control upon the range of meanings from which selection may be appropriately and relevantly made. In this approach, one's primary focus is upon systematic and functional variation in language. One is not concerned with all possible vectors of variation in situation; there is a firm rationale for limiting oneself to just those vectors which definitely correlate – causally and systematically – with linguistic variation. In the last resort, this is a strategy for imposing form upon that essentially formless thing – the extralinguistic situation, and the strategy yields variables which have been summed up (Halliday: 1975; 1976a) under three labels: i: the *field* ii. the *tenor* and iii. the *mode* of discourse. These three variables together make up the *contextual construct* (Hasan: 1973; 1975). The contextual construct is that part of the extralinguistic situation which bears relevance to systematic linguistic variation across texts of distinct genres. In any particular instance, these (highly generalized) variables are represented by some particular value(s); the totality of such values in one given case makes up the entity *'contextual configuration'* (CC). The difference between contextual construct and configuration is that while the former is entirely schematic (Firth: 1956) the latter is its concrete representation and, unlike the construct, is relevant to only one specific text genre.

2.2   Context and text-structure: some hypotheses

The claim is, then, that context is a determinant of the structural formula: the values within a CC determine what elements may occur in what configuration. To make these claims is to maintain that the CC relevant to a genre embodies the semiotics of that genre. I shall attempt to substantiate these claims by discussing some aspects of the structural formula associated with an imagined CC, whose values will not be stated exhaustively, the actual selection being motivated by the needs of the present discussion.

Variables	Values of the variables
field	{ professional consultation: medical; application for appointment ...
tenor	{ client: patient-applicant, agent for consultant: receptionist; maximum social distance ...
mode	{ aural channel: -visual contact: telephone conversation; spoken medium ...

The values in the right hand column are the values in a contextual configuration, to be referred to as CC1. Interpreted in every day language, the values of the CC state a situation in which a person (patient-applicant) telephones the receptionist at a doctor's clinic to fix a medical appointment. I shall assume that the context of culture for CC1 is the standard average European type and that the resulting verbal interaction produces a text – T1 – which is both complete and appropriate. Such an imaginary text will be presented below (4.1).

3   Some preliminaries

In the following discussion I shall need to make repeated reference to *channel, visual contact, social distance* and the concept of *role*.

By channel I refer to simply how 'the said' is made accessible to the addressee; whether it is presented visually or aurally. Between the two channels, there is normally a clear boundary, the said being either heard or read. The channel is independent of the medium, and vice versa. The difference between −/+*visual contact* is available, normally speaking, only when the channel is aural, though it would not take much ingenuity to think of some such situation as 'note-passing' in the class-room as a counter example.

3.1   Social distance

Social distance refers to the relationship between the interactants of the discourse (Hasan: 1973); the degree of social distance is determined by the frequency and the range of previous interaction between the interactants. (The term interactant is itself used to refer to persons involved actively in a verbal interaction). Social distance is a cline (Halliday: 1961a) as the various degrees of distance are ranged along a continuum, with the contiguous categories being less easy to distinguish though the end-points themselves are clearly perceived as distinct. I shall refer to the two end-points as minimum and maximum social distance. Minimum social distance obtains between interactants who have previously interacted fairly regularly in a wide range of differing fields; so they 'know' each other in a wide range of distinct roles. Intimacy is a function of such interaction; the interactants become aware of each other's idiosyncratic traits which distinguish them as distinct persons. By contrast, maximum social distance obtains between interactants who have either never interacted together previously or only very rarely in a highly restricted range of fields. This implies: the interactants are not known to each other – or only in a limited capacity – so that their distinguishing traits may not be recognized. Thus where maximum social distance obtains, the interactants 'know' each other primarily in the capacity of the holder(s) of some specific role(s).

3.2   Roles carried by the interactants

In the discussion of the context of situation, it has been normal till recently to talk of role as a unitary concept and to refer by this term only to the social role of the interactants. On the other hand, there is good reason for suggesting that every interactant in a verbal interaction carries at least three distinct types of roles simultaneously. These are *i.* textual roles; *ii.* social roles and *iii.* participatory roles.

There are two recognized (general) textual roles: those of *speaker* and *hearer* (for a discussion of how the degree of specificity for labelling the roles can be varied see Halliday: 1972 *a*). Generally, the textual roles are interchangeable, so that within the domain of the same interaction, the one who functions as speaker at one point in time will in all likelihood also function as hearer at another point in time, and vice versa. This unmarked state of affairs – notwithstanding lectures, speeches and the like – provides the justification for coining the term *speaker-hearer* and for referring to the interactants as *1st speaker, 2nd speaker* ... as if all the interactants do is to speak. The notion of turn taking (Sacks et al: 1974) is again closely related to the textual roles of speaker and hearer and the possibility of 'textual role-switch'.

By contrast, social roles – often thought of as *the* participant role – are not generally interchangeable within the domain of the same verbal interaction. Social roles are indicative of the rights and obligations of the bearers of the roles, often with particular reference to the transaction specified by the field; the two – the field and the roles – in these cases are mutually defining and together constitute the nexus of the transaction. It is possible to sub–classify the set of social roles into two classes: one, where the roles pair off hierarchically and secondly those where they form essentially nonhierarchic dyads. An example of the first category is teacher-pupil and of the second friend-friend or stranger-stranger.

Participatory role is determined solely by reference to the question: who set the interaction into motion? Whichever interactant does this, may be said to have the participatory role of *initiator,* while the one(s) whose move is a response to the initiator's move may be referred to as the *respondent.* It should be obvious that the roles of 1st speaker and initiator need not be carried by the same interactant; also cultures vary as to which social roles will coincide with the roles of initiator and respondent. Perhaps it is worth mentioning the generalization that when we have a clearly categorized social setting such as clinic, postoffice or courthouse, the respondent role is normally carried by interactants who have the function of maintaining the social nature of the institution. For example, in CC1 the respondent role is more likely to coincide with that of the receptionist than with that of the applicant-patient.

Significantly, these three types of roles relate readily to the three-part description of the text as a *verbal social event.* The textual roles arise because text is a social event of the verbal kind; the social roles arise because text is a verbal event of the social kind (Halliday: 1975 a; 1976 a); and the participatory roles arise because text is a happening, a doing, a piece of human behaviour like a handshake, a smile or an embrace.

4   Context and elements of text-structure

I will now consider the claim that the elements of the structural formulae are determined by the values of the CC pertaining to the genres in question. Given CC1 and the associated assumptions, I shall make a two-part statement. The structural formula associated with CC1 *must* contain the following elements: Identification *(I)*; Application *(A)*, Offer *(O)* and Confirmation *(C)*. These four elements are obligatory; any text belonging to this genre would be perceived as incomplete and/or inappropriate if one (or more) of these four elements were not realized in it. Secondly, the formula will also contain the following optional elements: Greeting *(G)*, Query *(Q)*, Documentation *(D)*, Summary *(S)* and Finis *(F)*. There are two noteworthy consequences of describing these elements as optional. The inclusion of optional elements in the structural formula implies that there will be some actual structures in the array in which one or more of these elements need not appear. Secondly, since such actual structures are permitted by the structural formula, a text which does not realize one or more of these elements will neither be regarded as incomplete nor inappropriate, though informally one might describe it as 'brusque', 'businesslike', 'bald' etc. Let me add also that the list of optional elements as presented here has been oversimplified. It is certainly possible to devise an alternative – and probably more viable – analysis in which the element *D* would be recursively related to *I*, and the element *S* to *O, C.* As the arguments for the recognition of recursive structures in texts are fairly complicated, I will not venture into them here, allowing the list of the optional elements to stand in their present oversimplified form.

With this proviso and without attempting to justify all aspects of my analysis, I provide an imaginary case of T 1, which is a text associated with CC 1. The symbol for an element appears within brackets, eg *good morning (G)*. Where a symbol appears repeatedly, this means that the element is discontinuous, and any one occurrence is only a partial realization of it. This is one reason why it could not be claimed that sentences enter directly into the structure of the text.

4.1   An imaginary T 1

The following will hopefully pass as a reasonable version of T 1:
- good morning *(G)* Dr Scott's clinic *(I)* may I help you *(Q)*
- oh hello good morning *(G)* this is Mrs Lee speaking *(I)* I wonder if I could see Dr Scott today *(A)*
- um well let me see I'm afraid Mrs Lee I don't have much choice of time today would 6:15 this evening suit you *(O)*
- yes, yes, that'll be fine *(C)*
- may I have your address and phone number please *(D)*
- 24 May Avenue, North Clyde and the number is 527.2755 *(D)*
- thank you *(D)* so that's Mrs Lee for Dr Scott at 6:15 this evening *(S)*
- mm yes thanks (F)
- thank you (F)

If it is correct that the only obligatory elements of structure are I, A, O, C, then a version of T 1 which contains only the realizates of these elements should be perceived by normal speakers of the language as a possible application for a medical appointment. I suggest that most native speakers will accept the following as complete though they may be disturbed by its brusqueness and baldness:
T 1 a
- Dr Scott's clinic *(I)*
- this is Mrs Lee speaking *(I)* I wonder if I could see Dr Scott today *(A)*
- um well let me see I'm afraid I dont have much choice of time today would 6:15 this evening suit you (O)
- yes yes that'll be fine *(C)*

4.2   Contextual control on elements of text structure

As space does not permit the examination of each element, I will concentrate only on element *I* to see how its appearance in the structural formula is determined by the values of CC 1.

The function of the element *I* is to establish that the interactants have, indeed, the potential of assuming the appropriate social roles. Much hinges upon what is meant by appropriate; I use it to mean 'suited to the CC under discussion' (McIntosh: 1961; 1965), so that the appropriacy of the realization of this element is judged by a consideration of the values of the CC, cumulatively. Obviously, *Sunshine Bakeries* and *this is the revenue department* are perfectly adequate identifications; but adequacy alone is not sufficient.

Given this function for *I,* it is reasonable to assume that the element would not be obligatory, if the potential for role appropriacy could be established by some nonverbal means such as the presence of visual contact. So, an initial hypothesis could be: element *I* is obligatory only if the CC contains the value *−visual contact.* If the hypothesis is correct and the causal correlation is absolute, then the element *I* should be unaffected by changes in other values of the CC and should not be allowed to occur if the CC contains *+visual contact.*

Imagine, then, a CC – CC2 – giving rise to a structural formula – formula 2 – which is identical with CC1 in every respect except that the aural channel is replaced by the visual one. Instead of a telephoned request for a medical appointment, we now have a written request. It is obvious that if this is the only difference between CC1 and CC2, then the element *I* would remain obligatory for formula 2, although its order vis a vis other elements in the formula may not be identical with that in formula 1 (see 6 below).

As a second step, imagine a CC – CC3 – whose values are identical with those in CC2 except in respect of field. Where in CC2 the value reads *professional consultation: medical; application for appointment,* in CC3 let it read *professional consultation, architecture; application for estimate of cost.* Such a difference across CC2 and CC3 will inevitably entail a change in the values of social role as entered for the variable: tenor. In CC2 the values of tenor are listed as *client: patient – applicant, agent for consultant: receptionist; maximum social distance;* for CC3 the values would have to read as *client: owner-applicant, agent for consultant: member architect; maximum social distance.* In the structural formula associated with this latter CC – let us call it formula 3 – the element *I* will still remain obligatory; moreover the potential for its order of occurrence within the formula would resemble that of *I* in formula 2 more closely than that of *I* in formula 1.

By these steps, all the values of CC1 have been replaced by some other value, except for *−visual contact* and *maximum social distance.* Imagine now a CC – CC4 – where all the values are identical with CC1 except *maximum social distance* which is replaced in CC4 by *minimum social distance.* In everyday parlance, the applicant is someone well known to the receptionist, perhaps a close friend. Associated with this CC, two possibilities exist; either we may have an opening such as T4a or T4b:

T4a – Dr Scott's clinic *(I)*
       – [oh Maria] it's me Julie here *(I)*
T4b – Maria, this is Julie *(I)*

The consideration of CC1–4 supports the hypothesis that the element *I* is controlled by the value *−visual contact.* If this control is causal and absolute, the element should not occur where the CC contains *+ visual contact.* Consider now a CC5 and 6, which are identical with CC1 and 4 respectively, in all respects, except that while 1 and 4 have — *visual contact,* 5 and 6 have +*visual contact.* In every day language the texts associated with CC1 and 4 are telephoned applications, while those associated with 5 and 6 are made in person by calling at the clinic. In CC1 and 5 there is *maximum social distance;* in CC4 and 6 the *social distance* is *minimum.*

Now, although the value + *visual contact* appears in 5, the possibilities for text-structure are close to those in 4, as shown by:

T5a – could I speak to Dr Scott's secretary *(I)*
    – I am the secretary *(I)*
    – well my name is Mrs Lee *(I)*

T5b – my name is Mrs Lee *(I)*

T5a is likely to occur if the clues provided visually are not sufficient to fix the social identity of the interactant and if the social distance is at its very maximum. T5b is likely to occur, if the visual clues sufficiently fix the identity of the receptionist and/or the applicant is someone who has visited the clinic before. The evidence from this CC begins to throw some doubt on the assertion that the element *I* is controlled absolutely by the value — *visual contact;* in CC5, we have the value + *visual contact,* but the social distance obtaining between the interactants remains maximum. It appears, then, that the element *I* is controlled simultaneously by the values of visual contact and social distance. This view is confirmed by CC6 where we have + *visual contact* and *minimum social distance:* the element *I* is not allowed to appear. If you are a personal friend of the receptionist's or an old patient of the doctor's having needed frequent consultation, you do not begin by announcing your identity.

The position can be summed up as follows:

(i) if the CC contains the values — *visual contact and also maximum social distance* (as in CC1–3) then, the structural formulae associated with each such CC *must* contain the element *I;* otherwise the text will be inappropriate and/or incomplete.

(ii) if both of these values are reversed, then the element *I* is not permissible as in any formula associated with CC6;

(iii) if only one value is reversed – either the CC contains + *visual contact* or *minimum social distance* as in CC5 and 4 respectively – then the structural formula must contain at least some part of element *I* (eg in T4b and T5b); the appearance of the element in some form is obligatory as exemplified by T4a–b and T5a–b.

Hopefully, the above discussion shows that the element *I* is controlled by the values of the CC. This control is not a simple one-value-one-element arrangement; rather, the presence or absence of the element is determined simultaneously by two values. The predictions (i) – (iii) regarding the occurrence of this element apply not only to the specific CCs discussed above, but if the reasoning is accurate, the generalization should hold universally.

4.3   Context and sub-elements

The position stated in (iii) above requires further examination. We note that in CC4 and 5, the array permitted by the formulae respectively allows actual structures T4b and T5b where the occurrence of *I* is qualitatively distinct from that in T4a, and T5a and T1. For ease of reference, let me tabulate the five possibilities below:

A. *Formula 1; structure T1:*
  – Dr Scott's clinic   – this is Mrs Lee speaking
B. *Formula 4; structure T4a:*
  – Dr Scott's clinic   – ... it's me Julie here...
C. *Formula 5; structure T5a:*
  – could I speak to Dr Scott's
    secretary
  – I am the secretary   – my name is Mrs Lee
D. *Formula 4; structure T4b:*
  –   – ... this is Julie
E. *Formula 5; structure T5b:*
                                                         – my name is Mrs Lee

In T4b and T5b we have a half-way position, where the realizate of the element *I* specifies only the identity of the initiator not of the respondent. I have commented above on the rationale for the selection of T5a as opposed to T5b. In both cases, visual contact is present but in T5a the 'seen' is not readily interpretable. In T4b, the situational setting is not 'seeable', as this is a telephoned request. Nonetheless, because the social distance is minimum, the initiator is in a position to make an accurate assessment of the possibilities: the eye of previous experience 'sees' without the evidence being physically available while the physical eye may not be able to interpret the seen without guiding experience from the past. Consider in this context the husband's *hello, darling, it's me* as a means of assuring his wife about the identity of the caller!

From these observations it is possible to generalize as follows. Wherever the value – *visual contact* appears in the CC, the interactant, holding the initiator role is in a position of greater advantage in the early stages of verbal interaction. The initiator has a clearer view of the details of the intended interaction, while the respondent is constrained to operate in the role entailed by the nature of the most likely field as expressed through the situational setting, surrounding the respondent. The more institutionalized and specialized such a setting is, the truer this observation regarding the respondent interactant. This explains why in T4a (despite minimum social distance) the utterance *Dr Scott's clinic* occurs. One may then view the personal address *oh Maria* as an instruction at a symbolic level to the respondent to revise her conception of the degree of social distance which is required for this particular interaction.

4.4   Constituency in text-structure

As the tabulation in 4.2 shows, the element *I* is, as if by the natural logic of the situation, divisible into two parts: one has the function of establishing role appropriacy for the initiator and the other, for the responding interactant. These two parts may be referred to as *II* (Initiator Identification) and *RI* (Respondent Identification), respectively. In the tabulation, the latter is realized by the 'bits' in the left hand column while the former is realized by the 'bits' in the right hand one.

If it is possible to divide *I* into two parts so neatly and discretely, is there any reason for retaining the more inclusive element *I*? Could the element *I* not be by-passed? There are strong reasons for rejecting this solution. As is implied by the predictions i-iii) in 4.2, we have established three sets of CCs, and four actual structural possibilities. These are:

sets of CC   position of the element I in actual structures
CC 1–3   formulae 1–3; where every actual structure in the array must contain both *II* and *RI*;
CC 4–5   formulae 4–5; where one set of actual structures in the array contains both *II* and *RI*; another contains only *RI*;
CC 6   formula 6; where the actual structures in the array are permitted to have neither *II* nor *RI*.

Out of the four actual structural possibilities, we need to refer to both *II* and *RI* three times; in all these cases the two parts are controlled together by the same set of values. Essentially, they function as if constituting one unitary element, a fact recognized by the postulate of element *I* which includes both *II* and *RI*. Secondly although there are actual structures in which a sub-element of *I* is not present, the conditions permitting this are stateable precisely; the nonappearance of one or the other subelement is non-random. The third and final reason for the recognition of the element *I* is as follows. If the inventory of obligatory elements for formula 1 is presented as *II, RI, A, O, C,* this makes it appear as if the relationship between *RI* and *A* is the same as that between *RI* and *II*, which is manifestly false.

It follows from the above that the element *I* consists of *RI* and *II*, while the sub-elements *RI* and *II* are constituents of *I*. In the SF model the 'consist of' relationship is displayed on a rank-scale (Halliday: 1961a; Huddleston: 1966; Hudson: 1971). Some concept analogous to that of rank-scale appears unavoidable for the description of the structure of the text, as Sinclair and Coulthard have found (1975); and as my own analysis of the narratives produced by children has demonstrated. However, the relationship that holds between the units on the rank-scale in the grammar of a language and that which holds between elements and subelements of the text is not identical in all respects. More work is required in this area to establish whether the number of ranks in text structure can be stated in isolation from specific genres or whether it varies from one genre to another.

5   Context and the order of elements in the structural formula

A structural formula is not simply a list of the elements of structure; it is a permitted configuration of such elements. Although elements within structural formulae do not necessarily have to be ordered (see for example Halliday's treatment of transitivity structures; Halliday: 1967; 1968), where text structure is concerned, I would suggest that at least a partial ordering is obligatory. There do not seem to be any genres in which all elements of the structural formula are free to occur in any sequence vis a vis all the others. By partial ordering I mean that the degree of mobility varies from pairs of elements to other pairs of elements; a given element may have to occur in a fixed sequence vis a vis another specific element but not vis a vis some other(s).

Such ordering as is present in a structural formula is imposed by the natural logic of the social event whose verbal expression is what we label 'text'. In other words, order in text structure is also a function of the values of the CC. For example, if we consider the obligatory elements in formula 1, their order may be stated as follows: $\Gamma[A]^{\frown}O^{\frown}C$. The square bracket indicates the fact that the realizate of the element A may be surrounded by that of the element I, as in: T1c: – Dr Scott's clinic

– *I wonder if I could see Dr Scott today* the name is Mary Lee. where the underlined is a realization of the element A and is surrounded on both sides by the realizates of the element I. This same structural formula can be used to display the fact of partial ordering; for this we move to the second rank elements RI and II (always keeping in mind the fact that the expression of the list as $R1$, II, A, O, C is descriptively not desirable unless we wish to imply that II belongs to the same rank as A, O or C. However, I show them in configuration with A, O and C as space does not permit the statement of the sub-elements of the last three elements). The partial ordering will be displayed if the formula is presented as: $R1^{\frown}(A^{\cdot}II)^{\frown}O^{\frown}C$, where the dot between A and II shows that these two elements are not ordered with reference to each other. The formula may be read as: the element C cannot precede O, cannot precede A or II, cannot precede RI but A may precede II or vice versa. In every day language, one cannot confirm an offer unless the offer has been made and the offer itself cannot be made unless an application has been lodged; to lodge the application, it is essential to know that the addressee is capable of granting the application ie that correct social roles are held. In terms of Austin's speech act theory (Austin: 1962; Searle: 1969), we have a series of illocutionary acts here, each of which demands certain preparatory conditions, before it can itself be appropriately undertaken.

By the logic of the social event, I do not mean simply the different stages of the transaction. The discussion of the above formula may have lead one to believe that the order of the elements is controlled by the nature of the field. However this would be a hasty and unwarranted conclusion. The order of the elements is determined by the values of the CC cumulatively, as a consideration of the structural formula 2 – associated with CC 2 – will hopefully show. Recall that CC2 differs from CC1 only in respect of channel: C2 has visual channel whereas CC1 has aural channel. The difference between the texts would be informally expressed as that between a written application and a spoken one. However, formula 1 and 2 show a great amount of difference. In the first place, not all the obligatory elements for the two are identical, the list for formula 2 reading as *RI, II, Ad*(dress), *A, F, Sig*(nature). Without further elaboration, I would suggest that the structural formula 2 could be expressed as follows: *RI^ ((AD^ (A˙ F)^ Sig)˙ II)*. So, the element *Sig* cannot precede the elements *A* or *F*, cannot precede *Ad*, cannot precede *RI; II* may precede *Ad* or follow *Sig* immediately. Note in particular that the element *II* may either occur between *RI* and *Ad* or text-finally, following *Sig*(nature). This last possibility is totally ruled out for any structure appearing in the array of formula 1. Hopefully this example shows how the order of the elements in the structural formula may be affected by such 'non-cognitive' values as *visual* v. *aural channel, maximum* v. *minimum social distance, written* v. *spoken medium, application* v. order v. *narrative.* Field is not the only determinant of the order of the structural elements in a formula. This is instructive, specially in view of our deeply ingrained belief that the primary function of human language is the cognitive one – to exchange or express 'thoughts' or 'facts' – and that all other kinds of meanings are an optional extra, riding on the back of the cognitive meanings (Leech: 1974).

5.1   Structural formula and array of actual structures

As is perhaps clearly indicated by now, a structural formula is seen as a generalized statement/expression of the structural potential for texts in a given CC. Each such formula allows a range of actual structures to the texts of the genre. For example, on the basis of the structural formula 2 (stated above), the following array of actual structures may be stated:

T2 i: RI^Ad^A^F^Sig^II
T2 ii: RI^II^Ad^A^F^Sig
T2 iii: RI^Ad^F^A^Sig^II
T2 iv: RI^II^Ad^F^A^Sig

It can be seen immediately from the above array that the number of actual structures is determined by the presence of those elements whose order of occurrence is not entirely fixed vis a vis some other(s). We may describe this phenomenon as 'optionality in ordering' of the elements. The second source of increase in the array of actual structures is the existence of optional elements. For lack of space I have confined myself here to the obligatory elements only; but the reader can have some idea of the increase in the number of actual structures in the array if three optional elements *X, Y, Z* are introduced in T2 which enjoy optionality of ordering with respect to the elements *Ad, A* and *F.*

5.2   Array of actual structures and genres

If we think of each structural formula as yielding an array of actual structures, we imply also that each CC is applicable to not just one single text but to a class of discourse. Another way of saying pretty much the same thing would be that any two or more texts realizing an actual structure from a given array would be regarded as belonging to the same genre. The terms 'register' and 'genre' as used here are then interchangeable. To allow for an array of actual structures accessible to one single genre is to imply that there can be non-registral structural variation across texts: the fact of belonging to the same register does not entail structural identity.

If CCs 1–6 are considered, not a single pair will be found members of which are totally different from each other in respect of every value. Since the values of the CC control the elements of the structural formulae, it is obvious that some elements will be shared across some genres eg the element *I* appears in five out of six cases. The important point is that variation across registers is not absolute, that registers cannot be totally 'sealed off' one from another; the difference is not a yes/no difference but a more/less difference. Thus CC 2 resembles CC 1 more closely than does CC 3; the degree of similarity is determined by the extent of similarity in the values – by what is common to both situations. To accept such indeterminacy as a part of one's description of register does not mean that the model is inadequate or that the concept of register is incorrectly expounded. The indeterminacy must be accepted because it exists; it is inherent in the data. And because it exists inherently, we require a model which is capable of describing this indeterminacy in an ordered and systematic manner. To construct a model which distorts facts by attempting to create clearcut boundaries where only fuzzy edges exist does not appear to solve any problems – at least not for very long.

6   Context, structure and texture

The above discussion has been concerned mostly with the facts of text structure. Although this discussion has been hurried and condensed I hope it still substantiates my claims regarding the centrality of context to the study of text structure. How do these facts about structure and context relate to texture? In what follows I shall content myself with very brief statements; in particular since a considerable amount of literature is available on texture I shall not describe the actual cohesive devices (Halliday: 1961 b; 1964; 1966; 1974; 1975; 1976 a; 1976 b; Hasan: 1961; 1964; 1971; Bowley: 1962; Sinclair: 1966; Halliday and Hasan: 1976; Gutwinski: 1974).

Texture is what makes the sentences of a text cohere. Such cohesion may be said to arise primarily from two sources (i) the stability of the CC and (ii) the inter-relatedness of the values occurring within a CC. The continuity of the values of a CC implies that the various kind of meaning relations ranging from identity of meaning to simple contiguity of meaning (Halliday and Hasan: 1976) must exist. The boundaries of a text can normally be determined by reference to the patterns of cohesion; and it is an interesting fact that the pattern of cohesion cannot continue undisturbed if the values of the CC have been altered. By the inter-relatedness of the values in the CC, I mean that the presence of a particular value within a CC often argues for the presence of some other value. The standard example here would be the inter-relatedness between some value of the field and the social roles within a CC, or the fact, for example, that the value – *visual contact* must normally occur if the channel is visual. Such inter-relatedness is quite obviously the basic motivation for the patterns of lexical organization in a discourse, involving both the identity and extension of meaning.

Again, the manner in which the values of the CC control the elements of the text structure also provides motivation for the presence of cohesive devices. It has been noted that one element can be controlled simultaneously by more than one value (eg the element *I*) and also that the same value may (partially) control more than one element in the structural formula (eg *minimum social distance*, which controls the elements *I, PA* (Personal Address) and *G*. As the realization of these elements must reflect their semiotic function, which is itself related directly to the values of the CC, it is not difficult to understand why at the realizational level there is a polyphonic quality in texts. Several strands of meanings are prosodically realized throughout the next: a sentence realizing any one element is not simply a realizate of that element and no more. Consider the difference between what is popularly known as conventional greeting and personal greeting: both realize the element *G* but the difference between the two is that in doing so the former also build in the value *maximum social distance* into the realization, while the latter build in the value *minimum social distance*. We note that *G* is an element simultaneously controlled by the values of the channel and the degree of social distance. But as *G* is not the only element which would be controlled by the values in question, the realizate of all other such elements as are controlled by these values will also contain 'evidence' of the value in it. So it comes to pass that the semiotics of the social distance will not be reflected in any one discrete place in the text but will appear prosodically throughout the text in the realizates of those elements which are affected by this value. Since there are various strands of meaning being thus realized in the next, this creates the polyphonic quality of the text. (Halliday: 1976a); and it is this quality which provides more than any other aspect the motivation for the selection of certain types of cohesive devices.

7   SF model, Context and text

If it is granted that context, structure and texture are closely related, the way in which the concept of context is integrated into the model, making contact with the lexicogrammatical categories, becomes highly relevant. In the SF model the link between context and lexicogrammar is established via the notion of macro-functions, which are said to provide a schema for the semantic level (Halliday: 1970; 1973; 1975; 1976a). If the semantic level is seen as representing the meaning potential of a language, this large area can be functionally divided into four distinct parts: i) the experiential; ii) the interpersonal; iii) the textual and iv) the logical type of meaning. In some manner or other, under some label or other, all of these functions have long been recognized in the study of human language. Thus, although in much of modern linguistics we find no interest in the textual type of meaning, it can perhaps be validly maintained that most of rhetoric was about textual types of meaning as much as it was about the interpersonal type.

The most significant contribution of the SF model is not that these functions have been suggested – they have long been recognized; it is that an effort has been made to show why these functions alone need recognition. Halliday maintains that with the give-and-take relationship that exists between the 'meanings' and the 'wordings' of a language, the two mutually justify the recognition of the categories at the two levels. So, if we start from the semantic level, it may be seen that each type of meaning potential represents an area which can be encoded by the grammatical options stateable in largely self-suffi-cient, self-contained networks of systemic options. For example, the experien-tial type of meaning is endoced by options that can be presented within the transitivity system network (this system states options which relate to such meaning distinctions as some linguists attempt to explain through case gram-mar). If on the other hand, we start from the examination of the lexicogramma-tical level in language, it would be found that some parts of the level are more closely related than others; for example, in general the fact of the verb being transitive or intransitive has little effect on whether the clause in which it occurs can be declarative, an interrogative or an imperative. And when we begin to examine these patterns from a functional point of view, it is found that each network relates to an area of meaning which is distinct from the others in ways which allow the setting up of the four areas of meaning potential mentioned above. This two-way relationship has been recognized since de Saussure and perhaps most effectively expressed in the work of Hjelmslev (1943) who saw the mutual interdependence of the sign and the 'signed' as the most important aspect of the organization of the human language.

7.1 Functions, lexicogrammar and context

The variables of the contextual construct are set up by reference to their systematic correlation with linguistic variation. It is perhaps not difficult to imagine how context could be related to the semantic and the lexicogrammati-cal levels of language. The linguistic variables must belong to some specifiable part of the lexicogrammar and these in turn would be related to the functional components at the semantic level. To oversimplify a great deal, the three variables of field, tenor and mode are set up because language is 'geared' to give information regarding precisely these aspects by virtue of the fact that the types of meanings languages are capable of encoding are experiential (relating to field), interpersonal (relating to tenor) textual and logical (relating to mode and structuring in general). There is thus a fairly close relationship between functions, lexicogrammar and context.

Human languages are capable of mapping all four types of meanings onto the same string of 'words'. Thus in *was it Mary who knitted this sweater,* we have all four types of meanings present and the sentence can be described as realizing four distinct types of structures derived from distinct networks; its experiential meaning is expressed by the relations that hold between *Mary, knit* and *sweater;* its interpersonal meaning is expressed by the fact that the clause is interrogative (rather than declarative or imperative); its textual meaning is expressed by thematic arrangement in the clause (Halliday: 1967; 1968) and by the occurrence of the demonstrative *this.*

Because of these relationships between functions and lexicogrammar on the one hand and between functions and context on the other, it can be seen that a chain of relationship is established which integrates both the notion of context and text into the model.

8   Concluding remarks

The exposition of the views on the study of text in the SF model has been very condensed. I have drawn heavily on Halliday's work. However, I claim responsibility for the views and interpretations presented here. The account is by no means exhaustive as it has not been possible to trace the history of certain other relevant developments. It is important to remark yet again that the model owes much to Firth and the present analysis of the structure of texts closely resembles a standard Firthian effort in this direction (Mitchell: 1975), though the details vary.

One final point needs to be made. The schema presented for the study of texts is not suited to texts in verbal art (Hasan: 1975); in particular the remarks that have been made about the relationship between the values of the CC and the elements of the text structure would seem not to apply to verbal artefacts and will give none but disappointing results if applied to Middlemarch or War and Peace. The schema seems best suited to small self-contained verbal interactions, and will probably pose some very interesting problems if extended to the analysis of texts which must display continuity either by explicit allusion to other verbal interactions as in the case of citing precedents in law or to such established events as, say, the broad cast of news.

References

1. J. L. Austin: (1962) *How to Do Things with Words,* Cambridge, Mass., Harvard University Press.
2. C. C. Bowley: (1962) *Cohesion and the paragraph,* dissertation for Diploma in General Linguistics, University of Edinburgh (unpublished)
3. T. A. van Dijk: (1972) *Some Aspects of Text Grammars,* The Hague, Mouton.
4. J. O. Ellis: (1966) 'On contextual meaning', in *In Memory of J. R. Firth,* C. E. Bazell, J. C. Catford, M. A. K. Halliday, R. H. Robins (eds), London, Longmans. pp 79–95
5. J. R. Firth: (1956) *Papers in General Linguistics,* Oxford, Blackwell.
6. M. Gregory: (1967) 'Aspects of varieties differentiation' *Journal of Linguistics,* 3. pp 177–198
7. W. Gutwinski: (1974) Cohesion in Literary Texts: *A Study of Some Features of English Discourse,* The Hague, Mouton
8. M. A. K. Halliday: (1961a) 'Categories of the theory of grammar' *Word,* 17. pp 241–292
9. –: (1961b) 'Descriptive linguistics in literary studies', Paper presented at IXth International Congress of Linguists, also in *English Studies Today,* G. I. Duthie (ed) (Edin. 1962). pp 25–40
10. –: (1966) 'Lexis as a linguistic level' in *In Memory of J. R. Firth* Bazell et al (eds), London, Longmans. pp 148–162
11. –: (1967/68) 'Notes on Theme and Transitivity in English', *Journal of Linguistics,* no. 3 pp 37–81, 199–244; no. 4 pp 179–215
12. –: (1970) 'Language structure and language function' in *New Horizons in Linguistics,* J. Lyons (ed), Harmondsworth, Penguins. pp 140–165
13. –: (1973) *Explorations in the Functions of Language.* London, Edward Arnold.
14. M. A. K. Halliday: (1974) 'Language as social semiotic: towards a general theory of sociolinguistics' in *The First LACUS Forum,* A. & V. Makkai (eds), Columbia, Hornbeam Press. pp 17–46
15. –: (1975) *Language and Social Man,* London, Longmans
16. –: (1976a) 'Text as a semantic choice in social contexts', in *Grammars and Descriptions,* T. A. van Dijk & J. S. Petöfi (eds), Berlin, de Gruyter, (in press)
17. –: (1976b) 'An interpretation of the functional relationship between language and social structure' in *Sprachstruktur – Sozialstruktur: Beiträge zur linguistischen Theorienbildung,* Uta Quasthoff (ed), Kronberg/Ts., Scriptor (in press)
18. M. A. K. Halliday, A. McIntosh & P. D. Strevens: (1964) *Linguistic Sciences & Language Teaching,* London, Longmans
19. M. A. K. Halliday & R. Hasan: (1976) *Cohesion in English,* London, Longmans
20. R. Hasan: (1961) *'The linguistic study of a literary text,* dissertation for Diploma in Applied Linguistics, University of Edinburgh, (unpublished)
21. –: (1964) *A Linguistic Study of Contrasting Features in the Style of Two Contemporary English Prose Writers,* Ph D thesis, University of Edinburgh, (unpublished)
22. –: (1971) 'Rime and reason in literature' in *Literary Style: A Symposium,* S. Chatman (ed), New York, Oxford University Press. pp 299–326
23. –: (1973) 'Code, register and social dialect' in *Class, Codes and Control, II,* B. Bernstein (ed), London, Routledge & Kegan Paul. pp 253–292
24. –: (1975) 'The place of stylistics in the study of verbal art' in *Style and Text,* H. Ringbom (ed), Stockholm, Skriptor. pp 49–63
25. Z. S. Harris: (1952) 'Discourse analysis' in *Language,* 28. pp 1–30
26. Z. S. Harris: (1963) *Discourse analysis: Papers on Formal Linguistics 2,* The Hague, Mouton
27. L. Hjelmslev: (1943) *Prolegomena to a Theory of Language,* Madison, University of Wisconsin
28. R. D. Huddleston: (1965) 'Rank and depth', *Language,* 41. pp 578–587
29. R. A. Hudson: (1971) *English Complex Sentences,* Amsterdam, North-Holland Publishing Co
30. J. J Katz & J. A. Fodor: (1963) 'The structure of a semantic theory' *Language* 39. pp 170–210
31. S. M. Lamb: (1964) 'On alternation, transformation, realization and stratification', *Monograph Series on Language and Linguistics,* 17, Georgetown University Instt. of Language and Linguistics. pp 105–122

32. G. N. Leech: (1974) *Semantics,* Harmondsworth, Penguins
33. D. G. Lockwood: (1972) *Introduction to Stratificational Linguistics,* New York, Harcourt Brace Jovanovich
34. J. Lyons: (1968) *Introduction to Theoretical Linguistics,* London, Cambridge University Press
35. Angus McIntosh: (1961) 'Patterns and ranges' *Language,* 37. pp 325–337
36. –: (1965) 'Saying' *A Review of English,* VI, no. 2, pp 9–20
37. T. F. Mitchell: (1975) *Principles of Firthian Linguistics,* London, Longmans
38. K. L. Pike: (1963) 'Discourse analysis and tagmemic matrices', paper read at LSA meeting; in *Advances in Tagmemics,* R. M. Brend (ed), Amsterdam, North-Holland Publishing Co. (1974) pp 285–306
39. J. S. Petöfi: (1975) 'Beyond the sentence, between linguistics and logic', in *Style and Text,* H. Ringbom (ed), Stockholm, Skriptor. pp 377–390
40. H. Sacks, E. A. Schegloff, & G. Jefferson: (1974) 'A simplest systematics for the organisation of turn taking in conversation', *Language,* 50. pp 696–735
41. J. R. Searle: (1969) *Speech Acts,* London, Cambridge University Press
42. J. McH. Sinclair: (1966) 'Beginning the study of lexis' in *In Memory of J. R. Firth,* C. E. bazell et al (eds), London, Longmans. pp 410–430
43. J. McH. Sinclair & M. Coulthard: (1975) *Towards an Analysis of Discourse,* London, Oxford University Press

Substitutional Text Linguistics*

Roland Harweg
Ruhr-Universität Bochum

1.

Wherever in the literature concerning text linguistics mention is made of a specifically substitutional approach within this discipline, the approach referred to is, as far as I know, the one developed by myself. I therefore feel compelled to deal, in this paper, mainly with this approach of my own.

2.

Although the text-linguistic approach known as substitutional text linguistics or substitution theory (cf. Lewandowski 1975: 702) is in fact essentially my own, it cannot, however, be overlooked that the use of substitutional models within linguistics as a whole is fairly widespread, and was so long before my own model was developed. But these traditional substitutional models are not – and, on account of their inner nature, cannot be – models for text linguistics.

To begin with, I shall try to show why these traditional substitutional models and the notion of substitution underlying them cannot serve as models for text linguistics and why, for text-linguistic concerns, we need a substitutional model and a notion of substitution that are of a principally different nature.

Among the substitutional models that I have classed as traditional, one may distinguish between two subtypes: a non-restricted and a restricted one. Both are – and therein lies their fundamental mutual kinship as well as their fundamental difference vis-à-vis the model developed by me – of a paradigmatic nature; that is to say that the notion of substitution underlying them designates an operation, or more precisely a substitution or replacement operation where the replacing and the replaced unit fill one and the same slot within a text or text portion, or more exactly, where the replacing unit fills precisely that position in the text which has been filled by the replaced unit before its replacement. But irrespective of the mutual kinship existing between the two types they display,

* I am indebted to my colleague Professor E.A. Hopkins for reading the manuscript, discussing some of the issues with me and suggesting several stylistic changes. Any remaining errors or inadequacies are, of course, my responsibility alone.

at the same time, a fundamental difference. Thus the notion of substitution underlying the non-restricted type of traditional substitutional models designates a symmetric-reversible kind of paradigmatic substitution operations, whereas the notion of substitution underlying the restricted type of substitutional models designates an asymmetric-irreversible kind of paradigmatic substitution operations.

If one designates the unit to be replaced by the term 'substituendum' and the unit that replaces it by the term 'substituens' (a terminology not to be found within the traditional substitutional models), then the substitution operation of the non-restricted substitutional models (an operation which plays a significant role above all with Fries 1952 and Harris 1951) can be described as an operation whose terms, the notions of substituendum and substituens, cannot be correlated in a general way with any definite classes of expressions. The notions are valid only with regard to concrete individual cases, and this implies that an expression which in some concrete substitution serves as the substituens may in some other concrete substitution serve as the substituendum – as a substituendum whose substituens might have been the substituendum of the first concrete substitution. The substitution operation, then, is reversible: the two expressions are, in one and the same textual position, mutually substitutable.

With the restricted substitutional model this is not the case. Within this model, the notions of substituendum and substituens do have assigned to them definite classes of expressions: they might be said to be of general applicability. True, the terms as such, as we have said, do not occur within the model under discussion, but for the terms occurring in their place, Bloomfield's (1933: 247ff.) terms 'ordinary' or 'replaced form' (in place of 'substituendum') and 'substitute' (in place of 'substituens') exactly the same holds: the opposition between ordinary form and substitute is asymmetric and irreversible. The two classes are invariable through all individual substitutions; none of their members may change from ordinary form to substitute or vice versa.

Within a paradigmatic substitutional model this restriction looks somewhat strange, at least at first sight. As a matter of fact, it can only be understood if one looks at it, instead from the angle of the substitution itself, from the angle of one its terms, and this is what Bloomfield, the founder of the restricted model under discussion, as well as all those who have followed him in his model, have done. They all look at the matter from the angle of the substituens, that is from the angle of what they call 'substitute'. This is particularly obvious when, at the beginning of his chapter on substitution, Bloomfield (1933: 247) begins by introducing the term 'substitution' and continues by defining[1] the term 'substitute'.

The choice of the substitute as the point of departure is, however, not implausible if one takes into account that the category of substitutes, apart from

---

[1] The definition runs as follows: "A *substitute* is a linguistic form or grammatical feature which, under certain conventional circumstances, replaces any one of a class of linguistic forms."

some marginal expressions, is identical with a certain time-honoured category of western grammar, namely that of pronouns – a category for which, by the way, the label of substitute was suggested as early as the beginning of the nineteenth century (cf. R. Crymes 1968: 23). The notion of substitution within the restricted type of paradigmatic substitutional models has, in the last analysis, no other function than that of elucidating the nature of the traditional category of pronouns, and it is obvious that it can do this only on account of its asymmetric-irreversible character.

Neither the restricted substitutional model nor the unrestricted one is of any use for the explanation of text-linguistic phenomena, particularly the explanation of text constitution. For this purpose one needs a substitutional model within which the terms 'substituendum' and 'substituens' do not, within the matrix of a text, occur instead of each other, but one after the other – a model which, by this fact, is able to account for the syntagmaticalness of text constitution. I have designated the notion of substitution underlying this model by the term 'syntagmatic substitution' (cf. Harweg 1968: 20).

But the notion of syntagmatic substitution as well has emerged from an attempt to describe the function of pronouns. Not, to be sure, the function of all pronouns, but certainly that of a certain subcategory of them, namely that which plays a decisive role in the constitution of texts: the category of the so-called anaphoric pronouns.

Interestingly enough, however, these anaphoric pronouns have already been thrown into relief as a prominent subcategory in the framework of the (restricted) paradigmatic substitutional model; already with Bloomfield they are, as anaphoric or dependent (1933: 249) or definite substitutes (1933: 252), set off from the other substitutes. As a matter of fact this, then, is a passage where it looks as if the (restricted) paradigmatic substitutional model, too, were suitable for the description of the constitution of texts, that is, text-linguistically fruitful, and there are even formulations which seem to imply that the anaphoric substitutes are identical with that category which I call syntagmatic substituentia. Mention is made, in this context, of so-called antecedents, and when these are defined as "the recently-uttered replaced form(s)" (Bloomfield 1933: 249) there seems to be no doubt that these antecedents, in their turn, are identical with the substituenda of my syntagmatic substitutional model. In fact, it seems as if we had secretly moved from the (restricted) paradigmatic substitutional model to the syntagmatic one.

But as Bloomfield's (1933: 251) statement

"In English, finite verb expressions are anaphorically replaced by forms of *do, does, did,* as in *Bill will misbehave just as John did.* The antecedent here is *misbehave;* accordingly, the replaced form is *misbehaved*"

makes abundantly clear, this is not the case. Wherever the opposite impression may arise, it is, except for certain passages in Dubois 1965, the result of imprecise or even misleading formulations, for it is not always the case that formulations about this topic are as clear and unambiguous as, for example, with Ruth Crymes (1968: 26, 34f.) – who, following Robert L. Allen (1961), explicitly states that even substitutes which refer to antecedents behave, from a substitutional point of view, paradigmatically. It cannot of course be denied that the recognition of a referential relation between substitutes and their antecedents is in any case a fact of text-linguistic significance, but it is equally obvious that this referential relation has not been formulated in substitutional terms, so that it does not touch the substitutional model in its innermost nature, but only from without.

But even if we suppose that by slipping from the (restricted) paradigmatic substitutional model into the syntagmatic one Bloomfield and his followers had re-interpreted the category of anaphoric substitutes as syntagmatic substitutes, that is, as what I call syntagmatic substituentia (with the antecedents as their – syntagmatic – substituenda), even then the result would not have been a text-linguistically efficient substitutional theory; for the class of these syntagmatic substituentia, identical as it would be with a category of substitutes stemming from a restricted paradigmatic substitutional model, would be by far too small. It is clear that not only the substitutes, but also the replaced forms of the restricted paradigmatic substitutional model, at least as far as they are replaced forms (not antecedents) of the anaphoric substitutes, would have had to be classed as syntagmatic substituentia.

3.

This conclusion is drawn in the syntagmatic substitutional model originally developed in Harweg 1968. Within this model we have as syntagmatic substituentia not only anaphorically used expressions like *he, she, it,* but also expressions like *the man* or *this woman,* expressions which are paradigmatically replaceable by them. In this model these expressions function as syntagmatic substituentia even when, instead of occurring as (textually not manifested) replaced forms, they occur as actual, textually manifested antecedents. This is to say that in a sentence sequence like *I asked a policeman, and the policeman told me. He was very friendly* not only *he,* but also its antecedent *the policeman* functions as a syntagmatic substituens and the only expression in this sequence to be interpreted as a syntagmatic substituendum is the expression *a policeman;* for *the policeman* could, paradigmatically, be replaced by *he; a policeman,* however, could not.

In Harweg 1968, I have categorized as among the (unambiguous) syntagmatic substituenda not only expressions like the non-generic *a policeman,* that is, nouns introduced by a non-generic indefinite article, but also non-generic expressions like *some women, several men,* and *three children,* that is, nouns introduced by certain indefinite pronouns or cardinal numbers, and even expressions like *somebody, something* or *somewhere,* that is certain indefinite pronouns and pronominal adverbs – expressions which, in the framework of the restricted paradigmatic substitutional model, as for instance with Bloom-field (1933: 249), are classed with the so-called independent substitutes. On the other hand, I have classed with the (unambiguous) syntagmatic substituentia not only the anaphoric pronouns *he, she, it, they, this,* and *that* as well as the anaphorically used pronominal adverbs like *there* or *thence,* but also nouns introduced by the non-generic definite article or the anaphoric pronouns *this* or *that*[2].

In a sentence sequence like *I asked Charles, and he told me* (in which *he* functions as a syntagmatic substituens), in the place of *he* there could also occur *Charles.* This implies that even proper names[3], or more precisely, certain positional types of occurrences of proper names, are able to function as syntagmatic substituentia. However, proper names, though able to fulfil the function of syntagmatic substituentia, are, from a morphological point of view, not unambiguous substituentia – just as the occurrence of *Charles* in the first sentence of the sequence under discussion, though functioning as a syntagmatic substituendum, is, morphologically, a not unambiguous substituendum: substituendum and substituens are, in the case of proper names, morphologically identical. Proper names are therefore, in Harweg 1968, classed as substituenda-substituentia.

By the same criterion, there are classed as substituenda-substituentia some other categories of expressions as well. Among these there are the nouns introduced by a generic article (in English frequently represented by zero), the nouns introduced by the universal quantifiers *all* and *each* (and, in the domain of negatives, by *no*), and finally all expressions used deictically.

Substituenda-substituentia of these categories are probably to be found in all languages; they form a universal category. In contradistinction, such substituenda-substituentia as are manifested by nouns in non-generic use are not universal. For nouns in non-generic use are in some languages (as, for example, in English) some of them substituenda and some of them substituentia. Generally speaking, one could say that those languages in which nouns in non-generic use are, even morphologically, some of them substituenda and some of them substituentia are the so-called article languages, whereas those languages in which such nouns are substituenda-substituentia are languages that do not possess articles. It seems, however, as though in these languages the said nouns were only optionally, not obligatorily substituenda-substituentia. The task of differentiating morphologically between substituendum and substituens in these languages, as for instance in certain Slavic languages, is performed by an unstressed variant of the cardinal number 'one' on the one hand and the anaphoric demonstrative pronoun on the other – the former serving as an

---

[2] Raible (1972: 160ff.), drawing on French literary material, especially Balzac, suggests a five-level substitution scheme, beginning with the substituenda as level 1 and ending with the anaphoric pronouns as level 5. Nouns introduced by anaphoric pronouns or the definite article represent levels 2 and 3, respectively.

[3] They form level 4 in Raible's (1972: 160ff.) scheme.

optional substitute for the missing indefinite article and the latter serving as an optional substitute for the missing definite article.

In Harweg 1968 the ascertainment of syntagmatic substitutions, that is of relations between a substituendum and its syntagmatic substituens or its syntagmatic substituentia, is based on the observation of referential identity or co-referentiality between these terms. That is to say it is based on the observation of a relation which in stating the relationship between antecedent and substitute has never played any role. The relation on which the ascertainment of the antecedent-substitute-relation has been based is, according to Bloomfield (1933: 251), either that of individualization of a species, together with an identification of the resulting individual, (this, according to Bloomfield, being the function of *he* with regard to the species designated by the antecedent) or it is the relation of lexical identity, a relation obtaining for example between the replaced form underlying Bloomfield's anaphoric substitute *one* and its antecedent[4]. In both cases, the antecedents, unlike most of my substituenda, have the form of a pure noun, so that for that reason alone the ascertainment of a referential identity relation is, at least in most of the instances, excluded. But whilst in the case of the anaphoric substitute *he* ascertainment of a relation of referential identity only requires the inclusion of, say, the indefinite article in the antecedent, ascertainment of referential identity in the case of Bloomfield's anaphoric substitute *one* is only possible if the combination 'adjective + *one*' is introduced by a definite article, but not, if (as in Bloomfield's [1933: 251] sentence *I prefer a hard pencil to a soft one*) it is introduced by an indefinite article. But even in the first of these two cases referential identity can only be recognized if the definite article and the adjective are included in the substitute. From all this it follows that the substitute *one* (and the same holds true for the corresponding zero-substitutes in languages like French or German) cannot, in the framework of my theory of syntagmatic substitution, function as a substituens.

There is still another category of Bloomfieldian substitutes whose members cannot function as substituentia, or more precisely as substituentia in the full sense: the restrictive relative pronouns, Bloomfield's (1933: 262f.) relative substitutes of the anaphoric type. For it is, at least on closer inspection, obvious that between them and their antecedents (regardless of whether the initial article is or is not considered part of the antecedent) there exists no referential identity in the sense in which it exists between the anaphoric substitute *he* and its antecedent. I have termed the substitutional relationship between restrictive relatives (or more precisely, restrictive relative clauses) and their antecedents 'micro-substitution', suggesting thereby that the combination of restrictive relative clause and antecedent as a whole may function as a normal substituendum or substituens (cf. Harweg 1968: 54f.).

---

[4] In this case Bloomfield (1933: 251) speaks of simple anaphoric substitutes.

There is, however, one kind of referential non-identity between syntagmatically related terms where I have retained the term of syntagmatic substitution. Of these syntagmatically related terms, the antecedent is (just as it is in the main type of syntagmatic substitutions based on referential identity) introduced by an indefinite article, and the subsequential form by a definite article, but their relationship is based on referential contiguity rather than on referential identity. In any case (and this must be stressed) the relationship is a referential one, not merely a lexical one, and it must be added that the contiguity relation, as a sort of abbreviation of a chain of identity relations, may in principle be transformed into the latter, though at the expense of linguistic naturalness. I have termed these contiguity relations 'substitutions of contiguity'. Examples are the substitutional sequences *a question : the answer, a flash of lightning : the thunder, a house : the windows,* and *a man : the neck-tie.* They manifest, at the same time, varying degrees of contiguity owing to the varying degrees of predictability of the substituens from the substituendum or, better, of 'impliedness' of the substituens by the substituendum (cf. Harweg 1968: 192 ff.).

4.

Syntagmatic substitution is, in my opinion, the basic text-building operation, that is, the basic operation building texts out of sentences. I therefore have based on it a definition of the notion of text, a notion that, in accordance with modern linguistic usage, covers both written and oral manifestations of verbal "successivity". According to this definition, a text is a succession of linguistic units (or more precisely of grammatical sentences) that is built up by an uninterrupted chain of syntagmatic substitutions (cf. Harweg 1968: 148). As to the terms of these substitutions, the substituenda and the substituentia, the former, provided they are not accompanied by substituentia (without substituenda in the same sentence), have the function of marking the beginning of a text, whereas the substituentia, as a means of connecting successive sentences, have the function of continuing the text. True, one can find, especially in modern literature, a great number of so-called texts which do not harmonize with this description. But this by no means invalidates the description; for these texts seem to be performances which, in deviating from our description, simultaneously deviate, as it were, from our text-grammatical competence (cf. Harweg 1973). Those texts that (as far as the above-mentioned functions of substituenda and substituentia are concerned) do harmonize with our text-grammatical competence I have called 'emic texts', whereas all texts of actual performance I have designated as 'etic texts', so that some of these etic texts are, at the same time, emic ones, whilst others are, at the same time, non-emic ones (cf. Harweg 1968: 152 ff.).

The discrepancy between substitutional "emicity" and substitutional "non-emicity" of a text can best be observed at the beginning of a text. As to the end of the text, it can only be described, at least directly, as an etic one; emically (that is as emic or non-emic) it could only be described indirectly, that is by having recourse to the beginning of all other texts.

These textological interpretations of the basic, and in a sense as yet rudimentary aspects of the syntagmatic substitutional model have been repeatedly criticized (cf. Harweg 1975). One of the main arguments of these criticisms has been the contention that the principle of syntagmatic substitution upon which my definition of the notion of text is based is but one among other possible text-building principles, so that, according to this argument, it is not sufficient for the constitution of texts. My answer to this is that it is surely not sufficient for the constitution of well-formed texts, but that it is sufficient (and necessary) for the constitution of what I call rudimentary texts[5] – so that it can and must be retained as the basic principle of text constitution (cf. Harweg 1975). In addition, it must be stressed that the contention as to the insufficiency of syntagmatic substitution for the constitution of texts can be viewed as an objection to my definition only in case the definition is considered a device for the generation of well-formed texts, but not, if the definition (as in my system) is looked upon in the traditional sense of furnishing the genus proximum and the differentia specifica of the definiendum, that is of furnishing the minimal set of the definiendum's identificational-contrastive properties.

In Harweg 1968 I have, within the area of emic text constitution, further distinguished between unambiguous and ambiguous emic text constitution. As unambiguous I have interpreted that form of emic text constitution which is based on syntagmatic substitutions that exist between unambiguous substituenda and unambiguous substituentia, whereas I have interpreted as ambiguous that form of emic text constitution which is based on syntagmatic substitutions existing between substituenda-substituentia (cf. Harweg 1968: 260 ff.). In addition, I have correlated these two forms of text constitution (at least with regard to the so-called article languages) with a fundamental text-typological dichotomy, namely the opposition between scientific and non-scientific, especially belletristic texts, arguing that scientific texts are mainly built up by syntagmatic substitutions between substituenda-substituentia and that they therefore manifest the ambiguous variant of text constitution, whereas the non-scientific texts are mainly built up by syntagmatic substitutions between unambiguous substituenda and substituentia and therefore exhibit the unambiguous variant of text constitution (cf. Harweg 1968: 331 ff.).

The ambiguity of text constitution turns out to occur less frequently than is suggested by my description in Harweg 1968 if one takes into account the role of stress in syntagmatic substitution. I have tried to show this, drawing on German examples, in Harweg 1971a. One of the results of this attempt has been that the unstressed substituenda-substituentia (unstressed in the framework of

---

[5]   These, though far from being well-formed, are nevertheless texts, not mere strings of sentences – just as Chomsky's sentence *Colorless green ideas sleep furiously,* far from being well formed as it is, is nevertheless a sentence, and not a mere string of words.

the normal, not the so-called 'emphatic' or 'contrastive' type of stress[6]) can be re-interpreted as unambiguous substituentia, and it is obvious that an increase in the number of unambiguous substituentia in a text increases the unambiguousness of the constitution of the text itself.

Taking into account the accentual properties of the substituenda, substituentia, and substituenda-substituentia has still another textological implication. It allows one to characterize even discontinuous stretches of speech (stretches of speech that are interrupted by longer intervals and/or other texts or portions of texts) as unambiguously concatenated by syntagmatic substitutions, and insofar as this is the case they are, despite their discontinuity, unambiguously emic texts. Imagine, for instance, a situation where a woman sitting at the dinner-table in the evening says to her husband: *Charles has written. He will come to see us. Tomorrow. He will arrive at ten o'clock in the morning,* and imagine further that Charles arrives, next morning, already at eight o'clock, when the woman and her husband are still sitting at the breakfast-table and that the woman, seeing Charles through the window, suddenly shouts: *Oh, look there! Charles is already here!* Then it is obvious, that, whilst the occurrence of the proper name *Charles* in the woman's former utterance is stressed, the one in her latter utterance is unstressed, and this shows that the latter utterance, through its unstressed occurrence of the proper name *Charles* functioning as an unambiguous substituens, is textologically linked up with the former – so that the two utterances are to be considered parts of one and the same emic text. I call an emic text of such an extension a 'large extension text'[7].

Large extension texts may, however, be still far more extensive. This is possible because of the double fact that proper names, textologically, may be traced back to generic names[8] and that this operation, since it has to go back before the moment of christening or even the person's birth (when the person was as yet only namable by some generic name such as *baby*), has to bridge over comparatively large intervals, intervals that consequently have to be bridged over by the large extension text as well.

The description of this phenomenon (which I have given in Harweg 1970, exemplified by Christian names) also affects the substitutional model: it requires a hierarchization of the notions of substituendum and substituens. Thus I have interpreted the combination 'non-generically used generic name *a baby* + predicative occurrence of the Christian name within the act of christening' as an absolute substituendum, whereas I have interpreted the later (non-predicative) occurrences of the Christian name some of them as relative substituenda and at the same time substituentia of the absolute substituendum and some of them as

---

[6] Strictly speaking, both types signal contrasts; the normal one signals paradigmatic contrasts, and the so-called contrastive one syntagmatic contrasts (as, for example, in the case of antitheses and corrections). Cf. Harweg 1971a: 129ff.

[7] The original German term is 'Großraumtext', the opposite term 'Kleinraumtext'.

[8] Raible (1972: 162ff.), too, speaks of the possibility or even necessity to trace back proper names to generic names, though not with regard to large extension texts. Cf. also Dubois 1965: 155f.

'absolute' substituentia, that is, as first-grade substituentia with regard to relative substituenda and as second-grade substituentia with regard to the absolute substituendum (cf. Harweg 1970: 27 f.). An example of such a relative substituendum is the stressed occurrence, an example of an 'absolute' substituens the unstressed occurrence of the two above-mentioned occurrences of the Christian name *Charles*.

Large extension texts are, deictically, characterized by what I have called temporal 'polytopy' (cf. Harweg 1969, 24 f.), that is, their constituent texts are produced at different times of utterance. This polytopy, however, is, as we have seen, no hindrance to the working of the principle of syntagmatic substitution, and equally little is the working of this principle hampered by the other deictic polytopies, be they of the local or the personal type, that is the type manifested in dialogues: syntagmatic substitution concatenates dialogic sentence sequences (cf. Harweg 1971 b) as well as monologic ones, yielding in both cases emic texts[9].

The phenomenon of large extension texts marks one of the directions in which the application of the principle of syntagmatic substitution transcends traditional ideas of the structure and delimitation of texts. This direction is, however, not the only one in which the application of the said principle has this effect. Another direction is the one that I have described in Harweg 1974 by means of the notion of text bifurcation.

Examples of text bifurcations are a) the branching off of foot-notes from the main text in written texts and b), in oral texts, the situations for example in which, in the case of a public lecture, two listeners take a certain remark of the speaker as a stimulus to begin a private discussion, a discussion which accompanies part of the continuing lecture. Text bifurcations, then, are a phenomenon by which texts that have begun unilinearly are extended to plurilinear ones.

For text bifurcations of the type of the oral one just described to be produced special presuppositions as to both the speakers and the hearers must be fulfilled. Thus, as has already been indicated, it is required that the speaker and the hearer of the side-chain branching off from the main chain of the text both have been recipients of the initial unilinear portion of the text. However, some kind of assumptions about speaker and hearer must, at least implicitly, have been made not only in the case of text bifurcations but already with regard to the concept of syntagmatic substitution as a text-building operation as such – a fact which, in the first phases of the development of my syntagmatic substitutional theory, I failed to call attention to. But when, in Harweg 1971 c: 338 ff., I suggested a distinction between a substitutional and a non-substitutional syntagmatic textology, this fact began to emerge plainly. For one of the main results of this study is the insight that text constitution, that is the progression of a text

---

[9] Whilst in my model, dialogic and monologic texts belong to one and the same hierarchical level, they belong to different hierarchical levels in the model of W.A. Koch. For Koch (1971: 36, 260 ff.) dialogic texts, which he terms 'bi-textemes' ('Bitexteme'), constitute a level above that of the (monologic) textemes.

on the basis of syntagmatic substitution, is only possible as long as the community of its actual producer and recipients does not progress, that is expand, but either stagnates or decreases or at least retains some constant nucleus. This in turn implies, too, that text-building syntagmatic substitution is more than mere co-reference. Co-reference for instance exists as well if somebody says to someone else: *I have bought a car* and if the addressee, meaning the same car, says later on to a third person: *So-and-so has bought a car* and thereby expands the speaker-hearer-community. Here we have co-reference between the two occurrences of the expression *a car,* but not syntagmatic substitution, and in so far as there is no syntagmatic substitution, there is no text constitution either, even no constitution of large extension texts.

The primary achievement of syntagmatic substitution is the concatenation of sentences to texts – rudimentary, not well-formed texts, it is true, but texts nevertheless. That, however, by no means excludes that by paying attention to the specific way in which the principle of syntagmatic substitution is applied one can observe that even certain internal segmentations and hierarchical organizations of texts or, in other words, the formation of intermediate hierarchical levels between sentence and text can be described in substitutional terms[10]. Thus, paragraphs and chapters of different hierarchical levels may originate from the fact that between a substituendum and its – first – syntagmatic substituens there are intercalated a great number of sentences[11]; for paragraphs and chapters are units which by the caesuras through which they mark off themselves from the subsequent units of the same hierarchical level extend the substitutional distances between substituenda before and substituentia after the caesuras (cf. Harweg 1973: 81 ff.) and at the same time cancel the distances between different substituenda within the boundaries of the paragraph or chapter. No matter whether a substituendum occurs at the beginning or at the end of a paragraph or chapter, the substitutional distance from its substituens at the beginning of the next paragraph or chapter of the same hierarchical level is the same.

5.

According to Dressler (1970: 64), substitutional theories have also been developed by Karlsen (1959), Roggero (1968), Palek (1968)[12], and R. Crymes (1968). This is true of Crymes and Roggero, but their substitutional theories, as we have already seen with regard to Crymes, are paradigmatic, not syntagmatic ones and therefore have, qua substitutional theories, no relevance for text lingu-

---

[10] For another approach to the hierarchical structure of texts cf. W. A. Koch 1968.
[11] The substituentia, in this case, have a special structure. Cf. Harweg 1968: 210 ff. Cf. also Gülich & Raible 1974: 94 ff.
[12] My reference in this paper is to Palek 1970, an expanded version of Palek 1968.

istics[13]. On the other hand, Dressler's statement is, stricto sensu, not true of Karlsen and Palek, but their theories, especially Palek's, nevertheless do have relevance to text linguistics.

What kind of theory are Karlsen's and Palek's theories? The answer to this can already be inferred from their respective books: Karlsen's theory is a theory of clause (or sentence) connection, and Palek's is a theory of co-reference or, as he himself terms it, of cross-reference[14].

Karlsen's theory could also be characterized as presuppositional (cf. 1959: 20 f.), for the connecting units, the so-called connecters, instead of substituting for a certain preceding expression, merely presuppose the existence of such an expression. This is particularly obvious with regard to ellipses functioning as connecters – which are Karlsen's chief concern –, but it can also be stated with regard to what he calls explicit connecters, as, for example, with regard to the comparative morpheme -er (1959: 26), the conjunctions (1959: 20), the definite article (1959: 26), or the limiting adjectives *this* and *that* (1959: 23 f.). Furthermore, Karlsen, though investigating the connection of clauses and sentences, does not deal with the notion of text as a higher hierarchical level; his concern is strictly speaking not a textual but only a contextual one.

Palek's concern, on the other hand, is, it seems to me, a textual one, and his theory, based as it is on the phenomenon of co-reference, comes fairly close to the kernel, that is the unextended original part, of my substitutional theory as set forth in Harweg 1968. But there is nevertheless a marked difference. This consists, apart from the different terminology, primarily in the fact that Palek's theory of cross-reference has no correspondence to my distinction between substituenda and substituentia and thus fails to possess the dynamic-directional component which is characteristic of my theory of syntagmatic substitution. Secondarily, of course, Palek (1970: 49), drawing on what he calls alterators and indicators (1970: 44), that is, on differentiating and identifying means of expression, introduces a distinction between modifiers, that is first units of cross-referential sequences, and subsequent units of such sequences – a distinction that, it is true, somehow recalls my distinction between substituenda and substituentia, but that, with the notion of text functioning as a mere frame of reference rather than as explicandum, is based on a quite different notional background, and apart from this, not exploited as to its textological implications, especially its inherent text-delimitational possibilities.

Beside the so-called cross-referential sequences there are, in Palek's theory, sequences that he calls alterational (1970: 50). These are sequences consisting of the first members, the so-called modifiers, of the different cross-referential

---

[13] The same seems to be true of the treatment of substitution in Gaatone 1972. Cf., with regard to
  · Gaatone, Meyer-Hermann 1975: 153.
[14] The two principles appear to be somehow combined in Viola Waterhouse 1963 who (1963: 45–54) distinguishes, among others, between sequential and referential dependent sentences – the latter, however, restricted to such dependent sentences as are marked by anaphoric substitutes of the Bloomfield type (1963: 48).

sequences of a text. In terms of my substitutional theory these sequences would be sequences consisting of the first members of substitutional sequences, that is of substituenda, and a certain type of such sequences I have dealt with under the heading of what I have called contiguity substitutions, substitutions whose substituentia are, at the same time, substituenda (cf. Harweg 1968: 197 ff.). But these substituenda are by no means the only substituenda whose introduction into a text has to be investigated by the text linguist; the investigation should rather be extended to the textual introduction of all types of new substituenda, and it should form a complementary part to the investigation of substitution proper (cf. Harweg 1968: 250 ff.).

Both substitution proper and the textual introduction of new substituenda, both of them text-building mechanisms that operate from left to right, that is horizontally, are, at least to a certain degree, guided by – as yet almost totally unknown – mechanisms that work, as it were, vertically, mechanisms that relate or convert the so-called thematic deep structure of a text to its concrete surface structure[15]. Of all these text-building mechanisms, and of many others as well, however, that of syntagmatic substitution is, to my mind, the most fundamental or even the fundamental one.

---

[15] Cf. Harweg 1973: 68 ff.; Dressler 1972: 17 ff., and van Dijk 1972: 130 ff., 273 ff.

References

Allen, Robert L., 1961. "The Classification of English Substitute Words", *General Linguistics* 5, 7–20

Bloomfield, Leonard, 1933. *Language,* New York: Holt & Company

Crymes, Ruth, 1968. *Some Systems of Substitution Correlations in Modern American English,* The Hague and Paris: Mouton

Dijk, Teun A. van, 1972. *Some Aspects of Text Grammars,* The Hague and Paris: Mouton

Dressler, Wolfgang, 1970. "Modelle und Methoden der Textsyntax", *Folia Linguistica* 4, 64–71.

Dressler, Wolfgang, 1972. *Einführung in die Textlinguistik,* Tübingen: Niemeyer

Dubois, Jean, 1965. *Grammaire structurale du français. Nom et pronom,* Paris: Larousse

Fries, Charles C., 1952. *The Structure of English,* New York: Harcourt, Brace & World

Gaatone, David, 1972. "Pronoms et substituts", *Études de linguistique appliquée* N. S. 7, 38–47

Gülich, Elisabeth & Raible, Wolfgang, 1974. "Überlegungen zu einer makrostrukturellen Textanalyse – J. Thurber, *The Lover and his Lass"*, in: E. Gülich, K. Heger, W. Raible, *Linguistische Textanalyse. Überlegungen zur Gliederung von Texten* (= Papiere zur Textlinguistik, Bd. 8), Hamburg: Buske.

Harris, Zellig S., 1951. *Methods in Structural Linguistics,* Chicago: The University of Chicago Press

Harweg, Roland, 1968. *Pronomina und Textkonstitution,* München: Fink

Harweg, Roland, 1969. "Zum textologischen Status von *wieder.* Ein präliminarischer Beitrag zu einer Theorie polytoper Texte", *Orbis* 18, 13–45

Harweg, Roland, 1970. "Zur Textologie des Vornamens: Perspektiven einer Großraum-Textologie", *Linguistics* 61, 12–28

Harweg, Roland, 1971 a. "Die textologische Rolle der Betonung", in: W.-D. Stempel (ed.), *Beiträge zur Textlinguistik,* München: Fink, 123–159

Harweg, Roland, 1971 b. "Quelques aspects de la constitution monologique et dialogique de textes", *Semiotica* 4, 127–148

Harweg, Roland, 1971 c. "Zur Textologie des Typus *ein Herr Meier*. Perspektiven einer nichtsubstitutionellen Textologie", *Orbis* 20, 323–346

Harweg, Roland, 1973. "Text Grammar and Literary Texts: Remarks on a Grammatical Science of Literature", *Poetics* 9, 65–91

Harweg, Roland, 1974. "Bifurcations de textes", *Semiotica* 12, 41–59

Harweg, Roland, 1975. "Nichttexte, Rudimentärtexte, wohlgeformte Texte", *Folia Linguistica* 7, 371–388

Karlsen, Rolf, 1959. *Studies in the Connection of Clauses in Current English,* Bergen: Eides boktrykkeri

Koch, Walter A., 1968. "Problems in the Hierarchization of Text Structures", *Orbis* 17, 309–342

Koch, Walter A., 1971, *Taxologie des Englischen,* München: Fink

Lewandowski, Theodor, 1975. *Linguistisches Wörterbuch,* Heidelberg: Quelle & Meyer

Meyer-Hermann, Reinhard, 1975. "Zur Textgrammatik von Verweisformen im Französischen", in: M. Schecker & P. Wunderli (eds.), *Textgrammatik. Beiträge zum Problem der Textualität* Tübingen: Niemeyer

Palek, Bohumil, 1968. "Cross-Reference: A Contribution to Hyper-Syntax", *Travaux Linguistiques de Prague* 3, 255–266

Palek, Bohumil, 1970. *Cross-Reference. A Study from Hyper-Syntax,* Praha: Universita Karlova 1968

Raible, Wolfgang, 1972. *Satz und Text. Untersuchungen zu vier romanischen Sprachen,* Tübingen: Niemeyer

Roggero, J., 1968. "La substitution en anglais", *La linguistique* 2, 61–92

Waterhouse, Viola, 1963. "Independent and Dependent Sentences", *International Journal of American Linguistics* 29, 45–54

Contributions to Textlinguistics in the Soviet Union

S. I. Gindin
Moscow University, Moscow

Without attempting to define "text" let us point out two of its properties whose investigation or use has provided a criterion for referring a particular work to the field of "textlinguistics" (elsewhere TL):

1. A text is a "quantum" of communicative activity possessing relative autonomy (distinctness) and unity (integrity).

2. A text is a higher unit than a sentence and possesses its own structure not reducible so that of a single sentence.

Furthermore, only investigations of properties and phenomena that may be, to varying degrees, present in all types of texts were included in TL, while works dealing with specific problems of text composition in various genres and types were excluded. However, even if these restrictions are applied, the number of Soviet publications on TL since 1948 (when such works as [16, ch. 2; 52; 61; 66] appeared) would exceed 700, and the present overview without purporting to be a history of the Soviet TL, is a brief listing of the more notable results obtained and the problems that have emerged.

1   Types and means of intersential links (ISL)

The early Soviet works on TL indicated a wide range of ISL means, including lexical [66; 16] and word-forming repetitions, coupling of different personal pronoun forms, division of a syntagm between different sentences [16] and semantic relations of the "whole/part" type [48]. However, in the years that followed (40s and 50s) the majority of works (see, for example, [35; 43; 14] concerned themselves largely with those ISL means which can already discharge their function within a sentence: conjunctions, pronominal adverbs with a spatial and temporal meaning, demonstrative pronouns and to some extent the sequence of predicate tenses and word order. In [66–67] the whole theory rested on the likening of intersentential relations to the relations obtaining between parts of a complex sentence.

Gradually, however, scholarly attention was shifting towards the types of ISL that have no parallel within a sentence. It was noted that the link between sentences in a text is effected primarily through thought transition and development and should therefore be manifested through interconnectedness and mutual "conditioning" of the lexical composition and tense characteristics in sentences [26, p. 215], while the use of conjunctions to express intersentential relations changes the character of relations by eliminating the inherent uncertainty [64, p. 294]. S. I. Bernštein renewed non-syntactic classification of intersentential relations [5]. In dialogic discourse, marked by a sharp weakening of syntagmatic organization of a single sentence [7, p. 50] a systematic description of the inner structure of the reply sentences [70] was found to be impossible without the notion of lexical repetition (LR), which is in this case a *bona fide* structural linguistic means (cf. the treatment of LR in [14; 18]).

Since the early 60 s students of ISL in monologic discourse, too, have been increasingly interested in the LR and the closely related phenomenon of substitution by personal pronouns. In [68] the most detailed analysis is given of the modes of using autosemantic words as ISL by a concrete language while the role of the repetition mechanism is not discovered yet. [56] made an important step towards revealing the textual role of the repetition mechanism in presenting the text not only as a string of sentences but as a combination of certain "objects of speech" denoted by repeated lexemes or substitute pronouns and successively represented in a string of sentences fusing it into a single entity. This suggested that text structure should be investigated in "two dimensions" taking into account not only the relations between sentences but also between lesser elements distributed over these sentences. I. P. Sevbo has used the position of LR in the subject and predicate groups to propose a method of graphical representation of the ISL system in texts and to isolate elementary types of combinations of several LRs and their functions in text structure. Finally, the study of German oral speech has revealed that persons with a free command of the language identify the ISLs not "by the intonation features" but by "the lexical-grammatical composition of the sentences" which "overrides" the perception of intonation [33, p. 40–41].

Because the relationship expressed through LR has no analogue within a sentence, its recognition inevitably leads to the recognition of the fact that a transition to the level of a whole text involves qualitative changes in the nature of syntactic links. An attempt was made in [18–19] to revert to the concept of a text as merely the result of a stringing of sentences and prove the basic similarity of intra-sentential links and ISL thus banishing the concept of LR from the ISL theory. The distinction of free and bound grammatical categories was taken as a basis, with any of the 7 categories (mood, tense, aspect, person, number, gender and case) considered free for a sentence if they are free for at least one element of the sentence. The relationship between sentences in a text consists and is manifested in that those categories in the sentence that are free when the sentence stands alone can be bound by categories selected in one of the other sentences.

B. M. Gasparov has extended the range of correspondences in the form of sentences regarded as means of ISL (formerly, the aspect and tense relations were largely considered [41]). However, the LR could not be banished from the

ISL grammar because the LR are implicitly present in the system in the shape of limitations on the categories of person, number and gender of the sentence governed. In many examples cited in [18–19] the presence or absence of the impact of the categories in one sentence on those of the other can only shown by assuming the presence or absence in these sentences of some repeated "objects of speech".

The discovery and study of LR pointed to the specific features of the ISL without, however, revealing the nature and causes of these specifics. The task was to explain it. The direction of the search was already indicated in [56] which described LR as a means of "conveying *meaning*". Analysis of the internal structure of the LR itself and the discovery that in the absence of LR formal grammatical correspondences are "semanticized" [21; 23] have led to the conclusion that suprasentential syntax is based primarily on the correspondence between semantic characteristics of the units of the preceding level [23].

Appeal to semantics, which fully accords with the intuitive perception of a single text as treating of a single subject, has stimulated the search for new types of ISL. Following the investigation into the logical derivability of sentences in a text [25], the concept of "semantic repetition" (SR) was introduced [60, pp. 75–76; 21–23] and defined as the repetition of a certain meaning, of a certain combination of semantic elements. The fact that the definition of SR is not tied to any means of external expression of the meaning repeated has enabled to reveal the functional identity of such ISL types, formerly treated separately, as the LR, use of synonyms and words of the same root, by isolating their common function of conveying meaning and to discover a number of new types of ISL, notably the vast sphere of "purely semantic repetitions". (The most detailed typology of SR, based on E. Sapir's division of the global meaning of a lexeme, and the analysis of SR's text functions are to be found in [23, Ch. 1]). The writers who proceed from the identity of the denotatum rather than of meaning [54; 36], in the end arrive at the same set of ISLs which they describe in a more fractional and less explicit way.

The study of the above-listed ISL types has permitted to pass on to the building of a general theory of ISL and to comparative investigations. As shown in [21; 23, ch. 1] all types of links involve the same structural mechanisms – repetition and "hook-up" (the role of the third mechanism suggested, that of "derivation" needs further scrutiny; it may be responsible, not so much for linking as for the meaning development within the text). A different classification of ISLs is proposed in [54]. A mathematical model of ISLs and distinction between actual and potential ISL is suggested in [22, § 1]. The ISL system for Russian mathematical texts is described in [44]. Comparison of the repertoires and frequency of ISLs used by different authors, in different styles and languages is found in [6; 9; 13; 17; 58] and the role of the "modus-dictum" dichotomy in dialogical ISLs is treated in [7]. Measurement of the strength of LR and SR and of their relevance for the structure of a given text is considered in [60, pp. 74–75, 86–88; 24, pp. 63–64, 86–88; 12].

2   Problems of Units Intermediate Between Sentence and Text

The direct experience of language speakers shows that a text is not a homogeneous combination of sentences but a structure comprising various intermediate units. Of the continous units, the *suprasentential entity* (SE) and the *paragraph* have come in for the largest share of attention in the Soviet TL.

The existence in the text of a "readily surveyable", i.e. relatively small unit intermediate between a single sentence and the whole text or such large units of text structure as, say, a chapter or part, was postulated in [52]. The relevance of such a unit for the apprehension and memorization of a text was proved experimentally by [61, ch. 5–6], and [26] proved that the presence of SE in the structure of a text is one of the main indicators of the mature mechanism of a written speech. Even so, the nature, status and structural characteristics of SE still require more study (as witnessed by the proliferation of names to denote it: complex syntactic entity, component, superphrase, sense segment etc., etc.).

Being a unit intermediate between the sentence and text levels, the SE should be delimited from the sentence (ranking below it) and from a sequence of sentences that do not form an SE, or, which is equivalent, from adjoining SEs in the same text (ranking above the SE).

In distinguishing the SE from a single sentence, the greatest challenge is presented by the compound sentence. Punctuation is no guide here because it often separates what would be more naturally treated as a single sentence (see, for example, [37]) and, conversely, joins several different sentences (see [30, pp. 63–73] on the English punctuation). The semicolon in Russian often stands between sentences in a homogenous string that are more closely linked with one another than with those members of the string separated from them by periods [29]. It was therefore proposed to consider as independent sentences any coordinated predicative units that have no common subordinate member [30, p. 76–130] or do not form between them a "closed" binary structure [11]. At the same time a search is under way for intonational [51] or structural [27] distinctions between a compound sentence and a set of independent sentences.

In [52] it was maintained that the upper boundaries of the SE are determined, among other things, by (1) semantic or syntactic (N.S. Pospelov wavered on that) autonomy and completeness it preserves out of context and (2) a special conjunctive *("prisoyedinitelny")* character of the links between sentences. Repeated attempts were made to elaborate property (1) by dividing sentences into dependent (synsemantic) and independent (autosemantic) sentences. It was assumed that the SE should contain one autosemantic sentence (and even begin with it) and all the synsemantic sentences dependent on it. However, because synsemantic indicators (initial conjunctions, substitutes, etc., see, for example [42]) are fairly numerous, each of them separately does not suffice for regular identification of SE, and when several indicators are present in the text, their scopes do not coincide and the boundaries between SEs are obscured. The most consistent criterion of this kind would seem to be to consider every sentence with grammatical categories undetermined by the context as marking the beginning of a SE [18]. However, as pointed out in § 1, it is unrealizable without a knowledge of the distribution of LR (or, more broadly, SR), and the use of the latter means passing to a different criterion (see below).

As to property (2) (conjunctive links), it was split into three different types of relations, each of them proposed as criteria of SE: a) relations between members of a "parcelled" structure, when a sentence member or a subordinate clause are made into an autonomous sentence (by a period in writing and by intonation in speaking); b) the relation between adjoining "complete" and "incomplete" sentences especially important for dialogical discourse, where incompleteness of sentences, notably replies, is a norm ([15]; S. N. Syrovatkin in [39, part 2, pp. 90–97]); c) the relation between sentences in which the second "complements" the content of the first, with the complementarity fixed in a special connector (*besides, in addition,* etc.) [67]. It turned out, however, that the first two types of relations generate units functionally equivalent to a separate sentence rather than a SE (as is especially apparent in dialogical speech where the question-answer unit is a minimum segment capable of forming an autonomous text). The third type of relationship, like other separate syntactic relations expressed by special connectors (e.g. pronouns, pronominal adjectives or adverbs signifying negation, generalisation, affirmation or comparison [34]), does not guarantee regular identification of SE. Nor is there enough power in the requirement that an SE should have at least one of the possible syntactic (in the sense of intrasentential syntax) relationships expressed [67].

Gradually, most of the definitions of the SE came to give increasing prominence to the unity (or community) of the meaning of component sentences, the presence of a special "micro-theme", [61], i.e. not so much the completeness and autonomy of the meaning of SE divorced from context [52] as the difference of its meaning from that of the adjoining SEs. By positing the existence in a string of sentences of a common "subject of utterance" (cf. "contextual subject" in [48]) N. I. Žinkin has been able to reveal the rationale of sentences being joined into SE by virtually spreading the concept of functional perspective on SE [26, pp. 146–147].

The validity and linguistic character of the approach to the definition of SE on the basis of unity and distinctness of their meaning flow from the thesis advanced in § 1 to the effect that the connection between sentences is manifested above all in the community of their meanings. The SE boundary is apparently a point where the ISLs weaken, hence it must lie in the places where semantic links decrease thus dividing segments with relatively different meanings. This approach can be rendered effective, if the concept of "unity and distinctness of meaning" is formalized with the help of LR and SR [21; 4]. An algorithm of segmentation of a text into SEs proposed in [8] takes into account the number of sentences connected by different repetitions. [12] proposes a coefficient to register the number of SR, and other relevant SR characteristics are discussed and used in [24]. A sentence that does not contain noun LR is considered to mark the end of SE in [49], which like [59] uses segmentation for the purpose of automatic indexing and abstracting.

Because the concepts of difference and autonomy of meanings are relative and permit of gradation, the said approach to the identification of SE leads to the conclusion [23, p. 46] that the SEs do not constitute a single or sole level but can form an entire hierarchy of telescoping units which have in common the quality of being "suprasentential" (cf. the two levels of SE in [67] and the grouping of SEs on the basis of the linking LRs in [8]). The number of levels in the hierarchy can vary from text to text and even between parts of the same text and depends on the length of the latter (cf. [60, p. 100]; S.I. Gindin in [47, part 1, pp. 73–74]). Besides, in at least some levels of the hierarchy the SEs may not only follow but also overlie and crisscross one another. The complexity of the SE system naturally explains the lack of uniformity in identification of the SEs registered in experiments in the perception of the text [61, pp. 210–212].

While the criteria for delimiting SE are arguable, the boundaries of the *paragraph* are always given in the text by "new lines". The use of the new line can and often is promoted by purely quantitative characteristics of human perception. There is, for example, a tendency to avoid paragraphs consisting of too few or, vice versa, too many sentences (cf. the analysis of trends revealed in "semantic grouping" of sentences during experiments [61, pp. 205–206]), the tendency to use a new line after particularly long sentences ([28]; it is significant that in oral speech, too, "a text consisting of long sentences is less monolithic" than a text made up of short sentences [33, p. 45]).

Nevertheless it is fair to assume that quantitative factors do not of themselves determine the division into paragraphs irrespective of the inner structure of the text but contribute to the choice of one of several divisions to which that structure (or, rather, its subjective reflection in the recipient's mind) lends itself. It was noted in [53, pp. 5–6] that paragraphing and other graphic divisions, which first arose as printers' devices, have later acquired a motivation and have been increasingly used to mark out real compositional and semantic boundaries and transitions in text structure (cf. the comparison of the principles of division into chapters by Pushkin and Turgenev in [40]). It cannot be gainsaid that at the present stage of the development of written and printed speech the distribution of paragraphs can be thought of by language speakers as being *more* or *less motivated* and that a "good" division into paragraphs is one that accords with the inner structure of the text, which involves among other things the division into SEs. "To accord with" does not mean "to coincide with" but rather "to coincide with or deviate *justifiably*". [45] shows that the division of one SE into two paragraphs tends to give expressive prominence to the part assigned to the second paragraph. The functions of the joining of two or more SEs within a single paragraph have not, to date, been as clearly defined, probably because the idea that there is just one SE level has obscured the fact that the joining of SEs yields other SEs and the specific pattern of paragraphing may depend on the level of SEs marked out by a new line (cf. the typically twomember paragraph structure in Heinrich Heine's *"Harzreise"* [57].

Because, as has been shown above, paragraphing "accords" with text structure the investigation of the use of the new line by recognized stylists could be instrumental in trying out various definitions of SE and procedures of its identification. Thus, the abundance of conjunctions, conjunctive words and anaphoric pronouns at the beginnings of paragraphs found in Lessing [57–58] seems to argue against the concept of SE as a combination of all the synsemantic sentences depending on the initial autosemantic one. By contrast, the view of SE as a combination of sentences having a common "microtheme" setting it off from the adjoining SEs is borne out by the analysis of initial paragraphs in Chekhov [50].It was revealed that in a descriptive discourse the initial names in all the sentences within a paragraph except the first one, are "dominated", i.e. denote objects already mentioned in earlier sentences or obviously connected with one of the earlier mentioned objects. It follows that any sentence with a non-dominated initial name in a descriptive discourse should start a new paragraph. This rule, even if it is the necessary condition for the use of a new line, is by no means the only one. The greater the distance from the beginning of the text, the greater it is likely to be the role of relative, as opposed to absolute domination of the initial name in the first sentence, when the dominating elements are absent not in the whole of the preceding text but only in the immediately preceding shorter segment, e.g. in the preceding paragraph. Besides, dissimilarity of the meanings of adjoining paragraphs can be achieved not only by the introduction of new "objects of speech", but by the removal of old ones (cf. the use of inverted word order in Old English texts, noted in [62] for sentences containing the last reference to a particular character and the "change of protagonists" factor in [28]), as well as by the change of text roles of the same subjects, e.g. their localization in the functional perspective of the sentence. When the semantic gap between adjoining paragraphs is relatively small, various types of transition sentences are possible (some of which are indicated in [55, pp. 104–105, 114–115]) which can equally be joined to any of the paragraphs linked.

In oral speech, the text can be divided by long pauses (the hypothesis about a special intonation of the beginning and end of each SE [67] in German has not been borne out [31]). The length of the pause alone is not enough for a clear qualification of the function of this pause in the text [31–33]. Like the new line, the pause may not coincide with the inner structure of the text. Still, the segments into which a text "falls semantically" are regularly shaped as "phonetic paragraphs" [32, p. 97] marked by a single "tension arc" and set off by considerable pauses followed by "expansion of the sentence diapason" [33, p. 44]. Because of the regular nature of this phenomenon, recipients regard all the pauses longer than 1.100 ms as dividing ones "unless pitch characteristics interfere (rise of pitch or its incomplete fall, with the result that the tension arc is not resolved)" [32].

Discontinuous intermediate text structure units, which include sentences located in different places of the text, have come in for less study in the Soviet TL than the SE and the paragraph. The only works dealing with the subject are [60, pp. 100–104; 1].

3   The Structure and Properties of a Whole Text

The ontological status of a text, the role of the speaker's intention and the situational and genre conditions and norms in ensuring the unity and distinctness of the text are considered in [21; 23] and by B. M. Leikina in [47, part 1, pp. 33–36]. The study of the signals of the beginning and end of text has revealed some interesting results for German oral speech [31, pp. 11–13]. It was found that the main intonation feature of boundary sentences is a "high degree of disjointedness", i.e. of tonal autonomy of the rhythmic groups within the sentence. Thereby the structure of boundary sentences approximates the so-call-ed "disjointed structure" in which all the rhythmic groups have an upward tonal curve and the last one a downward curve, a structure characteristic of sentences uttered in isolation.

An attempt to reveal the general principles governing the specification of well-formed texts of a given language is recorded in [23, ch. 1; 47, part 1, pp. 72–74]. An infinite set of texts can be specified in two different and independent ways. Let us call "subtext" any part of the text comprising the whole number of sentences. Then the "rigid" way involves the division of the potential aggregate of all possible subtexts into a finite number of classes and the setting of a scheme (or schemes) determining how the subtexts belonging to these classes should be disposed in the text. By contrast, a "flexible" approach rests not on the conformity of the types and order of subtexts to a certain scheme imposed on the text from without, but on the relationship between subtexts within the text: the subtexts themselves must have features signaling that they pertain to the same text. It is within the framework of the flexible approach that the opposition arises between a coherent text and an incoherent sequence of subtexts. The rigid approach is equivalent in power to the context-free grammar and is unfit to be a universal principle for organization of all well-formed texts: language offers just a general matrix, with various spheres of communication and genres establishing their own partitions of subtexts and rigid schemes. The far more powerful flexible approach is a universal principle for the specification of well-formed texts. (In sentence organization, on the contrary, the rigid principle is supreme [23, ch. 1]. This accounts for the basic change of nature of syntactic links on suprasentential level noted in § 1 above). By the same token, the coherence of flexibly-built texts being too weak a limit for the variety of texts, it stands to reason that when the number of subtexts is large, language speakers perceive as sufficiently "meaningful" and "normal" only a text in which the subtexts can be grouped into a much smaller number of coherent subtexts of a higher level whose sequence would meet a rigid scheme (logical, plot, etc.; cf. the distinction between the discursive and composite text levels by G. G. Pocheptsov in [39, part 2, pp. 8–15]). The fact that such a rigid scheme is formed by the recipient of the text is proved experimentally (see below).

The essence of the phenomenon of coherence in the above approach is revealed in its being opposed to a *priory* regulation of choice and disposition of text components. The first operational definition of a coherent text, which depends on mutual position of connected and unconnected subtexts for a distinction from an incoherent sequence of subtexts, was proposed in [38]. A more detailed analysis of intuitive ideas about coherence has revealed their lack of homogeneity and led to a more general theory (see [22]) involving, apart from the notion of coherent text (similar to that suggested in [38]), the concepts of everywhere coherent, everywhere motivated texts and texts with connected ISL graphs. In [22] theoremes are proved on the relation between all these classes of texts. Apart from the axiomatics of the coherence of a text with a fixed division into subtexts, [22] offers a typology of texts under a) reaction of their coherence characteristics to the elimination of certain subtexts in a given division and b) the relationship between their coherence characteristics relative to various divisions into subtexts.

In connection with the former typology the concept of "framework" of the text division is introduced, i.e. a system of subtexts in which there is at least one subtext connected with each subtext of this particular division. A typology of whole text structures based on the shape of the ISL graph of that text is elaborated in [60, pp. 90–99, 111–114]. All the types are here divided into the "proper" and "improper" ones depending on the presence in the ISL graph of a "main path" linking sentences in order of growing numbers in the text and covering more than half of the sentences in the text.

The study of the statistical properties of a single whole text just begins. [26, p. 151] pointed out that in the building of a text both the use of structurally very complex sentences and constant use of short and extremely simple sentences could be an obstacle to anticipatory synthesis (on this notion see below) of the segment to be written. [3] proceeds from similar consideration to show that the distribution of sentence lengths is regulated by the "relationship of parameters characterizing the relative weight of intrasentential and intersentential complexity". In [2] an attempt was made to prove that the widely discussed Zipf Law characterizes the statistical structure of the vocabulary not of language or sublanguage but of a single whole text.

Of great interest in terms of general semiotics is the approach to the study of "semiotic complexity" of a heterogeneous text involving several communicative systems at once [69] and the isolation, along with the hierarchic level interaction of text layers, widely studied in linguistics and semiotics, of parallel interaction of several coexistent "planes" in a text. The study of such "parallel" texts combined in a single text may provide a convenient way for treating particularly complex natural language texts, such as versed texts (cf. an approach to rhythm proposed in [20] and the investigation of the correlation between various layers and planes in versed text structure conducted by V. S. Bayevsky [39, part 1, pp. 33–39]).

A generative linguistic model for a whole text is proposed in [46]. The division of a text into interlinked sentences is here considered as a factor affecting the generation process at a very early stage preceding "not only the materialization of meaning in words belonging to a certain part of speech" but the categorization of meaning in terms of sentences and sentence members. The first component in the model generates a formula for an articulated meaning of the future text containing no information along the lines of Ch. Fillmore's deep cases and not limited in syntactic depth. At the second stage a single complex of articulated meaning is transformed into a coherent "proto-text" in a special procedure of "exposition". This operation is responsible for reducing the syntactic depth of each "proto-text" component to required level and is conducted in such a way as to ensure observance, in the subsequent stages of generation, of all the properties marking the structure of a coherent text. The model accomodates and explains many phenomena of so-called "functional sentence perspective".

Another important investigation of the process of text generation [26] is experimental in character. Elementary school children in grades 3 through 7 were asked to write a composition on one and the same picture, and comparison of these compositions offered many important insights into mature mechanism of text generation and on the ontogenesis of this mechanism. In particular, the role and operation peculiarities were revealed of so-called anticipatory synthesis, i.e. the degree to which a writer of a certain text segment foresees and takes into account the parts yet unwritten.

A comparison of [46] and [26] warrants a hypothesis to the effect that the initial "articulated meaning" (or intention) does not fully determine the structure and meaning of the final text, but each part is to some extent a function of the initial global meaning, the parts already formed and the design of the other yet unformulated parts.

Linguistic procedures for identification and presentation of whole text structure with the use of semantic dictionaries have been described in [4; 24; 12]. In [10] one finds a description of an experiment involving the restoration of the order of randomly mixed sentences and paragraphs of a text and a hypothesis to the effect that "the process of understanding a written text proceeds on three levels. The first is the level of montage, when the text being read is arranged in the mind from a succession of segments with relatively complete meanings. At the second level, proceeding simultaneously, text elements are compared and their initial correlation restored on that basis ⟨. . .⟩ At the third level, proceeding in parallel, a common meaning (concept) of the text is revealed. These levels are always represented in the process of understanding, but the role of each varies with the semantic peculiarities of texts". The process of dividing a text being read into groups of sentences on the basis of meaning has been the object of profound study [61, ch. 5–6; 63, §§ 4–7]. It has been established that sense "landmarks" or "props" are singled out in every such group to form a kind of semantic scheme of the text. The props themselves are not remembered and are not generally involved in the subsequent reproduction of the text [61]. Moreover, they need not be clearly fixed in internal speech, with a reduced hint of articulation being sufficient [63, pp. 134–139]. However, the singling out of prop points makes the speaker try to get at the meaning of the text thereby facilitating understanding and, consequently, memorization and reproduction [61]. Hence refusal to single out prop points [61] or difficulties in doing so due to the structure of the text ([63, p. 131 ff.] shows that they are easier to find in an argumentative discourse than in a descriptive one) impede memorization, down to complete inability to reproduce even the most general meaning of the text.

Such are the results and problems of Soviet TL that, in our view, deserve notice. Work on TL in the USSR is gaining scope and the growing concretization of the problems coupled with the emerging integration and comprehensive approach will, hopefully, bring more fruit in the near future.

References

[The order of titles follows the cyrillic alphabet]

Abbreviations of the most frequently mentioned titles and parts of titles: *AKD* – avtoreferat kandidatskoj dissertacii; *IJa* – Inostrannye jazyki; *inst* – institut; *"MP i PL"* – "Mašinnyj perevod i prikladnaja lingvistika"; *"NTI"* – "Naučnotehničeskaja informacija"; *ped.* – pedagogičeskij; *"RJaŠ"* – "Russkij jazyk v škole", *UZ* – Učenye zapiski; *univ.* – universitet.

1. Agraev V. A., Serebrjakova L. A. *O vozmožnosti smyslovoj kompressii dokumentov na osnove izvlečenija predloženij s jadernymi konstrukcijami.* – "NTI", serija 2, 1974, N 1, p. 22–26.
2. Arapov M. V., Efimova E. N., Šrejder Ju. A. *O smysle rangovyh raspredelenij.* – "NTI", serija 2, 1975, N 1, p. 9–20.
3. Arapov M. V., Šrejder Ju. A. *O zakone raspredelenija dlin predloženij v svjaznom tekste.* – "NTI", serija 2, 1970, N 3, p. 11–15.
4. Arnol'd I. V. *Tematičeskie slova hudožestvennogo teksta.* – "IJa v škole", 1971, N 2, p. 6–12.
5. Artobolevskij G. V. *Osnovy hudožestvennogo čtenija².* – In: Artobolevskij G. V. Očerki po hudožestvennomu čteniju. Ed. by S. I. Bernštein. M., Učpedgiz, 1959, p. 3–46. (1st ed. – 1940).
6. Arutjunova N. D. *K probleme svjaznosti prozaičeskogo teksta.* – In: Pamjati akademika V. V. Vinogradova. M., Moscow Univ. Press, 1971, p. 22–30.
7. Arutjunova N. D. *Nekotorye tipy dialogičeskih reakcij i "počemu"-repliki v russkom jazyke.* – "Filologičeskie nauki", 1970, N 3, p. 44–58.
8. Bondarenko G. V. *Raspredelenie povtorov v svjaznom tekste kak osnova dlja obnaruženija supersintaksičeskih edinic.* – "NTI", serija 2, 1975, N 12, p. 20–31.
9. Borodačenko O. A. *Mežfrazovye svjazi v različnyh stiljah pis'mennogo jazyka.* – "Matematičeskaja lingvistika", Kiev, 1973, [v.] 1, p. 14–25.
10. Brudnyj A. A. *K analizu processa ponimanija tekstov.* – In: Znak i obščenie. Frunze, "Ilim", 1974, p. 3–6.
11. Bunina M. S. *K voprosu o složnom predloženii.* – In: Voprosy sintaksisa i leksiki sovremennogo russkogo jazyka. M., Moscow Ped. Inst., 1973, p. 57–63.

12. Buhbinder V. A., Rozanov E. D. *O celostnosti i strukture teksta.* – "Voprosy jazykoznanija", 1975, N 6, p. 73–86.
13. Bělza M. I. *K voprosu o nekotoryh osobennostjah semantičeskoj struktury svjaznyh tekstov.* – In: Semantičeskie problemy avtomatizacii informacionnogo poiska. Kiev, "Naukova Dumka", 1971, p. 58–73.
14. Vardul' I. F. *O sceplenii samostojatel'nyh predloženij v japonskom jazyke.* – "Trudy Voennogo inst. IJa", 1955, vyp. 7, p. 3–16.
15. Vejhman G. A. *K voprosu o sintaksičeskih edinstvah. (Na materiale sovremennogo anglijskogo jazyka).* – "Voprosy jazykoznanija", 1961, N 2, p. 97–105.
16. Vinokur G. O. *"Gore ot uma" kak pamjatnik russkoj hudožestvennoj reči*[2]. – In: Vinokur G. O. Izbrannyje raboty po russkomu jazyku. M., Učpedgiz, 1959, p. 257–300 (1st ed. – 1948).
17. Gak V. G. *Russkij jazyk v zerkale francuzskogo.* Očerki 6–7. Struktura dialogičeskoj reči. – "Russkij jazyk za rubežom", 1970, N 3, p. 75–80; 1971, N 2, p. 63–69.
18. Gasparov B. M. *Principy syntagmatičeskogo opisanija urovnja predloženij.* – "UZ Tartuskogo univ.", 1975, vyp. 347, p. 3–29.
19. Gasparov B. M. *Struktura formalnoj svjazi predloženij v sovremennom russkom jazyke.* – "UZ Tartuskogo univ.", 1975, vyp. 347, p. 30–63.
20. Gindin S. I. *Vnutrennjaja semantika ritma i ee matematičeskoe modelirovanie.* – In: Problemy prikladnoj lingvistiki. Tezisy. Č. 1. M., 1969, p. 92–96.
21. Gindin S. I. *Ontologičeskoe edinstvo teksta i vidy vnutritekstovoj organizacii.* – "MP i PL", 1971, vyp. 14, p. 114–135; German – in: N 71, t. 2, S. 225–252.
22. Gindin S. I. *Svjaznyj tekst: formalnoe opredelenie i elementy tipologii.* M., 1971. 44 p. (Inst. russkogo jazyka. Predvaritelnye publikacii. Vyp. 24).
23. Gindin S. I. *Vnutrennjaja organizacija teksta. Elementy teorii i semantičeskij analiz.*Kandidatskaja dissertacija. M., 1972. 390 p. (typewritten).
24. Gindin S. I. *Opyty analiza struktury teksta s pomošč'ju semantičeskih slovarej.* Statja 1. – "MP i PL", 1972, vyp. 16, p. 42–112.
25. Dorofeev G. V., Martem'janov Ju. S. *Logičeskij vyvod i vyjavlenie svjazej meždu predloženijami v tekste.* – "MP i PL", 1969, vyp. 12, p. 36–59.
26. Žinkin N. I. *Razvitie pis'mennoj reči učaščihsja III–VII klassov.* – "Izvestija Akademii ped. nauk RSFSR", 1956, vyp. 78, p. 141–250.
27. Zaporožcev V. I. *K voprosu o razgraničenii komponentov složnosočinennyh predloženij i samostojatel'nyh predloženij.* – In: Voprosy grammatiki i stilistiki nemeckogo jazyka. Stavropol', 1972, p. 3–25.
28. Zarubina N. D. *O nekotoryh psiholingvističeskih osobennostjah vnutrennej struktury pis'mennogo teksta.* – In: Materialy 3-go Vsesojuznogo simposiuma po psiholingvistike. M., 1970, p. 76–78.
29. Ivanov M. N. *Stroenie abzaca i ego punktuacija.* – "RJaŠ", 1950, N 3, p. 16–20.
30. Iofik L. L. *Složnoe predloženie v novoanglijskom jazyke.* L., Leningrad Univ. Press, 1968. 214 p.
31. Kandinskij B. S. *Tekst kak intonacionnaja struktura.* AKD. M., 1968. 15 p.
32. Kandinskij B. S. *Celyj tekst i ego intonacionnaja struktura.* – "IJa v vysšej škole", 1968, vyp. 4, p. 93–102.
33. Kandinskij B. S. *Celyi takst kak intonacionnaja struktura.* – "UZ Moskovskogo ped. inst. IJa", 1968, t. 42, p. 35–52.
34. Kirpičnikova N. V. *O sposobah oh "edinenija predloženij v svjaznoj reči.* – "RJaŠ", 1960, N 5, p. 34–38.
35. Kobrina N. A. *Sintaksičeskie sredstva svjazi meždu samostojatel'nymi predloženijami v sovremennom anglijskom jazyke.* AKD. L., 1953. 20 p.
36 Krejdlin G. E., Padučeva E. V. *Vzaimodejstvie associativnyh svjazej i aktual'nogo členenija v predloženijah s sojuzom A.* – "NTI", serija 2, 1974, N 10, p. 32–37.
37. Kulagin A. F.*Bessojuznye sočetanija voprositel'nyh i pobuditel'nyh predloženij.* – In: Voprosy filologii. M., Moscow ped. inst., 1974, p. 117–126.

38. Leont'eva N.N. *O smyslovoj nepolnote teksta (v svjazi s semantičeskim analizom).* – "MP i PL", 1969, vyp. 12, p. 96–114.
39. *Lingvistika teksta.* Materialy naučnoj konferencii. Č. 1–2. M., Moscow ped. inst. IJa, 1974. 230, 212 p. (Partial German translation – in: N 71, t. 2, S. 7–56).
40. Lopatto M. *Povesti Puškina. Opyt vvedenija v teoriju prozy.* – "Puškinist", 1918, vyp. 3, p. 3–50.
41. Lunëva V.P. *O roli vido-vremennoj sootnositel'nosti v organizacii složnogo sintaksičeskogo celogo.* – In: Voprosy teorii i metodiki russkogo jazyka. Ul'janovsk, 1969, p. 273–280.
42. Lunëva V.P. *O stepeni samostojatel'nosti predloženija v složnom sintaksičeskom celom.* – "RJaŠ", 1972, N 1, P. 100–104.
43. Makarova M.M. *Sredstva svjazi predloženij v naučno-tehničeskoj reči sovremennogo nemeckogo jazyka.* AKD. M., 1960. 22 p.
44. Malov V.V. *Svjazočnye sredstva sceplenija samostojatel'nyh predloženij. (Na materiale matematičeskoj literatury).* AKD. Rostov n/D, 1970. 30 p.
45. Marov V.N. *Strukturno-stilistíčeskie modeli abzaca.* – In: Voprosy lingviskiki i metodiki prepodavanija IJa. Sverdlovsk, 1970, p. 71–77.
46. Martemjanov Ju.S. *Svjaznyj tekst – izloženie rasčlenennogo smysla.* M., 1973. 59 p. (Inst. russkogo jazyka. Predvaritel'nye publikacii. Vyp. 40).
47. *Materialy 5-go Vsesojuznogo simpoziuma po psiholingvistike i teorii kommunikacii.* Č. 1–2. M., 1975. 257 p.
48. Nikiforova O.I. *Rol' predstavlenij v vosprijatii slova, frazy i hudožestvennogo opisanija.* – "Izvestija Akademii ped. nauk RSFSR", 1947, vyp. 7, p. 121–162.
49. Novikov A.I., Jakušin B.V. *Algoritm indeksirovanija tekstov vzvešennymi ključevymi slovami po metodu semantičeskoj filtracii.* – "NTI", serija 2, 1972, N 6, p. 15–20.
50. Padučeva E. V. *O strukture abzaca.* – "UZ Tartuskogo univ.", 1965, vyp. 181, p. 284–292.
51. Peterson M.N. *Russkij jazyk.* M.-L., GIZ, 1925. 123 p.
52. Pospelov N.S. *Složnoe sintaksičeskoe celoe i osnovnye osobennosti ego struktury.* – "Doklady i soobščenija Inst. russkogo jazyka", 1948, vyp. 2, p. 43–68.
53. Reformatskij A.A. *Opyt analiza novellističeskoj kompozicii.* M., 1922. 20 p.
54. Ročnjak A.M. *Sposoby soedinenija makrosintagmatičeskih konstrukcij v tekste (na materiale sovremennogo francuzskogo jazyka).* AKD. L'vov, 1972. 20 p.
55. Rjadnova T.S. *Analiz abzaca kak komposicionno-sintaksičeskogo elementa jazyka hudožestvennoj literatury (na materiale "Vekfildovskogo svjaščennika" Goldsmith'a).* – "UZ Moskovskogo ped. inst.", 1961, N 165, p. 91–118.
56. Sevbo I.P. *Struktura svjaznogo teksta i avtomatizacija referirovanija.* M., "Nauka", 1969. 135 p. German transl. of an early version – in: N71, t. 2, S. 277–308.
57. Sil'man T.I. *Struktura abzaca v proze Lessing'a, Goethe i Heine.* – "Filologičeskie nauki", 1961, N 4, p. 106–116.
58. Sil'man T.I. *Problemy sintaksičeskoj stilistiki (na materiale nemeckoj prozy).* L., "Prosveščenie", 1967. 152 p.; German: Probleme der Textlinguistik. Heidelberg, 1974.
59. Skorohod'ko E.F. *Lingvističeskie problemy obrabotki tekstov v informacionno-poiskovyh sistemah.* – "Voprosy informacionnoj teorii i praktiki", 1974, N 25, p. 5–120.
60. Skorohod'ko E.F. *Semantičeskie svjazi v leksike i tekstah.* – "Voprosy informacionnoj teorii i praktiki", 1974, N 23, p. 6–116.
61. Smirnov A.A. *Psihologija zapominanija².* – In: Smirnov A.A. Problemy psihologii pamjati. M., "Prosveščenie", 1966, p. 7–352. (1st ed. – 1948).
62. Snegirëva T.A. *Porjadok slov kak sredstvo svjazi meždu predloženijami v drevneanglijskij period.* AKD. L., 1962. 18 p.
63. Sokolov A.N. *Vnutrennjaja reč' i ponimanie.* – "UZ Naučnoissledovatel'skogo inst. psihologii", 1941, t. 2, p. 99–146.
64. Steblin-Kamenskij M.I. *Porjadok slov kak sredstvo vyraženija svjazi meždu predloženijami v skandinavskih jazykah.* – "UZ Leningradskogo univ.", 1952, N 156, p. 282–299.
65. Figurovskij I.A. *Punktuacija celogo teksta.* – "RJaŠ", 1936, N 5, p. 143–147.

66. Figurovskij I. A. *Ot sintaksisa otdel'nogo predloženija – k sintaksisu celogo teksta.* – "RJaŠ", 1948, N 3, p. 21–32; German in: N71, t. 2, S. 111–154.
67. Figurovskij I. A. *Sintaksis celogo teksta i učeničeskie pis'mennye raboty.* M., Učpedgiz, 1961.
68. Haritonova I. Ja. *Rol' znamenatel'nyh častej reči nemeckogo jazyka (suščestvitel'nogo, glagola, prilagatel'nogo) pri ustanovlenii svjazej meždu samostojatel'nymi predloženijami.* AKD. M., 1965. 23 p.
69. Čerkasskij M. A. *K probleme semiotičeskoj složnosti teksta.* – In: Naučnyj simposium "Semiotičeskie problemy jazykov nauki, terminologii i informatiki". Č. 1. M., 1971, p. 106–109.
70. Švedova N. Ju. *Strojaščiesja na osnove leksičeskogo povtorenija vtorye repliki dialoga (repliki-povtory).* – In: Švedova N. Ju. Očerki po sintaksisu russkoj razgovornoj reči. M., Academy of Sciences Press, 1960, p. 280–362.
71. Jelitte H. (ed.) Sowjetrussische Textlinguistik. T. 1–2. Frankfurt/M., P. Lang; Bern, H. Lang, 1976. 278, 311 S.

Generative Discourse Analysis in America*

Susumu Kuno

1 Introduction

Current American research in generative syntax can be divided into two major categories: purely syntactic and primarily nonsyntactic. On the one hand, there are the serious attempts of many generative grammarians to arrive at an adequate theory of syntax solely on the basis of what they believe to be intrasentential syntactic factors. Research efforts within the framework of Extended Standard Theory, so-called "hard-syntax", Montague Grammar and Relational Grammar for the most part belong to this category. On the other hand, there is a growing number of generative grammarians who have come to the realization that many phenomena which have been regarded as purely syntactic are in fact often controlled by nonsyntactic factors: these researchers question the adequacy of theories that are built on incorrect syntactic characterizations of such phenomena.

It is interesting to consider the reactions of "mainstream" generative grammarians to developments in the latter area of research. I believe that Kiparsky and Kiparsky (1971) were the first generative syntacticians to explicitly discuss a correlation between syntactic and semantic phenomena. They divided complement clauses into two semantic categories – factives and nonfactives – and enumerated different syntactic behaviors displayed by the two types of complements. Their analysis was readily accepted by generative syntacticians for two basic reasons. First, factivity is a concept that can be formulated relatively precisely: whether a given complement is factive or not can be decided upon by a logical consistency test, as displayed below:

(1) *John regretted [factive] that Mary had left, but in fact she had not left.
    (contradictory)
(2) John believed [nonfactive] that Mary had left, but in fact she had not left.
    (noncontradictory)

Secondly, the factivity or nonfactivity of a complement clause can be dealt with formally in the lexicon by the use of a plus or minus marking on verbs that take

* Research represented in this paper has been supported in part by the National Science Foundation's grant to Harvard University (SOC-7412366). I am indebted to Robin Bechhofer and Linda Shumaker for the comments I received on the previous version of the paper.

complement clauses.[1] In other words, factivity is something that can be treated as an intrasentential syntactic phenomenon.

As far as I know, Cantrall's (1969) work on English reflexives was the first proposal to introduce a discourse factor which could not be formulated precisely within the domain of generative syntax. Cantrall endeavored to explain occurrences of reflexive pronouns in subordinate clauses on the basis of the speaker's point of view. He assumed that reflexives such as exemplified in (3) were "point of view" expressions:

(3) John said that there was a picture of himself in the post office.

In an attempt to treat the "point of view" problem within standard generative theory, he hypothesized that the underlying structure for (3) was something like:

(4) John said that there was *what he perceived as* a picture of himself...

For several reasons, Cantrall's work failed to receive the recognition that it deserved. Syntacticians were unwilling to give up their search for a precise syntactic formulation of complex sentence reflexivization in exchange for a vague concept such as the speaker's "point of view". Furthermore, the particular syntactic solution that Cantrall used in his analysis was ad hoc, and required deletion of such unrecoverable strings as *what he perceived as*.

Kuroda's (1973) work on the peculiar characteristics of certain Japanese syntactic patterns in nonreportive narrative style sentences was another attempt at discourse analysis within the generative theoretical framework. In Japanese, there is a fairly large class of verbals – all denoting sensation – that require their subjects to be first person when used affirmatively, and second person when used interrogatively. Thus, (5 a) is grammatical, in contrast to (5 b, c):

(5) a Boku wa hara ga hetta.   'I was hungry.'
        I   stomach emptied
    b *Kimi wa hara ga hetta.   'You were hungry.'
    c *Taroo wa hara ga hetta.   'Taroo was hungry.'

Kuroda noted, however, that (5 c) *is* acceptable as a nonreportive narrative style sentence in which the speaker has identified himself with the referent of *Taroo*. He generalized this observation by noting that the grammars of reportive and nonreportive style sentences differ from each other not only in their treatment of sensation words, but also in their treatment of reflexives. Unfortunately Kuroda's insightful observations were regarded by syntacticians as relevant only to the study of narrative styles, not to a syntax of everyday speech.

Another area of research which most generative grammarians have considered to be outside the domain of generative syntactic theory is the study of pragmatics – primarily because pragmatics treats phenomena which do not usually interact closely with syntactic rules. Consider, for example, the pragmatic implication of the following sentence:

(6) Could you pass me the salt?

---

[1] In fact, the concept of factivity is not quite so simple. See Karttunen (1971) for discussion.

One must recognize that this sentence (although syntactically a request for information) has an illocutionary force of a request for action.[2] It is possible for the researcher to examine the psychological processes that the hearer goes through in identifying the relevant pragmatic implications.[3] Beyond this, however, little can be done to relate the findings to syntax.[4]

Independent of efforts within the field of generative grammar to identify nonsyntactic factors relating to syntax, there has been a movement, led mainly by Czech and British linguists, to describe sentences in discourse from the viewpoint of theme and rheme. Studies in this field have grown out of Mathesius' original work (1939) on functional sentence perspective (FSP). European research in FSP has been limited primarily to word order and prosody study; the framework has mainly been used to describe well-formed discourse, rather than as a device for explaining the ungrammaticality or unacceptability of sentences. It is probably for such reasons that this important perspective, too, has been regarded with indifference by most generative syntacticians.

I believe that it was Kuno (1972 a) that first reexamined some of the central problems of generative syntax within the framework of discourse analysis. More specifically, the paper (Kuno 1972 a) demonstrated the functional sentence perspective of theme and rheme to be indispensable for stating constraints on both forward and backward pronominalization – phenomena which had defied previous attempts at characterization along intrasentential lines. The paper appeared at a time when some generative syntacticians were beginning to realize the inadequacy of a purely syntactic approach to many processes in English; it played the role of starting a new research trend in generative grammar known as "Functional Syntax".

Generative syntacticians are currently divided into two groups: those whose primary research objective is to arrive at generalizations statable within the syntactic component of transformational grammar; and those who are interested in discovering all factors, be they syntactic or not, which control the linguistic phenomena under examination. There is no conflict, a priori, between these two approaches: the former group must recognize the existence and influence of certain nonsyntactic factors; analogously, the latter group must recognize the fact that many linguistic phenomena *are* controlled by syntactic factors (although to a lesser degree than others might wish to believe). The difference between the two approaches lies more in the actual analyses of individual linguistic phenomena; the analyses, however, influence the determination of what kind of mechanisms are required by the syntactic component of generative grammar.

---

[2] See Gordon and Lakoff (1971).

[3] See Searle (1969).

[4] A notable exception is Ross's observation (1973) that patterns such as *will you be able to, are you able to,* and *do you have the ability to* have different degrees of illocuitional force of request for action, and that relatively speaking, it is easier to obtain the request for action interpretation when they are used in main clauses than when they are used in embedded clauses.

As an illustration, let us consider the phenomenon of Gapping. Gapping is the process assumed to be responsible for generating the structures underlying the (b) sentences below, from those underlying the (a) sentences:

(7) a. John ate roast beef, and Bill ate fish.

    b. John ate roast beef, and Bill ∅   fish.

(8) a. John wants to write a novel, and Mary wants to write a play.

    b. John wants to write a novel, and Mary   ∅   to write a play.

    John wants to write a novel, and Mary   ∅   a play.

(9) a. John persuaded Mary to donate $200, and he persuaded Jane to donate $300.

    b. John persuaded Mary to donate $200, and   ∅   Jane to donate $300.

What concerns us here is the unacceptability of sentences such as the following:

(10) a. *John gave Mary a nickel, and Jane [gave Mary] a dime.

    b. *John hit Mary with a baseball bat, and Tom [hit Mary] with a bicycle chain.

    c. *John persuaded Mary to donate $200, and Jane [persuaded Mary] to donate $300.

    d. *John wanted Bob to shave himself, and Tom [wanted Bob] to wash himself.

Does the unacceptability of these sentences result from the violation of a syntactic constraint? Operating under such an assumption, Hankamer (1973) proposed the following:

(11) *The No-Ambiguity Condition:* Any application of Gapping which would yield an output structure identical to a structure derivable by Gapping from another source, but with the "gap" at the left extremity, is disallowed.

According to this hypothesis, the ungrammaticality of (10b), for example, is due to the fact that there is a derivation of the same structure with a gap at left-peripheral position, as shown below:

(12) John hit Mary with a baseball bat, and [John hit] Tom with a bicycle chain.

Similarly, (10c) is ungrammatical because of the existence of the derivation shown in (9b). Note that the constraint stated in (11) requires a transderivational mechanism as part of the syntactic component of generative grammar.

There is, however, an alternative approach which can be taken; the Gapping facts can be examined under the assumption that many seemingly-syntactic phenomena are in fact constrained by discourse factors. It has been found that the process under discussion involves an interaction among the following four nonsyntactic constraints:[5]

(13) *Minimal Distance Principle:* The more recently a constituent has been processed, the easier it is to recall. As a consequence, the two constituents left behind by Gapping can most readily be coupled with the constituents in the first conjunct that were processed last.

---

[5] See Kuno (1976a) for details.

(14) *FSP Principle on Constraints Left Behind after Gapping:* Material left behind after Gapping must represent new information. When the first conjunct is pronounced without emphatic stress, the two constituents that appear in final position are ordinarily interpreted as representing new information. Hence, the constituents left behind after Gapping are most readily coupled with these.

(15) *FSP Principle on Constituents Deleted by Gapping:* Material deleted by Gapping must be discourse anaphoric. It is not sufficient that a copy of the deleted string be present in the first conjunct; what is deleted must represent subject matter which has been talked about in the preceding discourse, or which the preceding discourse (or nonlinguistic context) has led one to expect.

(16) *Subject-Predicate Interpretation Tendency:* When both an NP and a VP are left behind by Gapping, they tend to take on a subject-predicate interpretation; namely, it is readily assumed that the NP is (or is coreferential with) the underlying subject of the VP.

The unacceptability of (10a) and (10b) can be accounted for by the first two principles. Principles (13), (14) and (16) explain why (10c) and (10d) are unacceptable.

Note that it is possible to break the coupling pattern displayed in (9b) and (12). Observe the following contrast:

(17) a. *John hit Mary with a baseball bat, and Tom [hit Mary] with a bicycle chain. (= 10b)

b. One of the muggers hit Mary with a baseball bat, and another [hit Mary] with a bicycle chain.

Each conjunct in (17b) has an indefinite subject. Since indefinites ordinarily represent new information, *Mary* can easily be interpreted as representing older information than the subject. The sentence observes the FSP Principle (14), and is therefore acceptable to most speakers in spite of the fact that it violates the Minimal Distance Principle.

Similarly, observe the following discourse:

(18) a. Speaker A: Who hit Mary with what?

b. Speaker B: JOHN hit Mǎry (or hěr) with a baseball bat, and
JANE [hit Mǎry] with a bicycle chain.

Speaker A's question makes it clear that in (18b) *Mary* represents old information, and the stressed subject *JOHN,* new information.[6] Hence, the Gapping of hit Mary is consistent with the FSP Principle (14), and the sentence is generally accepted in spite of the fact that it, too, violates the Minimal Distance Principle.

The Subject-Predicate Interpretation Tendency manifests itself in the following contrast:

---

[6] See §2 of this paper for the distinction between the concept of "old information" and that of "anaphoricity".

(19) a. *John persuaded Mary to donate $200, and Jane [persuaded Mary] to donate $300. (= 10c)

    b. John promised Mary to donate $200, and Jane [promised Mary] to donate $300.

Few speakers accept (19a) when it is given in isolation and pronounced without emphatic stress. On the other hand, approximately 40% of native English speakers accept (19b). Note that in the specified interpretation, the *Jane* of (19b) is coreferential with the underlying subject of *to donate $300*, while the *Jane* of (19a) is not. Variations in judgments of acceptability can be attributed to idiolectal differences in the weights assigned to the three principles involved (i.e., [13], [14], [16]). (Note that while sentence (b) observes Principle (16), it violates (13) and (14).) Speakers for whom (13) and (14) are strongly inviolable principles find sentence (19b) unacceptable; however, those for whom (16) is stronger regard the sentence as acceptable.

The FSP Principle on Constituents Deleted by Gapping can be independently justified by the following observations. First, note the fact that (20) represents a well-formed discourse:

(20) a. Speaker A: Who hit who?

    b. Speaker B: John hit Mary, and Bill [hit] Jane.

The string deleted by Gapping is recoverable not only from the first conjunct of (20b), but also from (20a). Thus the acceptability of (20b) is at least consistent with the principle under discussion. Next, consider the following discourse:

(21) a. Speaker A: Who did what to whom?

    b. Speaker: B: ??First, John hit Mary, and Bill [hit] Jane, and next, Tom kicked Martha, and Jim [kicked] Margie.

Speaker A's question makes it clear that *hit* and *kicked* represent contextually new information. The marginality of (21b) seems to be due to the fact that Principle (15) is violated. Similarly, observe the following discourse:

(22) a. Speaker A: Did the boys hit the girls, or did they kick them?

    b. Speaker B: ??John hit Mary, and Bill, Jane, and Tom kicked Martha, and Jim, Margie.

Although *hit* and *kicked* are present in Speakers A's question, they represent contextually new information in (22b); if these portions of the sentence were garbled by noise, there would be no way for the hearer to predict which action was performed by whom. Hence the marginality of (22b).

The acceptability of sentences such as (17b), (18b) and (19b) demonstrates that the syntactic constraint given in (11) is not adequate, and that the unacceptability of (10a, b, c, d) should be dealt with not as a syntactic problem, but as a phenomenon based on perception and discourse principles. This analysis allows us to dispense with the requirement for a transderivational mechanism, making the theory of syntax less powerful, and hence, more desirable.[7]

The inadequacy of the purely syntactic approach becomes evident also when we examine Stillings' (1975) formulation of Gapping. The author is concerned only with sentences, such as (7b) and (8b), in which the subject remains after deletion; she regards sentences like (9 b) as having been derived, not by Gapping, but by another process which extracts leftmost common strings from conjuncts. In her paper, the following examples are presented as ungrammatical sentences:

(23) a. *I plan to talk to Mary a week from next Tuesday and John [plans to talk] to Fred [a week from next Tuesday].

   b. *Nancy thought Mike foolish for even talking to Sally and Cindy [thought] Alfonse [foolish for even talking to Sally].

   c. *John asked George to be the one to inform Mary of Ellington's death and Fred [asked] Sam [to be the one to inform Mary of Ellington's death].

   d. *The box certainly contained thumbtacks before Mary spilled them, and the carton [certainly contained] pins [before Mary spilled them].

On the basis of the "ungrammaticality" of these sentences, Stillings proposes that Gapping should be formulated so as to disallow deletions of noncontiguous strings.

However, a more careful examination of the data reveals that the unacceptability of examples (23 a, b, c, d) cannot be explained by such a syntactic constraint; rather, it is due to a violation of the FSP Principle on Constituents Deleted by Gapping. The deleted strings in these sentences are so semantically rich that few contexts would make the information old. Consider, for example, (23 a). It is hard to imagine a discourse which has been about "a week from next Tuesday". If we change the time to *tomorrow,* however, the sentence becomes acceptable.

(24) Í plan to talk to Máry tomorrow, and John, to Fred.

Time adverbs such as *today, yesterday, tomorrow, this year, last year,* and *next year* are much more likely to be contextually old (known) than adverbs such as *a week from next Tuesday.*[8]

---

[7] If it can be shown on independent grounds that the mechanism of transderivational constraint is needed in the theory of syntax, removing it only from the statement of Gapping might not seem to be too significant. However, the transderivational constraint embodied in Hankamer's No-Ambiguity Constraint is of a unique type because it claims that Gapping is blocked if the resulting output structure is identical to a structure that has the gap at the left extremity *even if the latter is ungrammatical.* Let us examine what this claim entails in connection with (i a):

(i) a. *Jack asked Mike to wash himself, and Sue to shave himself.

   b. *_____ and [Jack asked] Sue to shave himself.

   c. _____ and Sue *[asked Mike] to shave himself.

According to the No-Ambiguity Constraint, the reason for the ungrammatically of (i c) is that its structure is identical to that of (i b), which has the gap (i.e., *Jack asked*) at the left extremity, although (i b) is ungrammatical due to a violation of gender agreement of the reflexive. In other words, the transderivational constraint under discussion makes it necessary to examine derivations of ungrammatical (underivable) sentences. As far as I know, transderivational constraints with this added power have not been shown to be necessary anywhere else in syntax.

[8] Similarly, if the preceding context overtly shows that *a week from Tuesday* represents old information, (23 a) becomes acceptable:
Speaker A: What will you and John be doing a week from next Tuesday?
Speaker B: (?)I plan to talk to Mary a week from Tuesday, and John, to Fred.

Similarly, the deleted portion of (23b) *(thought ... foolish for even talking to Sally)* is too rich semantically. Compare (23b) to be following – an acceptable sentence to most speakers.

(25) Nancy found Mike attractive, and Cindy [found] Alfonse [attractive].

Likewise, the following sentence is acceptable, although it has the same constituent structure as (23c):

(26) John asked his father to do it, and Fred, his mother.

It is easy to assume that the preceding discourse has been about asking someone to "do it".

On the basis of the facts presented in (23), Stillings proposed the following statement of Gapping:

(27) NP V* C   AND/OR   NP V* C
      1   2   3   5   6   7
                                $\Downarrow$
                                $\emptyset$

V* is a string variable representing a string of verbs of indeterminate length; C is an unconditioned variable that must, however, be a constituent. Stillings claims that as a consequence of her statement of Gapping it is necessary to add to the theory of grammar two new mechanisms: a string variable such as V*, and a constituent variable. We have seen, however, that Stillings' characterization of Gapping is incorrect. Her claim that only a string of verbs can be deleted is falsified not only by examples (17b), (18b) and (19b), but also by the following sentence:

(28) John promised the fundraiser to donate $200, and Bill [promised the fundraiser to donate] $300.

In addition, the acceptability of gapped sentences such as the following invalidates Stillings' formulation of Gapping, and consequently, her claim that the theory of grammar needs the mechanism of a constituent variable:

(29) a. Yesterday, Tom took Mary to dinner, and today, [Tom took Mary] to a movie.

b. Yesterday, Tom came to visit me, and today, Bill [came to visit me].

By contrasting several analyses of Gapping, I have illustrated the danger inherent in analyzing linguistic phenomena on a purely syntactic basis. We see that a discourse-based approach to syntactic analysis can make a significant contribution in constructing a theory of generative syntax. In the following sections, I will present a brief survey of work done on discourse analysis of so-called "syntactic phenomena" within the framework of generative grammar.

2   Functional Sentence Perspective

Three concepts play important roles in this area of research: (i) old (predictable) information, (ii) new (unpredictable) information, and (iii) theme.

An element in a sentence represents old, predictable information if it is recoverable from preceding context; if it is not recoverable, it represents new, unpredictable information. For example, observe the following exchange:

(1) a. Speaker A: What does John like?   b. Speaker B: He likes fish.

In Speaker B's response to the question, *He likes* represents old, predictable information: even if that part of the sentence is garbled, it is recoverable from the preceding context. For this reason, *He likes* does not have to be included in Speaker B's response. *Fish,* on the other hand, is new, and unpredictable: it cannot be garbled or deleted without a loss of information.

There has been much confusion between the concept of "old, predictable information" and that of "anaphoric", and therefore, it will not be amiss to contrast the two here.[9] A noun phrase is "anaphoric" if its referent is uniquely identifiable either due to its previous mention in the discourse, or to the shared nonlinguistic knowledge. Observe the following exchange:

(2) a. Speaker A: Which of the two, John or Bill, won the race?

    b. Speaker B: John did.

In (2a), *John* is anaphoric in that both A and B can uniquely determine its referent, namely, the person named John that they both know. In (2b), *John* is anaphoric in the same sense, and also in the sense that it is coreferential with the *John* of (2a). On the other hand, the *John* of (2b) represents, not "old, predictable" information, but "new, unpredictable" information. If this part of Speaker B's response were garbled, there would be no way for Speaker A to determine what it was.

The concept of "theme" cannot be given any precise formulation. I can only say that the theme is what the rest of the sentence is about. Thus, the term is used in a sense that is very different from the way it is used by Prague School linguists (e.g., Firbas 1964) or by Halliday (1967). There has been a great deal of confusion, also, between the concept of "theme" and that of "old predictable information". The theme does not necessarily represent old, predictable information, although it often does. Compare the following two exchanges:

(3) a. Speaker A: What does your brother do for a living?

    b. Speaker B: John teaches music at a high school.

(4) a. Speaker A: What do your brothers do for a living?

    b. Speaker B: Well, John teaches music at a high school, Bill works for an insurance company, and Tom is a free-lance consultant in management.

---

[9] For example, note the following remark by Dahl (1976, P. 41):

"Kuno (1972, 271) introduced a concept of ANAPHORICITY which seems to be intended to cover the distinction between 'known' and 'unknown' in our own terms. He makes himself guilty of another confusion, however. There is another possible way of understanding 'old' and 'new', namely, in terms of PREVIOUS MENTION..."

In Kuno (1972a), I used the terms "old" and "new" exclusively as meaning "Predictable, recoverable" and "unpredictable, unrecoverable" from preceding context, and distinguished them from "anaphoric" and "nonanaphoric". As far as I can tell, there is no confusion here. The necessity for having "anaphoric" and "old" as two separate concepts is beyond any doubt.

In (3 b), John is the theme of the sentence because it is what the rest of the sentence is about, and it also represents old, predictable information. On the other hand, in (4b), *John, Bill,* and *Tom,* although they are the themes of their respective clauses, do not represent old predictable information. Note that if these portions of the sentence were garbled, there would be no way for Speaker A to determine what the subject of each clause would be. I use the term "predictable theme" in referring to *John* of (3 b), and the term "unpredictable theme" in referring to *John, Bill,* and *Tom* of (4 b).

The importance of the functional sentence perspective in analyzing syntactic phenomena is beginning to be realized by many generative grammarians in the United States. Below, I will touch upon various syntactic phenomena that have been analyzed in this perspective.

2.1 Pronominalization

Karttunen (1968) hypothesized that Backward Pronominalization in certain syntactic configurations is allowable only when the noun phrase to be pronominalized is discourse anaphoric. Kuno (1972 a) showed that discourse anaphoricity is a necessary condition, but not a satisfactory condition, for Backward Pronominalization, and that what is required is predictability of the referent of the pronoun from preceding context. For example, observe the following exchanges:

(5) a. Speaker A: Who is visiting John$_i$?
   b. Speaker B: His$_i$ brother is visiting John$_i$.
(6) a. Speaker A: Who is visiting who?
   b. Speaker B: *His$_i$ brother is visiting John$_i$.
(7) a. Speaker A: Who is visiting Bill$_j$ and John$_i$?
   b. Speaker B: *His$_i$ brother is visiting John$_i$, but I don't know who is visiting Bill$_j$.

In (5 b), Backward Pronominalization is allowable because the referent of *his* is determinable from the preceding context (namely, from [5 a]). On the other hand, (6b) is unacceptable because there is no way for Speaker A to determine who *his* refers to from the preceding context. The unacceptability of (7 b) shows that discourse anaphoricity is not a satisfactory condition for Backward Pronominalization. This can be seen by the fact that *His* is anaphoric to *John* of Speaker A's question, but that the sentence is still unacceptable because Speaker A cannot determine whether it refers to John or Bill. The following examples also illustrate the working of the predictability requirement for Backward Pronominalization:

(8) a. Tell me about John$_i$.
      Although Mary$_j$ dislikes him$_i$, she$_j$ is still seeing John$_i$.
    b. Tell me about Mary$_j$.
    ?? Although she$_j$ dislikes him$_i$, she$_j$'s still seeing John$_i$.

(9) a. If you see him$_i$, stop the policeman$_i$.
   b. *If you see him$_i$, stop a policeman$_i$.
(10) a. What did you do when you saw Harry$_i$ getting mad?
   (?)I calmed him$_i$ before Harry$_i$ did something rash.
   b. Which of the two, Mary or Harry$_i$, did you calm when you saw them getting mad?
   c. *I calmed him$_i$ before Harry$_i$ did something rash.

Gundell (1976) noted that there are acceptable sentences, such as those shown below, that violate Kuno's predictability requirement for Backward Pronominalization:

(11) Which of the two, Carter or Ford, do you think will win? Since he$_i$'s still ahead in the polls, I guess Carter$_i$ will win.
(12) In her Philadelphia speech earlier this week, Queen Elizabeth II thanked the United States for the lesson taught Britain by the American revolution. (Carden 1976)
(13) Do you have anything I can wear for Halloween?
   If you can find it$_i$, you can have my Greek sailor hat$_i$.
(14) When you have time for it$_i$, would you read my paper$_i$.

On the basis of the above observation, Gundell has hypothesized that Backward Pronominalization is dependent upon the topichood, and not the predictability, of the trigger NP. This hypothesis seems to solve hitherto unexplained instances of Backward Pronominalization noted by Carden (1976), where the trigger is indefinite:

(15) Because they wanted to know more about the ocean's current, students in the Science Club at Mark Twain Junior High School of Coney Island gave ten bottles with return address cards inside to crew men of one of New York City's sludge barges.
(16) At the conclusion of his sixth year of full-time service on the faculty of Capitol Institute of Technology, a faculty member was informed on August 1, 1974 that his appointment would be terminated.[10]

Kuno (1972a) also proposed that an NP that represents an exhaustive listing interpretation "x and only x" cannot be pronominalized intra-sententially. He later (cf. Kuno 1975a) generalized this constraint and hypothesized that an NP that represents an exhaustive listing interpretation cannot be pronominalized unless it is coreferential with the discourse topic. This constraint accounts for the contrast that exists between (17) and (18):

---

[10] If Gundell's hypothesis is correct, it seems to require reexamination of what qualifies as the theme of a sentence. Kuno (1973) hypothesized that only anaphoric NPs (including generic NPs, and NPs such as *the sun, the moon, my wife*, etc. whose referents are uniquely identifiable) qualify as themes. It might be that nonaphoric NPs qualify as themes if they are specific enough. Note the contrast that was observed in Kuno (1972a):
(i) a. *A boy was tall.
   b. ?A boy that I met yesterday was tall.
(ii) a. *A boy has an IQ of 160.
   b. A boy in my class has an IQ of 160.

(17) I have three children: John$_i$, Jane and Mary. John$_i$ is not terribly bright, but among John$_i$, Jane and Mary, he$_i$ is the brightest.

(18) I have three children: Jane, John$_i$ and Mary. Jane is clearly the brightest.
    *Between John$_i$ and Mary, he$_i$ is the brighter.

One might assume that the trigger for Forward Pronominalization in (17) is the *John* of among *John, Jane and Mary*. If that were the case, (18) should be an equally acceptable discourse because the *John* of *Between John and Mary* should equally serve as trigger for pronominalization. However, to many speakers of English, (18) is an incoherent discourse. This contrast can be explained on the basis of the fact that while the first part of (17) establishes John as the discourse topic, that of (18) does not. Similarly, observe the following contrast:

(19) a.   Among John$_i$, Jane and Mary, he$_i$ is the brightest.

    b.   ?Among Jane, Mary and John$_i$, he$_i$ is the brightest.

    c.   ??Among Jane, John$_i$ and Mary, he$_i$ is the brightest.

According to Kuno's hypothesis, the pronominalization pattern of (19) should be possible only when the pronoun is coreferential with the discourse topic. But if *John* is the discourse topic, then, it should appear at a prominent position in the list. The most prominent position in a list is list-initial; the second most prominent position is list-final. The list-medial position in the least prominent. We can attribute the unacceptability of (19 c) to the fact that *John,* which should be coreferential with the discourse topic, in fact appears in the least prominent position in the list headed by *Among.*

There are several other discourse-based constraints on Pronominalization. See Kuno (1975 a) for details.

2.2   Thematic Adverbs

Kuno (1971) hypothesized that some time and place adverbs originate in sentence-initial position in the underlying structure:

(20) a. Every year, many tourists come to Japan.

    b. Many tourists come to Japan every year.

Note that (20a) is unambiguous, but (20b) is ambiguous. In the former, *every year* has a higher scope than *many tourists.* If the latter sentence is interpreted as synonymous with (20a), the scope relationship is the same, but if it is interpreted as meaning "There are many tourists who come to Japan every year", then, the scope relationship is reversed. Kuno hypothesized that (20b) in its first interpretation is derived from the structure underlying (20a).

Kuno (1975 b) further generalized the observation and hypothesized that sentences such as (21) are potentially ambiguous between the thematic adverb interpretation (with the adverb originating from sentence-initial position) and the time- or place-specifying interpretation (with the adverb originating from VP-Internal position):

(21) a. John was in Paris *in 1960.*

    b. John was robbed *in Paris.*

There are sentences of the pattern of (21) that are not ambiguous. Compare the following two sentences:

(22) a. John was born *in 1960.*

    b. John was still a small baby *in 1960.*

The primary interpretation of (22 a) is that of when John was born. The time adverb *in 1960* is a nonthematic time-specifying adverb, and is assumed to originate as a VP-internal adverb in the underlying structure. On the other hand, (22 b) is not a sentence that tells us when John was still a small baby. It is a sentence that tells us how the situation was in 1960. In other words, *in 1960* of this sentence is a thematic adverb that sets the scene.

The above differences in the discourse functions of *in 1960* has various syntactic manifestations. For example, note that (23 b) is synonymous with (22 b), but (23 a) is not synonymous with (22 a):

(23) a. In 1960, John was born.

    b. In 1960, John was still a small baby.

In (23 a), *in 1960* is no longer a time-specifying adverb. The sentence is a statement as to what happened or how the situation was in 1960, and as such, has *in 1960* as a thematic adverb. Similarly, compare the following two sentences:

(24) a. Was John born in 1960?

    b. Was John still a small baby in 1960?

(24 a) has *in 1960* as focus of question, while (24 b) is a question about *still a small baby.* Kuno (1975 b) gives several other syntactic arguments for different functions that *in 1960* plays in (22 a) and (22 b). Reinhart (1976) adds some dozen more syntactic arguments for the distinction, and examines constituent structures of the two sentence patterns in further detail.

The distinction between thematic adverbs and nonthematic adverbs that I have briefly discussed above interacts with Pronominalization. Compare the following two sentences:

(25) a. *In John$_i$'s dormitory, he$_i$ smoked pot.

    b. In John$_i$'s dormitory, only he$_i$ smoked pot.

(25 a) is a sentence that is intended to state where John smoked pot. As such, it has *in John's dormitory* as a place-specifying nonthematic adverb, originating from the VP-internal position. Note that Forward Pronominalization after the preposing of the adverb produces an unacceptable sentence. On the other hand, (25 b) is a statement with respect to how the situation is in John's dormitory. As such, the sentence has *in John's dormitory* as a thematic adverb, originating from the sentence-initial position in the underlying structure. Note that Forward Pronominalization is acceptable in this sentence. Similarly, compare the following two sentences:

(26) a. *In John's portrait of Mary$_i$, she$_i$ found a scratch.

    b. In John's portrait of Mary$_i$, she$_i$ looks sick.

Jackendoff (1975) attributed the above contrast to the fact that *she* denotes Real-Mary in (26a), while it denotes Image-Mary in (26b). However, note that the same contrast exists between (27a) and (27b), both of which have *she* as Real-Mary:

(27) a. *From John's portrait of Mary$_i$, everyone thinks she$_i$ must have removed a stain.

b. From John's portrait of Mary$_i$, everyone thinks she$_i$ must have been sick.

It seems that the contrast should be attributed to the fact that while *in John's portrait of Mary* and *from john's portrait of Mary* are place-specifying non-thematic adverbs in (26a) and (27a), preposed from the VP-internal position, they are scene-setting thematic adverbs in (26b) and (27b), originating from sentenceinitial position in the underlying structures.

2.3   Topic-Comment Structure and Related Problems

Research results in the topic-comment structure in the framework of generative theory of grammar originates from Kuroda's work (1965) on *wa* and *ga* in Japanese. Detailed examination of what qualifies as a topic in Japanese and English are given in Kuno (1973). The role that the topic-comment structure plays in interaction with movement transformations and with left and right dislocation sentence patterns is examined in detail in Gundell (1974) and Kuno (1973, 1976b). Discourse conditions for appearance of the left dislocation pattern are examined in detail in Keenan and Schieffelin (1975, 1976). The concept of "predictable theme", which I referred to at the beginning of this section, is further developed in Kantor (1976).

The role that prosody plays in distinguishing various discourse-based sentence patterns (relating to topic-comment structure, contrast, exhaustive listing interpretation, presentational sentence structure, etc.), long recognized by scholars such as Bolinger (1957, 1958, 1965), has been reemphasized in recent works in the generative framework by Kuno (1972a, 1975a), Jackendoff (1972), Liberman (1975), Liberman and Sag (1974), and Schmerling (1973).

Hankamer and Sag (1976) classifies anaphoric processes into two categories: those that can be triggered only by antecedents that appear elsewhere in the linguistic structure (including wider discourse), and those that can be triggered by semantic units that appear in nonlinguistic discourse context. Observe, for example, the following examples:

(28) [Observing Hankamer attempting to stuff 12″ ball through 6″ hoop]

a. Sag: I don't see why you even try.

b.   *I don't see why you even try to.

(29) a. Sag: Why don't you stuff that ball through that hoop?

b. Hankamer: I'm trying.

I'm trying to.

VP Deletion, which leaves an auxiliary verb or infinitival *to* behind, requires a linguistic antecedent. This is why *I'm trying to* of (29b) is grammatical but not *why you even try to* of (28 b). On the other hand, null complement anaphora of *try* does not require a linguistic antecedent. Note that (28 a) has the nonlinguistic act of stuffing 12″ ball through 6″ hoop as antecedent of its missing complement.

2.4   Discourse Structure

Empirical studies of discourse structures, both for the purpose of better understanding anaphoric processes such as pronominalization, definitivization, and deletion, and for the purpose of developing computer systems that can deal with continuous discourse, are beginning to bear fruits. Hinds (1975) has analyzed paragraph structures of short newspaper articles, such as obituaries, that talk about only one topic. A paragraph consists of segments – the initial segment, which is the most important segment, and those that offer a motivation, a highlight, or an unexpected twist. Hinds argues that within each of these segments, there is one and only one sentence of particular importance, termed as the peak sentence. Hinds' analysis shows that it is within the peak sentence that full unpronominalized noun phrases occur, while it is within non peak sentences that pronouns occur.

Linde (1974) and Linde and Labov (1975) show that apartment layout descriptions have certain explicitly statable discourse structures, and that these structures are sometimes correlated with syntactic factors such as sentence boundaries, choice of subjects, and choice of subordinate structures. Work by Walker et al. (1975) and Deutsch (1974, 1975) on task instruction dialogues by computer also show that a discourse has an internal structure beyond that of the sentences that comprise it, and that processes such as ellipsis, pronominalization, and use of definite noun phrases are constrained by internal discourse structures.

3   *Points of View in Generative Grammar*

The problem of whose point of view the narrator takes in describing an event has long been a subject of study in the field of literary criticism. As I mentioned in § 1, Kuroda (1973) was the first who studied this problem systematically in the generative theoretical framework. Banfield (1973) examined direct speech, indirect speech, and free indirect speech from the same viewpoint. Recent work by Kuno (1972b, 1975a, 1976b) and Kuno and Kaburaki (1975) has demonstrated that the point of view perspective plays an important role in the generative syntax of everyday speech.

The speaker, in describing an event or state, can express his attitude toward the participants of the event or state in numerous ways. Assume that John and Mary are husband and wife, and that John hit Mary. The speaker can describe this event in numerous ways, which include the following:

(1) a.   John hit Mary.
   b.   John hit his wife.
   c.   Mary's husband hit her.
(2) a.   Mary was hit by John.
   b. ??John's wife was hit by him.
   c.   Mary was hit by her husband.

All the above sentences are identical in their logical content, but they differ from each other with respect to "camera angles". In (1a), it is most likely that the speaker is describing the event objectively, with the camera placed at some distance both from John and Mary. In (1b), on the other hand, the camera is placed closer to John than to Mary. This can be seen by the fact that the speaker has referred to John as *John,* and to Mary as *John's wife.* The situation is reversed in (1c), where the camera is placed closer to Mary than to John. (1b) and (1c) show one way (choice of descriptors) by which the speaker can overtly show from whose side he is describing the event. (2a) shows another device, namely, a transformational one, by which the speaker can express his attitude toward participants of the event that he describes in a sentence. Let us assume that Passivization is used when the speaker wants to describe an event from the point of view of the referent of the underlying object rather than that of the underlying subject. Under this assumption, (2a) is a statement in which the speaker describes the event under discussion from Mary's side rather than from John's side. (2c) utilizes two devices – choice of descriptor and application of Passivization – for overtly expressing the fact that the speaker is describing the event from Mary's side. The marginality of (b) can be accounted for as deriving from a conflict that utilization of these two devices can produce. Namely, the speaker, by applying Passivization, has overtly shown that he is describing the event from Mary's side rather than from John's side. At the same time, by referring to Mary as *John's wife,* and to John as *John,* the same speaker has overtly shown that he is describing the event from John's side, rather than from Mary's side. These two points of view are contradictory, and hence result in the marginality of the sentence.

Let us use the term "empathy" as representing the speaker's identification, *with varying degrees* (ranging from degree 0 to degree 1), with a person who participates in the event that he describes in a sentence. Identification to degree 1 takes place when the speaker (or the narrator) completely identifies himself with a person that he describes – this happens in nonreportive narrative style sentences where the narrator is omniscient. Identification of degree 0 takes place when the speaker describes the event objectively, with a camera placed at a distance. Empathy is a continuum between these two extremes. (1b) is a sentence in which John > Mary (the speaker empathizes with John rather than with Mary) holds, where the speaker's identification with John can vary anywhere from degree greater than 0 to degree 1 (the total identification, as a nonreportive narrative style sentence). On the other hand, in (3), the speaker's empathy with John cannot be of degree 1 because he is expressing his own action:

(3) I talked to John$_i$'s wife about him$_i$.

The empathy relationship that holds in (3) is: Speaker > John > John's wife.

Kuno (1975 a) and Kuno and Kaburaki (1975) have shown that there are several discourse principles involving empathy:

(4) *Ban on Conflicting Empathy Foci:* A single sentence cannot contain two or more conflicting foci of the speaker's empathy.

(5) *Surface Structure Empathy Hierarchy:* It is easiest for the speaker to empathize with the referent of the subject; it is next easiest for the speaker to empathize with the referent of the object; . . . It is next to impossible for the speaker to empathize with the referent of the by-agentive.

Subject ≥ Object ≥ . . . . ≥ By-Agentive

(6) *Speech-Act Empathy Hierarchy:* It is easiest for the speaker to empathize with himself. It is next easiest for the speaker to empathize with the hearer. It is almost impossible for the speaker to empathize with a third party at the exclusion of himself or the hearer.

Speaker ≥ Hearer > Third Party

(7) *Discourse Topic Empathy Hierarchy:* It is easier to empathize with the referent of a discourse-anaphoric NP than to empathize with the referent of an NP that has been introduced anew into discourse.

Discourse-Anaphoric > Discourse-Nonanaphoric

The marginality of (2b), as I have already mentioned, is due to the violation of (4), in connection with (5). The marginality of (8) is due to (6):

(8) ??John was hit by me.

Although the distance between the subject and object positions in the empathy hierarchy is in general small, and (5) can be violated very easily with respect to these two positions, there are verbs that *require* that empathy be placed on the subject, verbs such as *meet* (in the sense of "encounter"), *encounter, run into, marry, hear from, receive from,* etc. Observe the following sentences:

(9) a. ??A student heard from mě that Professor Smith has been hospitalized.

b. *An eight-foot-tall girl met (= encountered) John on the street.

(9a) is marginal because *heard from* requires that the speaker's empathy be placed on the referent of *a student* rather than on the speaker himself, in violation of the Speech-Act Empathy Hierarchy. (9b) is unacceptable because *met* in the sense of accidental encounter requires that the speaker's empathy be placed on its subject *an eight-foot-tall girl* rather than on *John,* in violation of the Discourse Topic Empathy Hierarchy. Observe, further, the following sentence:

(10) *The girl who the reporter met (= encountered) heard from him that Mary was a spy.

The main clause verb *heard from* requires that the speaker's empathy be placed on the subject rather than on the object. Hence, the empathy relationship 'the girl > the reporter' holds for the main clause. The relative clause verb *met* requires that the speaker's empathy be placed on its subject. Hence, as far as the relative clause is concerned, the empathy relationship 'the reporter > the girl' holds. These two relationships are contradictory, and violate the Ban on Conflicting Empathy Foci. The unintelligibility of the sentence in real time seems to be due to the fact that the sentence requires the hearer to be in two conflicting positions at the same time.

The above empathy principles interact with various syntactic processes in English. I do not have space here to discuss them. Details are given in Kuno and Kaburaki (1975) and Joseph (1976). Cross-language research shows that the empathy perspective is indispensable for a better understanding of numerous syntactic processes. Details are found in Kaburaki (1974) and Kuno (1976c) for Japanese, Yokoyama (1975) and Yokoyama and Klenin (1976) for Russian, Coppieters (1976) for French, and Thráinsson (1976) for Icelandic.

References

Banfield, A. (1973) "Narrative Style and the Grammar of Direct and Indirect Speech", *Foundations of Language 10*, 1–39.

Bolinger, D. (1957) *Interrogative Structures of American English,* Monograph of American Dialectal Society.

Bolinger, D. (1958) "A Theory of Pitch Accent in English", *Word 14*, 109–140.

Bolinger, D. (1965) *Forms of English: Accent, Morpheme, Order,* Harvard University Press, Cambridge, Mass.

Cantrall, W. R. (1969) *On the Nature of the Reflexive in English,* doctoral dissertation, University of Illinois; published as *Viewpoint, Reflexives, and the Nature of Noun Phrases,* Mouton, 1974.

Carden, G. (1976) "Backwards Anaphora in Discourse Context", presented at the 1976 Summer Meeting of the Linguistic Society of America, Oswego, N.Y.

Coppieters, R. (1976) *Point of View in French Syntax,* doctoral dissertation, Harvard University.

Dahl, Ö. (1976) "What is New Information?", in N.E. Enkvist and V. Kohonen (eds.), *Reports on Text Linguistics Approaches to Word Order,* Text Linguistics Research Group. Åbo Akademi, Finland, pp. 37–50.

Firbas, J. (1964) "On Defining the Theme in Functional Sentence Analysis", *Travaux Linguistique de Prague 1*, 267–280.

Gordon, D. and G.Lakoff (1971) "Conversational Postulates" in *Papers from the Seventh Regional Meeting of the Chicago Linguistic Society,* University of Chicago, pp. 63–82.

Gundell, J. (1974) *The Role of Topic and Comment in Linguistic Theory,* doctoral dissertation, University of Texas at Austin, Texas.

Gundell, J. (1976) "Stress, Pronominalization and the Given-New Distinction", *Papers from the Seventh Annual Meeting of the North Eastern Linguistic Society, M.I.T.*

Halliday, M.A.K. (1967) "Notes on Transitivity and Theme in English, Part II", *Journal of Linguistics 3*, 199–244.

Hankamer, J. (1973) "Unacceptable Ambiguity", *Linguistic Inquiry 4:1*, 17–68.

Hankamer, J. and I. Sag (1976) "Deep and Surface Anaphora", *Linguistic Inquiry 7:3*, 391–428.

Hinds, J. (1975) "Paragraph Structure and Pronominalization", mimeographed paper.

Jackendoff, R.S. (1972) *Semantic Interpretation in Generative Grammar,* MIT Press, Cambridge, Mass.

Jackendoff, R.S. (1975) "On Belief-Contexts", *Linguistic Inquiry 6:1*, 53–93.

Kaburaki, E. (1973) "Nihongo Saiki-Daimeisi *Zibun* nituite no Ikutuka no Teigen (Some Proposals Concerning the Japanese Reflexive Pronoun *Zibun*)", *Nebulous 2*, 19–52, Meiji-Gakuin Daigaku-in Eibungaku-Senkooka, Tokyo.

Kantor, R. (1976) "Discourse Connection and Demonstratives", presented at the 1976 Annual Meeting of the Linguistic Society of America, Philadelphia, Penn.

Karttunen, L. (1968) "Coreference and Discourse", presented at the 1968 Annual Meeting of the Linguistic Society of America, New York, N. Y.

Karttunen, L. (1971) "Some Observations on Factivity", *Papers in Linguistics 4, 55–69.*

Keenan, E. O. and B. B. Schieffelin (1975) "Topic as a Discourse Notion: A Study of Topics in the Conversations of Children and Adults", in Li, C. (ed.), *Subject and Topic,* Academic Press, New York, N. Y., pp. 335–384.

Keenan, E. O. and B. B. Schieffelin (1976), "Foregrounding Referents: A Reconsideration of Left Dislocation in Discourse", mimeographed paper.

Kiparsky, P. and C. Kiparsky (1971) "Fact", in Bierwisch and K. Heidolph (eds.), *Progress in Linguistics,* Mouton, pp. 143–173.

Kuno, S. (1971) "The Position of Locatives in Existential Sentences", *Linguistic Inquiry 2:3,* 333–378.

Kuno, S. (1972 a) "Functional Sentence Perspective: A Case Study from Japanese and English", *Linguistic Inquiry 3:3,* 269–320.

Kuno, S. (1972 b) "Pronominalization, Reflexivization and Direct Discourse", *Linguistic Inquiry 3:2,* 161–195.

Kuno, S. (1973) *The Structure of the Japanese Language,* MIT Press, Cambridge, Mass.

Kuno, S. (1975 a) "Three Perspectives in the Functional Approach to Syntax", in R. E. Gossman, L. J. San and T. J. Vance (eds.), *Functionalism,* Chicago Linguistic Society, pp. 276–336. Also published in Matejka, L. (ed.), *Sound and Meaning: Quinguagenary of the Prague Linguistic Circle,* University of Michigan, Ann Arbor, Mich., 119–190.

Kuno, S. (1975 b) "Conditions for Verb Phrase Deletion", *Foundations of Language 13,* 161–175.

Kuno, S. (1976 a) "Gapping: A Functional Analysis", Linguistic Inquiry 7:2, 300–318.

Kuno, S. (1976 b) "Subject, Theme and the Speaker's Empathy: A Reexamination of Relativization Phenomena", in Li, C. (ed.), *Subject and Topic,* Academic Press, New York, N. Y., pp. 417–444.

Kuno, S. (1976 c) "The Speaker's Empathy and Its Effect on Syntax: A Reexamination of *Yaru* and *Kureru* in Japanese", Journal of the Association of *Teachers of Japanese 11,* nos. 2–3, 249–271.

Kuno, S. and E. Kaburaki (1975) "Empathy and Syntax", in Kuno, S. (ed.), *Harvard Studies in Syntax and Semantics 1,* 1–73.

Kuroda, S.-Y. (1965) *Generative Grammatical Studies in the Japanese Language,* doctoral dissertation, MIT.

Kuroda, S.-Y. (1973) "Where Epistemology, Style and Grammar Meet – A Case Study from Japanese", in Anderson, S. and P. Kiparsky (eds.), *Festschrift for Mossis Halle,* Holt, Reinhart and Winston, New York, pp. 377–391.

Liberman, M. (1975) *The Intonational System of English,* doctoral dissertation, MIT.

Liberman, M. and I. Sag (1974) "Prosodic Form and Discourse Function", *Papers from the Tenth Regional Meeting of Chicago Linguistic Society,* 416–427.

Linde, C. (1974) *The Linguistic Encoding of Spatial Information,* doctoral dissertation, Columbia University.

Linde, C. ans W. Labov (1975) "Spatial networks as a Site for the Study of Language and Theught", *Language 51:4,* 924–939.

Mathesius, V. (1939) "On Information-Bearing Structure of the Sentence" (translated by T. O. Yokoyama and appended to *Harvard Studies in Syntax and Semantics 1).*

Reinhart, T. (1976) *The Syntactic Domain of Anaphora,* doctoral dissertation, MIT.

Ross, J. (1973) "The Penthouse Principle and the Order of Constituents", in Corum, C., T. C. Smith-Stark and A. Weiser (eds.), *You Take the High Node and I'll Take the Low Node,* Chicago Linguistic Society, pp. 397–422.

Schmerling, S. F. (1973) *Aspects of English Sentence Stress,* doctoral dissertation, University of Illinois. Also published by University of Texas Press, 1976.

Searle, J. (1969) *Speech Acts,* Cambridge University Press.

Stillings, J. T. (1975) "The Formulation of Gapping in English as Evidence for Variable Types in Syntactic Transformations", *Linguistic Analysis 1:3,* 247–273.

Thraínsson, H. (1976) "A Semantic Reflexive in Icelandic", *Papers from the Sixth Annual Meeting of the North Eastern Linguistic Society,* University of Montreal.

Walker, D. et al. (1976) "Speech Understanding Research", *Annual Technical Report,* Stanford Research Institute, Menlo Park, California.

Yokoyama, T. O. (1975) "Personal or Reflexive: A Functional Analysis", in Kuno, S. (ed.), *Harvard Studies in Syntax and Semantics 1,* 75–111.

Yokoyama, T. O. and E. Klenin (1976) "Semantics of 'Optional Rules': Russian Personal and Reflexive Possessives", in Matejka, L. (ed.), *Sound and Meaning,* University of Michigan.

List of contributors

Teun A. van Dijk, Instituut voor Algemene Literatuurwetenschap, Universiteit van Amsterdam, Herengracht 256, Amsterdam 1001, Netherlands
Wolfgang U. Dressler, Institut für Sprachwissenschaft, Universität Wien, Liechtensteinstrasse 46a, A-1090 Wien, Austria
Nils E. Enkvist, Åbo Akademi, Domkyrketorget 3, SF-20500 Åbo 50, Finland
Sergej I. Gindin, ulica Gorkego 26 kv. 56, Moskva 103050, USSR
Joseph E. Grimes, Department of Modern Languages and Linguistics, Cornell University, Ithaca, N. Y. 14850, USA
Ernst U. Grosse, Blumenstrasse 38, D-7800 Freiburg, Germany
Roland Harweg, Germanistisches Institut der Ruhr-Universität Bochum, Universitätsstrasse 150, D-4630 Bochum, Germany
Ruqaiya Hasan, School of English and Linguistics, Macquarie University, North Ryde, New South Wales 2113, Australia
Walter Kintsch, Department of Psychology, University of Colorado, Boulder, Colo. 80309, USA
Susumo Kuno, Department of Linguistics, Harvard University, 5 Divinity Avenue, Cambridge, Mass. 02138, USA
Stephen Levinsohn, Robert Longacre, Summer Institute of Linguistics, 1500 W. Camp Wisdom Rd., Dallas, Texas 75211, USA
Winfried Nöth, Englisches Seminar der Ruhr-Universität Bochum, Universitätsstrasse 150, D-4630 Bochum, Germany
Bohumil Palek, Zdena Palková, Vinohradská 103, ČSSR 13000 Praha, Czechoslovakia
János S. Petöfi, Fakultät für Linguistik und Literaturwissenschaft, Universität Bielefeld, Postfach 8640, D-4800 Bielefeld, Germany
Ellen F. Prince, Linguistics Department, University of Pennsylvania, The College, Philadelphia, Pa. 19104, USA
Hannes Rieser, Fakultät für Linguistik und Literaturwissenschaft, Universität Bielefeld, Postfach 8640, D-4800 Bielefeld, Germany
Emanuel A. Schegloff, Department of Sociology, University of California, Los Angeles, Cal. 90024, USA
Siegfried J. Schmidt, Universität Bielefeld, Kavalleriestrasse 26, D-4800 Bielefeld, Germany
Götz Wienold, Fachbereich Sprachwissenschaft, Universität Konstanz, Postfach 7733, D-7750 Konstanz, Germany

Index

Research in Text Theory
Untersuchungen zur Texttheorie

Volume 1

Grammars and Descriptions
Studies in Text Theory and Text Analysis
Edited by Teun A. van Dijk and János S. Petöfi

Contributions in English, French, and German. 1977. Large-Octavo. x + 404 pp. With 3 foldout plates and numerous tables. Cloth DM 148,–; $ 65.80. ISBN 3110057417

Since the mid-sixties more and more studies devoted to problems arising from the grammatical analysis of texts have been published. Most of these studies also argue for the necessity of constructing a text grammar according to the methodological principles of modern linguistics. The primary function of this volume is to present a wide choice of different text-grammatical concepts and/or different methods of linguistic text descriptions. The unusual and challenging task of having the same text (THE LOVER AND HIS LASS by J. Thurber) analyzed by different scholars promises a maximum of variety and concentration at the same time.

Volume 3

Text Processing
Papers on Text Analysis and Text Description
Edited by Wolfgang Burghardt and Klaus Hölker

This volume contains the papers delivered during an international conference, organized by the Centre for Interdisciplinary Research of Bielefeld University. It included the following topics: Theoretical aspects of text processing; theory of action, and dialogue in text processing; analysis and description of ethnopoetic texts; aspects of computerized text processing. Contributions in English and German – To appear in 1978

Volume 4

Text Theory
Empirical and Methodological Aspects of Text-theoretical Research
Edited by János S. Petöfi and Siegfried J. Schmidt

This volume contains discussions of the following main subjects: Motivations for the construction of text theories; empirical research into the structural properties of texts; methodological problems in the construction of text grammars and formal text theories. The twenty-four papers provide a representative and systematic treatment of the grammatical foundations of text theory.